For Frankie and
Stanley with affection
and respect.
Sidney Jan 30/84

Sidney Bernstein

by the same author

FORTUNE'S HOSTAGES
THE LETTERS OF FREYA STARK:
SOME TALK OF ALEXANDER (ed.)
TRAVELLER'S EPILOGUE (ed.)

Sidney Bernstein

A Biography

Caroline Moorehead

JONATHAN CAPE
THIRTY BEDFORD SQUARE LONDON

First published 1984
Copyright © 1984 by Caroline Moorehead

Jonathan Cape Ltd
30 Bedford Square, London WC1

British Library Cataloguing in Publication Data
Moorehead, Caroline
Sidney Bernstein
1. Bernstein, Sidney, *Baron*
I. Title
791'.092'4 PN2597

ISBN 0-224-01934-1

Printed in Great Britain by Thomson Litho Ltd, East Kilbride, Scotland

For Martha

Contents

Illustrations

Illustrations

Cartoons

Preface

IN EVERY FIELD, whether art, medicine, the sciences or technology, there are a few figures who stand out, not only for their personal achievements, but for the way that they always seem a little in advance of what is about to happen. It is at times as if they were possessed of a kind of prescience, a prophetic understanding of what should come next. For Sidney Bernstein, born in 1899, that foresight was applied to the world of entertainment.

Heir to a small chain of cinemas showing silent movies, he adapted them first for the talkies, then for colour film and Cinemascope. In the late 1920s, when most cinema exhibitors were trying to adjust to the miracle of sound, Sidney was building super-cinemas, vast Italian and Spanish Renaissance palaces as exotic and overwhelming as the Hollywood epics they showed. At the same time, he was a founder member of the Film Society, and one of the first people to bring to Britain the great classics of the European and Russian cinema.

In the 1930s, he turned his attention to the stage, building a theatre of his own, the Phoenix in the Charing Cross Road, which he opened with Noël Coward's *Private Lives*, while campaigning energetically for a National Theatre. He spent the war showing how important and how far-reaching film could be when used as an instrument of propaganda. Then came his own experience in film production: five years as producer with Alfred Hitchcock.

His major achievement, in which all his earlier dreams and experience seemed to fuse, was the creation of one of the first four British independent television companies. In its time Granada has initiated some of the most exciting experiments in the medium. To this day, the station bears his unmistakable stamp.

In the spring of 1979 Tom Maschler of Jonathan Cape asked me whether I would like to write a biography of Sidney. He had tried before to convince Sidney to allow such a book to be written, but Sidney had always insisted that his life did not merit one. Being a shy man, he was also reluctant to permit any intrusion into his privacy. But now he was prepared to discuss the idea. As the daughter of old friends, my intrusion possibly seemed less alarming.

However, as he explained at our first meeting, he was not to feature in the biography very prominently himself, for the object of the exercise was to show how lucky he had been and how, in particular, he had had the good fortune to meet, work with and become friends with a number of remarkable people who had influenced him, and his life, very strongly. The book was to be about them, the people who really mattered, and not about himself.

I agreed to write the book, but explained that I could not guarantee how it would turn out, or where the story would lead me. With that, Sidney gave me total access to his private papers and to a unique archive of music hall, film, theatre and television material that goes back to before the First World War. Over a period of eighteen months, he also spent many hours answering my questions.

Inevitably, things did not turn out the way he planned. The book I came to write is largely about him. Every friend, acquaintance, colleague or employee to whom I talked only added to my sense of an immensely strong and influential man.

London, 1983   C.M.

Acknowledgments

TO THE PUBLIC, whose lives he has done so much to enliven, Sidney Bernstein is an unknown figure, largely because of his diffidence in playing a public role. To his friends he seems formidable and leaves his mark wherever he goes. I would like to thank the following, all of whom helped me to chronicle a life that began in a London suburb in the last year of the nineteenth century:

Eric and Joan Ambler, Julian Amyes, Dame Peggy Ashcroft, Professor Michael Balfour, Robin Barry, the late Vernon Bartlett, Cedric Belfrage, the late Ingrid Bergman, Alex Bernstein, Charlotte Bernstein, David Bernstein, Lady Bernstein, Connie Bessie, Sir John Betjeman, Paul Bevan, John and Roy Boulting, Dallas Bower, Brenda Bracey, Natasha and Peter Brook, Kay Brown, James Cameron, Leila Cannon, Molly Castle, Victor Chapman, Brenda Christiansen, Betty Comden, Sir Alistair Cooke, Jeremy Croft, Ian Dalrymple, Sir John Davis, Professor Thorold Dickinson, Cecil and Mary Elsom, George Elvin, Sir Denis and Lady Forman, Jack Freeman, Fred Friendly, Norman Frisby, Frank Gardiner, Kenneth Gladstone, Walter Goetz, Lord Goodman, Jules Goodstein, Derek Granger, Adolph Green, Sir Hugh Greene, Bill Grundy, Deborah Hall, Major Edmund Hall, Reginald Hammans, John Hamp, Kitty Hart, Barrie Heads, Lillian Hellman, Jane Hill, Lord Hill, Lady Huxley, Brian Inglis, Enid Isaacs, Jeremy Isaacs, Henry Kaplan, Sir George Kenyon, Harry Kershaw, Maurice King, Teddy Kollek, Lord Lever, Bernard Levin, Mark Littman, QC, Philip Mackie, Reginald Mander, Eileen Maremont, Sir William Mather, Ivor and Helen Montagu, Malcolm Muggeridge,

xiii

Acknowledgments

Janet Murrow, Eileen O'Casey, Lord Olivier, William Paley, Sir Edward Pickering, Alan Pinnock, David Plowright, Dilys Powell, Nicholas Pronay, John Rayner, Martin Savitt, Lawrence Scott, Irene Selznick, Bernard Sendall, Lydia Sherwood, Milton Shulman, Hugh Stewart, Sir Michael Stewart, Lady Stone, Charles Stringer, George Malcolm Thompson, Marietta Tree, Ralph Tubbs, Joe Warton, Harry Watt, Lord Weidenfeld, Sir Harold Wilson and Lord Zuckerman. Graham C. Greene and Tom Maschler of Jonathan Cape have given me constant support.

I am grateful to Sir John Betjeman for permission to reprint his unpublished poem on pp. 120–1, and to the late Lord Clark, Michael Foot and Sir Hugh Trevor-Roper for permission to quote from letters they wrote to Sidney Bernstein. The quotation from Hansard for 28 September 1938 on p. 110 is reproduced with the permission of the Controller of Her Majesty's Stationery Office.

The cartoons in the text are reproduced by kind permission of: Associated Newspaper Group Ltd (*Daily Mail*, 25 June 1958), p. 263; Sir David Low/the *Standard* (*Guardian*, 21 June 1958), p. 307; and *Punch* (June 1959), p. 278. I would also like to thank the following for permission to reproduce copyright photographs: Associated Newspaper Group Ltd (Copyright *News Chronicle*), no. 21; BBC Hulton Picture Library, no. 22; and Camera Press Ltd: photo by Horst Tappe, no. 29.

1

Ilford and the London Suburbs

THE FIRST DOCUMENT in the room full of the papers Sidney Bernstein
has kept since he was a young man is a pale-blue card, frayed and
beginning to crumble. It is a faded certificate of medical discharge, a
declaration that the bearer is 'permanently and totally disabled for
service'. The date is 24 September 1917; the issuing office, the 67th
Regional District of London. Sidney was then eighteen, and this
rejection slip marked the end of a prolonged campaign to enter the war.

The disability was not as incapacitating as the bald words suggest. A
kick delivered by mistake during a football game at school had injured a
bone, the septum in his nose, making breathing difficult. The
treatment for it, however, was both drastic and extremely painful: a
two-hour chisel and hammer operation, without anaesthetic, to
straighten the bone. To enlist, Sidney was forced to endure it; it failed,
leaving an indented and slightly battered-looking nose, ever since
affectionately and on occasion scathingly referred to as a 'boxer's nose'.
The whole event taught him, he says, not a fear of death, but a
permanent terror of pain.

The reason he struggled so hard to join up was not so much the
prevailing climate, when every apparently able young man feared to be
thought a shirker, as the fact that his elder brother, Selim, had died at
Gallipoli in September 1915 of wounds from a dumdum bullet. To fight,
Selim had braved the anti-Semitic mood of the times: volunteering for
the smart gold-epauletted Middlesex Imperial Yeomanry he had given
his name as Burns, having been told that someone with the Jewish name
of Bernstein might not be accepted. When war broke out his regiment

I

was on manoeuvres. Every young man in it responded to the call for overseas volunteers. When the names were read out before the departure for the Dardanelles, Selim requested that he should be listed formally and publicly as Bernstein. Before his death, he was twice mentioned in dispatches.

Sidney was the second son, separated from his elder brother by two girls, Rae and Beatrice. He was the half-way child, the result of a reconciliation, family history has it, when his mother Jane packed her bags after a row one day and disappeared to Brighton, to a hotel the Bernsteins often visited. It took Alexander, his father, an anxious twenty-four hours to find her. After Sidney, another gap; then five more children: Ida, Cecil, Max, Beryl and Albert.

The first home Sidney remembers is Cleodora House, in Bathurst Road, Ilford. There was a balcony in front from which the smaller children used to let down invisible black cotton threads with small objects attached, to baffle passers-by. Behind, the garden ran down to the river Roding; beyond lay the green stretches of Ilford golf course.

In the early years of the century Ilford was still an Essex village, surrounded by agricultural land, a ward of Barking parish, but fast growing from the 'small village, where there are some agreeable houses' as noted by an early-nineteenth-century chronicler into a suburban corner of Greater London. Today, following the diminishing numbers, Bathurst Road stops suddenly at number 80 on one side, number 73 on the other. Cleodora House has gone, demolished in the 1920s together with all those that lay beyond to make way for a more modest stretch of terraced houses.

It was to Ilford that Alexander Bernstein had come from Sweden in the 1880s, together with his mother and sister, while three brothers had gone to make their fortunes in America. Why he chose to come to England, or why he settled in Essex, is unknown. Neither parent ever spoke to Sidney of the past. He discovered that his father was a naturalised Swedish subject only when, already grown up, he saw his passport. All he knew as a boy was that on 6 August 1893 his father married Jane Lazarus, daughter of two Russian immigrants, and that, as children multiplied and family finances grew, so the family had moved into ever larger houses, always in Ilford.

Not that Alexander Bernstein, in these early days at least, was a particularly successful businessman, though he tried his hand at many ventures, from stone quarries in North Wales, at Betws-y-coed, which he and his wife would visit perched on donkeys, to property deals on the fringes of London. When doodling, he would write the figures £68,000 – a morose reminder of a lost consignment of goods, a shipment bound for South Africa and the Boer War, which went down at sea. He had an office in Finsbury Square and caught the Great Eastern Railway most mornings from the halt station outside Ilford to Liverpool Street. When the children were not at school they went to see him off.

The Bernstein finances may have been erratic but the income was sufficient and Alexander, with his silk hat and tubby good humour, imparted a sense of security to his growing family. Portraits, with Victorian backdrops of leafy lanes, the boys in starched Eton collars, the girls in matching pinafores and the babies in lace, suggest a lively, harmonious group. By all accounts his wife Jane, a large and handsome woman with heavy, rather frizzy hair, standing several inches taller than her husband, was an able housekeeper and a careful seamstress, taking in dresses to pass down from one girl to the next. Her father, Isaiah Lazarus, was a tailor, a man with a red beard and a teasing sense of humour, and he made suits for the boys. There was not much music in the house, and not much attention paid to art, but there was a good deal of fun. Friends were always turning up for meals and aunts and uncles who came to visit often stayed – for Ilford was then considered a definite journey to the country. The home was Orthodox Jewish, with strictly observed dietary laws, and a rabbi came regularly to teach the children Hebrew. There was no synagogue in Ilford; Sidney recalls walking several miles to one in Romford.

Though half the Bernstein clan had settled permanently in America, there were visits from across the Atlantic. The best remembered, one small fragment of family lore, was the surprise arrival of Alexander's youngest brother Jack, who made his presence in the house known only by sending a visiting card in with the maid on a silver salver. 'Bloody fool,' exclaimed Mrs Bernstein fondly, her choice of words causing surprise among the children. Jack's visit was fixed firmly in Sidney's memory when he banished the boy – then aged five or six – to the cellar of the house for refusing to eat his peas. Though affectionate and for the most part good-tempered, Sidney could already be stubborn.

But Jack also brought excitement. Alice, Jane Bernstein's sister, was staying in Ilford at the time. He soon wooed her away from an engagement to a man working in South Africa, and the two were married, in a great family gathering, under the traditional Jewish canopy in the garden of Cleodora House.

School was just up the road, a ten-minute walk along the fringes of the Ilford golf course, past the matching terraced houses, past the new buildings and the newly bought-up sites, signs of encroaching London. For Sidney, schooling came before family prosperity made a private education possible. Highlands was free, a Board school that is still there today, a late-Victorian building with weathercock and bell tower, of yellow and grey brick with windows placed high to stop pupils gazing out. The playground is large, bare, somewhat forbidding.

At the turn of the century the school attracted a humane and ambitious headmaster, Alfred Kemp, who instituted a system of colours and caps, had the word 'Board' removed from the name, and fostered a public school team spirit. Under his aegis Highlands became famous for its scholarships. One of these, in 1911, went to Sidney, who can recall those years only for the kindliness of the headmaster, who used to talk to him, with interest rather than disapproval, during the many hours he spent in punishment standing in the big central hall, banished from his classroom for being distracted and refusing to concentrate. Sidney was not a keen student, particularly when faced with historical dates and Latin verbs. But he was bright and quick and intensely curious, and he had a certain agility in mental arithmetic: when school inspectors came to visit, he was pushed to the front to perform.

Coopers Company School, Tredegar Square, Bow, where the scholarship took him on 22 September, has left no memory at all, except a dim recollection of a journey on the Great Eastern Railway. Soon afterwards, in any case, the family moved, north across Romford marshes, round the City of London and up to Cricklewood. Sidney, his younger sister Beryl remembers, would have preferred the cachet of St John's Wood, which suggests a remarkable intuition about social complexities in a boy so young. Their parents felt the area to be wrong, too professional, too withdrawn, not suited to the untidy and sprawling domesticity of their ways, and settled instead on a roomy double-fronted Edwardian villa with a small drive in front and a large garden behind. The younger children took their bicycles out into the street. Alexander Bernstein, recalling his own Swedish childhood, constructed a sauna by the garage. The long, dark room is there still, though 187 Walm Lane is now a boarding house, the marble stairs carpeted over, the stained-glass windows replaced by frosted panes, and the attic sealed off. Then, the six-bedroom house was always noisy with people. There was a lavatory on the landing, though in keeping with Victorian niceties no one drew attention to its presence.

By now Sidney was already standing a little apart from the other children. Physically there was something distinct about his appearance, taller, leaner, more conventionally good-looking than the other boys, with his very bright eyes and his pale skin. There was also a slightly fastidious strain in his character, so that he always looked scrubbed, his clothes seldom scuffed or dishevelled. He rarely fought or scrapped with other boys. Photographs taken of him at the time show an alert, faintly quizzical smile, as if he was thinking of something odd or funny.

In politics, Alexander Bernstein was dedicated to the Liberal Party. Before they moved from Ilford he explained to Sidney, with some pride, that theirs was the largest constituency in England. He took the boy to hear Lloyd George speak at Ilford Town Hall. Jane Bernstein supported the suffragettes. She also gave her time to an organisation that met young girls arriving from Poland and Russia via the Hook of Holland and Harwich in search of a new life, in an effort to prevent them from being taken off to Buenos Aires and the White Slave Trade. When George Lansbury resigned as MP for Poplar in 1912 and stood again as a suffragette candidate, the Bernsteins gave both money and support. (Though his campaign drew the most enthusiastic meetings ever seen in the division, Lansbury was beaten by 749 votes and later, after speaking at a great demonstration in the Albert Hall, he was charged under an act of Edward III as a 'robber or a piller beyond the Seas' and sent to Pentonville Prison.) They were not quite so pleased when Rae, a studious, somewhat earnest girl, responded to an appeal in the newspaper by the suffragette movement for young volunteers to hand out leaflets: she was locked in a bedroom until she agreed never to take part again.

One afternoon, after a large and convivial City lunch, Alexander Bernstein went along, as he often did, to a property auction. Among the other lots there was one for an estate in Manor Park, Ilford. He bought it unseen and found himself the owner of some six hundred houses, currently being let out at 5s. 6d. and 6s. 6d. a week. Even for the early years of the century the price was low. He soon discovered why. The estate was ragged, even derelict, and in need of drastic repair. Characteristically, he set about improving it, installing bathrooms and offering prizes for the best-kept gardens, and sacks of coal at Christmas to tenants who paid their rent on time. He brought gas to the neighbourhood. To counter the high local crime rates he also advertised free houses for policemen, hoping that their presence would deter the criminals. It was an example of his particular brand of humour that he chose to rename the streets after famous judges and prisons of the day. They bear them still: there is a Selbourne Street and a Darling Street and not far away stand Walton and Parkhurst.

This was the start of a modest investment in property. Next came something more serious. In 1906 Alexander Bernstein had bought a piece of land in Edmonton. He inspected the site and concluded that it was ideal for shops, but that to entice shoppers you needed something more. A music hall seemed the most likely answer, and with this momentous decision the Bernstein family entered entertainment.

Alexander Bernstein knew nothing about variety halls, but was soon

5

introduced to George Adney Payne, a leading impresario and the controlling voice in a chain of London music halls, known as the Syndicate Halls, which included the Tivoli, the London Pavilion and the Oxford. The two men entered into a gentleman's agreement. Bernstein would build a theatre at Edmonton, near to shops, and Payne would run it. The whole notion appealed to Alexander Bernstein's sense of adventure; within months he had engaged Bertie Crewe, a distinguished theatre architect, to draw up plans, and Kirk and Kirk the builders to carry them out. All was set to proceed when Payne casually announced that the site no longer seemed to him quite so appealing – he was going to build a theatre in the adjoining suburb of Tottenham.

Bernstein was a man of considerable temper, quick to rages and quick too to recover and laugh, with round, rimless glasses and a small moustache that gave him a stern, even severe look. He did not wish to see his plans collapse at that point. 'Go to hell,' he is reported as saying, 'I'll run it myself.' Wandering, afterwards, down the street he began to have doubts. It was all very well putting up a vast variety theatre on what had once been a rubbish dump – but who was now to run it? Somewhere down Charing Cross Road he was stopped by a young man whose face seemed familiar and who introduced himself as Harry Bawn, George Adney Payne's assistant. 'Young man,' Alexander Bernstein is said to have asked, 'do you want a music hall?'

Thus began a partnership. Alexander Bernstein went ahead and built, equipped and furnished his Edmonton Empire, across the way from Lower Edmonton Station; he then let it out to Harry Bawn and his partner Jesse Sparrow for £900 a year. The Bawn family had the advantage of being old music hall hands: Harry's American wife, Mae Rose, was a much-loved star, appearing for her act as My Fancy in a little Lord Fauntleroy suit and doing a sand dance. Sidney, aged eight, seeing her for the first time at the Palace Theatre, found her extremely beautiful.

On Boxing Day 1908 the Edmonton Empire held its official opening. On the bill was a troupe of elephants, and there had been considerable and rather pleasurable alarm among those buying tickets that, given the refuse-dump foundations of the Empire, the weight of the beasts would bring the building down. The Bernstein children, decked out in their sailor suits, were driven over by carriage from Ilford for the occasion. It was to Sidney's lasting shame that he was made to stand in the gallery handing out sweets to local children as they filed in.

Unwittingly Alexander Bernstein had hit on something financially very good; it was a marvellous moment to be in entertainment. The boom in music hall building had started around 1880 and was now reaching its peak. Night after night the public turned out to watch acts, variety, performing horses and juggling tenors. Every suburban main street wanted its theatre: architects and builders could not turn them out fast enough.

As the music hall became more respectable so it had to be grander and ever more luxurious. (One great improvement had come in 1905 when smelly and suffocating gas lighting was replaced by electricity.) It wasn't just the style and architecture which had, by that time, become almost grotesquely exotic: the Horace Jones Musical Hall in the Surrey Zoological Gardens in Southwark which seated ten thousand had, for instance, staircase towers topped with Turkish kiosks and a zinc-covered roof suggestive of Palladio's Basilica in Vicenza. But the spectacle itself had to be ever more fabulous, and showmen vied with one another to devise acts to astonish and confound. No performance was deemed a success without a constant murmur of incredulity from the stalls.

In 1901, Sir Edward Moss, one of the great showmen, had opened the Hippodrome as a circus water-spectacle music hall. The theatre itself was decorated to remind the audience of the Flemish Renaissance, all voluptuous swirls and heavily decorated figures. But what was new was the water tank, a contraption made of steel boiler plates, which weighed 400 tons when full and could be filled with 100,000 gallons of water in just over a minute. Into this, high divers plunged from the ballustraded central dome, which opened to reveal the sky, and twenty elephants slid down chutes into the water. There was an act called Siberia, in which a horse-drawn sledge – Hengler's Plunging Horses – was pursued by wolves (dogs, made up) and leapt into the water to escape. Tallyho featured a fox hunt with hounds and horsemen swimming a river. The Redskin showed Indians in canoes shooting rapids seventy feet high (some of the audience complained of sea sickness). It wasn't all water. There were also sea lions and polar bears, a performing Bengal tiger and a horse that skipped. A Miss Mina Alix looped the loop in a motor car to the accompaniment of a big roll of drums.

Sir Edward Moss's extravaganzas were highly popular: several thousand people turned up twice a day for the set performances. In 1904 the architect of the Hippodrome, Frank Matcham, agreed to turn his hand to a second Pandora's box, this time for Oswald Stoll. The Coliseum rejected a water tank in favour of great revolving stages round which actors performed Roman chariot races and ran the Derby. The Coliseum prided itself on its hydraulics: lifts took visitors to their seats – bookable, a wholly new concept – and the Royal Box was connected to a special Royal entrance by a carriage that glided by on rails.

Even the straight theatre was engaged in a constant quest for splendour. When Oscar Asche staged *As You Like It* in a London theatre he signed a contract with a firm of Covent Garden florists, who agreed to provide and maintain two thousand pots of fern and large clumps of bamboos, together with cartloads of autumn leaves for the Forest of Arden scene. At one point the actors were walking through beds of ferns two feet high. 'It was admitted', commented one critic somewhat drily, 'that there had never been a more natural forest scene on the stage before.'

By the time Alexander Bernstein and Harry Bawn opened the Empire it had become usual to include at least one bioscope on the programme. Film was, as yet, no serious threat to variety and drama, but it was rapidly catching on. It was barely ten years since the Lumière family had opened the first ever public auditorium for films in Paris, in a basement of the Grand Café on the Boulevard des Capucines, but already the public was beginning to clamour for these crude, flickering images, some of them lasting barely a minute. (Since many were based on music hall gags, part of the excitement lay in wondering whether the film would peter out before the joke had been completed.)

It was in this atmosphere that Sidney was growing up, and it entranced him. He remembers playing truant to see his first film, Edward VII's funeral, in a converted shop in Ilford; as the cortège passed by on the screen he doffed his cap, a gesture which earned him a box of chocolates from a lady standing behind who was impressed by his manners. When there were no trips – the Bernstein family were regular pantomime-goers – he escaped from school to visit the new world of entertainment. In the early days it was to the Ilford Hippodrome matinees; later, further afield, to anything he could find: straight drama, variety, films. One day he saw Diaghilev at the Coliseum and he soon discovered that if he hung around the doors of the Covent Garden Opera House he stood a good chance of free tickets in the gods, on condition that he applaud a chosen artist vigorously.

The Edmonton Empire proved a financial breakthrough for the family and Alexander Bernstein, enjoying his new role as showman, began to expand. In the next five years, leading up to the First World War, he built four more cinemas, for by now the public passion for movies was extraordinary. In barely fifteen years enterprising businessmen had demonstrated that the flickering celluloid need no longer be relegated to the fairground booth. And so he joined the boom in cinema building that saw, between 1908 and 1914, the opening of at least 300 new halls in London devoted exclusively to film. At the start of that period three exhibiting companies, with a total capital of £110,000, had registered themselves with the authorities; six years later the combined capital of the 1,833 companies on the books stood at £11,304,500. Film exhibition had become commercially respectable.

There was money to be made on the fringes as well. Once his cinemas were flourishing, Alexander Bernstein started a company called Film Agencies Ltd which rented out film prints, and manufactured cinema equipment and all its accessories.

It was at this point that Sidney decided to leave school. He was fifteen, impatient, a tall, rather ungainly boy with very formal manners, sharp blue eyes that seemed to have a permanently inquiring look, and an authoritative manner, a little intimidating even to those considerably older. No amount of parental reasoning could stop him. He seemed always to know, with surprising clarity, precisely what he wanted; and having decided to leave school, he simply left.

He wanted to join his father's cinema business immediately, but here Alexander Bernstein was not to be moved. The boy was sent instead as an apprentice engineer to a company belonging to friends, Simon Engineering. As assistant to one of the workmen, Sidney carried tools and tapped boilers. The apprenticeship did not last long, Sidney finding it all intensely boring and irrelevant to the grander schemes in his imagination. Having failed to enlist, he persuaded his father to let him work for the cinema side of the business. His purposefulness was already very persuasive, particularly since he seldom let go of an idea once it had formed in his mind. He was preceded into the business by his sister Rae, who had started to help her father with the letters and the books at the age of seventeen. Cecil, with precise and courteous manners so like Sidney's own, and Max, round-faced and smiling, were both to follow him in.

Sidney soon showed every sign of possessing his father's business acumen. He was very quick to distinguish a good deal from a bad one, and seemed to have an extraordinary ability to see the consequences of transactions. What was more, he was always full of ideas, always agitating for responsibility. But his real interests lay elsewhere. Alexander Bernstein decided to continue to control the building side of his business; Sidney, ostensibly junior to and working for his father's two partners, now really took over the films themselves. Father and son, very alike when it came to quickness of temper and both astonishingly obstinate, fought, breaking into sudden explosions, while the younger children, far less irascible and considerably more pliant, watched with awe. After one violent argument conducted over the lunch table at Walm Lane, Sidney dashed from the room and stormed noisily out of the house, while his father, mute with fury, slowly and deliberately picked up the plates from the table and hurled them to the floor. After these brushes Sidney would write his father long, intense letters, begging to be allowed to pursue some new plan, some scheme for expansion, returning by pen to whatever argument he had failed to win with words. Seeing the pages, with their spiky handwriting, waiting for him on his desk, Alexander Bernstein would moan to his wife: 'Can't you stop that boy writing to me?'

Film Agencies Ltd – which included Kinematograph Equipment Ltd – had its London office at 19 Cecil Court, conveniently near to Wardour Street, then rapidly transforming itself from its past as a centre for print and ivory sellers to the heart of the film industry. The Cinematograph Exhibitors Association had settled there in 1912, under the presidency of the eminent Irishman T. P. O'Connor; the renters followed them there in 1915 with their Kinematograph Renters Society. It was the right place to be. And it was from here that Sidney set off, every morning he could get away, for the trade shows and the West End first runs, with a bag of sandwiches, to find out what was good and what was not, what was right for Edmonton and what better suited to West Ham.

In 1920, by now running the cinemas and a director of the company, and finally though cautiously entrusted with a good deal of responsibility by his father, Sidney embarked on a totally new project. It could have marked the start of a different life; instead, it opened possibilities that were never, really, to be explored. Casting about for further expansion he put a small advertisement in a magazine called *Advertising Weekly*: 'Bring the success of Cinematography into your business. Kinematograph Equipment Co. 10 Cecil Court'. He received only one reply. It was from the major US oil company Phillips, part of Esso and Standard Oil, asking him to call on their London representative in Queen Anne's Gate.

The young man in charge was, like Sidney, full of notions about the future of film. 'Could you produce something on our petrol coming from America?' Sidney was just twenty-one. He engaged a cameraman and took off north for Barrow-in-Furness to film the arrival of the Phillips tanker from the USA, followed that with scenes of the petrol being pumped out, then transferred to jerrycans and from there to the Esso Depots. It was then that he heard of a new American invention – a mechanical pump for transferring the petrol. He contacted the company in America and asked them to put a pump on board the next ship to England. When it arrived, he filmed what it could do. To round off the film, he prefaced the footage he already had with a shot of oil lighting up the sky as it burnt off.

Phillips were delighted with the film. To what other use could cinematography be put? Sidney is less proud of his second film. Phillips had an oil stove called the Valor Perfection that they were trying to promote. It fell to him to think up a selling idea for a film. He came up with a simple story using subtitles. (It was still seven years before the first commercial talkie.) A man, recently married, comes home one evening to find his home full of smoke: the gas cooker is playing up again and his distraught young bride is not handling it well. In disgust, he leaves home again, slamming the door behind him. The next evening he returns to find a gleaming kitchen, a mouth-watering dinner and no smoke – she has been out to buy a Perfection oil stove. The experience amused him, but for the time being Sidney had had enough of film production.

In any case, he had other plans. He had never been abroad, even though his father was a keen traveller, going regularly to Vienna which he loved, or up and down the coasts of England and Scotland by steamer. Early in 1921 Sidney caught a train, then a ferry, for France; next morning the intense blue Mediterranean light woke him in his couchette. It was all very different from the London suburbs. He was with David Blairman, a slightly older friend who had served in the RAF and been reprimanded when he celebrated the end of the war by flinging official papers out of the window at headquarters into the Strand below. The two of them smoked their pipes, marvelled at this new world, and were annoyed when they had to pay for a new carpet in their hotel in Nice because the old one had been singed by ash.

This expedition to France, lasting barely three weeks, was soon eclipsed by many others. During the 1920s and 1930s, it was rare for Sidney not to visit three or four countries a year. After this first taste he became a passionate traveller, walking all over Europe with a rucksack on his back for pleasure, looking, asking, watching: feeling always that he had a lot to learn.

His manner, with adulthood, had become more restrained, less impetuous. To the invariable, and on occasion rather elaborate, courtesy had been added a certain gravity of manner that made him appear far older than he was. Strangers, who warmed instantly to his attentiveness, were none the less a little disconcerted by the resolution with which he seemed to pursue his life. With close friends he could be funny, light-hearted, though usually he preferred to listen than to talk, to encourage others rather than to contribute himself. Increasingly, there seemed to be an air of detachment about him, a self-protective withdrawal from too easy commitment. He was busy observing the world, unsure as yet about what really mattered.

On 4 June 1921 he caught a Cunard liner, the *Aquitania*, for New York. His diary of the crossing is terse. 5 June: 'Mod. breeze. Sea fine. Clouds.' 10 June: 'Light breeze. Slight sea and fog.' Nothing about the passengers, the ship, what he did all day. No mention of Noël Coward,

Jeffrey Amherst or Lorenz Hart, fellow passengers and soon to become friends.

All he remembers of the experience is sharing an inside cabin with a man who shaved every morning not with a razor but by applying some kind of cream to his face and scraping it off with a fine bone blade. Despite his Jewish upbringing, it was many years before he discovered that this was in fact the practice among Hasidic Jews.

For a young man infatuated with film, bred on a diet of almost exclusively American movies and involved in running a chain of theatres and cinemas, America was a country of dreams. Nothing could have prepared Sidney for the experience that awaited him in New York. It was not merely bigger, more advanced, more exciting, brash; there were a million different things going on. He wanted to see them all.

He was met by his father's American family and installed in the Commodore Hotel above Grand Central Station. There were no Empire State Building and Chrysler yet to dominate the skyline, but already blocks towered above the city, gleaming in the midsummer sunshine, while the elevated train, the El, perched on superstructures high above the heads of pedestrians, clanked its way up and down the main avenues.

A golden decade was just beginning for the cinema, not only in America but all over the world, in Germany, Italy and Russia. In New York and California it was at its most exuberant. And part of this exuberance proclaimed itself in an intensive cinema-building boom. The USA, remote from the war in Europe, was ahead of the game. By the time Sidney reached New York, well over 25,000 cinemas were running throughout the country, showing films to some six million people a day.

The picture palaces were not to reach their fullest glory for another four or five years but New York already had cinemas of which to boast, with more marble, more arcades of mirrors, longer galleries of oil paintings and more coloured electric lights than a young man from Europe could have imagined. That summer, entire theatre fronts were frosted over like ice compartments, steaming mist-like in the haze, to advertise the desirable arctic chill inside.

There was the Rialto to visit, 'The temple of the Motion Picture', where an orchestra of forty performed four times daily, together with wonder dogs and jazz bands in funny hats, as an accompaniment to the regular movie shows. Ushers wore scarlet tunics piped in gold, looped with tassels, and carried swagger-sticks with mother-of-pearl tips that lit up in the dark. The head usher sported a bugle. Outside, on the façade, whirled a continual pinwheel of electric light that seemed to cast a shower of sparks as it spelled out the word Rialto, while an eagle flapped its wings and Old Glory shone above.

Nearby stood the Rivoli, with its terracotta columns and a pediment from the Parthenon, and the Capitol, where it was said that a team of skilled charwomen specially imported from Baltimore came to scrub the sweeping white marble staircase during the night. It was all overpoweringly opulent, and designed to dazzle; in the search for ever more alluring details, fierce rivalry was encouraged between the cinemas. When the Rivoli hired a giant in a gendarme's uniform to stand by the box office, the doorman at the Grand was put into a burnous of the Foreign Legion, while not far away the Tivoli employed a midget dressed as a Keystone cop.

These were absurd and heady days and Sidney lost no time. When he had seen what he could of New York he set off with his Aunt Alice – who had married Jack and settled in New York – on a train tour of the country. They slept on board each night, in considerable comfort, alighting every morning in a new city where Sidney had introductions to people in the film and theatre world. Each night, they returned to the station and moved on again. The trip lasted a month, and Sidney and Alice went as far as Colorado before turning back. 'It was', he says, 'like drinking champagne all day.' Wherever they went the tall young man with his flattened nose and extravagant Englishness – he was sensible enough, despite the June temperatures, to wear his bowler hat and carry a rolled umbrella at all times, as well as accentuate his accent – was much fêted. The Americans were accustomed to youth and drive; they marvelled at such sophistication. And back in the train each night he sat in the front car where the talkers gathered and listened to the European immigrants as they spoke of their work, and their pleasure in the limitless opportunities of the new world.

He came home, on the *Berengaria*, not only forever marked by what he had seen but with new authority. The sophistication that had singled him out among the young Americans was not lost on those back home, and his descriptions of new developments and ideas on how to adapt them to England drew increasing interest in the film industry. In September 1921, he was asked by a member of Lloyd George's staff whether he could provide some entertainment for the Prime Minister, currently on a trip to Scotland discussing unemployment with local mayors and in dire need of distraction. Sidney's memory was still full of the brilliance of the slapstick comedians: he suggested an evening of Charlie Chaplin, then the youthful hero of the New York screens.

Lloyd George was staying at Gairloch, where there was as yet no electricity. Sidney caught the overnight train from London to Inverness with a projectionist, picked up a generator and motored on to

Gairloch. On the way, the party stopped at a country pub where they met Lord Riddell, one of Lloyd George's Liberal Party backers; he and Sir Emsley Carr, who owned the *News of the World*, told Sidney that they expected trouble at the Gairloch meeting.

In the event, all was quiet. Sidney and his projectionist installed their generator in the small house where Lloyd George was staying, causing havoc among the furniture, and on a chilly early autumn evening the political gathering settled down to a programme of Chaplin burlesque, to the soothing rhythmic stutters of the projector. Lloyd George loved it.

In December, when the Royal family had gathered at Sandringham in Norfolk for the Christmas holidays, Sidney was asked to organise a Royal film-show. It was an extraordinary honour for a young man of twenty-two and indicated his growing stature in the world of Britain's show business. Once again he suggested a Chaplin film, *The Kid*. The equerry detailed to supervise the performance agreed. Since Chaplin had a London representative, Hi Winik of Western Electric Import Company, Sidney approached him for permission to show the film.

At 6.30 in the morning, on 29 December, Sidney motored down to Sandringham. He spent the day supervising the setting up of the equipment in a long gallery and retired to dine with an aide-de-camp. Then a message arrived from the Lord Chamberlain's office: *The Kid* was not suitable for the Royal family – it showed a baby in nappies. Could that scene be cut?

No, said Sidney, it could not. *The Kid* was not his film to tamper with, and in any case there was no time. Did not Royal babies wear nappies? Reluctantly the Lord Chamberlain gave in.

The showing was a success. King George and Queen Mary were not at all disgusted by the nappies. Once the film was under way Sidney walked back down the gallery to see that all was well with his projectionists. Glancing out of the windows behind them, he saw five fire engines parked in the courtyard below, their water hoses aimed at the makeshift cinema. The lessons of the great cinema fire in Paris of 1897, in which more than a hundred people, many of them children, had died, and the still considerable perils of inflammable nitrate film, had not been forgotten by the Lord Chamberlain's office.

Winik had wanted to see Sandringham and Sidney took him there one day. On the way they passed the Jewish Home for Incurables, a tall and imposing building in Tottenham. Winik asked what it was; Sidney explained, adding that it was a charity regularly supported by the Bernstein family, but that he, personally, had always objected to the word 'incurable'. Winik was a strange man. A few weeks later he asked Sidney to take him round the Home, and announced: 'Sidney, I can cure those people by laughter. I'm going to show them Chaplin's films.'

The Home's administrators were pleased, but suggested that the more usual charitable gesture was to offer a special lunch for the patients. Winik insisted. And after a showing of *The Kid* and *Shoulder Arms*, much enjoyed by the patients, he rose to his feet and delivered a speech. He did not believe, he said, that there was such a thing as an 'incurable' illness. 'Any patient who forgets that he is incurable and walks from here to my office in Wardour Street will receive a considerable sum of money.' Several of the inmates tried; all were retrieved, exhausted, from along the way. Winik himself was eventually incarcerated with religious megalomania.

Sidney was now in the right business at the right time. He was moving confidently in a field where there were, as yet, no experts, only a great deal happening and much to be learned. More important, perhaps, he was beginning to meet people, make friends quite unlike those who inhabited the cinema exhibitors' world. The only question was in which direction to go.

There was no time to work it out. Alexander Bernstein had not been well for some time. Doctors had long advised surgery, fearing cancer of the stomach. He had refused until it was too late. He was rushed to a Harley Street clinic; the older children remember giving him oxygen. Within days he was dead. Everyone missed him; for all his short temper, he had been a popular, much loved man.

There were no immediate financial worries. But there were five younger children, all living at home and two still at school. Cecil had by now joined the company on the building side. Whatever thoughts Sidney might have had about his own future, there was now no choice: the moment had come for him to manage his family's affairs.

2

The Music Halls, Bloomsbury and the Film Society

HARRY BAWN WAS a charming, good-looking man but he was not a worker. The Edmonton Empire soon ran down; in lieu of rent the Bernsteins accepted shares in the company. Then Bawn died and another charming young man took over, only this one was a golfer, who preferred the links to managing a music hall. One night, not long after his father's death, Sidney was driving past the theatre on his way to Hertfordshire to have dinner with Tom Davis, English representative of Chaplin, Mary Pickford and Douglas Fairbanks, who wanted advice for friends who were building a cinema in Shrewsbury. Looking out of the car window he noticed that the Empire was unnaturally dark, exuding gloom and disrepair. He stopped, went in and found that many of the lightbulbs had been removed to save money. The place was half-empty and indescribably seedy.

Next morning he went to call on the family accountant and trustee, Ernest George Bygrave, a lasting friend of and influence on the Bernstein family, and asked him to find out whether Mrs Bawn was prepared to sell back the lease. She was: she longed to retire to a bungalow in Ramsgate. Next he visited Maurice King, the son of a former business associate of his father's, who was in the liquor business. 'If I buy a music hall will you run the bars?' he asked.

The three men inspected the Empire, noted its dereliction and decided that they could make it pay. The theatre had three bars; Maurice King reasoned that there was money to be made from them. Sidney then went to Barclays Bank (he had been introduced to them by his father while still in knickerbockers), borrowed some money and the deal was signed. Sidney's first independent business move had now been made.

From late in 1922, when the Edmonton Empire reopened, smartened up and as lively as its new owners could make it, until 1927, Sidney ran the theatre as a music hall. The redecoration had been only one small part of the problem; a far larger one was that of the 'bar system' then widespread in the more prestigious music halls of signing acts in such a way that they were then barred from appearing in nearby areas or other circuits. The Empire was ill organised in the 'bar system' and had lost many of the more talented performers. Sidney now cast about for a way of breaking the ban.

He asked his booking agent, Leon Pollock, to arrange a lunch with Harry Masters, booking manager for the Palladium and an important voice in the variety theatres. Taking his travelling friend David Blairman with him, Sidney went to the appointment at Verreys, a then fashionable restaurant in Regent Street, and waited nervously for the far older and much more established man to turn up. Eventually, Masters appeared. Sidney asked him what he would like to drink. 'Mumble, mumble,' came the reply. Sidney interpreted this as champagne and called for a bottle of the best. That soon vanished. 'Would you like another drink?' Another mumble; more champagne. By the end of lunch, Masters had agreed to see that the bar would be waived.

Now began an enjoyable interlude in Sidney's life. He set about learning the music hall business: the list of those who appeared on the boards of Edmonton in the 1920s is a lexicon of the stars of the day. There was G. H. Elliot (The Chocolate Coloured Coon), Harry Champion (Quick Fire Comedian), Gus Elen (Coster), Ernie Lottinza (PC 49), and Ella Retford, who arrived at the theatre each night in a different fur coat; there were the male impersonators, Vesta Tilly and Hetty King, and the groups like Fred Karno's Mumming Birds (Karno was Chaplin's mentor) and Lew Lake and Co., the Ten Loonies.

Sandow the Strong Man used to advertise his act in the street outside the Empire by linking his arms between the reins of two pairs of brewers' shire horses and holding tight, while their drivers urged them in opposite directions. The animal acts would arrive at the theatre from across the green, walking past the Cross Keys pub to be stabled behind the Empire. One night a stable man rushed into the pub and called for help with the elephants, one of which was trumpeting and rapidly becoming uncontrollable. Bernard Fitch, the publican, rang Lockhart, the elephants' owner, for advice. 'It's probably colic,' said Lockhart calmly. 'Give him a drop of whisky.' The drop turned out to be two bottles, administered in a bucket. The elephant gave no more trouble.

On another occasion, the Police Minstrels, fifty bobbies all blacked up as 'Massa Bones', decided to install a giant organ weighing several tons for their annual charity show. It arrived by rail, along the tracks that ran behind the theatre. As the 1920s wore on, local people came to cherish the Empire, with its blind accordion player providing music until the doors opened each day and the trams rumbling past up and down New Road Hill. Fifty years after it opened, Sidney was still receiving letters full of fond anecdotes of its early days.

It was at the Empire, not long after Sidney took it over, that Marie Lloyd, possibly the most loved of all the music hall stars, died. Marie Lloyd was the public's sweetheart, with her dazzling white teeth and risqué ballads. (Sarah Bernhardt once disconcerted a London gathering by declaring that Marie Lloyd was the best living British actress.) The Edmonton Empire billed her as the 'Queen of all comediennes'.

One Monday night in October 1922, Sidney was telephoned by the manager of the Empire. Marie Lloyd was ill, but refused to go home, since in those days not to appear would have meant forfeiting a night's pay (she was making between £250 and £300 a week). 'Tell her that she needn't go on, and that I'll pay her the salary just the same,' said Sidney. The message had no effect: Marie Lloyd went on stage.

On Tuesday, Sidney visited the first house at 6.30. He found her huddled over the stove in her dressing-room, her teeth chattering. He tried to persuade her to go home, but again she refused, so he called in a doctor to give her a calming injection.

In the interval, walking around the lobby and the bars, he heard people saying: 'She's wonderful, but she's very drunk.' News of her illness, however, got out, and next morning the *Star* reported admiringly that she had 'pulled up her skirts and danced and laughed and winked in her inimitable way'. On Wednesday she insisted on appearing again, sang her most lastingly popular song, 'I'm one of the ruins that Cromwell knocked about a bit', and collapsed. She was carried to her house in Golders Green. Two days later, she died.

Over 100,000 people came to see her grave, which gives some indication not just of her personal fame, but of the extraordinary popularity of music hall stars in the 1920s. Room 108 of the Empire theatre, the dressing-room she had used, was kept locked in her memory for over ten years.

Sidney was a regular visitor to the Empire. Whatever Monday he was free, he, Maurice King and E. G. Bygrave, three rather formal figures in their city suits, would meet in the lobby, make their way to the special box reserved for them, and watch the show. Afterwards they retired to an office above the theatre, sent out to the pub for steaks, beer and cigars and reviewed the performance, usually concluding that it was 'no damned good'. Invariably, Sidney would add: 'Never mind. It's great fun.' But he could, already, be tough; employees soon learned that he would tolerate no shoddiness and that he despised fawners.

It was at these late-night meetings, a little lightheaded on beer and cigars, that Sidney and Maurice King dreamt up ever more improbable stunts with which to lure new audiences. E. G. Bygrave, the accountant, would sit and listen. This was Sidney at his best: inventive, irreverent, canny. Sometimes, he seemed to be driving the whole operation simply by the force of his own exuberance. One of the most inspired and shortest lived ideas was a lottery, with numbers printed on every programme (3d. each); local shops had been persuaded to donate prizes. The gimmick caught on fast with the public: there were queues around the block for every performance. The trouble was that it was also illegal and after a few weeks of great profitability Sidney, Bygrave and the Manager – though not the more established businessman King – were summoned before a magistrate's court. The case of Sidney's illegal lottery tickets, minor and frivolous as it was, and soon dismissed by the magistrate, was the first episode in a lifetime of litigious behaviour.

The Empire took only a small part of Sidney's time. By the summer of 1922 he was already moving in other, more ambitious directions, feeling his way, always tentatively, but with purpose. Some time that spring a producer from Paramount Pictures USA, Walter Wanger, arrived on a visit to London; he had been preceded, as all Hollywood celebrities were, by a sheaf of telegrams of introduction to people in British films and theatres. One of them, indirectly, led him to Sidney, and the two men, Wanger five years the older, became friends. At this stage in his life, most of the people, men and women, with whom Sidney spent his time were noticeably more successful than he was.

Walter Wanger was an unexpected figure to find thriving in the Californian movie world: an Ivy League graduate, a theatre producer on Broadway, with a quiet voice and steady dignity that singled him out from the louder and more flamboyant of his contemporaries. Jesse Lasky, vice-president of Paramount, had recently employed him to seek out acting talent for the studio.

Wanger invited Sidney round to the house he had rented in Charles Street and questioned him closely about the state of the London theatre. When he heard that the Covent Garden opera house had been forced to close down after two disastrous seasons he came up with an idea that appealed to Sidney's showman side, and the two went into partnership. Wanger's idea was to use Covent Garden as a temporary cinema-cum-theatre, making use of its size and prestige, and to invite

Eugene Goosens to conduct the Covent Garden Symphony Orchestra to accompany the films and ballet, starring Lydia Lopokova and Léonide Massine. They also showed *Atlantide* and *Theodora*.

The first performance took place, with much publicity, on 19 December 1921, after Sidney's company, Film Agencies Ltd, had built a projection box in the Grand Tier. The main feature was *The Three Musketeers*, and it was presented by Douglas Fairbanks. All would probably have been well had it not been for an unforeseen technical hitch. Once the film was going, the box heated up so excessively that the projectionist began to wilt. Sidney hastened to construct a second makeshift box behind, which he filled with ice, and then placed a fan designed to train the chilled air into the booth. There was now ventilation – but no oxygen. As an experiment, the cinema season at Covent Garden had been a failure. Wanger and Sidney both lost their money.

In the autumn of 1922 Sidney went to Shrewsbury for the opening of another Empire; the theatre was not a Bernstein property but the owners had asked him to supervise its reconstruction and manage it. During the evening he spent time with the secretary of Shrewsbury's Flower Show, who told him about a local family he had been billeted on in the war, a gipsy-like mother whose daughter was mad about films. Later, Sidney met the girl. Her name was Iris Barry. It was the start of an immensely important friendship that lasted until her death in 1969.

Iris Barry was then twenty-six, three years older than Sidney. She was tiny, extremely thin, with blue eyes, rather sallow skin and black hair cut in an Eton crop. She had been brought up by her grandparents, who were dairy farmers in Worcestershire, sent to a convent and would have gone to Oxford had the war not intervened. As it was, she learnt typing and shorthand, took a wartime job in a Birmingham post office, and wrote poetry in the evenings. Some of it reached Ezra Pound who summoned her to a meeting in London. By the time she met Sidney, Iris Barry was already friends with T. S. Eliot, the Sitwells, and through them Liam O'Flaherty and Wyndham Lewis, by whom she had had two children. It was into this Bloomsbury world, of poetry, literature and erudite conversation, that she now began to draw Sidney.

She introduced him to Liam O'Flaherty, who, in turn, introduced him to other Irish poets and playwrights. She took him to a hall in Chelsea with a group of friends to see one of the first performances of Edith Sitwell's *Façade*: a white sheet had been draped across the back of the hall with a hole cut in the centre in the shape of a gramophone record, through which Edith Sitwell declaimed. Sidney can remember that one guinea bought the signature of one Sitwell on a book; three guineas, all three. A letter that Iris Barry wrote to him early on in their friendship gives some idea of the doors that she was opening for him:

> Dearest Sidney, a small party here on the evening of the 8th would be vastly improved by your presence – and if you can bring a lovely young woman so much the better. I seem rather short of them. 10 pm and after. There is a dim hope that Galsworthy might come but I doubt it. Rebecca West, Vyvyan (Holland), Elsa (Lanchester) and perhaps C. (Laughton), the Lavers, perhaps the Cochrans perhaps not, and so forth. Do come my angel.
>
> Yours
Iris

He, in return, asked her to review films at the trade shows for his cinemas, and introduced her to the Strachey family, John and Amabel and their father, St Loe Strachey, who ran the *Spectator*. In 1924 Iris Barry became the magazine's film critic – one of the first serious critics of the cinema to be appointed in Britain. She later married the paper's literary editor, Alan Porter.

Iris Barry was many things that Sidney was not: she was an intellectual, who talked to him of books and paintings, and a musician, who had a fine contralto voice and played the piano, while Sidney was singularly unmusical. She made an enormous impression on him.

One of Iris Barry's friends was a young man called Ivor Montagu, son of the banking family the Samuel-Montagus, who, like her, was passionate about films. Some time in 1924 Montagu went to Berlin for *The Times* to write about the German film industry and the UFA studios. On his way home he met Hugh Miller, the actor, in the corridor of his train. The two men stood discussing their German experiences – Miller had been filming for a joint Anglo-German production in Munich – lamenting the unadventurousness of the British cinema, the fact that a combination of boorish censor, American film domination and a timid film industry had effectively put a stranglehold on all experimentation. What was needed for films, they agreed, was something like the Stage Society, which tried out new playwrights not deemed sufficiently commercial on Sundays when the theatres were closed. Why, they asked each other, were there no specialised societies putting on some of the exciting new German, French and Italian films? Why were there so few decent critics? Why was it always assumed in Britain that no one serious could possibly be interested in cinema?

Not long after this conversation, Iris Barry and her new husband Alan Porter gave a party in their ground-floor flat in Guilford Street. To it came Ivor Montagu and Hugh Miller, Adrian Brunel, the film director they were trying to involve in their deliberations, Walter Mycroft, film critic of the *Evening Standard*, and the sculptor Frank Dobson. Sidney was there as well and discussions went on late about how to set up an equivalent to Louis Delluc's Ciné Club in Paris. In the early hours of the morning Sidney and Ivor Montagu left together, in the pouring rain.

Out of this evening was born the Film Society, with the aim to bring films from abroad, uncut, properly titled and with musical accompaniments – for all films, in the mid-1920s, were silent. Its manifesto, issued in June 1925, stated:

> The Film Society has been founded in the belief that there are in this country a large number of people who regard the cinema with the liveliest interest and who would welcome an opportunity seldom afforded the general public of witnessing films of intrinsic merit ... This cannot but affect future production, by founding a clearing house for all films having pretensions of sincerity, irrespective of origin or immediate mercantile interest.

There was another, more selfish, reason as the founders laughingly agreed. They themselves greatly wanted a chance to see what was going on in the international cinema. But the silent movies needed their musical scores, and how otherwise than with membership fees to pay for a full orchestra – sometimes as much as £50 – to play them? As Ivor Montagu puts it: 'We were all devotees of Chaplin – but we wanted to see something else.'

Each of the founders, who described themselves in the articles of association as 'a writer, a film director, an actor, a sculptor, a zoologist [Montagu had studied zoology] and a cinema exhibitor', brought something different to the society, other than a love of films. Ivor Montagu, who became its chairman, though aged only twenty-one, was enthusiastic, sociable and possessed of considerable energy: he went out and canvassed for prestigious supporters, the kind guaranteed to keep the authorities from too much interference. His forays brought in H. G. Wells, Bernard Shaw, Maynard Keynes, Roger Fry, J. B. S. Haldane, Julian Huxley and Lord Swaythling. Iris Barry contributed her critical skills and her wide knowledge of existing films; McKnight Kauffer, the designer, agreed to produce a logo for the Society, 'a much admired, bold FS with a tiny attenuated figure attached, deciphered variously as a Cupid and a Red Indian'.

Sidney brought his experience of renters and exhibitors, and he brought contacts. It is arguable that without him the Society would never have been formed, never found its way through the labyrinths of

LCC rules and censorship permissions or the industry itself, which viewed him already with a mixture of respect and fear – respect for his business abilities and his generosity, fear because he was friends with the people most likely to complicate their exclusive way of running things. In the Film Society, Sidney was the bridge to them. His manner was unobtrusive, but it inspired confidence; at twenty-six, he radiated steadiness. He was not easily awed, either by grandeur or by bullying. He was rarely talkative, even among the joking and the laughter, of which there was a great deal, but when he did talk, in his light, staccato voice, making short and emphatic statements and occasional funny rejoinders, people listened.

Sidney also brought, through his connections, the use on Sunday afternoons of the New Gallery Kinema in Regent Street, said to be the most comfortable cinema in London. On 25 October 1925, 1,400 people – 900 members, the rest guests – gathered to watch Chaplin's *Champion Charlie*, a Bronco Billy melodrama, a study in cinema futurism, a parody of a news film and Paul Leni's *Waxworks*. The crowd that flowed out on to the pavement afterwards, in bright, bohemian clothes, arguing loudly, made the occasion seem rather like a party in Chelsea.

Somewhat to its Council's surprise, the Film Society did not receive a very warm welcome. The trade chose to see in it a threat, an implication of criticism (to such an extent that Adrian Brunel had to dissociate himself from their activities, lest he be labelled too highbrow). The press, which might have been expected to greet any such venture with enthusiasm, called it 'snobbish' and 'intellectual'. 'Nothing of this kind', wrote C. A. Lejeune in the *Manchester Guardian*, 'can be of any use unless it is open to the public.'

Worse, the Society fell foul of the Censor at its first performance. In the 1920s the British Board of Film Censors regarded its role as that of protector of a profitable and innocuous kind of family entertainment, barring, in the process, the showing of 'white men in a state of degradation amidst native surroundings', 'British social life held up to ridicule', 'police officials leading a double life', or 'the impugning of the honour of members of the medical profession'. *Waxworks*, argued Brooke Wilkinson, the Censor, with whom Sidney was to tangle again on later occasions (and who now said to him crossly, 'Don't talk to me about art, young man; I knew Ruskin'), should not contain a figure called Jack the Ripper, since that was a real criminal and to use his nickname infringed censorship rules. (He proposed instead 'Spring-heeled Jack'.)

The Society won a temporary dispensation for the first performance and then acted fast. Ivor Montagu rallied his eminent cast of

23

supporters; Sidney, Iris Barry and Walter Mycroft lobbied the members and, by a close margin of fifty to forty votes, the LCC gave the Society a licence to show films under bona fide private society conditions, with annual membership and no censorship. Not that Wilkinson did not continue to rumble his misgivings. When *The Cabinet of Dr Caligari* was shown uncut early in the Society's life, he objected that some of the audience were bound to have relatives in insane asylums and would imagine that the conditions they were observing on the screen were those of British mental hospitals.

Since there were as yet no international film archives or catalogues, it fell to the Council members to search out films. Each of the founders travelled abroad whenever possible, and brought back prints from the studios and directors they visited. Sometimes it was a case of smuggling a reel past wary and hostile customs officers. Sidney had the inspired idea of getting Nancy Cunard to bring over Buñuel's *Un Chien Andalou* from Paris in her hat box. He had met Buñuel, who had complained bitterly to him that his first French audience had thrown eggs at the screen, in Paris. 'Isn't that what you wanted?' Sidney had asked. 'Yes,' replied Buñuel, after some thought. 'Exactly what I wanted.'

At other times it was a question of detective work. One day, on a whim, Sidney opened the telephone directory and found a 'Ben Hur' listed. He put it out of his mind until a few weeks later when the Film Society Council were discussing a Ben Hur film and Sidney, jokingly, told them about the entry. Prompted by their interest, he followed it up. The address took him to a pub in Stepney where the publican, a Jew, told him that he had taken the name for his strong-man act. What was more, he had a film of *Ben Hur*. It turned out to be a rare and early print of a one-reel film made in 1907 on Manhattan Beach by Frank Oakes Rose and Sidney Olcott, which Sidney arranged to have shown at the Film Society.

That first year, 1925-6, the Film Society put on thirty-nine films, of which twenty had never been seen in England before. The following year, they showed Fritz Lang's *Dr Mabuse*, Erich von Stroheim's *Greed*, and G. W. Pabst's *Joyless Street* with Greta Garbo, three films now considered among the classics of the silent years. By this time the Sunday viewings were very much part of London's social and intellectual life. Augustus John came to them, with a bottle of brandy in the game pocket of his long overcoat; Bernard Shaw, Arnold Bennett, H. G. Wells and Baroness Budberg, his mistress and former friend of Gorki and Bruce Lockhart, often turned up, lured by occasional free tickets. Usually the audience cheered and applauded what they saw, gathering afterwards in little huddles down Regent Street picking over the various films; sometimes fights broke out, or the staider members walked out in disgust. H. G. Wells solemnly left the cinema when Fernandel as the village idiot in *Le Rosier de Madame Husson* spent his prize money on a prostitute. The *Daily Express* summed up at least one strand of hostile public feeling when it said of one Sunday showing:

> The most diverse and peculiar collection of people I have ever seen in London ... A good many had no hats, but to make up for that they had, believe me, a quite astonishing number of hairy chins. Plus fours, queer coloured flannel trousers and immaculate morning coats were inextricably jumbled.

Whatever else, this attack was not aimed at Sidney, who never wore anything but suits. After the showing, the founders and their friends dispersed in groups, some to go to Adrian Brunel's select 'hate parties', élite gatherings of cinema buffs where conversation centred around everything in the film industry people most hated – the Censor, the critics, the exhibitors.

It was with its fourth season that the Film Society ran into harder opposition. That winter, 1928–9, they decided to bring over the great Russian films, hitherto unseen in Britain and already described by the Censor (who may have been aware of Lenin's remark, 'Of all the arts, for us, the cinema is the most important') as being 'tinctured with political propaganda'.

Pudovkin's *Mother*, put on in October, angered no one. But then, on 3 February 1929, the Society screened *The End of St Petersburg*; after it was over, Pudovkin, who was on a visit to London, addressed the members on his film-making techniques and his views on sound film. There were noisy arguments among the audience, many of whom had cheered when 'All power to the Soviets' had come up on the screen. Later, questions were asked in the House of Commons – the Conservative Party was already agitating about the growth of 'revolutionary Soviet film propaganda'.

This was the moment for which some critics had long been waiting. The *Sunday Pictorial* was the first to attack. Under the headline, 'What we are tolerating: Propaganda efforts behind latest Russian Importation', Walter Mutch declared:

> ... we are a strange people. We suffer fools gladly. We tolerate the intolerable. The BBC with its supposedly rigid censorship, saw fit the other day to permit a young man to broadcast the sneer that the Russian film *Potemkin* had been exhibited in every enlightened country save our own. This was the speaker who declared that all British pictures were dull and stupid ...

Is the LCC entirely satisfied with the result of granting a licence to the Film Society?

The 'young man' in question was Sidney, who had recently given a talk on the radio declaring that British directors and producers needed to become familiar with the Russian techniques, and all new techniques, if Britain was ever to have a thriving film industry of its own. He now issued a writ: Bernstein and others v. the *Sunday Pictorial* and another. A long battle was out in the open.

Before the case came to court, the *Sunday Pictorial* settled and printed an apology, as did the *Sunday Express* not long after, when the Fleet Street critic G. A. Atkinson wrote that the Society had been formed 'to communise the country by showing Soviet films'. Atkinson had long been feuding against the Society, who knew him to be a crook in the film world, taking money from the American companies in return for a promise of a good review in the *Express* for their films. (There was a car on the market called a Straight Eight; Atkinson's limousine was jokingly known as a 'Crooked Eight'.) Atkinson, however, continued to regard himself as one of the Film Society set. It pleased Sidney greatly when one day, as he was leaving the Ivy Restaurant, he bumped into George Atkinson. The two men decided to walk towards the Strand together. As they approached Lincoln's Inn, Sidney stopped. 'I shall have to leave you here,' he said. 'I'm going to see my solicitors to find out how my case against you is going.'

None of these writs checked the hostility of the newspapers, however, who continued to wage an anti-Film Society crusade well into the 1930s. In October 1930 the *Express* repeated that 'knowingly or unknowingly [it] is engaged in furthering the subversive propaganda of the Bolsheviks ... some of these films are definitely anti British. Others are semi blasphemous. Others are frankly indecent. All are designed to ferment social and political unrest.'

All this was obvious nonsense and everyone knew it. If the Society did not take the libels too seriously, it was that the Council members were having fun, that they were young – most still in their twenties – and that the Society itself was well respected in the circles they admired. When the LCC, seeking to penalise them for the Russian season, proposed an exorbitant new minimum subscription of 10s. it was Bernard Shaw, H. G. Wells and Bertrand Russell who came to their defence, declaring: 'The view that the rich are not open to moral corruption whereas the poor are is an insult to the masses of the nation.' By 1930, too, the idea of specialised film societies was fast spreading to other cities and both Leeds and Glasgow had already formed their own, modelled on the London Society. It was not only in London that there was a growing appetite for the better foreign films.

The Film Society was also having a considerable influence on a very wide range of people. Its programme notes, started by Ivor Montagu, were models of clarity and erudition, while its superimposed titles were precise and apt, the Council members having discovered that poets could handle them better than writers since they had a keener sense of space with words. The Society kept trying things out, experimenting with film in an exciting way, even if some of the experiments had comic results. On one occasion Dziga Vertov, the Russian director famous for his documentaries, brought over a print of his film *Enthusiasm* which included a primitive sound track. For the showing on Sunday, he sat in the back row of the Dress Circle clutching the sound box, with its red and black buttons for controlling the volume. During the second half of the last reel, when the film was showing the triumphs of Russian nationwide industrialisation, with howling wirelesses, blaring sirens, clattering of Bessemers and clanging of factory machinery, Vertov seemed to go beserk. He started pressing the red button over and over again until the building trembled and members of the audience, half-demented by the hoots and roars and jangles, fled the cinema. The manager lunged towards Vertov, to seize the box; Vertov hung on grimly. There was chaos; Thorold Dickinson, the director, by then a Film Society devotee, tried to hit him. It had no effect. Only when the reel finished in a cacophony of industrial sound, did Vertov, evidently well pleased with his sound effects, and uttering a loud grunt of satisfaction, yield up the box.

The screening of Eisenstein's *October* also presented a daunting technical problem. Edmund Meisel's score, written not for the original but for a cut German version of the film, was found to be forty-five minutes shorter than the full film, and Ernest Irving, the musical director at Ealing studios who had agreed to conduct it, had only one day with the orchestra to rehearse his adaptations. By Sunday afternoon when *October* was due to be shown, he was only half-way through. The first part, up to the interval, flowed smoothly. The second was sheer improvisation: Irving kept up a shouted commentary, beating time and turning the pages of his score backwards and forwards. The orchestra played gamely, but some were so busy flicking pages that they missed out passages altogether. Inevitably, Irving reached the end too soon and had no choice but to make the orchestra repeat the last chords of the score eleven times, very slowly, before the end titles came up on the screen. At this point, he hurled his baton high into the air, and the audience stood and cheered as if it had been the last night of the Proms.

By this time, the Society was a force in the British film world. Any film person with pretentions to seriousness now came to their gatherings, and many new and original film-makers, like the New Zealand animator Len Lye, who was using colour and design and marrying it with discs of music in a way never done before, had their first showings in the New Gallery on a Sunday afternoon. (Sidney and Ivor Montagu had come across him living on a barge on the Thames.) Even abroad the Society's voice was respected: when the city of Stuttgart banned the film *Battleship Potemkin*, Sidney arranged for the mayor to be inundated with foreign telegrams. Eventually he agreed to a performance, provided it was put on without Meisel's music, which he considered *staatsgefährlich*, dangerous to the state. These were strange times for the movies.

In the autumn of 1929 Sergei Eisenstein, whom Sidney had met in Moscow a couple of years before, came to England on his way to California. He gave a series of talks at the Society on how to handle space and setting on a screen, and described at length the minute technical details of his camera work. Sidney never forgot the lectures. One night he gave a party for the Russian director, and for Grigori Alexandrov, his assistant, and Edouard Tissé, both of whom were going with him to Hollywood. It was a memorable occasion, with a special feast of Russian food, and all the Film Society grandees whom Sidney could muster, as well as some of his new friends, like Liam O'Flaherty and J. M. Keynes.

The Russians spent some weeks in London, with the Society's founding members doing their best to provide entertainment and work: they had come out of Russia with just twenty-five dollars each. Jack Isaacs took them to the theatre. Herbert Marshall showed them the City. Ivor Montagu, Eisenstein's closest friend, took him to Whitehall Court to call on Shaw, who recounted to his guests the story of Einstein's recent visit. Shaw had said to him that he had never been able to master the Law of Relativity. Einstein had smiled: 'Never mind, Mr Shaw. *Ce n'est pas votre métier.*'

Sidney became close to Eisenstein, though others found him to be a cold, somewhat difficult man; they had a perfectly companionable relationship, and one which happily was not marred by a slightly unpleasant incident that took place the afternoon *Potemkin* was screened. The Society had decided to show it in the same programme with John Grierson's *Drifters*, since Grierson, the British documentary film-maker, had worked on editing the Anglo-American version of Eisenstein's film in New York. After the performance was over, and Sidney was walking away down the theatre, both Eisenstein and Grierson caught up with him. 'You shit!' called out Grierson, believing that Sidney had put the films together precisely in order to question the originality of his work. Eisenstein was not much better pleased. He too wondered whether the Film Society was ridiculing him. It was a mark of Sidney's standing within the Society, however, that it was on him that the two men turned.

The Film Society had been a remarkable creation. As Sidney Cole, the writer and film director, was to write: 'One can say that it opened up for a generation of film-makers the prospect that there were virtually no bounds to what cinema, at its best, might achieve ...' On Sidney, its impact had been enormous. It had introduced him to films he might otherwise never have seen, to techniques and experiments that were later to influence him in everything he did; more than that, it altered his life, placed him at the fringes of a group of people who were thinking, talking and writing in ways very different from anything he had previously encountered.

Until 1925 Sidney continued to live at home at Walm Lane in Cricklewood. What was surprising perhaps was that he managed to combine bustling family existence lived at very close quarters, with its Jewish celebrations and its sense of intense loyalties, with a very different outer life of professional encounters and intellectual demands. With the younger children Sidney was both charmingly avuncular and something of a tyrant. Beryl, many years younger, can recall being taken to the circus by him and David Blairman, who brought along his younger sister, two elegant young men escorting their sisters out for a treat. She remembers, too, being conducted by him to her school in Switzerland and the way he questioned the headmistress in the most precise manner about what she was to learn, so that ever afterwards whatever she did the staff would say: 'Now, you know your brother wants you to ... ' He followed the younger children's education closely, almost as if to make up for the lack of his own, urging them on to greater studies, discussing with his mother the course of their careers. When Max was failing to make progress at the Haberdashers School in 1926, it was Sidney who took him away and found a job for him in Germany with an electrical engineering business. When Albert, who had a bad stutter, seemed not to be improving, it was Sidney who sent him to Dr Emmanuel Miller, the child psychiatrist, to help him. It was also Sidney who broke the deadlock reached by his elder sister Beatrice over her marriage. She had long wanted to marry a young man her parents deemed absolutely unsuitable. While Alexander Bernstein was alive there was no question of her doing so (and as a younger brother Sidney had spent many afternoons as a chaperone). But when their father died, Sidney, reasoning that she would never otherwise be happy – though he didn't approve of her choice either – persuaded their mother to consent to the match.

As for his own romantic affairs, he kept those very private indeed. Friends and company employees who knew him then describe a young man very attractive to women and much courted by them, who went to many parties and first nights. But just of whom Sidney himself grew fond, no one can say.

He was also a conscientious and loving son, dining at home every Friday night that he could in his father's place, even if he was far from Orthodox Jewish in his beliefs. 'She was', Sidney says of his mother, 'a kindly, *gemütlich* mother', and he remained very attached to her, anxious not to upset and displease her, and admiring of her strength and determination. He did the family things that needed doing himself, preferring not to delegate to others. Not that his mother relied very heavily on him. She was an independent woman by nature, and, as trustee of the Alexander Bernstein Trust, had taken on the task of paying unexpected visits to the Bernstein theatres to ensure that all was running smoothly. Edmund Hall, who was then a trainee manager in the West Ham Empire, can still recall the Rolls-Royce drawing up unannounced at the door and a matronly but very upright woman dressed in black, thick frizzy hair escaping from beneath a wide hat, alighting on her own to make a thorough inspection of the premises, right down to the ladies' lavatories.

Sidney himself, though not particularly well off, was beginning to develop a style of his own and it was something very different from Cricklewood. It was never flashy; but already there was a tinge of luxury about it all. In the early 1920s he was eating regularly at the Savoy, having his dress suits made at Leslie and Roberts in Hanover Square and buying his shirts from Sulkas; he drove (very badly: he was constantly having minor crashes) an Austin, with a cobalt body, loose grey covers and a leather hood. Studio portraits show an almost foppish elegance, hair short, slicked down and impeccably parted, tie nonchalantly neat, white handkerchief fashionably ruffled; but the quizzical smile is still there, and the shining eyes look determined.

He had also become an energetic and inquiring hiker. France, Germany and Spain, he found, were the best places to walk. He and whatever companion he was with would rise at dawn – most often severely bitten by bed bugs from the country inns – start the day with a nip of the local brandy, and set off with their rucksacks in the half-light. If they had felt in a particularly lighthearted mood and marked their hotel forms with a very facetious entry, they would find themselves occasionally pursued by an indignant and mystified policeman on his bicycle. The morning walk lasted a couple of hours, preferably across country, away from roads. Then they would start looking for a village shop or a farmhouse where they could buy food, before taking a long siesta in a field. Italy in the 1920s was very poor: the distances from one village to the next, in some of the wilder stretches of countryside, were enormous, and few of the local farmers had food to spare, even for money.

The 1920s were very much a time of travel. Sidney's passport for those years reads like a travel brochure. 1923: Bentheim in Germany; Göteborg, Sweden; Copenhagen, Denmark; Boulogne; Switzerland. 1925: Calais; Lithuania; Latvia; Germany; Switzerland. In 1923 he was in Germany when his train to Koblenz was stopped because the French had just marched into the Ruhr. Sidney had been warned this might happen and providentially had taken money to hire a car for the journey. He was twenty-four; nothing seemed to confuse him. The car cost the unbelievable sum of a million marks, packed into the game pocket of the ankle-length greatcoat he wore.

He had always been curious to look at what other countries were doing with their theatre, cinema and ballet. The Film Society provided him with the extra impetus, and in November 1925 he toured the continent. The newspapers, on his departure from England, described him as 'the young and energetic managing director'. In Germany he saw Erwin Piscator's pioneering work using film within the theatre, the first time he had ever seen them combined successfully and something in which he had long been interested; in Russia he talked to Meyerhold, the theatre director. Everywhere, he looked at equipment and lighting. Lithuania in particular caught his attention. It was at the height of its artistic development, with thirty different theatres – Yiddish, Russian, Polish, German – running simultaneously and political émigrés passing backwards and forwards through Riga on their way in and out of Russia. 'At one time', he says, 'there wasn't a theatre in Europe that mattered that I had not seen.'

In 1926 he went back to Russia, travelling with Ernest Fredman of the *Daily Film Renter*: the Russian films had a particular fascination for him. In Moscow he had the good fortune to be given an interpreter, Madame Blagovitch, who really knew and cared about the arts. She took him to meet Eisenstein, then working on his first film, *Strike*. He visited the studios, and later spent several hours talking to Stanislavsky, the great Russian teacher of drama, who wanted news of what was happening in the theatre abroad. One day, having separated from his guide, Sidney took refuge from the cold in a tea room – it was February – and an American started a conversation. It was Victor Hammer, whose brother Amand owned a pencil factory in Russia. He invited Sidney to a party at his home. When he got there, the next day, he found it was all rather like Bloomsbury, except for the caviar and the footmen waiting to brush the snow off the guests. No one spoke to him. (This was the period of the New Economic Policy: Lenin, trying to develop industry, had guaranteed that any foreigner who invested money in the country could take it out in goods. When the Russian Government bought the factory from the Hammers, they paid for it in Fabergé objects: these were the beginnings of the New York Hammer Galleries.)

On his return to London he moved at last into a house of his own at 46 Albemarle Street. It was here that his style became more marked. He hired a butler-cum-valet, and rode every morning in Rotten Row, returning home to find his bath run and North waiting to pull off his boots. While he breakfasted, a secretary arrived with the mail, after which he would walk to his office at 197 Wardour Street – the Bernsteins had moved there in 1923 – smoking Sullivan and Powell cigarettes, a special mixture of Turkish and Virginian tobacco. In the afternoon, when not working or visiting theatres, he went to *thés dansants*; in the evening, he danced at Ciros or the 400.

There was, of course, a more serious side to his life. Some evenings, he would meet Raymond Mortimer, H. G. Wells and his walking companions Laz Aaronson, Jack Isaacs and David Blairman at the Café Royal, the English equivalent in the late 1920s and 1930s of the Dôme in Paris. Augustus John sometimes turned up, and so did the critic James Agate, and Jacob Epstein. On Sundays, the group might go to Epstein's studio in Hyde Park Gate; other days they went to Sidney and Violet Schieff's house in Cambridge Square, where they might find Wyndham Lewis, T. S. Eliot and Iris and Alan Porter. It was an extraordinarily rich intellectual life. If Sidney didn't wholly belong, it was that he was always a little different; rather shy, preferring to listen rather than to talk. The luminaries liked him, even if they marvelled at his affluence, and sometimes mocked, behind his back, his business concerns. But Sidney, with his eagerness and intelligence, was not a figure to dismiss too lightly. He exuded stability, not only financial but mental, the very adult kind of confidence that comes with understanding your own nature and abilities, and he was never ingratiating. However inadequate he must at times have felt, he did not fawn.

In May 1926, the General Strike stopped the country. It was typical of Sidney that he immediately offered trade unionists the use of his theatres for meetings, despite the fact that the local councils threatened to take away his licence. Already, politics, friends, business interests, all lived in compartments; they rarely clashed.

The fluidity of his life, the way he appeared to be everywhere, making friends, signing deals, running his family's affairs, and also travelling extensively, was helped by the fact that in the 1920s Sidney still had no clear idea of where exactly he was heading. Theatres were a great delight to him, and all the elaborate business calculations that went with his company, but then so were films and the cinema. Even while the Film Society was continuing to take up a great deal of his time – there were many meetings at which, as Ivor Montagu puts it, Sidney was the 'wise counsellor' – he now became entangled in another kind of project. He took over, for one season, the Court Theatre in Sloane Square with Arnold Bennett and the Russian director Theodore Komisarjevsky.

Komisarjevsky was a strange figure. He was not an easy man, but he was exceptionally talented in a wide variety of areas and he has left a legend behind him in the theatre world. He had trained early in his youth as an architect in Moscow before the revolution, then had risen under Lenin to be managing director of the Moscow Grand State Theatre of Opera and Ballet; he had founded his own acting school in 1910 and also made a number of films praised for their beauty and originality. (At Sidney's party for the Russian film-makers in Albemarle Street, Eisenstein had asked to be introduced to Komisarjevsky: 'It was because of you', he told the theatre director and designer, 'that I became a film-maker. I was trained as a chemist and then one night I saw one of your plays. I decided I had to change my life.') In 1919 he had left Russia and settled for a while in Paris where, in 1925, he started the 'Arc-en-Ciel' Theatre.

It was there that Sidney met him, a slight, balding man with rather protruding eyes and immense charm, who exercised an enormous fascination over women. They had a mutual friend, Jeanne de Casalis, an actress and writer, herself a bizarre and talented woman, who was a great friend of Arnold Bennett's, and who was later to invent a highly popular radio character called 'Mrs Feather'.

Sidney and Komisarjevsky spent many hours talking about the theatre. Sidney had always imagined he knew a great deal about the Russian playwrights; he now found his knowledge to be sketchy. Komisarjevsky talked and talked; it was an enjoyably educational time. At some point Sidney evidently pressed him to come to England to work, for shortly afterwards Komisarjevsky wrote to him:

As for myself, I am not in a hurry, but I have to think about my work ... I prefer to work in London and in England because ... it seems to me the English stage has something to say in the future (if someone will give a push to the English producers and actors).

These were words that could not fail to appeal to Sidney, who loved the notion of challenge, the vision of change: and was fast becoming someone eager to push others in directions he believed they should go.

33

Komisarjevsky turned up shortly afterwards in London, having found an opening at the Barnes Theatre where his friend Philip Ridgeway was the director. Here Komisarjevsky staged a succession of refreshingly new and different productions of the great Chekhov plays, *Uncle Vanya*, *The Three Sisters*, *The Cherry Orchard*, using colour and movement in ways that English audiences had not seen before. When he could, Sidney lent his help. Most often this took the form of being a go-between, as Komisarjevsky was always ringing him up and pleading: 'Sidney, please go and talk to ... '

Komisarjevsky was also a friend of Arnold Bennett and Dorothy Cheston, the actress by whom Bennett had a daughter and whom he was later to marry. Some time in the summer of 1927 the three of them talked about running a season of plays: Komisarjevsky favoured the Russians, Dorothy wanted an 'international' selection. Eventually she and Arnold Bennett talked Komisarjevsky round and an agreement was reached: Komisarjevsky was to guarantee up to £500, and the other two £1,500 between them. Komisarjevsky was also to have full control over the cast, the posters, the publicity and the choice of plays. But they still needed a further backer, preferably someone who knew about theatre management in England. Komisarjevsky, remembering Sidney's enthusiasm and his experience, now turned to him for help. Sloane Productions Ltd was launched, Sidney's friend Maurice King who had the public house next to the theatre having agreed to put up some of the money. Arnold Bennett recorded an early meeting with Sidney in his diary on 21 August:

> Bernstein, the 'business man' in Komisarjevsky's and our 'Sloane Productions Co. Ltd' which is to run at the Court Theatre in the autumn, was to have come down for lunch today. He arrived – scarcely hoped for – at 3.25, and stayed for tea. [It can't have been an auspicious start: Bennett was almost pathological about punctuality.] He proved to be all right, *sympathique*, young, some artistic perceptions and some artistic blindnesses. Thus he could see *nothing* in 'Malbrouck s'en-va-t'en guerre'. Before dinner I read Merezhkowski's 'Paul 1st' and decided that it would do for the Court Theatre. Tonight I wrote to this effect to both Komisarjevsky and Bernstein ... I have been very gloomy; I began to be gloomy yesterday. Dorothy pointed out to me that my liver is out of order, and I think it certainly is.

The early autumn of 1927 was spent preparing for the opening of *Paul 1* on 1 October. Sidney took charge of the company's business side, negotiating costs and contracts, and came to rehearsals when he could, sitting silently and self-effacingly in the stalls. The cast included Charles Laughton as Count Pahlen, whom Komisarjevsky had first tried out as Osip in Gogol's *The Government Inspector* in Barnes, and whom Arnold Bennett had approved in a five-minute interview on 8 September. Dorothy Cheston was to play the lady-in-waiting to the Empress. Lydia Sherwood, a young actress whom Komisarjevsky had bumped into on the stairs of the house he shared in Bloomsbury (Maynard Keynes and Raymond Mortimer lived there too), had been invited to be the Grand Duke's wife Elizabeth.

Paul 1 opened on time, to good notices, despite its relentlessly dark mood, and Arnold Bennett got on with rewriting for the stage his novel *Mr Prohack*, the story of a henpecked Treasury official who suddenly becomes heir to £100,000. But by early November the company was falling to pieces: Komisarjevsky complained that Dorothy Cheston was impossible to deal with, and wasn't best pleased when Arnold Bennett called in his old friend Beatrice Stella (Mrs Patrick) Campbell to coach her. He got a doctor to sign a note saying that he was suffering from 'general nervous debility' and took off for a two-week holiday in France, leaving all financial control in Sidney's hands. Reliability was not Komisarjevsky's strongest suit.

On his return, there was more ill feeling. Komisarjevsky wrote to Arnold Bennett, declaring that the agreement that he should be 'sole and autocratic artistic director and producer of the company' had been broken; that the cast – and Dorothy Cheston in particular – were altering his scenes without consulting him, that he wasn't getting the billing that he had been promised, and that he had been slighted over the matter of what constituted 'English dresses'. 'The point is', he wrote shortly before the opening of *Prohack*, 'that according to *my* idea and *my* rules of the Theatre, which I have been enforcing on my companies for the last 20 years, an artist who changes anything in my production and then refuses to obey my order *must give up the part* ... '

In all these rows Sidney acted as arbitrator. Both sides wrote to him, complaining of the other: Komisarjevsky, in great untidy handwriting, on scraps of blue paper, in different inks, with blobs and splashes, that Dorothy Cheston was intolerable; Arnold Bennett, by typewriter, on headed paper, in reasoned terms, that there would be no company at all without her since her presence on the stage was one of the major reasons for forming it. 'I find Komis', he told Sidney, 'too difficult to work with and do not consider him to be a good producer of English comedy.' Sidney soothed, placated. (He himself found Dorothy Cheston somewhat silly.) 'There was never anything aggressive in his manner,' remembers Lydia Sherwood, who became a friend of Sidney's at the Court, and has remained so ever since, 'but you knew that he had power.' The rows went on. 'I put on my hat and I go,' stormed Komisarjevsky, in his accented English.

None the less, *Mr Prohack* opened on 16 November with Dorothy Cheston firmly in her part as Lady Massulam. Arnold Bennett was not there, having decided to spend the evening entertaining friends at the Yacht Club. They left at 10.35 and he drove to the theatre. Later he recorded in his diary:

> The curtain had just fallen. It kept going up again while I was in the wings or near the wings. Much satisfaction in the wings, on the staircases and in the dressing rooms. Charles Laughton very pleased with himself, as he had the right to be, seeing he had had a great triumph. Everyone who 'came round' professed the greatest enjoyment of the play. I almost believed in a success. Especially as, going into the theatre, I saw Komisarjevsky outside in the dark entry. I said: 'Is it all right?' He said: 'Oh yes, it's all right.' Dorothy said she had not played very well, but she was not depressed.

The evening had been, as Arnold Bennett rightly perceived, a great personal success for Charles Laughton, whose blinking, sleepy, heavy manner was ideally suited to the character of the Treasury official. It was his first major success and he was never to look back. He was in high spirits, being at the start of a love affair with Elsa Lanchester, the red-haired actress who had been engaged to play Mr Prohack's secretary Mimi. (They later married.)

At the last moment he had decided to model his appearance on Arnold Bennett himself and appeared for the first night dressed and made up to resemble the author as closely as possible, moustache and all. The likeness was unmistakable. 'A piece of gross impertinence,' Bennett rebuked the 28-year-old actor, ' ... unwarrantable effrontery.'

The play turned out to be a box-office success, well reviewed, except by *The Times*. Even Sidney, who had been dubious about it earlier, now viewed it with satisfaction. *Mr Prohack* would certainly have lasted for a longer run, had not the lease on the Court Theatre run out in early January and Laughton departed for a new engagement, offered as a result of his excellent reviews for Prohack, in Benn Levy's adaptation of Hugh Walpole's novel, *A Man with Red Hair*, before another empty theatre could be found. *Mr Prohack* was the start of a long friendship between Sidney and Charles Laughton.

To celebrate the whole venture Komisarjevsky gave a great party in his top-floor flat early in the New Year, and Sidney sat on the stairs until four o'clock in the morning talking about the theatre with Lydia

Sherwood and Jeanne de Casalis. Sloane Productions Ltd had not made him any money – when totted up, the overall losses came to £926 12s.2d. – but it had given him a lot of pleasure.

3

Komisarjevsky and the Super-cinemas

ONE OF THE more remarkable sides to the new business of cinema was the sheer speed with which it seemed to catch on. One year, the public craved the cosy familiarity of the music hall, with its tumbling clowns and bawdy crooners; the next, it demanded film, and nothing but film, the flicker on the screen, albeit silent, black and white and often abysmally naïve. There seemed to be no limit to the public appetite for it. In 1927 there were three million cinema tickets sold every week in London alone; the entire population of the city came to only eight million.

That year, the film industry, surprised and delighted by the way things were going, announced that £2.5 million would be spent on building cinemas in the capital, or converting old ones, to provide a total of well over 52,000 seats. Some of the cinemas would have dance halls attached; others, tea rooms and cafés.

The message was not lost on Sidney. That same month, February, he made an announcement of his own. He intended, he told the trade press, to build a new cinema opposite Sadler's Wells, to rebuild the Empires at Edmonton, Willesden and West Ham, and to demolish the Empire at Plumstead, putting in its place an elegant and completely redesigned palace of entertainment. In April, he declared that he also planned to rebuild the Rialto in Enfield and to take over the lease of the Lewisham Hippodrome. The battle for the audience had begun. With it, a new note was entering Sidney's manner, a more authoritative one. There were many things he might do, but his immediate future, it was now clear, lay with the cinema.

Before announcing exactly what form his alterations would take he made one more trip to America. It was the natural place to go; from earlier visits he had no doubts at all that America was far in advance in all that concerned the cinema – Hollywood was now turning out some seven hundred features each year. Some of its more extravagant ideas would never suit Britain, but they could not be ignored. Before sailing on the SS *Olympic* on 8 May he wrote to J. C. Graham, at Paramount Pictures in London, to ask him for introductions to American theatre people. He wanted, he told him, to 'discuss the internal organisations of their theatres' with someone.

Sidney reached New York at a critical moment in the cinema world. On the technical side, it was the year that sound was born: though *The Jazz Singer*, the first feature 'talkie', was not yet on the screen, sound was being used experimentally by most of the major companies in 'shorts' and newsreels. As for cinema building, the Roxy, the most ambitious and spectacular cinema, in a city now dotted with Parthenons, Renaissance cathedrals and Moorish palaces, had just opened its doors on Seventh Avenue.

It was precisely there, a few days after his arrival, that Sidney witnessed for the first time the effect of sound on an audience, and something of the kitsch of the new cinema culture. During the second show at the Roxy, on 27 May, the performance was interrupted by a message flashed on to the screen: Lindbergh had arrived safely in Paris after his crossing of the Atlantic in the *Spirit of St Louis*. While the audience was still applauding, Fox's Movietone newsreel of Lindbergh's take-off from Roosevelt field came on – with sound recorded on the spot. Six thousand two hundred and fourteen people watched as the frail, heavily laden plane wobbled its way down the runway in the misty Long Island dawn, its engine spluttering as it skimmed over the high-tension wires and up and away. Then Samuel Rothafel, 'Roxy', the great New York impresario himself, appeared on stage and asked the audience to get down on their knees and offer up a prayer for Lindbergh's safe journey. Row after row sank down, but not, however, Sidney, who stood, a little embarrassed, watching.

Afterwards, Sidney got a chance to take a closer look at the Roxy. Through mutual friends he had been introduced to Samuel Rothafel, who was delighted to show the young Englishman round every inch of his super-cinema, the magic of which, he explained, lay in the combination of really expensive entertainment with the plush and marble glamour of the setting. The movies had given the public a taste for the exotic; here, at the Roxy, they were going to get more of it than they had ever dreamt.

The Roxy was, indeed, splendid. Outside it looked like a Renaissance palace. It was larger, glossier, more flamboyant than anything Sidney had ever seen. Inside, it had washroom facilities for ten thousand people, including sixty complete bathrooms; indicator lights to guide people to their seats; fourteen Steinway pianos; and a miniature hospital equipped for minor surgery. There were page-boys, elevator operators, doormen, streetmen and footmen, a team so highly trained and polished that a *New Yorker* article of the time referred to them as 'young men of far greater beauty and politeness than any other clique in the City'. Crowds thronged the lobby and stairways for the daily Changing of the Ushers, when two by two 125 of these young paragons marched to their positions to the sounds of a bugle: all this before the show itself, with its three organ consoles played by organists in green velvet smoking jackets, its orchestra of 110 musicians and its stage shows of dancing girls. Sidney could hardly fail to be impressed, even if he returned to London and commented to a reporter, somewhat wryly:

> Never have I seen such rubbish presented in such ornate surroundings. It isn't the picture which draws the public, but the cinema. In the Roxy Theatre, for example, a man can have a luxurious seat for 75 cents. He can hear wonderful music, including a choir of one hundred voices, see remarkable presentations, and if he falls ill with appendicitis he can be operated on in the medical wards.

As a showman he appreciated the splendour of what he had seen, and had every intention of drawing on its lessons. It was the rubbish on the screen that he deplored and now intended to fight.

1927 was a strange year in the history of British cinema. Never before had so many people wished to see films, yet British production was well on the way to extinction: only 5 per cent of the films shown were actually British. Film production had virtually come to a halt in this country during the First World War; and by the time war was over and the British studios were ready to reassert themselves they discovered that the public had learnt to prefer the more expensive and technically superior offerings from Hollywood.

While France had Réné Clair, Jean Epstein and Abel Gance, Germany Fritz Lang and Ernst Lubitsch, Russia Eisenstein and Pudovkin, all turning out what are now regarded as masterpieces, those films that were being made in England seemed to be forgettable, tawdry and drab. (When Paul Rotha surveyed the industry in 1929 all he could find in the way of worthwhile British contributions were John Grierson's *Drifters*, Miles Mander's *The Firstborn* and the early work of Anthony Asquith.)

By the mid-1920s Sidney was already a strong figure in the politics of the industry. His European and American travels, his involvement with the Film Society, his increasingly close friendships with the young American moguls – Walter Wanger, Jesse Lasky, David Selznick – gave him an authority and a voice that far exceeded the actual business potential of his small cinema circuit. People had simply stopped remarking that he was still only twenty-six.

He was also a member of the Cinematographic Exhibitors Association, and though often in a minority with particular views, he now joined forces with other interested people to try to break the American stranglehold and promote the birth of a genuine British film art. This, he kept saying, could be done only by legislation and the forcible curbing of American imports.

The Government finally responded to the growing pressure from the British film world by introducing the Cinematograph or Films Act, making 'blind' (the block booking of American films by British exhibitors unseen, and in bulk) and advance booking illegal, and imposing a quota on the showing of foreign films, while enforcing a percentage of British films on a graduated scale. The measures had come late, but at least something had now been done, and for the moment it looked as if a total takeover by the Americans had been averted.

The Act had another result, and one which was to have a more important bearing on Sidney's particular business. Until the Act provided a stimulus for the production of British films, integration of the industry – as in America, with producers, renters and exhibitors combining – had not been practical. Now, however, two large-scale film combines rapidly formed. One was British International Pictures, later renamed Associated British Picture Corporation; the other, Gaumont British Picture Corporation, financed by the merchant-banking house of Ostrer Brothers, and including the distributing companies Ideal Films and W. and F. Film Service, as well as a production side in the form of Gainsborough Pictures.

On the exhibiting side, Gaumont British had the seventeen cinemas of the Biocolor circuits through the simple process of buying up smaller independent exhibitors. In January 1928 Sidney, because of the way the structure of the industry was changing, and because he now needed to spread the family money to other businesses, merged the Bernstein theatres with Gaumont British, receiving in return over a quarter of a million pounds from Isidore Ostrer. The merger bore all the shrewd hallmarks of his deals. The Bernstein family held on to 49 per cent of the shares and Sidney himself remained managing director, at £5,000 p.a., advising Gaumont on booking films and running the cinemas. 'One effect of mergers', Sidney told the *Kinematograph Weekly*, which ran a long article describing him as the 'bright young ambassador of the British Cinema industry', 'will be the elimination of bad pictures.' Groups, he said, would now be able to employ expert advice in a way they could not have afforded as small circuits, and far more attention could now go into the booking of serious films.

The Empire, Edmonton, had been a variety hall for fourteen years when, on Easter Monday 1927, it began its new life as a cinema. 'I think', declared Sidney at the time, 'the day of the suburban music hall is dead. How can they hope to compete with a film show which gives the public twice as long a programme and without any waits between the turns?' By July work had started on the Rialto, in Enfield, where £8,000 was allocated to modernise the cinema and rebuild more comfortable and elegant stalls, as well as to house a new wonder organ, built by Messrs Norman and Beard, Organ Builders to the King, which was to contain 2,800 pipes and 35 miles of wire; the distance, so the publicity leaflets said, from Enfield to Southend. A new heating and ventilation plant, designed to ensure 1,000 cubic feet of fresh air per person, had also been ordered. In September, one Saturday night, Sidney bought the Hippodrome, Willesden; on Monday morning 200 men started work on the conversions. It was a time for sensational gestures, for business deals that could have been straight from the Hollywood movies themselves.

It was some time during this summer that Sidney took a momentous step, and one that was to transform rapidly the scale of his operations. He asked Theodore Komisarjevsky to become the art director of all the Bernstein theatres. The two men could not have been more different: Komisarjevsky, brilliant, unreliable, sometimes plaintive, particularly about money, with his pale face and large brown eyes, always, and very publicly, mad about women (theatre friends had given him the nickname 'Come-and-seduce me'); Sidney, restrained, discreet, absolutely purposeful. Yet the alliance was to prove enormously fruitful. Sidney had the experience and a perfectly tuned sense of what people responded to; Komisarjevsky had flair.

There was, however, at least at first, something lackadaisical about Komisarjevsky's approach to the job. For one thing he was deeply scornful of the cinema, even if his language tended always towards exaggeration. 'The popular cinema', he wrote in *The Theatre and a Changing Civilisation*, 'does not only cater for imbeciles. It breeds them. Lured into kine-palaces and forced to look at the insipidness shown on the screen, people cannot help becoming shallow pates, incapable of seeing life as it is, cannot help developing the complexes of sexual maniacs and gangsters ... ' Strong words for a man about to devote most of the next four years of his life to the construction of these very kine-palaces.

During the first months of the new partnership the correspondence between the two men was in fact marked largely by ever more frantic and reproachful tones from Sidney about Komisarjevsky's failure to meet deadlines, fulfil contracts and deliver plans, and by nonchalance on Komisarjevsky's part. Sidney was reluctant to decide anything without Komisarjevsky's approval, sensing, probably quite rightly, that every detail was part of a grandiose scheme it would be crass to alter, yet at the same time he was haunted by the dates of fast-approaching openings that he had to meet. 'Chairs mauve carpets pinkish terracotta,' Komisarjevsky cabled him in June about the Willesden Empire from Turin, where he had suddenly vanished to produce *Cosi fan tutte*. Later he wrote, once again on his invariable scraps of tattered paper, but soothingly, 'I am going to do your cinemas. I am going to stay in London all the summer. And I do hope that you will be generous and pay me £150 for each of the cinemas.' Sidney, mollified, replied asking him to look in Italian antique shops for mirrors and furniture, both for Albemarle Street and for the theatres, where, 'I want things that look more interesting than they are valuable.' With Komisarjevsky, it was as well to stress the point.

Komisarjevsky's dilatoriness was not Sidney's only concern. He had an expanding business to run with not a great deal of help, even if by now his younger brother Cecil had come to join him and was on the verge of assuming responsibility for much mundane but essential business activity, thereby leaving Sidney free to roam and experiment. As with Komisarjevsky, this was to prove a strong and absolutely vital partnership.

At the end of the 1920s, however, Sidney still felt totally in control, with a style of work which, under pressure, sometimes verged on the dictatorial. He conducted his business from the offices in Wardour Street, with great impatience when there were delays, working a six- or seven-day week, always arriving beautifully but soberly dressed, in white shirts and dark-blue suits with a black-and-white checked tie and a black Homburg. Whenever he could he dropped in on his cinemas without warning, arriving in his Minerva, springing from the car, dashing up the stairs and into the manager's office: 'How's business? Where are the publicity posters?' It was sudden and explosive, and the younger managers were terrified. Major Hall, by then manager at the Plumstead Empire, remembers the cinema page-boy, detailed to keep his eye out for the Minerva, tearing across the lobby one day: 'Sid's here.' Sidney heard him, and laughed. 'How did you know that I was Sid? By my nose, I suppose?' It was this manner – ruthless, sometimes almost bullying and then equally suddenly charming – which made most impression on his employees.

It was about this time that Sidney's passion – there is no other word for it – for detail took over. The cinemas had not only to look good, they had to be perfect; the best. A long list of memoranda, usually to Cecil, who had by now become an essential partner to Sidney, bears witness to a ferocity of purpose, a clarity of vision that is sometimes daunting. 2 May: 'The man who sells the Ice Cream is still in a white overall. This looks horrible and must be stopped.' 2 June: 'I think Angels' uniforms are unsatisfactory at most theatres . . . You promised to deliver a tennis cup to Enfield by Tuesday. What is being done regarding this? . . . I notice the border has been left off the 16 sheet. This should be replaced . . .' 13 June: 'All theatres should now be hanging baskets of greenery and flowers outside their canopies.' 20 August: 'Things for attention: A letter should be sent to all Managers regarding rubber heels for the staff . . .' They never stopped, these nagging notes: nothing, it seemed, was too small to escape attention.

The small Bernstein circuit, full of original ideas and marked with a strong sense of showmanship, might well have gone on as it was, had it not been for the next step in the development of cinema. This time the move did not come from Sidney. In the autumn of 1927 the days of silent cinema came to an abrupt close. On 26 October in New York, when Al Jolson elbowed his way across a screen and sang out 'Dirty hands, dirty face' before holding up his hand and uttering the never to be forgotten lines: 'Wait a minute! Wait a minute! You ain't heard anything yet!', the fortunes not only of the Warner brothers, whose film *The Jazz Singer* was, but of the movie industry as a whole changed overnight. Until this moment, sound on screen had been no more than an interesting experiment, arousing curiosity. It was now essential. Its importance and its impact cannot be exaggerated. It was more like magic than progress, as startling as if the very pictures on the walls had begun to speak.

From that moment, in America, the race for sound was on. Theatres all over the country competed to install the necessary equipment, as Fox began issuing regular Movietone Talkie newsreels. By 1929, ninety-four sound systems were being advertised in the *Film Daily Yearbook*. They spelt, at the same time, the end of the great era of American vaudeville. Almost within months, it seemed, the orchestra pits of the great theatre-cinemas emptied, the live stage spectaculars began to diminish in size and then disappear, and the theatre managers turned from flashy impresarios into ice-cream salesmen. They spelt, too, the end of a certain pattern in the American entertainment world. The point about the silent cinema had been, in a country with so many immigrants, its universality. Now, to enjoy the cinema, these people would have to learn English. On his return from America Sidney had announced that he had become a director of the Phonofilm Company, manufacturing the British Talking Picture system, an amplification process pioneered by Lee de Forest before the First World War, but only now synchronised to images. But at first he remained, like many others, a little dubious of its full worth. 'Full-length speaking films', he told an assembled audience of exhibitors, even while the sound revolution was exploding in America, 'would necessarily be a great strain on an audience ... I feel convinced that the human ear cannot stand long periods of mechanically produced music, sound or dialogue ... As a permanent attaction I do not see that, at any rate for the moment, they in any way threaten silent films.' It was one of his rare errors of judgment, and when *The Jazz Singer* opened, a year later, in London at the Piccadilly Theatre, he was very quick to see it. Within weeks he had committed his entire circuit to sound.

It was not a decision to take lightly. The 'talkies' cost an extra £100 a week in running costs and the rental of a sound film was three times that of a silent one. The Bernsteins were rich, and becoming richer, but they were also financially cautious, and Sidney was utterly determined to waste nothing that could be ploughed back into the expansion of the business. Over the question of the talkies, however, he really had no choice. As he explained to a Mr F. H. Featherstone of Leytonstone who had written to him lamenting the disappearance of the old music halls, 'We can no more stop the revolution of Talkies than anyone could stop the development of wireless.' And, characteristically, he was already having a good deal of fun. He arranged for people to be planted in his cinema audiences primed to ask questions out loud just before a figure on the screen was due to reply to it. 'What's that?' his stooge would shout out at the given moment. And a voice from the screen replied. The effect on audiences was electric.

It was now obvious that the age of the super-cinema had come to Britain, that all the fiddling about with reconstruction and conversion that had been going on in Plumstead, West Ham and Edmonton was a mere prelude to a great building spree. Sidney had just been waiting his moment. Komisarjevsky had never been to America, but as an architect and a theatre designer he knew intimately the great ages of European art. Together he and Sidney now set about designing a series of cinemas the like of which had not been seen in England before and would never be rivalled. They owed, of course, much to the American dream-palaces of the 1920s, to the Roxy, to the marble and gilt edifices of New York. But they were also totally individual: Sidney, as a showman and a businessman, knew exactly what he wanted to do: bring the fabulous glamour of the imaginary to places where people led lives of apparent drabness. (His instinct in this as in so much else was right. When the New Victoria opened in Wilton Road, with E. Walmsley Lewis's muted art deco motifs of a mermaid's palace, Sidney commented: 'People don't want this sort of thing: they want architecture with marble columns, gilt and mirrors. This won't pay.' It didn't.) In Komisarjevsky he had found the perfect partner, and if the strange Russian theatrical genius was not the only architect in the Britain of the 1930s to dream up such fantastic buildings he was arguably the most brilliant.

In 1929 Sidney and Cecil began a cinema-building project in Dover. Cecil Masey was the architect; Bovis the builders; Komisarjevsky the interior designer. Later, it was always assumed that the current talk about a Channel tunnel had lured them to that part of the coast, but in fact they settled on Dover for the simple reason that here was a town full of people in need of a new cinema.

A plot of land was bought from Levy and Company, the brewers, and work started on the 'County Theatre and Tea Room' as it was to be called. Half-way through building, Sidney and Cecil decided that 'County' was hardly glamorous and catchy and that a more dashing name was called for. Sidney remembered, fondly, a walking tour of southern Spain. The name 'Granada' came up. A few weeks before the opening in January 1930 posters appeared all round the town: 'Start saying Granada'. Nothing else; no explanation of what this meant. Only on 28 December did the *Kent Gazette* reveal what a 'Granada' actually was.

To finance this cinema the Bernstein brothers had gone to Barclays Bank, as they had done seven years before for the Empire in Edmonton. They borrowed enough money to see them through the building stage and then replaced the first temporary bank loan with a long-term loan from an insurance company. When the Dover Granada was ready, a company was formed (a separate company for each cinema until Granada Theatres Limited was floated in 1934) and outside money was brought in by long-term loans and mortgages. This same financial pattern was used for each of the cinemas. In 1929 capital costs came to about £25 per seat – or between £50,000 and £100,000 per cinema.

The Granada, Dover, opened its doors on 9 January 1930. The entire town came to gape at a décor of such splendour that an admiring critic was reduced to describing it as a compromise between Russia and Spain. There was an enormous entrance hall, overlooked by a balcony with carved stone balustrades; there were Moorish arches and a feeling of 'infinity beyond'. The Mayor of Dover officiated at the opening ceremony, which was presided over by a well-known local toast master,

Mr Knightsmith, 'in red dress jacket and black trousers, holding his wand of office'. Critics of the occasion found the place 'gay but not gaudy', and marvelled at its 'warm shades of red, gold, green and yellow', its 'stark balustrades relieved by brilliant Spanish shawls hanging carelessly', its chandeliers of cut glass and etchings of the Alhambra.

Next came the Granada at Walthamstow, which looked very like a Moorish court with wrought-iron columns and a fine metal canopy over the entrance. Inside it had heavily patterned walls, 3,000 seats upholstered in alternate deep-claret and dark-orange corded velvet, the stage curtains a delicate pale-green silk with a 'deep embellishment of orange, black, green and white'. A grand piano stood in the foyer, so that patrons could listen to music as they stood waiting for their seats. Banks of sweet-smelling pot plants lined the walls, put there by Constance Spry, a friend whom Sidney had encouraged to give up her job as headmistress of Homerton Day Continuation School, in order to start her own flower shop, by promising her the contract for the flowers in the foyers of the Granadas.

And so the building programme got under way. Often, it was a case of Sidney and Komisarjevsky keeping their nerve, relying on some intuitive sense that what they were concocting, this incredible and often grotesque blend of art, this hotchpotch of styles and colours with its mirrors and chandeliers and architectural jokes, was actually going to work.

At Woolwich they nearly foundered. Komisarjevsky had chosen a set of colours based on early church manuscripts with lines of gold, grey and red. At nine o'clock, two nights before the cinema was due to open, the two men went to watch the ceiling scaffolding come down. They stood together in the aisle, staring up at an overpowering impression of green. Finally Sidney said: 'Let's go.' They drove, in silence, to the Savoy where they ordered two large whiskies. They both knew that the ceiling was wrong. Next day, the scaffolding went back up; thirty-six hours later the Granada Woolwich opened, looking very different (and giving birth to the legend that Sidney disliked the colour green).

The talkies, Sidney soon found, were greatly increasing profits. But he was careful not to shed the past too quickly, remembering the lure of the very varied programmes provided by the great American super-cinemas. Each programme continued to contain a balance of film, music and acts. A list of costs for acts touring the Bernstein theatres in 1929 gives some idea of what these were like: Three Bostonians (£10 for nine performances); Eight Dainty Maids (£12 for twelve performances); the Tiny Town Follies (£55 for fifteen performances); and Les Georges (£6 for nine shows). There was also a cat that did a 'famous mouser' turn. Programmes changed mid-week. Sidney himself was full of ideas for improvements. One week he arranged for twelve pianolas to be put on one of the Granada stages, with no one sitting at them, but so wired up that they appeared to play themselves, with spotlights picking out the moving keys. Among managers, there was intense rivalry about stunts of this kind, much encouraged by prizes given each week to the most ingenious ideas. One man came up with a lion in a cage in the foyer to advertise a jungle film (until the Captive Animals Defence League objected); another borrowed an aeroplane to announce a coming war film; yet another put two wax dummies holding handcuffs, ostensibly burglars, in the foyer for a week, and then replaced them with identical male figures, only alive, for the next. At East Ham, a camel was hired to walk the local streets with a placard saying 'There's plenty of leg room at the Granada'.

And then there were the organs. In America, Sidney had watched with some amazement the way the Mighty Wurlitzers rose silently out of the depths of the super-cinemas and burst into music that seemed to bubble up and fill the vast auditoriums. These organs, it seemed to him, were an essential part of the cinema's power of make-believe and on his return to England he ordered one for each of the new Granadas.

When properly played, the Wurlitzers could do more than any other single instrument; they were more versatile than pianos, and the perfect substitute for a full orchestra. These incredible new organs had been invented by Robert Hope Jones, an Englishman looking like Liszt in his white wig who had devised ways, by opening and closing the valves of the pipes, of producing completely new voices. Sadly, he committed suicide before his mighty machine caught on. By the time Sidney became interested in them the Wurlitzers were capable of imitating all the usual instruments, plus many no one had ever heard before, so that a skilled organist could summon up grand pianos, drums, triangles, saxophones, banjos, gongs, bells and castanets. From these came nightingales, fire-engine sirens, smashing crockery and steamboat whistles, until there was no mood or theme in a silent movie that an able organist couldn't enliven with some musical effect.

The skill lay in coaxing such sounds from the instrument, and in this Sidney was lucky. The taste for organs in England came at a time when interest was already dying down in America. So it was to New York, and to Canada, that he turned for organists. He couldn't get Jesse and Helen Crawford, but Harold Ramsay, whose act consisted of emerging from the pit in a variety of masks – 'Mr X', as he was known – was at once immensely popular with English audiences.

During the last years of the 1920s, when his building programme had been successfully launched, Sidney decided to become more involved in the wider politics of the cinema industry. He was already a solid voice among exhibitors on both sides of the Atlantic but he wanted to do more, and in particular, he wanted to boost the ailing British studios. In a talk he gave on the BBC radio at the invitation of Lionel Fielden, he hit out at English film production in most unflattering terms ('My chief complaint is the lack of initiative and originality ... Most British films suffer from an obvious indecision of purpose ... ') before urging a return to the creative British spirit that once gave rise to Shakespeare, Swift and Dickens. There was no need, he said, for the British studios and directors to take such a supine role. With the new Quota Act they should now stand up and challenge the American and continental dominance, make films that were creative, original and worth while. The talk was widely reported.

It was not surprising, then, that Sidney was seen increasingly as a spokesman for the industry. He was decisive, argumentative and very knowledgeable; what was more he looked impressive, so that he carried weight when he spoke, and he had many friends. It was a time of lunches and dinners, discussions and launches. On one occasion Michael Balcon the producer wrote to ask for his help in luring Arnold Bennett to a dinner being given at the Savoy in the presence of the Prince of Wales to announce a programme for the selling of British films overseas. All other leading British writers had accepted: only Bennett had refused.

Sidney forwarded Balcon's letter straight to him. Immediately he received a reply: Bennett agreed to come to the dinner, but only if Sidney would sit next to him, and if the two could meet first for a drink. Sidney sent Balcon a cheque for two tickets.

On the day of the dinner, Sidney was held up at his office. He reached the bar where he was to meet Bennett slightly late: Bennett was distinctly annoyed. 'First of all,' he said irritably, 'you're late. And secondly, where are we sitting? I always like to know where I'm sitting at a public engagement.'

Sidney went into the Savoy ahead and looked up their names on the place list: he was appalled to discover that not only was Bennett not at the high table, but that he was intended to sit with Sidney on one side and Gordon Craig, the rugged and decidedly unliterary head of Movie-tone News, on the other. Bennett was furious. As dinner started he asked Sidney where he had been recently. 'America,' said Sidney. 'What did you read there?' 'I made another serious but hopeless attempt to conquer Dickens,' replied Sidney, 'but I failed.' For Bennett, this came as the last blow. 'Sidney,' he declared mournfully, before relapsing into silence, 'this is the final dampener on the whole evening.'

49

It was not only in England that Sidney was earning respect. One day at about this time he received a cable from a cinema entrepreneur in Hollywood: 'Am in contact with a brilliant film executive ... who can form remarkable combination of great stars, directors, writers, technicians and others to make films in England ... thus making you the Zukor of England.' Though nothing came of this particular plan, it is revealing that it was to the 29-year-old Englishman that a number of studios were now turning, despite the fact that Sidney spent so much time trying to curb American cinema supremacy and promote British interests.

They had good cause to do so. Sidney was starting to do some very interesting things. One of these was his attempt to discover the reasons why people went to the movies and what they liked best once they got there. The first of what became a much-celebrated series of Bernstein questionnaires was organised by a friend of Sidney's called Angus McPhail and sent out to 250,000 people in March 1929, probably the first time a piece of market research of this kind had ever been carried out in England.

The questionnaire was divided in two. First came the replies from 'prominent persons in various walks of life (the Peerage, the House of Commons, Society, the Clergy etc. etc.)'. Analysing the answers, Angus McPhail wrote scathingly that these replies 'demonstrated in an illuminating manner the attitude of those who hardly ever enter a cinema and of those who are actively hostile to films in general'. Five Bishops replied that they were not in the habit of going to the cinema; thirteen Peers said they never went at all; two Peeresses declined to reply; of the many Members of Parliament canvassed, two wrote that they were too busy to answer questions and one, Rhys Davies, 'sees so much tragedy in daily life that he never goes unless he is sure of a good laugh'. As for the Spanish Ambassador, 'he is unable to reply' (doubtless for diplomatic reasons). Individually, Lord Fitzwalter replied that he thought he had been 'to a cinema twice and does not think he will ever go again'; Earl Howe declared that he had not been 'able to attend a cinema or even to read about them for very many months now', and the 'late Lord Swaythling' said that 'all he required was a comfortable seat in which to smoke and as good air as possible'. The upper classes obviously still viewed the cinema with extreme contempt.

The second section of the questionnaire was filled in by ordinary patrons. They were considerably less snooty. Angus McPhail noted approvingly that their 'answers are free from the snobbery or ignorance' of the gentry. Male patrons revealed that they liked adventure, comedy, Society drama, 'Historical, Melodrama and War', and Mystery – in that

1 Sidney as a baby

2 Sidney as a small child

3 The Bernstein children in 1907 *(from left to right)*: Beatrice, Sidney, Cecil, Max, Selim, Ida and Rae

above left 4 Alexander Bernstein,
Sidney's father

above right 5 Jane Bernstein, Sidney's
mother

left 6 Selim Bernstein, Sidney's
brother, 1914

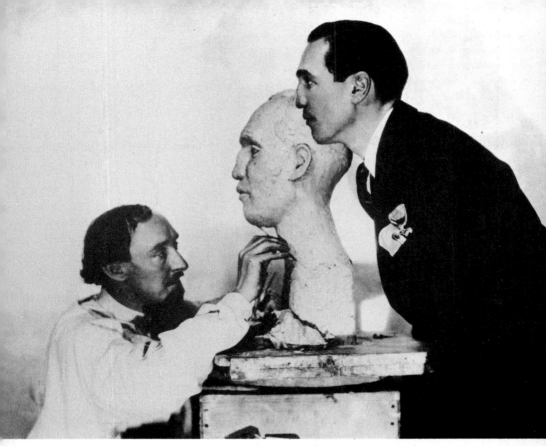

above 7 Frank Dobson at work on a
sculpture of Sidney, 1929

right 8 Sidney with a ski instructor,
St Moritz, 1929

9 Sidney at Long Barn, dressed for a wedding, 1934

order; women that they liked Society drama best and Historical and War least. Both men and women put Betty Balfour as their favourite female star, followed by Constance Talmadge, but while men chose Adolphe Menjou as their favourite man, women preferred Ivor Novello. Some resentment at the 'Americanisation' of the movies was voiced, as well as doubts about a long-term future for the talkies. John Gielgud admitted that he did not particularly care for the talkies except as a means of making a living.

More questionnaires followed, in 1928, 1932, 1934, 1937 and 1946-7. The results, every time, were widely reported. It was not that in themselves these questionnaires were very sensational; what was surprising was that there was someone in the industry then who felt such questions should be asked. It was one more step in the direction taken by the Film Society towards turning film into an art form that merited serious criticism and analysis.

The same spirit of inquiry prompted Sidney, early in 1928, to set up film shows for children. Cinemas had always been conceived of as family outings; but Sidney had long taken the view that it was not fair to sandwich the type of film that appealed to children into the middle of an adult selection. He launched his new idea one day at the Savoy over a lunch. His guests included Arnold Bennett, Gordon Craig and Sir John Foster Fraser, and he invited Miss Jean Harvey, secretary of the Film Society, to be responsible for putting together suitable programmes. The first screening took place a few weeks later at the Empire in Willesden, where on a Saturday morning at 10.30 a.m. 2,000 children gathered to watch *Robinson Crusoe*. The price of the tickets was 3*d*. Dr J. S. Bridges, Chief Education Officer, and the Dean of Willesden both attended. When, during the film, a mother reported that her child had got lost in the crowd, the manager flashed a message across the screen, and the boy was quickly found.

The children's matinees were widely praised in the newspapers – it had been only weeks earlier that Ernest Betts was lamenting in the *Daily Chronicle* that 'no single theatre in the capital had pledged itself to such an ideal' – and were soon extended to all the Bernstein theatres. By mid-July 30,000 children – called, by now, Granadiers – had taken part. Once again, the managers were needled into thinking up enticing stunts; Edmund Hall asked Pritchards of Enfield, the bakers, to make an enormous cake (it cost three shillings per hundredweight) and each child coming to the Edmonton Empire got a free slice. By March the following year, other cinemas had started their own series of children's matinees.

None of these respectable projects had dampened Sidney's taste for legal battles. Some time in 1929, as part of the building programme, the

Bernstein brothers had decided to add to a one-floor cinema they owned in Stratford. They jacked up the roof, to add a Circle, and prepared to reopen. To do so, they needed a new licence from the Fire Brigade which, under the Cinematographic Act of 1909, was still responsible for the safety precautions; it was all to do with the inflammable nitrate film of the period. To their extreme astonishment, their application was turned down.

A few days later, while brooding on what to do, Sidney met another local cinema owner and told him what had happened. 'You'll never get your licence, Sidney,' his acquaintance told him. 'You didn't give the Fire Inspector a present at Christmas.'

'No,' replied Sidney, 'that is our policy. No bribes.' He decided to open the cinema at Stratford, without a licence.

The local Fire Inspector instantly appeared. 'This is a breach of the law. Where is your licence to show inflammable film?'

Sidney had prepared his reply. 'Where is the inflammable film? These are *non*-inflammable.'

'Very well. Give me a piece to analyse.'

'I can't. It's not my film. You can't just chop it up.'

The Film Inspector departed. This game lasted several months, Sidney enjoying himself enormously. Finally the Inspector came up with a ruse of his own. He visited the distributors' offices in Wardour Street and made off with a piece of film that had once been shown at Stratford. It was, of course, nitrate and inflammable, as the analysis soon showed; there was no other sort of film in the late 1920s.

The case came up before the Magistrates' Court in Stratford. Sidney had taken the precaution of retaining a renowned Counsel of the day, Sir Henry Curtis Bennett, QC, a tall, distinguished figure much respected in legal circles, and had briefed him carefully about the bribes. 'Young man,' said Curtis Bennett, 'you sit behind me and if I say anything wrong, tug my gown.'

The first witness to be called by the prosecution was the Fire Inspector himself. Bennett started asking him deft questions about how he ran his department, with well placed innuendoes about Christmas presents. Within minutes the Town Clerk, who was part of the prosecution, asked for the case to be adjourned. There was a private meeting afterwards, the Corporation withdrew the summons and Sidney got his licence, having agreed to install two fire extinguishers.

It was in no one's interest to broadcast the Fire Brigade's behaviour too widely. The case had one amusing consequence. Five years later Sidney applied to the Fire Inspector of Manchester for a licence for a new cinema there. The Inspector asked Sidney to come and see him. 'I know all about *you*, young man, from my friend at Stratford.' He paused, expectantly. Sidney did not: 'Are you going to behave in the same way?' The Inspector said nothing; and Sidney said good day to him. The licence came through.

There was one other battle to fight; the issue of Sunday openings. Under the first Cinematographic Act of 1909 loopholes had been left to cover matters other than fire regulations. One of these was the question of whether or not cinemas should be allowed to open on Sundays. Passions ran extremely high over the subject, the Church bodies arguing that it was lacking in piety to have entertainments on the Lord's Day, the police countering by saying that it would give young people something to do. By the late 1920s, the Church lobby was in the ascendant and all cinemas had to stay shut on Sundays.

Sidney now gathered together what support he could find and after intensive lobbying prevailed on Herbert Morrison, the former Labour MP and then active in LCC affairs, to lobby for a Bill through Parliament. The outcome was not entirely satisfactory, as the Bill ruled only that there should be a public meeting and a referendum on the subject in every town in the country.

The whole Bernstein organisation was pressed into service. On the days of the public meetings, cars were commandeered to drive around the streets mustering voters. They were numbered to start at a hundred, thereby giving the opposition the impression of formidable troops. Sidney also returned to the stunt that had worked so well before: he commissioned a film in which an actor was ready with replies to questions about Sunday openings – what sort of films, staff bonuses, alternative days off and so on – put to him by a stooge in the audience. The battle for Sundays travelled from town to town and reached its height in Dover, where the Lord's Day Observance Society won the first round only to have the ban reversed when Cecil arranged for every theatre and cinema in the town to be fully lit up on a Sunday, with all attendants present and instructed to turn away audiences with the explanation that it was all by order of their own council. Local protest soon reversed the decision.

By the time the Dover battle was being fought Sidney was in fact in California, paying his first visit to the capital of the movie world. For a man whose life was so intimately linked with films it was perhaps surprising he had not been there sooner. But the film production companies' headquarters were all in New York, where scripts were read and contracts signed, and Sidney had met the Warner brothers, the men from Paramount, MGM and United Artists on their frequent visits to the East Coast and when they had come to London. Hollywood in the late 1920s was not much of a lure, as Iris Barry, on a visit there, wrote to tell him:

Your nice wire was very welcome: I am most frantically disenjoying Hollywood ... How right you were not to come out here: there is nothing at all but exactly what you see on the screen – a lot of good workmanship and a lot of abysmal stupidity.

And of course the people – the society – the conversation – all is unimaginably awful. You know what chorus girls are like, or don't you? Let us argue that you do, and it's just like that. The men are worse than the women.

California itself is fun – I spent a day at the lake up in the mountains, and enjoyed every second, even motoring home at night along the most hairpin of serpentine roads ... It is only the film community which is so vile, so deadly boring, and so exhausting. They never talk of anything but films, and not at all intelligently, and *all* of them, good and bad, are most bloody self important ...

The respectable citizens despise the film people beyond anything the *Daily Mail* ever imagined and so, I found, do all normal Americans.

By mid-1930 Sidney's Film Society friend Ivor Montagu was also in Hollywood, working with Eisenstein, Alexandrov and Tissé on a possible film for Paramount. (The three Russians were on a year's leave from the Soviet Union, partly as a reward for their films *Battleship Potemkin* and *October*, partly because the switchover to sound technology in Russia had caused a temporary halt in movie production.) Sidney had been largely responsible for the visit, having introduced Eisenstein to Jesse Lasky in London, and arranged for them to travel across to America on the same ship, as well as lending them all money to buy proper formal day and evening clothes for the voyage.

In October, just before setting sail on the *Majestic* from Southampton, he received a cable from Iris Barry, by then living in New York: 'Don't miss the boat this time ... eagerly waiting so is Capone who wants you to decorate all his new beer parlours with Tintorettos.'

Sidney reached New York on 27 October after a trying journey, as he wrote to Will Evans, head of Gaumont British: 'The boat was very ugly and much uglier passengers ... New York is altered considerably. Business is hopelessly bad ... the films they are showing are dull and uninteresting. Nobody quite knows that to do and everybody is afraid to make a decision.' To Ernest Fredman of the *Daily Film Renter*, he added: 'Everybody is talking depression, just as they used to talk prohibition. Nobody ever mentions prohibition nowadays – they just offer you a very good drink.' He also remarked that the New York Theatre dressing-rooms were palaces compared to the Hippodrome and that 'miniature golf courses are all the rage'.

A few days later he caught an overnight train to Chicago, spent several rather unsatisfactory days there – 'boring', he commented, though he was able to see some of the Balaban and Katz movie palaces, where the key note was opulence and which had been dubbed by their creators 'shrines to democracy' – and boarded the *Chief*, Southern Pacific Railways' East Coast train, for Hollywood. The *Chief* was the train favoured by the film people, agents, actors, directors and producers, who spent a great deal of their lives on three-day journeys backwards and forwards between film studios and company offices. It had all the old-fashioned romance of a film set itself, with superb drawing-rooms and private bathrooms in mahogany and plush, and excellent food: fresh trout would be ordered ahead by wire from Denver and white fish from Lake Superior. Though there was no air-conditioning, wet sheets were strung up through the dining car to lower the temperature. There were parties every night, and by day passengers read scripts, discussed deals, played cards or simply sat at the cocktail bar in the observation car at the rear, watching the scenery recede over Manhattans and daiquiris. From time to time the *Chief* would stop to allow passengers to stretch their legs.

It was a strange moment to arrive for a first visit to Hollywood. The depression which had by the autumn of 1930 put more than four million Americans out of work had caused considerable anxiety throughout the film industry and few of the original pioneering figures now held financial control of their own companies (though motion pictures were now the sixth largest industry in the United States). The switchover to sound was almost complete and solidly-built wood and brick studios, light- and sound-proofed, had replaced most of the original glass-covered sheds. The early moguls – L. B. Mayer, the Warner brothers, Carl Laemmle – were being jostled by three boy geniuses, Irving Thalberg, David Selznick and Darryl F. Zanuck, former script-writer for Rin Tin Tin and now, at $5,000 a week, head of production at Warner's. Sam Warner himself, the man who could be said to have officially launched talkies with *The Jazz Singer*, was dead, having collapsed the night before the première. The Hays Office Code (under the presidency of Will Hays, an abstemious Midwestern Presbyterian and Postmaster-General for the Harding administration) had just been formally adopted by the Motion Picture Producers and Distributors Association of America, thus bringing to an end a series of scandals that had beset Hollywood in the 1920s and enforcing a morals clause in all studio contracts. Anyone could now be dropped for immoral conduct, and a blacklist of 'unreliables', people addicted to drink or drugs, had been circulated throughout the studios.

The carnival of the 1920s was over.

But it was all, still, very glamorous. The stars had built themselves palatial villas around the suburbs of Los Angeles, at Bel Air and Beverly Hills, with colonnades, inner courts, pools, waterfalls, pergolas and porticoes (Dorothy Parker called the style 'early marzipan'); immense gardens and private golf courses rivalled each other in perfection of lawn and display of tropical flowers. Inside, the houses were kept very open – with 334 days of sunshine a year they could afford to – with galleries and niches designed to show off the furniture and bric-à-brac collected in Europe and the Far East as well as personal mementoes from particular films. Cars were longer, sleeker, more absurd than anywhere else (Rudolph Valentino had a cream Mercedes-Benz with a silver snake for the radiator cap). Despite prohibition, many had bars.

Sidney arrived to an impressive collection of invitations. Ten years in the movie business had made him good friends: people like Walter Wanger and Jesse Lasky, who now pressed the young Englishman to make the most of Hollywood. In a letter written earlier that year, Wanger, after letting Sidney know that Paramount had signed a contract with Eisenstein and thanking him for his help, had said: 'The more I think of it, the more I feel that one of these days you ought to join us in our operations. Has the thought ever occurred to you? . . . I am sure it would be to our mutual advantage. This is not just a letter, so take it very seriously.'

Sidney took a room at the Beverly Wilshire Hotel, dined at the Trocadero on Sunset Boulevard and met Buster Keaton, went to a party given by Charles Boyer who had just arrived from Paris, where he was introduced to Ginger Rogers, Anatole Litvak, Joseph Kessel and W. P. Lipscomb. He played Monopoly – the new craze – and ping pong. One night he went to a dinner given by William Randolph Hearst for his seventy-fifth birthday at which the guests all wore Spanish costumes and San Simeon had been turned into a Spanish village. Another night, he dined with Sam Goldwyn. Several days running he went to visit Hollywood's own exotic collection of super-cinemas, where the great gala premières took place, with their Hindu, Persian and Romanesque motifs, among them the recently opened Grauman's Chinese with its pagoda roofs and varnished dragons – the rival to the Roxy in New York – which featured the footprints of the Hollywood stars cast in cement, and where gongs summoned people to their seats. The ceremony of a foot imprinting was an impressive sight, with the whole of smart Hollywood invited, and the public gawping from the sidewalk.

Because of the reliable climate, many Hollywood cinemas were open, with doves trained to circle the balconies, stuffed peacocks glued to the organ grilles and a plethora of brilliantly coloured gazebos, trellises, columns and arches, mostly made out of cast plaster.

There were the Montagus, Eisenstein, Alexandrov and Tissé to visit, living in a rented, Spanish-looking house in Cold Water Canyon above Beverly Hills. Eisenstein, who was in charge of the finances, kept the others on a tight budget, choosing to dish them out pocket money rather than hand over the agreed fees allocated to each of them by Paramount. He was a strange man. One of his favourite jokes was to wait until someone offered him a drink, and then look shocked and say: 'No. No. I wouldn't dream of disobeying the American laws.' He was in fact a teetotaller.

One day there was an unexpected call for Sidney from Kono, Charlie Chaplin's Japanese butler, asking whether he would like to meet Chaplin at his studio at 8.30 to see his new film, *City Lights*. Sidney arrived to find Chaplin alone in a surprisingly modest studio, and was told to sit at the back of the room. Chaplin himself walked forward and sat down at the piano. *City Lights* came on; Chaplin played throughout. Sidney thought it was wonderful and said so and Chaplin asked him to stay on for a second sitting and not to reveal to anyone that he had seen it already. Then arrived Nick Schenck of United Artists, Sam Goldwyn and a collection of top Hollywood tycoons. Sidney sat down with them, feeling something of an interloper. When the show was over, Chaplin whispered to him to stay on and when the tycoons left he took Sidney back for dinner to his house at Laughlin Park, where an architect had designed a swimming pool as an exact replica of the famous bowler hat. Another night, he and the Montagus dined with Chaplin, and played tennis and charades. This was the start of a close and important friendship which lasted until Chaplin's death on Christmas Day 1977.

After ten days Sidney had seen enough. He found the glamour seductive but it was not exactly his world: too many parties, too much frivolity. When, at a casting party one night, a director had asked him, 'Which girl would you like?' he had been shocked. One day Hell, Ivor Montagu's wife, asked him whether he was enjoying his stay. 'No,' he replied, 'I feel about it what I do about food I don't like. I want to send it back.' It was a very characteristic remark: there was then, and there remained, something very straightlaced about Sidney, a sort of puritan modesty that recoiled from such brazen ostentation, and which made him, at times, appear fastidious, even aloof. It was all part of his sense of complete privacy, his desire that no one should know anything of his personal affairs. After a diet of Hollywood exotica he was in fact more prone than ever to push the idea of British production. 'Bear in mind', he wrote to David Selznick, Louis B. Mayer's son-in-law and a growing power at Paramount, 'the few moments' talk about London and film production there. I have no doubt that European – and especially

English – production will assume an importance in a few years' time that today may seem fantastic.'

Just as he was preparing to leave, Eisenstein's deal with Paramount fell through. For various reasons – tyranny of the studios, rivalry, the question of budget, Eisenstein's 'foreignness' – the contract to make a film in Mexico had collapsed amid much unpleasantness with its sponsor, Upton Sinclair, and the trio now planned to return to Moscow. The venture had been, it seemed, doomed from the start. Of an earlier suggestion that they should make Theodore Dreiser's *An American Tragedy*, Sidney had written sadly to Wanger: 'Why – oh why, Walter, did you allow it to happen? Of course I have not told them I think it is a tragedy – I have no doubt they will make something of the subject, but in my opinion it is not an Eisenstein story.'

Eisenstein himself had not been altogether enchanted by Hollywood, and foresaw a rapid decline in the quality of films emerging from it. One night, Sidney saw him at one of the monthly Mayflower dinner dances where all celebrities and leaders of the film industry collected: as the two men passed each other on the dance floor, Eisenstein said to Sidney: 'If a bomb went off right now, it would be the saving of Hollywood.' Sidney looked around and saw that they were surrounded by all the current Hollywood film celebrities and studio heads.

Sidney left America with the Montagus, once again on board the *Aquitania*. On the first day out he caught his fingers in the cabin door, and for the rest of the crossing played bridge with his arm in a sling, the cards spread over a chair alongside. He told friends that the wound had been caused 'by testing prohibition liquor'. The *Aquitania* docked at Southampton shortly before Christmas, in time for the finishing stages of his most ambitious single project yet.

The opening of the Granada, Tooting, the show-piece of the Bernstein circuit, had been announced for October 1931. So fast did Komisarjevsky and Cecil Masey proceed, however, that it was ready by September. Komisarjevsky had said, somewhat grandiloquently, that he 'intended to paraphrase accurately a whole architectural style in one auditorium by means of solid composition'. Sidney had put it more simply: the decoration, he said, would be 'in a style never before attempted in any country in the world'. The public waited.

At 7 p.m. on the night of 5 September, sixteen trumpeters from the Life Guards blew a fanfare from the steps of the brilliantly lit, Italianate façade, and four thousand invited guests surged inside, while many thousands more gazed from the street.

Komisarjevsky had indeed excelled himself. What the audience found on entering was an immense foyer, designed after a medieval baronial hall with minstrels' gallery, carved panelling and heavily beamed ceiling, with oak and gilded Gothic side-tables and chairs. Heraldic Venetian lions stared down from above. A 150-foot-long Hall of Mirrors, with Italian Renaissance marble columns, led the guests on through an arched cloister to the vast splendour of the auditorium.

Here, Sidney and Komisarjevsky had made real their finest dream. Everything was the colour of deep, antique gold. The ceiling had been embossed in rose and gold moulding, while the walls were lined by row upon row of cloistered arches and delicate tracery. A series of cusped Gothic pendants clustered on the proscenium, which was also shrouded in rich draperies. In the recesses were murals by Vladimir Polunin of courtly fifteenth-century figures, troubadours and damsels in wimples. Nearby were stained-glass windows and wall paintings simulating illuminated manuscripts. Where there wasn't marble on the floor, there were deep carpets of rose and mauve. The Grand Canal in Venice, the Ca D'Oro, the Palazzo Cavalli, and the Palazzo Foscari, all had had their say; so had thirteenth- and fourteenth-century French Gothic. It was hardly surprising that next morning a stunned press labelled it the 'Cathedral of the Talkies, one of the seven wonders of London'.

Neither was the première itself a disappointment. The curtains parted at 7.30 to show a scene depicting the outside of the theatre itself: a motor car drove sedately up on to the stage, was received by bowing, uniformed commissionaires and opened to set down a very small girl. She was presented with a bunch of flowers and then declared the Granada, Tooting open, in a voice perfectly audible throughout the building – a tribute to its amazing acoustics. Next came the parade of all those who had helped in the building (a by now standard Bernstein procedure on gala nights) filing, one by one, on to the darkened stage, their names announced over the loudspeakers. Sidney did not join them; nor did he throw any sort of ostentatious party for the occasion, but it was an important evening in his life and he watched and listened, with satisfaction, out of sight. Then was shown a short, impressionistic film, suggesting mechanisation and labour, in appreciation of the workmen, before Alex Taylor rose up out of the pit triumphantly sounding forth on his Mighty Wurlitzer. Finally, the audience settled happily down to *Monte Carlo*, Jack Buchanan's first talkie.

The interval was no less pleasurable. It was then that the audience had time to look more closely at the fabulous detail, make out the carved and painted figures on the wall, parade in the Hall of Mirrors, their reflections thrown a hundred times about themselves, before going to inspect the novelty of a large dog kennel and a nursery for babies. (Later, Sidney had to employ a man to check the nursery after the last performance: people took to leaving their babies behind.) Some had 'snacks', something American and quite new, in the café with its

Hollywood-like menu of waffles and buckwheat.

The Tooting Granada was Sidney's third cinema in under two years, and certainly the most extraordinary and ambitious ever built in London. (When Roxy came to London a few weeks later, Sidney showed him round the newly opened cinema. He was evidently greatly impressed. As he left again for America, he told a reporter: 'Entertainment in England will survive while Sidney Bernstein and Noël Coward are around.') It had been expensive – not much less than £200,000 – and there had been local protest when six shops, twelve houses and four flats had had to be demolished to make way for it. Clearly it was going to be hard to run – to replace the hundreds of lightbulbs behind the crenellated openings, men had to crawl along parapets a hundred feet above the stage; and purists were bound to complain that it was nothing but an architectural joke. But that night, four thousand people inside and many others outside marvelled and cheered, none of it mattered very much.

4

The Theatre Years

THE EARLY 1930s saw a pause in Sidney's cinema activities. They were a time for the theatre, no longer the music hall but the 'legitimate' theatre, and for friends. The great building phase of the super-cinemas was still on, but by now others were in control of the details. This was the moment for a change of direction.

One day, while the finishing touches were still being put to the Granadas at Tooting and Walthamstow, Sidney received a visit from Sidney Gluckstein, Chairman of Bovis, the firm of builders he had used for each of his theatres. Bovis were in difficulties, Gluckstein told him. They had entered into a deal with a financier to put up a new theatre on the site of a disused factory in Charing Cross Road. The plans were turning out to be impractical, the scheme was foundering: would Sidney help?

Sidney already had some small experience of the legitimate theatre. His association with Arnold Bennett at the Court Theatre had resulted in some fairly ambitious productions, and they had not made money. Better than anyone he knew that the moment was terrible, that after an exciting and experimental decade, with the new plays of O'Casey, Galsworthy and Shaw, and the Russian and Shakespeare revivals, the theatre had reached a moment of uncertainty, as new cinemas opened weekly and fickle audiences showed every sign of deserting to film. Everywhere, people were losing money, particularly in new theatres. But here, suddenly, seemed a chance that Sidney might never again have of combining all he most enjoyed: the expertise he had acquired in the construction of settings that in themselves attracted audiences together with an opportunity to indulge his own love of theatre. He took it.

The possibility of a total disaster was of course reduced by the fact that by now Sidney had a highly experienced team to call on. There were the builders, Bovis, and Cecil Masey, the architect, all of them well versed in the details of his requirements; there was Komisarjevsky, who reacted with understandable pleasure when presented with an opportunity to try out his splendid and bizarre designs not on theatres in the far reaches of the suburbs, but in London's West End; there was Vladimir Polunin, Diaghilev's pupil and teacher of decorative design at the Slade, pleased to move on from Tooting's murals to entire Renaissance panels, derived from Sellaio, Tintoretto and Giorgione.

'I took most of my ideas from Raphael, Giulio Romano, Girolamo da Carpi and Giovanni da Udine,' Komisarjevsky explained to the *Sunday Times*. 'The gangway at the back was adapted from the Loggia in the Villa Madama built by Raphael in 1519. I must confess that I was not above stealing certain details intact and unaltered ... The designs for the fittings, carpets and upholstery I made from various Italian originals.' As for the underlying inspiration behind the new theatre, that was to be found in Sidney's declaration: 'The Phoenix Theatre', he wrote, 'has been built in the belief that there is a necessity for a distinctive theatre in London ... It is hoped that the theatre will be used for every variety of experiment as well as for those plays which follow the more traditional paths.'

As work on the Phoenix went on, Sidney became immersed in details. Italy, Spain and Portugal were combed for master plasterers able to reproduce the elaborate details envisaged by Komisarjevsky. He was even concerned to produce the perfect booklet for the opening night, now a rare collector's item, with essays by Komisarjevsky and Jack Isaacs and its twelve pages of detailed architectural photographs. Sidney approached his friend Francis Meynell, the designer, responsible for the Nonesuch Press, who spent two days on the most elegant of engraved programmes (and later refused all payment, saying, 'I've done something for you I have never done for anyone else: given up two days at Lords'), and persuaded Ted McKnight Kauffer, who drew for him a rising Phoenix for the cover.

When the building was nearing completion, the architectural plans suffered a sudden setback: no one could produce a satisfactory design for the Phoenix's frontage. The area involved was very small, wrapped around an awkward corner of two streets. The builders and Cecil Masey produced nothing imaginative enough, and Komisarjevsky stuck to his interiors. Sidney, just thirty and at the height of his confidence, went to call on Giles Gilbert Scott, the eminent architect, designer of the

Liverpool Cathedral. When he explained what he was looking for, a design for an eighteen-foot area at the front of the theatre, Gilbert Scott expressed disbelief: 'Have you come to ask me only for that? Not for the whole theatre?' 'I'm afraid not.' 'What are the rest of your plans?' Sidney told him. Gilbert Scott followed them, detail by detail. 'I like your cheek, young man,' he said finally. 'I'll do it.' What had impressed the master architect, as much as anything, had been Sidney's obvious love of and obsession with architecture, for there was no doubt that Sidney knew about buildings with an understanding and a curiosity that went beyond the amateur's ordinary appreciation. That Sidney might have been an architect himself had never before really seemed a possibility: but it was becoming an increasingly important element in his life now.

As the day for the opening approached, Sidney heard that Noël Coward had just finished a new play, so wrote to ask him whether he might read it. Coward sent him *Private Lives*.

Sidney read it and was delighted: here was the very play with which to launch his theatre. But when he approached him again with an offer, Coward replied: 'I don't want it put on at a new theatre. New theatres are unlucky.' Sidney urged him at least to come and look at it. At the end of a conducted tour, past the Tintorettos, the Titians and the Giorgiones (Polunin was just back from a visit to Italy where he had been delighted to find the real Renaissance colours were precisely as he had imagined them), round the special noiseless fans, through the magenta-coloured upholstered auditorium, and down to the cloakrooms with their 1,200 hatracks, one for every seat, he changed his mind. 'But I'll only do it for three months,' he warned Sidney. 'After that I will have had enough of the London public.'

Charles Cochran, the most adventurous impresario of the day, presented *Private Lives*, the comedy of two honeymooning couples, which opened at the Phoenix on 24 September 1930. Apart from Coward himself in the role of Elyot Chase, the cast included Adrianne Allen, Laurence Olivier, Everley Gregg and Gertrude Lawrence, for whom Coward had conceived the play while on a trip to the Far East the previous year. The audience was the smartest that London could turn out. Sidney took his mother, as he often did to his first nights, and found that he had seats under the central candelabrum; he spent the entire evening wondering whether it would fall on their heads. In the interval, walking through the bars, he was overwhelmed by praise from all sides. Laurence Olivier, who remembers with pleasure acting in a theatre of such old-fashioned red and gold warmth, was not alone in welcoming a change from the prevailing art deco.

The critics, too, were full of praise. They had long been awaiting the event, carrying bulletins almost daily towards the end on progress of the building, and they were now universally enthusiastic. They loved the play and acclaimed the actors; they were also lyrical about the theatre's designers, architects, and Sidney himself, whom they called 'a rich young man of exquisite taste'. Coward was well satisfied with the evening:

> Gertie was brilliant. Everything she had been in my mind when I originally conceived the idea in Tokyo came to life on stage: the witty, quick silver delivery of lines, the romantic quality, tender and alluring, the swift subtle rages ... Adrianne played Sybil with a subtle tiresomeness and a perfect sense of character ... Larry managed, with determination and much personal charm, to invest the wooden 'Victor' with enough reality to make him plausible.

Cochran officiated at the opening ceremony, because both Gordon Craig, Ellen Terry's designer son, and Bernard Shaw had refused Sidney's invitation to do so. Shaw had replied that he was away at Malvern, writing, and Craig had answered Sidney's telegram by saying: 'Until considered fit to work in an English theatre am not fit to open one', a reference to his ostracism by London managements because of his strange and highly opulent approach to stage production. During his opening speech Cochran announced that he would be asking Craig 'to produce for me whatever play he likes, with whatever company he chooses'.

A week later, by which time the entire three-month season had been sold out, Sidney left for America. While he was away he lent his house in Albemarle Street to Gordon Craig, who was already planning another play for Cochran at a theatre near the Elephant and Castle and had complained that he hated his current bachelor digs in Duke Street. He told Sidney that all he wanted was a bed and a lot of coffee when he woke up: instead he spent the days giving enormous parties.

Sidney was away just over four weeks. The evening he returned to London he hastened to the Phoenix: the performance was excellent, the theatre packed, the audience enthusiastic. Afterwards he went round to congratulate the cast. The first person he saw was Gertrude Lawrence. She called him into her dressing-room. 'Thank God you're back. Noël doesn't speak to me.'

Sidney was surprised: 'But I just saw him, tonight ...'

'No,' said Gertrude Lawrence. 'When he comes off stage he cuts me dead.'

'How long has this been going on?'

'A couple of weeks.'

Sidney visited Noël Coward and invited him out to lunch the next day. The story came out. Gertrude Lawrence was playing her part as Amanda Prynne differently at each performance, changing scarves and shawls, altering positions and gestures. Coward had waited a few days and then said to her: 'Gertie, if you're going on doing that I won't talk to you.' And, he now told Sidney, she had gone right on changing things and so he had stopped talking to her.

Sidney went back to see Gertrude Lawrence and had a long and tactful conversation with her; at the end of it she swore she would behave. She did, but the same thing happened the following year when she was rehearsing Granville-Barker's *Take Two From One* at the Haymarket Theatre. Komisarjevsky, who was directing, came to Sidney and begged him to talk to Gertrude who, he said, was ruining the play by drawing attention to herself at the crucial moment when all focus should fall on the lover walking off-stage at the back. 'She's your friend, Sidney. You talk to her.' Again, Sidney went and delivered a long and reasoned speech, and again Gertrude Lawrence promised faithfully that she would stay still. At every rehearsal she kept her word; the dress rehearsal was perfect. On the opening night, at that very moment in the play, her shoe somehow fell off.

When Sidney had been in Moscow in 1925 Stanislavsky had pressed him not to miss seeing a performance of the Habima, a group of Russian Jewish actors who worked under the direction of a former favourite pupil of his, Vachtangov. Sidney had been immensely impressed, particularly by the beauty and distinction of Hanna Rovina. Now, in December 1930, he invited the company to come for a two-week season to follow *Private Lives*. It was quite a risk to take: all the plays, *The Dybbuk, Twelfth Night, The Golem, The Crown of David, Jacob's Dream, The Deluge* and *As You Like It* were performed in Hebrew.

The Habima season opened on 29 December. Chaim Weizmann was in the audience. Few could understand the words, but critics responded to the acting and the two weeks were a modest box-office success, though Sidney reported in a letter to Elfreida, Komisarjevsky's wife, 'Artistic sense (?) – yes. Financial (?) – no.' (Sidney brought the Habima players to London a second time, in 1937, for a month at the Savoy Theatre. *The Dybbuk* was chosen by the BBC as one of its first televised dramas and Sidney introduced it from Alexandra Palace.)

After this, the fortunes of the Phoenix changed. *Frailties* by Dion Titheradge, which opened at the end of January 1931, lasted only four performances. *Strictly Dishonourable* by Preston Sturges, a play about speakeasies which had just completed a long and extremely successful run in New York, was greeted by one critic as a 'poor shallow play'. It was slightly hard for Sidney to receive a letter, in February, from Noël

Coward in New York:

We're an absolutely smash hit and everything is fine and dandy. How is the dear old Phoenix going? You might drop me a line some time and let me know what is happening. Or better still you might hop over and come and see a little play we're doing called *Private Lives* ...

On 17 April, Sidney replied:

The theatre is still dying and the King of Spain is to all intents and purposes dead. It is so strange this world. *The White Horse Inn* (which beyond its spectacular value is dull beyond description) première and Sir Alfred Butt's resignation from Drury Lane have completely eclipsed the drama of Spain. After all, the theatre is more dramatic than life. That is, if Sir Oswald and Sir Alfred are the theatre.

The Phoenix has not yet been reduced to its original ashes but *Strictly Dishonourable* ends on Saturday after rather a halting ride of six weeks. Three weeks of film shows and then *Speed*, produced by Leslie Henson and Austin Melford. A comedy of drama and motor racing. Who knows ... ? We read without envy I swear but just a wee wee tinge of regret the success of *Private Lives*.

On 22 April, to bridge the gap until a new play could be found, Sidney put on a talkie. Having heard from friends that René Clair's second spoken film, *Le Million*, the story of a penniless artist who wins a million-francs sweepstake and loses the ticket, was a great new Paris success, he flew over to see it. Again, it was something of a risk: the dialogue was all in French. But somewhat to Sidney's surprise it was immediately greeted by critics as a very welcome alternative to American talkies. 'Mr Sidney Lewis Bernstein as an entrepreneur has probably done as much for the film industry in great Britain as anyone,' wrote Sidney Carroll in *The Times*. 'He has introduced to us some of the most remarkable, interesting and artistic films the world has ever seen.' When the Film Society could not get the use of the Tivoli to show Ilya Trauberg's *The Blue Express* with music by Edmund Meisel, Sidney immediately offered the Phoenix, and was not put off when an anonymous letter threatened that the theatre would be blown up if he allowed such pernicious Russian propaganda to be shown.

He also let his theatre be used for charitable functions. The Queen was present at a matinee in aid of the British Hospital for Mothers and Babies and the National Training School for District Housewives

when Miss Vacani's pupils put on a dancing display and Society ladies
and their children staged tableaux of pictures by famous players: Lady
Dunn posed wearing a green pyjama suit; Lady Nunburnholme
appeared in an evening dress of silver sequins, holding a baby in her
arms, with her three-year-old son peeping out from the folds of her
skirt.

In July, when the Phoenix had been open for nearly a year, R. D.
Blumenfeld, the American-born managing Editor of the *Express*, asked
Sidney whether he would allow a midnight charity performance of a
play currently running called *Late Night Final*, the proceeds to go to
the Newspaper Benevolent Fund. Shortly before the appointed date,
Sidney was looking through the list of tickets sold to see how the house
was being dressed when he noticed that Beaverbrook's name was
missing. It was perhaps not surprising; Beaverbrook, an avowed
enthusiast for films, had long admitted that he didn't care for the
theatre.

Sidney telephoned a mutual friend and told him that he thought it
shocking that a newspaper figure like Beaverbrook, who by now owned
the *Evening Standard* as well as the *Daily* and *Sunday Express*, was not
supporting his own trade. A little later he received a call from
Beaverbrook. 'I understand that you are very cross with me, Sidney.'
Sidney replied that he was and went on to explain why. 'All right,'
answered Beaverbrook, 'I will come. Providing there is a box available
and you will have a drink with me in the interval.'

The relationship between Sidney and Beaverbrook, who had friends
in common, was a strange one. Beaverbrook had been overheard to refer
to 'that impudent Jew, Bernstein' – this was some time before
anti-Semitism of this kind became wholly unacceptable – and he was
known to resent Sidney's assumption that they could talk to each other
on equal terms. Equally, he allowed his newspapers to print extremely
libellous things about him. Sidney, for his part, sued, whenever he saw
the chance. And yet the two men were friends, of a sort, and continued
to help each other when the occasion arose.

For the charity performance of *Late Night Final* Beaverbrook
bought tickets and Sidney made certain that he was given a box. During
the interval, just after Sidney had arrived with a bottle of champagne,
Beverley Baxter, of the *Express*, knocked on the door. Sidney knew him
from Film Society days when he and Ivor Montagu had been to dinner
with him at his rooms in Lincoln's Inn to complain that George
Atkinson, the *Express* film critic, was a crook. (Sidney had been
shocked when Baxter had told them that he knew Atkinson took what
amounted to bribes from the American companies but that he kept him
on because he wrote an engaging column.) Now, Baxter turned to

67

Beaverbrook: 'Max, I want to have a word with you. Privately', looking at Sidney. Sidney didn't move. He felt no need to in his own theatre. Beaverbrook nodded. 'You can trust Sidney.'

Baxter then revealed that Bobby Shaw, the son of Lady Astor by a previous marriage, had just been arrested and charged with importuning a guardsman. The Astors had asked *Express* newspapers not to print the story.

Beaverbrook turned to Sidney. 'What would you do?' Sidney replied that not being in the newspaper world, he wouldn't know. After a lengthy discussion between Baxter and Beaverbrook, the decision was made, against Baxter's advice, that *Express* newspapers would not print the story. Baxter objected that 'if anything happened to your boys, they would go ahead and print', to which Beaverbrook replied: 'My boys aren't buggers.' Some weeks later, Peter Aitken, Beaverbrook's youngest son, was arrested for being drunk while driving. Baxter later told Sidney that only an Astor paper had carried the story.

That summer Sidney and David Blairman rented a house called Cowslips at Mickleham, near Dorking in Surrey. They took it for ten weeks, at twelve and a half guineas a week, 'to include plate, linen and gardener's wages'. The house had a tennis court, the garden was full of vegetables and the owner wrote to say that the tenants were to have all the flowers they wanted. In July Sidney extended the lease for another month.

It was a summer of house parties and tennis matches, games of bridge and long rides up Leith Hill. Sidney now used Cowslips to repay some of the hospitality he had received from friends. Arnold Bennett had died in March. (Sidney was there shortly before his death and found straw laid down outside the flat in Baker Street – the last time straw was laid down to deaden the noise of carriages. In the hall he had encountered H. G. Wells, who lived in the same block of flats. 'Poor Arnold,' Wells had squeaked in his high-pitched voice. 'Never understood women . . . Not like me.') But there were new friends, like Mark Gertler the painter, and Liam O'Flaherty, who brought great parties of Irish friends to Cowslips and shocked everyone with stories about the sexual needs of leprechauns. Angus McPhail came and Ivor and Hell Montagu with Jeanne de Casalis, Koteliansky and James Stephens, and later the economist Laz Aaronson and Julian and Juliette Huxley. Lady Huxley remembers great elegance, good food and considerable luxury, and a long ride on Sunday morning through the woods, when Julian Huxley's stallion tried to mount Diana Winyard's mare and, unnerved by the rearing horses, she decided to ride quietly home. Sidney, always the perfect host, always exquisitely dressed, whether in white flannels or tailored riding britches, accompanied her.

Another new friend was Sean O'Casey, whom Sidney had met earlier at a performance of *Juno and the Paycock*. O'Casey had been in London at the time of the Film Society's season of Russian films, and Sidney had invited him and his actress wife Eileen Carey to the party he gave in Albemarle Street for Eisenstein. (Eileen O'Casey remembers meeting O'Flaherty there and not much taking to him. Sidney, she says, was an attentive host, introducing the O'Caseys to everyone.) Sidney was now able to help him over a disagreement he was having with the Censor, Brooke Wilkinson, over the film Alfred Hitchcock wanted to make of *Juno*.

The shooting of the film had already begun at the Ealing studios when the Censor raised various objections to it. Hitchcock asked Sean O'Casey to go and talk them over with him. O'Casey refused. Hitchcock then turned to his friend Sidney, who he knew had already had a number of dealings with Wilkinson over the Film Society, and asked him whether he would talk to Wilkinson. Sidney accepted, on condition O'Casey accompanied him.

The two men went to call on the Censor and found Wilkinson sitting at a desk with a list before him. He turned to O'Casey and began running through the lines in the play he wanted changed. O'Casey sat silent. Wilkinson then turned to Sidney, who delivered his prepared speech, pointing out that *Juno* had already been accepted on stage, and that a film version could hardly be more shocking. Wilkinson now appealed directly to O'Casey. 'Couldn't you just take these words out altogether' – referring to the many swear words – 'and put in a few "begorras" instead?'

Without saying a word, in complete unison, as if the scene had been rehearsed before, Sidney and O'Casey rose to their feet and in total silence left the office. In the event, the film of *Juno* was passed by Wilkinson, but not before Sidney's contempt for him – already considerable because, although nearly blind, he exercised the most ferocious censorship over material he could barely see – had grown enormously.

Sidney admired O'Casey greatly and grew very fond of him over long conversations they had together in O'Casey's house at 19 Woronzow Road in St John's Wood. It was a curious friendship, O'Casey so profoundly literary, Sidney so much part of a wider, less intellectual world, but there was no doubt the affection was mutual. One day Sidney received a letter from him. 'Dear Sidney. I hear you're seeing too many people who interrupt your work. Don't see them. Keep them away. When Eugene became successful he put a notice outside his door: Stay away. I'm working. Don't come near me.' 'Eugene' was Eugene

O'Neill. Sidney was flattered.

When not at Cowslips, Sidney was away in Dorset staying with his American friend Warren Vinton who was editing *Psycho*, a scientific magazine about spiritualism, with C. K. Ogden. (Sidney had been the best man at his wedding in 1929.) At one point he went off on a walking tour of the Black Forest, down the Danube, with Laz Aaronson, hiking several hours each day, catching buses when they grew tired or bored, staying at remote country inns. Aaronson was married to Lydia Sherwood, the actress who had played a small part in the Court Theatre productions. Every evening the two men would drink a toast to the beautiful Lydia.

When they got back to London they discovered that Lydia was being courted by Komisarjevsky, whose passion in life was not simply pretty women, but preferably married ones. (He would then marry them himself, in order to be able to leave them.) Aaronson suspected, wrongly, that Sidney had known about the affair and wrote him reproachful letters which he pushed under the door at Albemarle Street. Komisarjevsky, whose suit with Lydia was not going entirely smoothly, also pushed notes under Sidney's door, begging him to intercede with Lydia. Sidney, whose role with friends was rapidly becoming the one he had with the Film Society, that is to say a conciliator and arranger, paid no attention to either of them. He counselled Lydia to move into a flat of her own for a couple of months while she decided which she liked better, and offered to pay the rent for her. She listened, but decided to go off with Komisarjevsky after all.

On evenings he was not working late, Sidney nearly always went to the theatre or the cinema, often going on to parties or dinners afterwards. He was regularly accompanied by women, invariably elegant and some of them well-known actresses, but none was known to be linked with him for long. Already in his early thirties, he surprisingly showed no sign of a lasting attachment. Diaries from that time show a regular series of invitations to first nights. One, from Nancy Cunard, to a private showing of the Buñuel and Salvador Dali film *L'Age D'Or*, was addressed 'Mr Sidney Bernstein-Archangel', with a characteristic touch of period whimsy. When the Covent Garden opera season was running, he automatically took two seats for every first night: the perfect way, he had found, of repaying the hospitality of visitors from abroad.

He was also busy buying books: a bill from Maggs Brothers in Conduit Street of that summer gives some indication of his interests. There is Proust's *Time Regained*, Hughes's *Story of the Theatre* and a copy of *The Soviet Five Year Plan*.

On 28 December 1931, Sidney boarded the *Andalucía Star* for

Buenos Aires. He had friends in Argentina, made one winter at St Moritz when he volunteered to act as the brake for the Argentinian team on the Cresta run. His name was not on the passenger list – he had long since discovered that it led to unwelcome invitations. That he was capable of leaving England on such a trip – a jaunt, on his own, to South America, which he had never before visited – at a time when the Phoenix was losing money and three new cinemas had not been open many months, says much about his nerve as well as his extreme restlessness. After a week at sea he wrote to his secretary, Miss Mason, about the spring cleaning of Albemarle Street and concluded, 'Another eight days to Rio – and oh hell it's dull.' From there, came: 'Rio I found delightful but this tour so far is disappointing. My next move is uncertain.'

Buenos Aires, too, failed to live up to his expectations and he soon left for a week on an estancia belonging to Joe Trail, an Englishman whose family had come out to settle in Argentina a few generations earlier. Sidney reached the estancia at the time of an enormous plague of locusts. He was astonished to discover that Trail's daughter spoke no Spanish, just as he had been appalled earlier to find that the Hurlingham Club in Buenos Aires allowed no Argentine young men on the premises on the days that the English girls came to swim. As a way of life, none of it was likely to appeal to him. He found, however, that his reputation in the film world had preceded him even to Latin America and he was asked to give an interview to the *Herald*. In it, he did what he always did on such occasions: he declared, in fulsome tones, that the British film industry was flourishing.

At Valparaiso, where he went next, there was a cable waiting for him from Noël Coward, urging him to catch up with him at La Paz, so again he hastened on, this time by train which almost immediately came to a halt when a quarter of a mile of line was washed away by floods.

He reached La Paz, only to discover that Noël Coward and Jeffrey Amherst (with whom he was travelling) had moved on the day before. Finding the American and English colony 'the most unpleasant lot of boozers', he too moved on, catching the only train out, which went to Arica in Chile, where he took a room in a sumptuous hotel overlooking the harbour, erected during a boom in the economy and now, at the height of a slump, deserted. The baths were made of marble, but there was no water; there was a vast restaurant, but no food. Sidney bought the fur from the knees of llamas and had it made into a rug.

Finally, in an old fashioned pension in Arequipa, run by a woman called Tia Bates to whom Sidney had an introduction, he caught up with Coward and Amherst. Now the trip improved greatly. The food was excellent and there was a magnificent garden. The three of them stayed five days then flew on to Lima, found rooms at the Country

Club, went to a performance of *Tosca* and had tea with the English and American Ambassadors. From Lima, they caught a boat to Panama. There Noël Coward and Jeffrey Amherst transferred to a ship bound for California, while Sidney decided to go to New York via Cuba and Florida.

He spent two uneventful and largely unremembered days at the National Hotel in Havana, but he did bump into Nathan Burkan, an American lawyer of some influence within the Democratic Party in New York, whom Sidney had met with Charlie Chaplin. Hearing that Sidney was stopping in Miami on his way to New York, Burkan gave him an introduction to friends staying in the same hotel, the Ronay Plaza.

Sidney reached Miami in the late afternoon and to fill in the hours before dinner decided to introduce himself to Burkan's friends. They invited him down to an enormous suite overlooking the sea, where he found four very tall men playing cards and drinking. One was Mo Annenberg (father of Walter, later Ambassador to London), another was Joe Bannon, with newspaper and racing interests in Chicago. The others were introduced as 'judges'. (Sidney only discovered hours later that they were judges of racing.) The four took him to a restaurant which was just recovering from a police raid, and later in the evening Joe Bannon, by now singing Irish songs, persuaded Sidney not to catch his train for New York. The party lasted all night. The next day they gave another party for Sidney and when it was over finally allowed him to leave the city. (Just after the war, Sidney received a cable from Mo Annenberg: 'Congratulations on winning the war.' It came from prison. Annenberg had finally been caught for tax evasion.)

Sidney returned to England, after a few days in New York, on board the *Europa* with Charles Laughton. He embarked somewhat depressed and extremely cold after the warmth of South America but was soon sufficiently embroiled in Laughton's problems to forget his own. 'He was very excited,' he reported in a letter to Walter Wanger, 'receiving wireless messages from Lasky, who, in the usual Paramount manner, made up his mind to engage Laughton on the day he, Laughton, actually arrived in England.'

'I found England much more full of energy than the New World,' he went on, 'and London restaurants enjoying a boom. Business generally is down on last year, but, compared with other countries, very satisfactory. The West End Theatre is still in the doldrums and there have been few real successes ...

'Non stop variety, in various forms, has caught on. There are now six West End theatres with this type of show and at least four of them are reputed to be making money.'

The time had clearly come to get out of the 'legitimate' theatre. The only person who seemed to be making money was Coward – with *This Year of Grace*, *Bitter Sweet*, *Private Lives* and *Cavalcade*. Everything else seemed doomed to make a loss. A group of theatre owners, anxious about the way audiences seemed to be defecting, proposed to Sidney that he join them in a theatre pool, lowering seat prices and acting together rather than in competition with one another, but it was too late. In April Sidney sold the Phoenix to a man he described to Walter Wanger as a 'fat but kind gentleman'. It was his last personal large-scale investment in the theatre. The building itself had been a virtually undisputed triumph and, like everything Sidney was ever involved with, rooted firmly in practicalities. As he explains: 'We only spent money where the public could see it ... At the back of every circle was an exit, but behind those doors was only ever painted brickwork, never plastering.' It is a revealing remark: in his thirties, Sidney was capable of dreams, but he never forgot the cost.

To all requests from friends that he join them in fresh theatrical ventures he now replied that he was no longer interested. On 4 August he wrote to Archibald Selwyn, a producer of plays in New York who had been lamenting the American theatre depression:

> Frankly I do not want to be tempted to do anything ... There's tons of money in England lying in the Bank not earning one percent, but the owners seem to have fish hooks in their pockets and it would take a greater man than you Gunga Din to get anyone to invest in Shows'.

When Sidney Carroll wrote to ask him to take a share in a syndicate for a Regent's Park Open Air Venture to put on Shakespearian comedies and pastoral plays out of doors, he declined, repeating his 'resolution not to invest in anything related to theatre'. All he would agree to do, and that extremely reluctantly, was to buy 250 shares in the Cochran Corporation Limited, a new company his old friend Cochran had set up in which to merge all his separate theatre interests.

On 4 July 1932 Sidney rented Long Barn for the summer from Harold and Vita Nicolson. It was a fifteenth-century, L-shaped, barn-like house with mullioned windows and a tiled roof, and Vita Sackville-West had spent most of the 1920s there writing while Harold Nicolson was abroad on diplomatic postings. 'You're making a big mistake,' Nicolson warned Sidney. 'It's cold and miserable here.' The Nicolsons had moved to Sissinghurst Castle after a poultry farmer had threatened to turn the fields surrounding the house into chicken runs. The rent was £6 a week to include furniture, silver and books.

But when the two months were up Sidney and David Blairman, who had once more come in on the renting, approached the Nicolsons about buying it; they had fallen in love with the curious, rather dark house covered in creepers and its remarkable garden. Vita Nicolson had explained that it was not for sale since she was planning to give it to her eldest son, Ben, when he reached twenty-one, so an arrangement was now drawn up to suit both sides. Sidney would take Long Barn until the end of 1934, with options to 1936 and 1941, and the lease would be a repairing one. The Nicolsons would also now be free to remove the most valuable bits of furniture and silver.

From the start, relations between landlady and tenant were not easy. Slightly to his annoyance, Sidney soon discovered that along with the magnificent garden Vita Nicolson had left him at Long Barn, she had made him custodian of a number of extremely valuable and temperamental plants, brought back with her from two visits to Persia. That in itself would not have mattered had Sidney not sensed that the gardener she had left to tend them was not doing his job properly. He wrote to tell her so.

In reply Vita Nicolson appeared at the house. It was autumn and bitterly cold; she came looking like a character in a Russian novel, her legs tightly bound in newspapers. Sidney found her formidable. Somewhat acidly, she pointed out that while she herself was an extremely knowledgeable and experienced gardener, he was not, and that the man she had employed was doing an excellent job. She then departed.

Sidney may not have been much of a gardener, but he was tenacious and not easily cowed. Three months later he wrote again, repeating his fears and suggesting a compromise: as both of them were members he would pay for an official of the Royal Horticultural Society to come down and adjudicate. The official came; he declared in Sidney's favour and the Nicolson gardener was dismissed. In his place Sidney hired a man called Hook, second gardener at Mereworth, a large Palladian house with gardens nearby, who was getting married and wanted the cottage the job would carry. Hook was a success; he nurtured the Nicolson plants and in time followed Sidney on to his own house.

The garden was not the only irritant. Vita Nicolson interpreted her landlady's clause very generously in her own favour. When Sidney was away she came round and removed rugs, linen and books, leaving the house, as he described it crossly, 'shabby' and 'denuded'. Sidney complained. Later, he received a letter objecting to something someone at Long Barn had said to her over the phone. It carried a postscript: 'I must add, that it did strike me as not quite an educated voice that answered – though it did not occur to me that it might be a servant's voice.' Miss Mason, Sidney's secretary, scrawled at the bottom: 'Still can't understand this mystery'; Sidney in pencil added: 'Such snobs too.' When Vita Nicolson also objected that her maid Louise was getting over-burdened with work, Sidney tartly replied that at the last weekend there had been four servants and seven residents.

None of the altercations marred life at Long Barn. Sidney loved it there and resumed the pattern he had started so successfully at Cowslips: weekend parties with the Huxleys, Sean O'Casey, the Montagus, occasionally the Gertlers. Charles Laughton came when he could, and so did the American actress Sally Eilers, as well as Oliver Messel, the young designer, who was becoming close to him. Sidney was now establishing what was to be the pattern for his future life. He was, and preferred to be, host, enjoying his friends' company in a setting he could control. He took great pleasure in providing excellent food and wine (one early guest, to this day, also remembers the admiration she felt for the fine embroidered linen pillow-cases), and if there were few sporting activities to amuse them, there was a great deal of good talk. Meals lasted for hours; after lunch the guests sat on the terrace or walked.

Some time that summer Sidney and David Blairman drove down for a weekend to Bournemouth. They stayed at the Branksome Towers Hotel, on the sea front overlooking Poole, and it was there that Sidney met Zoë Farmer, a strikingly good-looking and elegant girl. There were three Farmer sisters looking after themselves; their parents had died while they were young, leaving them to be brought up by a governess on the Isle of Wight. Kathleen, the eldest, was now working at the hotel, which belonged to friends of her father's, as a receptionist, and had taken Zoë, aged twenty, with her.

Zoë soon moved to London and took a flat opposite Claridge's in Adam and Eve Mews. Molly Castle, who was working as a columnist for the *Daily Express*, had known her since childhood. When Beaverbrook asked her one day to find someone, preferably a pretty young woman, to read the papers to him at 6 a.m. every day at Stornoway House (his sight was bad) she thought of Zoë, knowing that she needed work and wanted to join a paper.

A month later, Beaverbrook, who was famous for his powerful likes and dislikes, sent for Molly Castle. 'I don't like her voice,' he said irritably. 'Send her away.' Molly Castle objected that this would put Zoë out of work. 'Well, find her a job on the paper,' Beaverbrook replied. Zoë went to work on the Women's Page, first as Molly Castle's assistant, and later, having proved her worth, as editor of the beauty section. She was funny and beautiful and she had great style, with an oval face and high cheek bones and a look that was at once rather knowing and slightly amused. She rarely wore the bulky trousers then in fashion, preferring tailored suits and high-necked silk blouses.

Zoë was soon a frequent visitor at Long Barn. She played little part in the domestic arrangements. But the fact that she came so often and that Sidney appeared increasingly fond of her was in itself noticeable: up until now he had always been extremely private about his private life, escorting invariably rather glamorous women to the many first nights he attended, but remaining detached and rather solitary. He had many close women friends, like Iris Barry and Lydia Sherwood, but they remained precisely that. Zoë carried down with her to Long Barn the gossip of Fleet Street which he enjoyed and friends like John Rayner, then features editor of the *Express*, Tom Driberg (as William Hickey, the columnist) and Cedric Belfrage, the theatre and film critic. Generally Molly Castle or her sister Kathleen came with her, and the two young women, keen but not intrepid riders, would take their horses into Knole Park where there was a steep hill at the end of a long gallop, reasoning that it would draw up any bolting horse. Robin Barry, Iris Barry's son by Wyndham Lewis, whom Sidney invited to Long Barn, remembers at the age of twelve admiring the smart young men and the pretty girls.

Sidney did not neglect his family. Max, after a spell in Germany in an engineering firm, had been dispatched to train at the Paramount Public Theatre Managers' Training School in New York. Since the normal entry age was twenty-seven and Max barely twenty-three, Sidney had had to use his substantial Paramount connections to secure him a place and now wrote exhortatory letters about hard work and good behaviour. 'If you do not get promotion in one of Paramount's theatres, take my advice and return to England immediately. There is no point in wandering around New York lazing your time away and living on your capital.' He could be loving, but he was also exceedingly firm.

Albert, whom Sidney had sent to his friend Dr Emmanuel Miller for treatment for his bad stammer – at the same time asking him whether he could get hold of a copy of Freud's *Interpretation of Dreams* for him – was sent to Paris to improve his French. (His eldest sister's son Selim Tafler was also sent by Sidney to Dr Miller, who recommended a special school, 'an open air nature cultivating place in wooden huts', on the same lines as Russell or Neill.) It is true of the Bernstein family generally that whenever they moved about at this period they wrote each other long letters about the plays and films they had seen and the theatres they had visited. Sidney, it was accepted, needed this information. By the summer of 1932 both Cecil and Beryl were married, Cecil to Myra Lesser, and Beryl to a young doctor called Joseph Stone, but not before Sidney had exercised a fairly tyrannical elder-brother control over her movements. To their cousins in

America, where she had gone on a trip, he had cabled: 'Where the devil is Beryl stop cabled nine days ago asking her plans unchaperoned return not agreeable.'

The big family house at Walm Lane had finally been sold and Mrs Bernstein had gone to live with the younger children at 8 Abbey Lodge, in Regent's Park. (Before she moved in, Sidney got his friend Lesley Blanche to paint panels in the drawing-room.) Sidney, whose relationship with his mother remained close and loving, had long promised to take her to see Selim's grave at Gallipoli and in the spring of 1933 he asked the War Graves Commission to help him arrange the trip. For part of the way, Beryl accompanied him, and on 14 April the two were lunching in Paris with H. G. Wells and Frederick Voigt, the political correspondent for the *Manchester Guardian* in Berlin.

From Istanbul, where Mrs Bernstein met them, they took a Turkish steamer overnight to Chanak, a somewhat disconcerting experience since the boat was carrying a thousand lambs and goats on its decks and the carcasses of three hundred more hanging from every available piece of rigging. At Chanak they were met by the Australian who was in charge of the cemetery and one of the three White Russians who cared for the graves. There, among the long white lines, beautifully tended, they found Selim's. It was the only one with a Star of David.

Before returning home, Sidney was to have had a meeting with Trotsky, then living on Prinkipo. Just before the date fixed, Mrs Bernstein fell ill and Sidney and Beryl decided to leave at once for England. Sidney never did meet Trotsky.

Sidney in fact continued to travel a great deal in the early 1930s, spending two to three months abroad each year. One autumn he was in Berlin where, wandering down a street by the canal, he saw in an art gallery a picture he greatly liked. He went in and asked, in bad German, the name of the artist and the price. The assistant couldn't understand what he wanted and called the proprietor, Alfred Flechtheim. The picture he liked was Paul Klee's *Blumen in Zimmer*. Sidney had never heard of Klee and didn't have the £70 in German marks that Flechtheim was asking but he cabled Cecil for the money and, while waiting for it to arrive, Flechtheim invited him to have breakfast with him at his house overlooking the Wannsee. The two became friends and later Sidney helped Flechtheim to get his paintings out of Germany and to set up in England, introducing him to Norman Haire, the gynaecologist, and Eisenstein, with whom Flechtheim used to go off to watch wrestling and boxing at a club near the Thames. *Blumen in Zimmer* was the first Paul Klee picture to come to England.

Sidney was always wandering, restless to get away, to keep moving even when demanding transactions were being conducted back at home. More and more he was now able to leave these to Cecil and others, whose grasp of the intricacies of the film industry was rapidly becoming greater than his own. In the winter of 1934 he decided to miss another English Christmas, an occasion he had always dreaded, and to go and spend the time instead in a place where there could be no trace of festivities. He took a train to Genoa, a boat to Port Said and then a car on to Cairo and to Mena House near the Pyramids. He stepped out to be confronted by the largest Father Christmas he had ever seen, made out of cotton wool.

He returned home by a P & O liner and objected strongly when he was asked to dress for dinner. The food was disgusting, never something Sidney would easily accept. The day before the ship reached Marseilles Sidney prepared a list of the best fresh food he could imagine and gave it to the Chief Steward with some money and a request that it be bought and given to the Chef to prepare for him. The P & O officials refused to countenance the order. Eventually Sidney threatened to leave the ship and do the shopping himself, and they capitulated. He was not an accommodating passenger.

But his real passion was, and remained, walking. The journeys on foot that he took seemed to him the best way of escape, those weeks when no one could reach him and he moved on as the whim took him from one remote area to the next. Invariably, his walking companions were men. In the mid-1930s a new one appeared in the shape of Cedric Belfrage who planned to do a series of travel pieces for the *Express*. The two men had been drawn together by the conversations on politics they had had, late into the night, at Long Barn.

Now, in 1934, Belfrage decided that the moment for his world tour had come and Sidney offered to accompany him on its first leg, a walk through Spain, starting at Gibraltar and finishing up in Majorca. Later, Belfrage wrote an account of the trip in *Away from it all*, giving Sidney the pseudonym Bernard Stone. The trip finished up with a disastrous visit to Robert Graves and Laura Riding in Majorca, unsuccessful in that Graves made plain his disapproval of the two unkempt and politically minded hikers while Sidney and Belfrage took against the 'carefully built up prim atmosphere of his hermitage', and found the man both had long considered a hero and a model to be cold and unfriendly. Of the two, Sidney was the more disappointed.

On Sidney's return to London the critic James Agate invited him to a party. There was a lot of talk about Spain, and Sidney was questioned closely about his opinion. 'There's going to be no fighting,' he declared emphatically. The next week the Spanish Civil War broke out.

It would be wrong to give the impression that the selling of the Phoenix

Theatre was the end of all Sidney's theatrical ambitions. For he was, throughout the 1930s and indeed 1940s and 1950s, closely involved in the creation of a National Theatre for England; it was a matter in which he had no financial interest, but it took a great deal of his time and he fought extremely hard to ensure not only that the scheme got off the ground, but that it produced a theatre worthy of its backers' dreams. Just how hard he fought and the kind of ideas he put forward reveal his foresight in anything to do with entertainment, as well as his ferocious determination when it came to seeing ideas he personally believed to be right actually carried through.

By the time Sidney entered the movement, the idea of a 'National Theatre' was nearly two hundred years old. In the middle of the eighteenth century David Garrick had pleaded for one to be built, while Matthew Arnold, in 1879, had stated the case in words that have since become legendary: 'The people *will* have the theatre; then make it a good one ... The theatre is irreversible; organise the theatre.'

Arnold had in mind a theatre either supported or owned, like many foreign theatres of the time, by the state or the sovereign. Since neither seemed likely at the turn of the century the idea was born of setting up a theatre by private gift or public subscription – to be 'national' in much the same way as great museums and libraries were national.

In 1908 a public meeting was called to discuss the setting up of an adequate memorial to Shakespeare on the occasion of the approaching Tricentenary; unanimously it voted for a National Theatre as a monument to the playright, and not long afterwards an anonymous donor offered £70,000 towards it. This benefactor turned out to be Sir Carl Meyer, a German Jewish banker, and Dame Edith Lyttelton later told Sidney that she had persuaded him to part with the money by promising him a baronetcy from the then Prime Minister Herbert Asquith. Before the money could be spent, however, the war intervened and the plans for a National Theatre went into abeyance until the early 1930s.

On 17 June 1932 Sidney received a letter from the Secretary of the recently revived Shakespeare Memorial National Theatre Company, Geoffrey Whitworth, inviting him to become a member. Whitworth was a remarkable and now forgotten man, a short hunched figure who founded the British Drama League and gave the best part of thirty years of his life to the National Theatre. Sidney accepted the invitation, and found himself joined by Lewis Casson, Sir Bronson Albery, Dame Sybil Thorndike and Bernard Shaw. By the time the Committee launched its major appeal in 1935, it had been signed by everyone of any stature in the political, literary and theatrical worlds.

Being young and enthusiastic Sidney soon discovered that he had been co-opted on to one group to debate the logistics of the new theatre, from size of corridor to type of stage (Frank Collins, general manager of Drury Lane, and Robert Atkins, from the Stratford Theatre, both came, on Sidney's urging, to advise), on to another, detailed to find premises for the new theatre, and on to a third to decide its programme. The last was the least demanding since those involved soon agreed that the theatre should run on a repertory basis, with two plays in the bill each week, and nine new productions each year, of which three would be Shakespeare. In his report, Sidney did not include the works of Bernard Shaw, who came to him and said: 'Sidney, where are my plays in all this?' There was really no answer; Sidney was extremely embarrassed. 'You wait, young man, you'll see, it will be my plays that will pay for your deficit.' (Words that came, very nearly, to be proved right.)

One of the strongest forces on the committee was Dame Edith Lyttelton who was constantly asking Sidney to go out and inspect possible sites. When he could, he made detailed visits, reporting back that those selected were too small, too cramped, in the wrong place or too expensive. Occasionally he was more concise. To a suggestion put to him by a fellow committee member, Sidney Carroll, that they could do worse than take the Winter Garden Theatre, since Bernard Shaw had put his new play on there and 'if the theatre is good enough for Shaw it ought to be good enough for us', he replied somewhat cruelly, 'Shaw is 78 I believe and does not mind where his "swan song" plays appear.'

The Charity Commissioners finally intervened, protesting that in their opinion the Memorial Committee had failed since a theatre had still not been built. Sir Frank Meyer, Sir Carl's son, replied instantly that he would return the baronetcy if they returned the £70,000. Nothing more was heard from them.

Eventually a site was found by Sidney, a plot just across the road from the Victoria and Albert Museum. Though feeling that it was probably too small for their plans, he urged the Committee to buy and start building, because only when the public actually saw progress would they take to the cause. They did so.

Now came the question of an architect. Every member of the Committee except for Sidney voted for Sir Edwin Lutyens. It was not that Sidney didn't admire him as an architect, simply that he did not believe that Lutyens had either the technical experience or the patience to handle all the minute details of theatre building, of which he was now an impressive master. Lutyens got to hear of Sidney's objections and came to see him. Sidney liked him immediately, all the more so when Lutyens told him that he had just lost a contract to rebuild the Bank of England by doodling unflattering pictures of the Board of Governors during his meetings with them, and unfortunately leaving them behind on the table when he left. Lutyens soon made Sidney a generous suggestion: he told him that he would be delighted to work on the theatre in partnership with any architect whom Sidney deemed to be capable of the necessary technicalities. Sidney proposed his own theatre architect, Cecil Masey, and everyone now threw themselves into the work, even Shaw, who was called on to try and dissuade the local council from poaching back, for a pavement, a bit of the land they had bought.

Before work could progress far, war broke out. To carry the story to its end, Sidney was in North Africa in 1943 when he heard from Geoffrey Whitworth that the LCC were suggesting that the V and A site be exchanged for a larger one on the South Bank. He wrote back encouraging the Committee to consider it.

Still plans for the National Theatre dragged on. It was not until Gerald Barry had persuaded Herbert Morrison that what was needed to boost British morale was a Festival of Britain, and set it up on the South Bank of the Thames, thereby overnight making the National Theatre site attractive, that the scheme finally made serious progress. The Committee then asked the Queen (the present Queen Mother) to lay the foundation stone, and on 14 July 1951 at an enormous opening ceremony, attended by the entire acting profession, she did so. (Some time later, the stone was found to have been laid in the wrong place. Permission had to be sought from the Queen to move it, and this was then done secretly, in the dead of night.)

The National Theatre now needed a new architect. Brian O'Rorke had acquired a certain popular reputation for his interiors of a P & O liner and was now invited by the Committee to submit plans. From the first, Sidney considered the drawings to be hopelessly inadequate; not only technically unimaginative, but strongly élitist, segregating pit from gallery and providing only one restaurant, and an expensive one at that.

There followed a series of acrimonious Committee meetings, at some of which O'Rorke himself was present. Then came the day that Sidney presented his argument that the National Theatre should include a projection booth at the back of the theatre and somewhere for television cameras, in case directors wanted to use snatches of filmed material in their productions; he talked about Piscator's work in Germany that had so impressed him many years before. O'Rorke interrupted. 'I know what *you* want, Mr Bernstein. *You* want a cinema.'

Sidney was on the point of an explosion when Tyrone Guthrie, a recent member of the Committee and a good friend of his, led him from the room. 'This is all nonsense, Sidney. You're wasting your time.

What you need is this.' And he settled down with a rough piece of paper and a pencil to sketch out the theatre he believed to be right. Though never used for the National Theatre, these ideas later formed the nucleus of the plans for the one at Stratford, Ontario, in Canada.

These scenes marked the close of Sidney's official dealing with the National Theatre. He resigned from the Committee. He had been a member for twenty-four years. As he explained to Sir Bronson Albery in his letter, it was the one way left to him to register his protest:

First, there is the incontrovertible fact that there is a great deal of experimental production in the theatre which incorporates the use of film into a live production. I do not say that this is either a good thing or a bad thing, but simply that it surely must be taken into account in planning a National Theatre, which should offer the producer all the flexibility which can be gained through the many technical devices which today lie ready to do our command ...

Secondly, there will be many occasions to which the Committee will want to admit a far greater audience than can be contained within four walls. For no outlay and at no practical or aesthetic inconvenience this need can be met in advance by preparing sites for television cameras. Not to do so would be to confine the great occasions of the National Theatre to a few hundred people within reach of the West End of London, instead of broadcasting them to the Nation and perhaps, bearing in mind the rapidity of technical developments in television, to the whole of the English speaking world.

In short, I find the Committee's present attitude intransigent and short-sighted, and since mine is a solitary voice, I feel obliged to offer my resignation.

The story is not quite finished. In July 1959, Lord Chandos, Lady Lyttelton's son, and now Chairman of the Joint Council of the National Theatre and the Old Vic, wrote to tell him that he was trying to get the support of the television companies for the new theatre. Sidney's answer was somewhat sharp. 'I am still an ardent supporter of the National Theatre, but really I cannot ask Granada TV to do anything until the points I raised are dealt with.

'You might also find it difficult to get support from the other television companies if they know that the plans of the National Theatre exclude the possibility of the use of television.'

In the end, Sidney won. The words of capitulation are contained in a letter from Sir Kenneth Clark, dated 9 November 1960. The National Theatre had still not been built, but a new constitution had been

10 Long Barn, 1932-6, the house Sidney rented from the Nicolsons, with its garden designed by Sir Edwin Lutyens. Visitors in the 1930s included:

11 Tony Butts and Oliver Messel 12 Julian Huxley 13 James Stephens and Koteliansky (with Red)

14 The Phoenix Theatre, Charing Cross Road, which opened in 1930 with Noël Coward's *Private Lives*

15 The Granada, Tooting, the most exotic of the super-cinemas which opened in 1931

above 16 North Africa, 1943: Sidney
with Hugh Stewart of the Army Film
Unit, an RAF Liaison Officer and
Anthony Kimmins of the Royal Navy

right 17 Sidney, 1945

left 18 Alfred Hitchcock with Ingrid Bergman, in London for the filming of *Under Capricorn*

below 19 Alfred Hitchcock with Sidney

drafted, and with it new instructions for the architect. 'Your idea of installing facilities for cinema projectors and television cameras is obviously right,' Clark wrote, 'and when we come to consider the mechanics of the two theatres I will see that it is done.'

It was not until 1976, some seventy years since a public meeting had voted for it, that the National Theatre was finally opened. Denys Lasdun was the architect. The projection booth and the television cameras were there, but it had not been a simple assignment. Lasdun met Sidney one day and said to him: 'I have given twelve years of my life to that theatre. I have been all over the world and seen every theatre. I thought that there was nothing I had overlooked. But there was. I overlooked Harold Pinter.' Sidney asked why. 'He has so many perceptual pauses. During his plays you can hear the air going through the air ducts.'

5

Politics in the 1930s

WHEN SIDNEY CAME back from his first visit to Germany in the autumn of 1921 he brought with him presents for his family. Among them was a green marble desk-set which, his father being out at the time, he laid on the table in the first-floor study to await his return. Some time later he heard a shout of outrage: 'Who put that writing-set on my desk?' Sidney came to the bottom of the stairs. 'Take it out of the house immediately,' said his father. 'It's German.' The scene left its mark. In time Sidney himself was to develop the same reflex against all things German, refusing to buy German wine or drive a German car.

That his father should have felt so strongly is not surprising: most Jews arriving in Britain from Europe in the 1880s brought memories of oppression. More revealing perhaps is the fact that Sidney had not yet, at the age of twenty-two, understood the depth of his father's feeling: the Bernsteins were not people to indulge easily in self-revelation, and deep personal discussion played no part in family gatherings.

Politics however was safer ground and Sidney grew up from early boyhood in an atmosphere of liberal politics and considerable intellectual tolerance. Support of Lloyd George was natural, and when at the age of seventeen Sidney decided to join the Labour Party he was doing no more than was expected of him. It was more characteristic of him personally that in 1925 he should choose to contest a seat on the Middlesex County Council: the Bernsteins owned a cinema in Willesden and Sidney had been arguing with local councillors over the ever recurring question of Sunday opening. Unable to beat them, he decided to join them.

The incumbent county councillor for Willesden Green was a Liberal lady of many years standing in the party called Margaret Royle. To her great surprise, Sidney beat her in the next local elections by the narrow margin of 169 votes, becoming, at twenty-six, one of the youngest county councillors in the country.

His pleasure in his political appointment was soon checked by discovering himself not only to be considered too young, but totally isolated well to the left of all seventy-four of his fellow councillors. Sir Herbert Neil, KC, the Conservative chairman, took one look at the tall, brash, radical young councillor and decided that the way to prevent him from making trouble was to keep him off committees, the only place real decisions were made. From the side lines, Sidney fought an ineffectual but valiant war to keep the land on both sides of the Great West Road under the ownership of the Council so that the benefits of any development would go to the taxpayers. He was unable to influence a single decision but soon too Neil found it impossible to ignore him altogether and so offered him a place on the Maternity Committee, where, he judged, Sidney could do least harm. He was undoubtedly right, but rapidly Sidney wormed his way across to the considerably more powerful Education Committee and here, at last, he made some mark. It took him five years, but by the time he resigned his seat late in 1930, every school assembly hall in the county had a platform with rudimentary theatrical equipment and curtains so that children could perform plays rather than sit reading Shakespeare at their desks. It was an achievement that Sidney was pleased with, but the many hours of political wrangling had convinced him that there was no place for him in conventional party politics.

From that day on, membership of the Labour Party was to be enough, though his allegiance did have one brief moment of uncertainty in the early 1930s. As a friend of John Strachey's – around this time he was spending several weekends at Portmerion with the Stracheys, Clough William Ellises and Alan and Iris Porter – it was not surprising that Sidney was regarded as a possible recruit for Mosley's New Party, one of the rich and prominent younger men whose support Mosley was so anxious to gather. In the spring of 1931, Strachey wrote to Sidney asking him whether he knew of 'portable talking picture equipment' which could be loaded on to lorries and used for political meetings. Sidney inquired into the existing equipment, then wrote back telling Strachey that nothing really reliable had yet been produced.

Out of this came an invitation to lunch with Mosley, to hear more about the New Party's Manifesto and its views on 'British production in the new conditions prevailing in the world'. A lot of what the New Party was saying appealed to Sidney, as it had to the

85

seventeen Labour MPs who had signed the Manifesto: there was something energetic and wholesome in all this talk of action and priorities that could hardly fail to sound attractive to a man like Sidney whose desire to get things done was one of the strongest forces in his nature. But the Mosley lunch was too much for him. On arriving at the politician's house in Smith Street, Sidney saw that he had been placed in the seat of honour, next to the leader. 'Those awful eyes, bright and pig like', as he remembered later, were too chilling; they suggested fanaticism and Sidney backed instantly away.

Even had he joined the New Party, the association could only have been short-lived. At the time of the lunch Mosley was still voicing an active policy of racial equality, but by the summer of 1932 he had started his negotiations with existing fascist groups, with the idea of uniting them under his leadership, and this for the first time brought him into contact with the anti-Semitic fringe of British politics. On 24 October 1932 Mosley made his first recorded anti-Jewish remark, when he referred to hecklers at a political rally as 'warriors of the class war – all from Jerusalem'.

This, Sidney could never have accepted. While personal faith has never played a very strong part in his life, his mother's family was profoundly Orthodox and the lessons of his childhood had marked him deeply. They could hardly have failed to, growing up when and where he did: Ilford lies on the edges of London's East End, and it was in those London boroughs – Hackney, Stepney, Bow, Bethnal Green and Shoreditch – that the immigrant Jews had settled in the eighteenth and nineteenth centuries, and that were to become the settings for the anti-Semitic battles of the 1930s.

By 1933 he was becoming ever more involved in anti-Nazi campaigns. As a friend of Frederick Voigt, and close to other overseas journalists, he was among the first to hear reports of Jewish persecution in Germany. Among these friends was a Russian critic and writer called Koteliansky, whom Sidney had first met some years before with James Stephens and the Huxleys. Koteliansky was a short, bear-like man, always on the edge of utter penury. In July 1933, he wrote to tell Sidney about a film produced by a Russian friend of his, S. Liberman, and financed in France by Baron d'Erlanger. The film was to be a 'Jewish reply to Hitlerism' and Koteliansky was wondering whether there was a 'chance of getting Gaumont or any other film producing company in England interested in the idea of making an English version?'

Sidney's reply, written two days later, is revealing:

My dear Kot,
    I would like to meet Mr. Liberman but his proposition is

impossible because the British Board of Film Censors have already stated they will not pass any film dealing with the Hitler regime, at least showing the Nazis in a bad light.

Gaumont British producing unit submitted three scenarios to the Censor for his approval dealing with anti-Hitler propaganda in a mild form, but the Censor was adamant despite political pressure.

These two paragraphs alone say much about the climate of the day.

Now began, for Sidney, a period of intense political activity. It was not that he had the time to spare – the Bernstein circuit demanded as much of him as ever – but he simply added this work to all the other claims on him. There came a period during the 1930s when most of his private letters were dated 'Midnight' and contained apologies about lateness and brevity of reply. The first important piece of anti-Nazi work to concern him was the London counter-trial of the Reichstag Fire, and here his support, both moral and financial, as well as his organisational drive proved invaluable.

On the evening of 27 February 1933 the German Parliament building in Berlin had caught fire. When the flames died down one man, a Dutchman called Marinius van der Lubbe, was led from the smouldering building and confessed that he, alone, had started them. No one believed him. A search began for his accomplices. To this day, no one is quite certain precisely what happened in the Reichstag fire, whether, as Goering claimed, it was a 'communist outrage', the signal for communists to begin their revolution in Germany, whether the Nazis themselves had started it to give themselves the opportunity they needed to move against their opponents, or whether in fact, as van der Lubbe insisted throughout, it was the act of one lone figure, despairing at the lack of fight shown by Hitler's critics.

Whatever the truth, the Reichstag fire gave the Nazis the chance to act. Claiming that an identification card of the Dutch Communist Party had been found on van der Lubbe, they now arrested Ernst Torgler, chairman of the communist block in the Reichstag, and the hundred communist deputies, as well as three Bulgarian communists, Georgi M. Dimitrov, Blagoi Popov and Vassili Taner. From there, they moved on to pacifists, liberals, democrats, anyone, in short, who had expressed opposition to their aims. Van der Lubbe, Torgler and the three Bulgarians were arraigned for trial.

Willi Munzenberg, a Reichstag deputy, one of the early founders of the German Young Communist League and head of the huge Munzenberg Trust, with its newspapers and film companies, was near the Swiss border as the Nazis started their programme of arrests. He managed to cross into Switzerland before they got to him. From there he moved to Paris, where he set up, first in the Rue Montedour near Les Halles and later in Boulevard Montparnasse, the offices of a world-wide anti-fascist campaign, which within months was initiating a great number of committees and organisations devoted in different ways to the fight against Hitler and, later, Franco. One of these was the Reichstag counter-trial. (Whether Munzenberg was or was not run by the Comintern and acting solely for the communists, as was later suggested – Arthur Koestler called his campaign a 'unique feat in the history of propaganda' – is not really relevant here. Munzenberg never pretended to anyone that he was not a communist.)

In London, there already existed a group of people ready and capable of undertaking the sort of tribunal Munzenberg envisaged in the form of the Committee for the Victims of German Fascism. Ivor Montagu was a member, and so was Sidney. It was to them that Munzenberg now turned, using his secretary and assistant, Otto Katz, a Czechoslovakian refugee, and already known to the London Committee, as go-between.

The Commission of Inquiry into the Burning of the Reichstag was now formed, presided over by 'an International Committee of Jurists and Technical Experts'. Denis Nowell Pritt, KC, agreed to act as chairman, Arthur Garfield Hays, legal adviser to the American Civil Liberties Union, came over from America, and Holland, Sweden, France, Denmark and Belgium each sent a representative.

The London counter-trial opened formally on 14 September 1933 at the Law Society headquarters – exactly a week before the German trial was due to start in Leipzig. Sir Stafford Cripps gave the opening address to a tightly packed audience that included H. G. Wells. Bernard Shaw had refused to come, saying that 'whenever a prisoner is used as a stick with which to beat a government his fate is sealed in advance'. There was a great deal of behind-the-scenes activity, and in this Sidney was much involved. There was the publicity to handle – the Committee realising all too well that only the most intensive reporting of the case could possibly have any bearing on the forthcoming German trial – there were hundreds of documents to translate, type and distribute. Sidney and Ivor Montagu called on their linguist friends to help, and were now joined by Heinrich Fraenkl, who had been Berlin correspondent for the film magazine *Variety* until the day that he had gone to the station to collect his foreign newspapers and seen that the cover of the current *Variety* bore an obvious attack on Hitler, with the words 'by our Berlin correspondent'. He had left overnight for England. Fraenkl was bilingual, having been interned on the Isle of Man, at the age of sixteen, in the First World War. There was also Ellen Wilkinson, the energetic women's rights campaigner, a friend of

Sidney's and a frequent guest at Long Barn, who now entered the campaign with the same zeal.

Every day, witnesses were called and statements made. Every evening, sitting in the bathroom of the flat that constituted the Committee's headquarters, with a typewriter perched on the lavatory seat, D. N. Pritt would type up the day's position, while the other Committee members milled about discussing the trial. Each of those involved felt sure that the case against the Nazis was beyond dispute. As a new Chancellor, Hitler had only three of his followers in the Cabinet, as against eight belonging to the von-Papen-Hugenberg group. He needed a clear majority of seats in the coming elections and it was obvious that the communists would take at least a hundred of the deputy seats. Only by wiping them out would he gain supremacy. Day after day, more incriminating evidence came to light, including a document, the Oberfohren Memorandum: a direct indictment of the Nazis (later believed to be a forgery).

When, ten days after the counter-trial had opened, the jurists pronounced, it was to lay all blame for the fire squarely at the feet of the Nazis. 'No connection whatsoever can be traced between the Communist Party and the burning of the Reichstag,' the Committee of Inquiry concluded, and went on to say that 'the documents tend to establish that van der Lubbe cannot have committed the crime alone . . . that the happening of such a fire at the period in question was of great advantage to the National Socialist Party; that for these reasons and others pointed out . . . grave grounds exist for suspecting that the Reichstag was set on fire by or on behalf of leading personalities of the National Socialist Party.'

The verdict was widely publicised; all over the world newspapers and radio stations had carried daily reports of the trial, many of them at great length. When, at the end of the month, the real trial opened in Leipzig it seemed, to the delight of those in London who had worked so hard, to have to spend much of its time refuting evidence examined by the English court. Its own verdict, fifty-seven days later, was not surprisingly a mirror-image of the London one: all blame attributed to communist arsonists. Ernst Torgler and the three Bulgarians were acquitted but van der Lubbe, whom many considered a half-witted and disturbed youth, incapable of such precise action, was sentenced to the guillotine. Shaw had been right. Van der Lubbe was executed on 10 January 1934.

What bearing the counter-trial had on the Leipzig verdict is impossible to say, but the proceedings threw up a hero, in the form of the Bulgarian Georgi Dimitrov, who, everyone involved believed, gathered a great deal of the remarkable courage and resolve he showed when day after day, conducting his own defence, he stood up to the prosecution, and for several days to Goering himself, from the knowledge and understanding that the case had been examined in judicial fairness abroad. So outspoken was Dimitrov in fact that foreign reporters declared that he was turning the proceedings into a trial of the National Socialists themselves. (Dimitrov spent a few months in prison in Leipzig, before being given a Russian passport and deported. In 1972 Sidney was presented with a medal in memory of the ninetieth anniversary of Dimitrov's birth for 'outstanding services given in defence during the Reichstag Fire Trial of 1933' by Alexander Yankov, the Bulgarian Ambassador to London.)

No sooner was the London counter-trial over than Sidney was caught up in a second, equally demanding, campaign. This involved the boycott of German goods, and had been a subject under much discussion throughout Europe in the preceding months. It was not an easy issue. That people should be steered away from buying goods produced in Nazi Germany seemed on the face of it an excellent idea – but what if the boycott backfired on the Jews inside Germany? The Berlin Jewish Community had in fact cabled the Jewish Board of Deputies in March 1933, protesting against the boycott: 'Spreading reports tends only to do harm to lessen the regard in which the German Fatherland is held and to endanger the relations of the German Jews to their fellow citizens stop Beg you emphatically to work for a cessation of all atrocity reports and boycott.'

Sidney was on the side of the boycotters. A public letter of appeal, written from his office at 197 Wardour Street and signed by himself and two other Jewish film exhibitors, Phil Hyams and Theodore Fligelstone, explained why:

> For six months now Germany has been persecuting the Jews with ever increasing fierceness.
> Appeals and indignation voiced all over the world by men and women representative of every religious sect have been in vain.
> The persecution goes on.
> Words have been proved useless. Anglo-Jewry must take action in self defence of its co-religionists in Germany.
> Many measures have been considered but it is clear that no other way remains for Anglo-Jewry than a rigid boycott of all German goods.
> A large number of exhibitors in this country are apparently unaware that the carbons and other electrical goods they are now using are, in many cases, of German manufacture. By refraining from making any further contracts and so ceasing to buy such German products the boycott will be ensured a large measure of success, and exhibitors will

be rendering a vitally important service to Jews in Germany.

This letter is written at the request of a number of exhibitors who have already imposed a ban on German goods so far as their own businesses are concerned and now look to you to follow their example.

Germany must be made to realise how much the world resents the appalling campaign of persecution.

A little later, replying to a letter he had received from Boris Morros, of Paramount in New York, urging him to take some sort of anti-Nazi stand, Sidney wrote:

I get daily reports from Germany which show that although the persecution of Jews continues, especially in smaller towns, the government are officially taking steps to reduce this because of the effect of the economic boycott. Therefore it is more important than ever that the boycott continues ...

Like many campaigns of its kind, the boycott was doomed to have little effect. As the Board of Deputies was quick to realise, 'The Jewish purchasing public is so tiny compared with the world purchasing public that if no individual Jew ever again bought any German goods the German industry would be barely affected.' Individuals like Sidney, and organisations like the Jewish Representative Council, fought on, wherever they could, lobbying politicians, producing stickers ('Buy British Goods – Boycott Everything German'), and setting up 'vigilance' committees in the different trades. But just how successful – or unsuccessful – these were is revealed in the words of a letter written after the President of the Board of Deputies of British Jews, Neville J. Laski, KC, went to call on Viscount Cecil at 15 South Eaton Place on 26 September 1935. Laski had gone to urge Cecil 'and other men of distinction in the different activities of English life' to join as cosignatories in a protest against the treatment of German Jews, and to discuss the idea of proclaiming a general boycott in Britain of German goods.

Shortly after this visit, Laski received a letter. It came from Marjorie I. Johnson, Private Secretary to Sir Austen Chamberlain, and it read:

Like Lord Cecil, he shares and sympathises with the indignation of Jewry, but feels that the present moment is not a good one for raising the question and thinks it would be probably inexpedient to proclaim a general boycott, though if he were a Jew his feelings would cause him to refuse to purchase any article of German manufacture.

There was too much going on for Sidney to pause and rail at any one faltering campaign. From all sides, as his sympathies became more widely known, poured in pleas for help, both financial and personal. When he could, he wrote letters, signed petitions, effected introductions or invited people to stay at Albemarle Street; almost always, he sent donations, though sometimes the demands on his charity now seemed so enormous he had trouble meeting them.

It was a year of constant activity. A little later that summer Sidney joined with Leonard Woolf at the Hogarth Press to bring out a pamphlet written by his journalist friend Frederick Voigt called *The Persecution of the Jews in Germany*. Two months later, he was circulating friends to find new members for the Committee for Co-ordinating Anti-Fascist Activity. Interestingly, the secretary of the Committee was John Strachey, who had now abandoned Mosley, and the main thrust of the Committee's message was an attack against the man who had by now already formed his British Union of Fascists. 'It is obvious to everybody that Mosley hopes to win a tremendous amount of support by his anti-semitic propaganda', Sidney wrote in the letter he sent out, 'and this committee is taking special steps to deal with this side of the Fascist campaign.'

It is important to remember that at a time when few people in this particular fight had much money, Sidney did. During the 1920s Sidney had stood out among the Film Society group not so much for the actual amount of money he possessed as for his ability to keep making it. Now, in the 1930s, he was still richer than most if not all of his companions in the fight against fascism, and once again extraordinarily generous. This openness with money made him friendships he never lost; he rarely turned down an appeal and was always among the first to contribute, anonymously, where money was needed. Often, the calls on his help came from acquaintances; in the course of the gift or the loan, they turned into friends. A perfect example was the inexhaustible Ellen Wilkinson, who asked Sidney for £20 in the summer of 1935 to go towards a trip to Finland. He evidently sent the money, for at the end of August he received a long letter from her, describing what she had seen:

> I have just got back. The next country to go Fascist is apparently to be Finland. The Nazi influence is everywhere. About 90 per cent of the university students are fascist, with pressure from the authorities ... You are a brick. As things turned out I simply do not know what we should have done without your help.

It was the start of a long and close friendship.

Throughout Europe the position of the Jews was growing worse. It was hardly surprising, then, that when the *Daily Express* ran a story in the William Hickey column with the words 'Sidney Bernstein, that rarity almost unique: Jew who is employed by Adolf Hitler', Sidney reacted with all his old impetuosity. The writer had muddled him with Sidney Beer, the conductor of the Berlin Symphony Orchestra.

None of Sidney's *Express* friends were in London. Tom Driberg, editor of William Hickey, was on holiday; Arthur Christiansen, the Editor, and Dick Plummer, a director of Beaverbrook Newspapers, were abroad. Sidney waited. Finally a very contrite managing director, E. J. Robertson, phoned to ask what action he planned to take. Did Sidney want the writer sacked? No, replied Sidney, he did not. But he demanded that he be allowed to draft his own apology, which he took great pains with, trying to imitate Driberg's style. The piece ended with the words 'keen sense of humour, for which William Hickey is indeed grateful'. It was a dig that even Beaverbrook was likely to enjoy.

Sidney has always been a man to take offence remarkably quickly, and not only offence directed towards himself. At about the same time as the William Hickey affair, the London Police Court Mission sent him a booklet containing some of their cases, together with an appeal for financial support. Before sending anything, typically, Sidney read the booklet from one end to the other. At the very back he caught sight of the words: 'Romance? She was highly imaginative and deeply in love with a Jewish boy ... On demand of some tangible proof of her wealth (which was his chief interest) she stole from her employer ...' He returned the booklet, with no cheque, but with a furiously indignant letter. Others might have shrugged their shoulders and ignored it.

By the mid-1930s people in Sidney's position were definitely nervous. German anti-Semitism had by now become so violent that no Jew of his standing could safely find himself in Nazi territory. In the autumn of 1935 Sidney went to Moscow to find out what was happening in the Russian film industry and to see something of his old friends Eisenstein and Alexandrov. He carried with him an introduction to Mr Shumiatsky, the chairman of the Central Board of the Film Industry, and was hoping to settle certain difficulties that had arisen with Russian films at the Film Society.

On arriving at Croydon airport he discovered that Tom Driberg was to be on his plane – the friendship between the two men had not been dented by the mistake in his column – and they envisaged a rather agreeable journey together. After taking off on the second leg of the journey it was announced unexpectedly that the plane would be coming down in Berlin. Sidney was instantly very apprehensive. When the plane touched down a British journalist friend was phoned and summoned to come and collect the travellers. He stayed with them that evening, guarding them like a sheepdog, locked them into their hotel rooms that night, and saw them back on to the plane again next morning.

On his return to London Sidney posted watercolours and books of reproductions of Matisse paintings to two new Russian painter friends, Lebeder and Tischler, who had lamented the appalling shortage of materials in Moscow. Not long afterwards came a letter of thanks and a few words from Eisenstein, who wrote to say that he had smallpox. 'Some people consider them as smallpox. Other medicine men think them to be great pox. You can be sure that according to my style I vote for great pox.'

Towards the end of 1936 Sidney decided to carry the campaign against fascism to America, where he would try to raise money and publicity among his New York friends and the rich movie-makers in Hollywood. He wanted a break from Europe, and now agreed at least to investigate some of the invitations that had been reaching him from the Californian studios. Urged to do so by Charles Laughton, who had by now settled in Hollywood, Irving Thalberg, the genius of MGM, wrote to ask him to come and look over his studios and perhaps do some work for him. Sidney, cautiously, accepted, and set about planning a trip.

This time, he decided, he would see something more of the country, and instead of catching the *Chief* from Chicago would drive through the Southern states, stopping in Scottsboro, Alabama, to see the black teenagers awaiting execution for the rape of two white women. Kingsley Martin, at the *New Statesman*, had agreed that Sidney should write about the case. For such a journey, he needed a second driver and he invited Edward Porter, Alan Porter's younger brother who had come to work at Granada, to accompany him. Edward Porter was obviously a charming figure, managing to span both Sidney's more elegant, intellectual world and that of his blunter, genial younger brothers. He was a protégé of Laz Aaronson's; a quiet young man with a beautiful voice and a pale face who wore bow ties and did an imitation of Hitler, using a small black comb for a moustache. Everyone loved him.

They set sail from Southampton on the *Île de France* on 12 February 1936, with one enormous set of well-wishing telegrams, and docked in New York on the 18th with another. The crossing was uneventful and Sidney reported to Komisarjevsky that 'smooth seas made it possible to enjoy every meal'. New York was in the grip of its coldest winter for many years and nothing could be seen of the Statue of Liberty, wreathed in driving snow, as the *Île de France* steamed up the Hudson River. 'The streets here,' Sidney wrote on disembarking, 'are miniature Rocky Mountains with twelve inches of frozen snow . . . ear muffs are de rigueur. But there are skaters in Central Park and the sun shines with an alien brilliance.'

Sidney and Edward Porter had booked rooms at the Plaza, where they found a cable from Charles Laughton. 'Beloved stop Letter despatched stop Described you as fair and foul weather friend of many years understanding stop How am I doing Charles', to which Sidney immediately replied: 'Thank you for the perfect description sweetheart stop What a scriptwriter somebody's lost stop Ice melting but heart heavy.' He took the time off to write a furious and reproachful letter to his new butler in London, Donovan, complaining about the faulty packing of his shaving cream and the fact that his suits had not been properly brushed, as well as a jovial cable to Christiansen: 'Exclusive new chain Granadas being erected New York built of ice blocks neo eskimo gothic style', before setting out on a ferocious round of plays and films. Business on Broadway, he noted in his diary, was 'brisk'. 'The depression seems a thing of the past.'

After a couple of days at the Plaza Sidney rented Warren Vinton's flat on East Fifteenth Street; Vinton had separated from Helen, from whom Sidney had recently received a sad and charming letter:

> The real reason I haven't written all this time is because it's tough to write [to] your best man that the marriage is over ... I never was as happy as I pretended to be, and finally the whole strain wore me down so that the doctor made me face the truth.

While with Vinton, Sidney lunched one day with an old movie acquaintance, Winnie Shehan, the former head of production at 20th Century Fox, and his wife Maria Jeritza in his suite at the top of the St Regis Hotel. After lunch Shehan was called to the telephone. He came back saying that he had a tip for Sidney: 'Buy American Can and Can shares: they'll pay for your whole trip.' Sidney replied as he always did on such occasions: that he was no gambler.

On the way down in the lift he was overcome by greed and on reaching the lobby phoned his New York stockbroker, a man named Plant McCaw, and instructed him to buy American Can and Can. He named a figure. McCaw seemed taken aback. Could Sidney raise the money, because he had to pay in cash? Yes, indeed he could, replied Sidney, somewhat irritably.

Next morning, while lying in the bath, Sidney thought back to the transaction and a terrible realisation came to him: in converting dollars into pounds in his head he had so managed to confuse the sum that he had asked for five times the number of shares that he wanted or indeed could pay for. McCaw was already on the floor of the Exchange when

Sidney reached him, buying American Can and Can for all he was worth. He was halted before the full sum was reached but not before Sidney was greatly out of pocket and had to cable Cecil for money.

Furnished with introductions from Vinton, who was now in the Government Housing Department, Sidney and Porter bought a Buick 'open tourer', a convertible sedan, and set off with Ernestine Evans, an old *New Yorker* writer friend of Sidney's, first to Washington, where they met 'some of the New Dealers – experts in the art of inefficient government' and then across the Appalachians to Knoxville, where the Tennessee Valley Authority under the guidance of David E. Lilienthal was at work on the Norris Dam. Sidney thought it the 'most impressive effort being made in the US today'. They were a lively party, with Ernestine Evans, apparently a bulky lady, perched in the back among the bags, and Porter at the wheel. To friends in the film industry in England, Sidney wrote that every small town seemed to have its Roxy or its Rivoli, but that only the vast canopies on the outside had any grandeur – inside, the cinemas were small and dirty. After Tennessee, the three of them struck southwards, as he reported in a long letter to Sam Eckman, head of MGM in England:

. . . Into increasingly warmer weather and more Southern country. Painted wooden houses with front porches and rocking chairs, soft lazy accents, fruit trees in bloom, slow moving towns and people. In Montgomery, Alabama, I stayed with a real Southern family, who gave me partridge and quail, strawberries and cream for breakfast.

In Montgomery too, I saw the Kilby Jail (the Alabama State prison). It was very much like the prisons we've seen so often on the screen; and the Deputy Warden showed us with gusto the Condemned Cell and the Electric Chair.

The Chair was painted a brilliant yellow, and the D.W. explained to us in precise detail the procedure. It was interesting to see that there is discrimination between Whites and Negroes even in prison: they occupy different sections and the dining room is partitioned into two sections.

Then to New Orleans, where the natives speak a bastard French, and through the Evangeline country into Texas. We drove into Texas by night, but the pervading smell of oil and the light of petroleum flares advised us where we were.

So to the prairies where men are still men and cowboys wear ten gallon hats. Here we picked up a young hitchhiker, Charles William Edward Morgan, aged seventeen ex Western Union Messenger, American patriot, devotee of Texas, on his way to Los Angeles to make a fortune selling newspapers. He accompanied us all the rest of

the way and proved an engaging lad. When we had crossed the
Arizona border he remarked: 'Maybe I oughter have told you, but it's
a criminal offence to take a woman or a minor across a State Border.'
Such merry confidences quickly endeared him to our hearts.

From the prairies we climbed the hills amongst the giant cactuses,
the vultures, the rattlesnakes, the mountain lions (we encountered
none of them). Then down to the prairies again and suddenly, just
round the corner, the desert with wind whipping across the road and
making the car sway from side to side so that at first we thought the
steering had failed us.

California greeted us with rain. First we climbed the Sierras at
night, with patches of dense white fog and a precipitous curved road:
then we came down into San Diego and found the Exposition washed
out. But on the last lap to Los Angeles and Beverly Hills the sky was
bright and sunny, the Pacific was blue and everything in the garden
was lovely.

What he did not tell Eckman was how shocked he had been to see for the
first time chain-gangs, mostly of blacks, manacled to one another in the
sugar fields, or the strange saga of his visit to Alabama. Sidney had had
what he took to be the good fortune to be given introductions to the
Alabama Attorney General who was married to the sister of a *New
Yorker* friend of his, Sheila Hibben. The Attorney General invited the
travellers to stay, and delayed their trip by insisting on giving a big
fancy-dress ball in their honour, to which the Southerners came in their
bustles and crinolines, and the old colonnaded mansion was lit by flares
and candelabra. The Attorney General assured Sidney that he had
arranged for the visit to the jailed black boys for the following morning.

When Sidney arrived at the prison next day, the boys had gone. The
Warden expressed surprise at Sidney's visit, saying that they had been
moved, as planned, a couple of days earlier, but that he could not say
where to. The appeals, retrials and reconvictions of the nine youths
were rapidly turning into an international cause célèbre, and no
Southerner wanted a figure like Sidney reporting on the case in a
London magazine.

There was one other curious interlude during the journey. After
Ernestine Evans left them, Sidney and Porter called on the man who
was now living in the New Orleans house in which D. W. Griffiths had
filmed *The White Rose*. They found him very ill in bed, and a strange
macabre scene going on about him. A number of priests in black
soutanes were walking up and down the garden, while what looked like
a coffin was being heaved down the main staircase. Uncertain as to
whether these were all undertakers, a seminar of priests or a gang of

looters, Sidney and Porter fled the scene. It was all more like Hollywood than Hollywood itself.

They reached Los Angeles and took rooms in the Beverly Wilshire Hotel. As before, a great pile of invitations awaited Sidney. One was from Walter Wanger, asking him to celebrate Henry Fonda's birthday on stage three of the Paramount studios. Others came from Myron Selznick, David's agent brother, and from the head of production at Columbia, asking him to a preview of Frank Capra's *Mr Deeds goes to Town*. He wrote to Ernest Fredman:

> The village looks more like Golders Green than ever, but not quite so much like Wembley – some of the statues to milkmaids, page boys, automobile tires, silk stockings etc have been removed. But have no fear, you would still know your way about . . .
>
> Everyone is talking colour and no doubt next year at least one quarter of the big pictures will be in colour, whether people like it or not.

To David Blairman, he added:

> What I particularly note about Hollywood and what I hadn't noted before – is that there are no pedestrians. It's just like a race of people living in cars. Nobody walks and even the newspaper boys stand in the middle of the road and sell their papers not to people but to cars.

Before getting down to work, and to escape the fog and rain that had now spread over the city, Sidney took off for a long weekend on his own to Palm Springs, the oasis in the desert where the stars went to rest. Walter Wanger had recommended what Sidney now referred to as a 'dude ranch' and here he settled down for what he hoped would be four uninterrupted days of solitude, broken by rides in the desert. Almost immediately, he was approached by a man who introduced himself rather mournfully as William Powell, the actor. 'You're English, aren't you? This film business is a terribly lonely occupation. While you're making a movie you're close to people. When it's over, you never speak to them again. That's what you must keep remembering if you come here, you'll be lonely.' As it happened, Sidney was never lonely; he liked being on his own.

He got back to Hollywood to find that David Selznick, by now hard at work on *The Garden of Allah* with Charles Boyer and Marlene Dietrich, had kept his promise and arranged for an anti-fascist fund-raising lunch at the Beverly Wilshire Hotel. Sidney duly gave his prepared speech about the worsening position of the Jews in Germany, and all went agreeably until someone raised a question about blacks. At this, recalling his drive across the Southern states, Sidney began berating the assembled moguls, seated about him comfortably smoking their cigars in their handmade suits, about the way they never used black actors in their films. 'Why do you only make them into lavatory attendants? Why don't you use a coloured lawyer for once? And come to that why are priests in your films always Roman Catholics? Why is there never a rabbi? Why don't you have a hero with a name like Bernstein?' It was all a bit too close to home. Hollywood, with its high proportion of foreigners and Jews, was quite outstandingly conservative. Sidney had said things no Hollywood producer would have dared to. It didn't really matter; he was only an Englishman.

The time had come to call on Irving Thalberg. By 1936 Thalberg was already a legend in Hollywood, his dedication to making serious films, known as 'prestige pictures', having turned MGM into the most respected studio – as the slogan put it, the one with 'More stars than there are in heaven'. He was a hard man to see. The seats in his office were called by the locals the 'million dollar bench' because of the entire days highly paid executives perched there awaiting an audience.

Sidney, the Englishman, had no trouble. Thalberg, though only thirty-six, was already almost corpse-like in appearance, waxy faced and seemingly so tired he could scarcely move from his desk (he was to die later that year). 'Sidney, I want you to read a book and advise my script department whether it would make a film. It's *Goodbye Mr Chips*.' Sidney confessed that he had never read it. 'Well, go away and read it and then tell me what you think.' Sidney bought the book and sat reading it in his hotel. He found it sloppy and boring, and saw no prospects in it for a film. A few days later he summoned up his courage to tell Thalberg not only that he didn't like *Goodbye Mr Chips* but that, on further reflection, he didn't really want to work for the studio at all. The two men parted amicably. *Goodbye Mr Chips* was subsequently made into a highly successful movie, proving to those who believed in Thalberg that, commercially, his judgment was seldom wrong. (In Hollywood, Thalberg was always contrasted with Harry Cohn, who also seemed to have a magic touch with scripts, but whose style differed so markedly from his own. Cohn is reported to have said: 'I have a foolproofed device for judging whether a picture is good or bad. If my fanny squirms, it's bad. If my fanny doesn't squirm, it's good.')

Sidney now stayed on mainly to enjoy himself, first fulfilling the one obligation that he had brought with him to California, which was to introduce the works of his eccentric and brilliant colour film-maker friend, Len Lye, to Walt Disney. Sidney showed Disney two experimental reels of *Tusalava* and *Kaleidoscope* he had brought with him, and the American was highly impressed. He also took a job, of sorts, with Walter Wanger, acting as his assistant producer on *The Trail of the Lonesome Pine*, the first outdoor film ever to be made in technicolour. Henry Hathaway was the director, Henry Fonda the star, and Sidney, who did not have a very arduous or specific role, spent a great deal of time observing the workings of a Hollywood production. The experience was to come in very useful later.

Sidney was always slightly hesitant about parties, preferring to spend his time with small groups of people whom he knew well. But there was something remarkable about Hollywood. Here the parties were famous for their extravagance and exoticism, and the Hays Code had done nothing to dent their splendour. Sidney, puritanical as he was in his personal affairs, was not averse to enjoying the spectacle. One night David Selznick invited him to the monthly Beverly Wilshire Mayflower Ball, a charity function of immense grandeur, and asked him whom Sidney would like to take as partner. Sidney happened to be leafing through *Spotlight*, the casting directory, and saw a photograph of Tom Douglas, a young actor who had appeared in *Fata Morgana* on the London stage. 'Tom Douglas,' he said. David Selznick, for a moment, looked apprehensive; there was always something so elusive about Sidney, that it was impossible not to have doubts. 'All right then,' said Sidney, laughing, 'Louise Brooks.'

There was little that a Hollywood mogul could not do, and Louise Brooks, with her square-cut black hair and pert manner, queen of half a dozen epic silent Hollywood films, was now invited as Sidney's partner. On the night of the ball, Sidney found that she was at first very drunk indeed, and later, totally comatose. It was the height of Prohibition: no one moved without a flask. Eventually Selznick offered Sidney his car and chauffeur to take her home. Louise Brooks slept throughout the journey. On reaching the gates of her house, she woke abruptly and instructed the driver to take them instead to the house of her former husband, the English film director Eddie Sutherland. A few minutes later, she climbed out, peered through the huge plate-glass windows and banged on the door. Sutherland opened it and, catching sight of Sidney, shouted: 'You shit', then reluctantly invited them in for a drink. He had a girlfriend in the sitting room. Twenty minutes later, the Sutherlands were deep in conversation. Sidney turned to the girl: 'There's nothing for us here.' They got up and left; it was a typical Hollywood occasion.

Another night he went to a preview of Fritz Lang's *Fury*, the story of an innocent man being lynched in a Southern state. The German director was having a tough time with MGM, who insisted on changing the main scenes. When the film had run through, Sidney, who had been greatly impressed, congratulated Lang, but asked why, since there was to be an ending as shocking as a lynching, had the man not been made guilty? Lang explained his reasoning; Sidney gave his; the discussion lasted late into the night. (In the end, *Fury* was hacked about a good deal by MGM's editors. When it came to London, Sidney saw that it received as much publicity as he could raise, receiving in return a long and grateful letter from Lang, who swore that never again would he work under contract for a Hollywood studio.)

By now, Sidney was beginning to tire of Hollywood. Though he had rented a house of his own in Bel Air, the most expensive and exclusive of Los Angeles's suburbs, he reported in a letter to Ernestine Evans that it had a

... unique uncomeliness. I don't recommend California to the traveller as pleasure. The food is atrocious, the houses are lath and plaster, the fruit grows large but has no taste, the flowers no smell; the landscape is made up of oil derricks and transplanted trees and HOLLYWOOD-LAND in great white letters on the hillside; no one walks but everyone drives hellforleather in their powerful automobiles; the people flit from home to home, from job to job. Everything, so to speak, flows but nothing seems to get anywhere.

He spent the last weeks rather forlornly inspecting the Hollywood cinemas and reporting back to his managers in London about car parks and lotteries, advertising and organs. After a while nothing pleased him: the previews were too long, the radio programmes too dull. It was as with every visit Sidney ever made to Hollywood, starting full of excitement, ending with a longing to escape. At the end of May, considerably earlier than he had expected to, he returned to meet Zoë, who was arriving in New York on the *Queen Mary*, having been asked to write about the maiden voyage for the *Express*.

This was the first time Sidney and Zoë had been in New York together. It was now becoming plain to many of Sidney's friends that he was greatly drawn to Zoë with her gaiety and her absolute refusal to be in any way intimidated by him. Zoë loved having fun; Sidney was a master at turning occasions into celebrations. Together they laughed a great deal. There was, however, a major obstacle to any future plans they might have together: Zoë was not Jewish and Sidney, who, fond as he was of his mother, remained somewhat nervous of her strong opinions, was aware how much such a marriage might upset her. But now, in New York, it was late spring, the weather was perfect and there were a great many friends to see. Orson Welles was in Harlem with his black production of *Macbeth*, one of the outcomes of Roosevelt's New

Deal Federal Theatre projects, and the two of them travelled uptown to the Lafayette Theatre to see *Macbeth* set on the island of Haiti in the early-nineteenth century with the witches as voodoo priestesses.

When Sidney reached Southampton he found that a fresh crisis in the film industry had blown up and he was instantly immersed in letters, memoranda and committee meetings. Eight years had elapsed since the last Film Act, and a new one was in the making, but it was still far from clear what needed to be said. The curb on foreign films had proved helpful to the British industry, and indeed at one point it had looked as if a genuinely profitable British enterprise had begun. Alexander Korda's *The Private Life of Henry VIII*, made in 1933, was the first British film to rival the lavishness and range of the American spectacles, and on the wings of its immense international success, British film investment had become, overnight, a good risk. Money had flowed into the studios. Everywhere, people started believing in its future.

They had little real cause to do so. There was something inherently wrong in the very structure of the British film industry, and as the financial difficulties of the late 1930s worsened, so it became ever more apparent that British films would never be able to capture a big enough share of the world market – particularly in the one place that it mattered, America. Costs were too high, and not helped by the fact that American stars had been put under contract to British producers at costs far above what they were actually worth. With these stars went big, expensive sets and big, expensive publicity campaigns. Just at the very moment the film studios were in fact reaching their peak of production, turning out some two hundred films a year, disaster struck, with confidence of investors falling, studios having to close down and film finance generally falling into disrepute. Contempt for the industry, never in short supply, was voiced by people like Sir Thomas Beecham, who told the *Sunday Times* that he could not work with the film industry because he found 'the mentality of all film people to be as singularly and exotically different from that of the rest of humanity as some fabulous legends of antiquity'. What could you expect, he went on, when you wandered into a cinema, and in the space of fifteen minutes, saw a 'battle at sea, a train wreck, a fire on the 130th storey of a San Francisco skyscraper, the abduction of at least 25 young women ... accompanied from beginning to end by the Good Friday music of Parsifal?'

This was hardly fair, and most people knew it, but it is a good example of the contempt in which many of the intelligentsia continued, right into the late 1930s, to hold the movie world.

Now, fighting for a way out of the chaos, and trying to influence the coming new Film Act, Sidney began to lobby for stronger regulations, more realistic quotas and some sort of sense of direction and guidance from government. In November 1937 he joined Charles Laughton, Robert Donat, Anthony Asquith, John Grierson, John Maxwell and Isidore Ostrer in signing an appeal for a film commission to direct the British film industry, something that had been suggested by the Moyne Committee, set up in 1936 to consider the position of British films. After the signing, Sidney told the *Evening News*:

> It would be a most serious thing if the British film business were ever to be controlled by American films and we believe that a good British film organisation is perfectly possible if only the various sections of the trade – which must always have conflicting ideas – can be brought together and can take a long view of the problems instead of considering only their individual interests. Cows need a milk board and pigs need a pig board and it looks as though films need a co-ordinating body as well.

Throughout 1937 and early 1938 the arguments rumbled on: should there be quotas? financial inducements? a Films Bank to handle film finance? In 1938 the third Films Act was passed. Nothing very new or very radical was said in it, but it was clear to everyone by now that if British film production was going to survive at all it was only going to do so as a protected industry.

If the industry itself was in trouble, the same was not true of Granada which, in October 1933, had moved its main offices from Wardour Street to a handsome office block in Golden Square, just off Piccadilly Circus. British films might be ailing, but for film exhibitors the late 1930s were a marvellous time: eighteen million people were going to the cinema every week, and the Bernstein brothers were building super-cinemas steadily to keep pace with their demands. (The great Roxy himself had been to visit the Granada at Tooting and pronounced it splendid.) When Granada Theatres Ltd was formed as a private company to take over from Bernstein Theatres in July 1934 there were nineteen cinemas in the circuit, including the Denham eight which were still managed by Sidney. Seventeen months later, when Granada Theatres became a public company, there were twenty-one, three of which were in Rugby and had been owned by a consortium under the chairmanship of an accountant, Halford Reddish, later chairman of Rugby Portland Cement. (Reddish joined the Board of Granada, and Sidney that of Rugby Portland Cement.) By the end of the decade the number had risen to thirty, making Sidney one of the largest existing independent circuit owners, with a voice in the industry that far exceeded the power of his actual investments. There were far richer and more influential exhibitors: but none was quite like him, and none bridged as he did the worlds of film and political and intellectual life. The high point of the Granada building programme came towards the end of 1936 when, on average, a new Granada was being opened every three months. In January 1937 there were five new cinemas in the pipeline.

In each case the pattern was the same. Sidney and Cecil would learn about an area that appeared in need of a cinema. They would then send in teams of market researchers (usually out of work film-makers from the documentary movement) with long questionnaires as to the tastes, occupations, expectations and habits of the local inhabitants. If those sounded promising they would bid for a site, then gather together their usual team of architects, builders and designers, though by 1936 Komisarjevsky was married to Peggy Ashcroft and had largely moved over to theatre direction. Much of the interior work of the theatres was now in the hands of Ted McKnight Kauffer, Frank Dobson, Roger Furse and Vladimir Polunin. (For the opening of the Granada in Manchester, which Sidney had in fact already sold to Gaumont British, and in which Komisarjevsky had been involved, he cabled Sidney: 'Greetings and best wishes from Bramante Michelangelo Vognola Palladio Raphael the Bibiena family and the Komisarjevsky family the dog included Eviva Il Duce').

As in the early days, every new cinema was overseen personally, step by step, detail by detail, always by Sidney, and now often by Max. Cecil was ever more in control of the business side, but he too was beginning to be affected by Sidney's drive for detail and perfection that verged at times on the ludicrous, as a memo to staff of the mid-1930s shows: 'Mr Bernstein requires that each member of the staff should make a note of anything that happens every day, about which he would normally be told, and a sheet containing such notes should be given to me before 10 a.m. every morning, relating to the previous day.' It was said that Sidney would take his camp bed to the site of a new cinema for the last few weeks before its opening, in order to be permanently there to watch over what was going on, not a move greatly welcomed by those working on the building. He also had a trick of announcing an opening for three weeks ahead at a time when no one involved believed that it would be possible to complete the job in time. It always was.

The most memorable of all the Granada openings was probably the one at Greenwich, which took place on 29 September 1937. A military band had been booked with six trumpeters, and the Dagenham Girl Pipers. Maureen O'Sullivan was to officiate at the ceremony. On the 28th she fell ill. Sidney searched, ever more frantically, for a replacement. Then he thought of Gracie Fields, whose first show, *Mr Tower of London*, Sidney had brought to the Edmonton Empire for its first appearance in the south so many years before. He called on her. Would she open his Granada? 'I'll give a cheque to any charity you name,' Sidney told her. Gracie Fields thought for a minute, and said she would open it but that she wanted nothing at all.

Gracie Fields arrived at Greenwich shortly after the other star attraction, the Charlton Athletic Football Team. Hitching up the skirts of her long dress, she took a kick at their football and sent it bouncing off the ceiling and into a tray full of champagne glasses. The roads, for miles around, were jammed with crowds, trying to get close to her. Mounted police arrived to help control them – the Granada stood at the intersection of five major roads – and finally Sidney ordered the loudspeakers to announce that Gracie would come out if they promised to disperse quietly afterwards. Gracie Fields then clambered out on to the canopy high above the entrance, with an electrician clutching her ankles, and bawled out, in her rich Lancashire voice, to cheers that could be heard for a long way down the river, 'I never cried so much in all my life' and 'Sally'. (Later, Sidney sent her a blank cheque. She filled it in for £1,000 – and sent it to a charity.)

Early in the 1930s Sidney had instigated a system of reports: every week, the manager of every cinema in the circuit had to write a letter with news of the week's events. From these documents, some funny, some awkward, some apologetic, there emerges a striking and clear picture of cinema life in the London suburbs in the last years before the war.

Music hall acts were still popular though Walthamstow reported to head office that Scottish humour was not to local taste and that the 'Scotch patter act' should be dropped. The manager complained that no one ever told him what to expect: he had been led to believe that Alda and Doret were a dance act, and had billed them accordingly, only to find when they arrived that they were sword balancers. From Tooting, a Mr Hutchinson added that the 'staff usher singing a solo went very big'.

Stunts and competitions had reached new heights of inventiveness. To advertise *Night Flight*, the Rialto Enfield organised a squadron of planes to fly over the cinema, and asked audiences to estimate the height and speed of the planes, the prize being ten free flights. For *The Fire Raisers* they brought in the local fire chief and his brigade to patrol the lobby.

Hot summers spelt disastrous attendances: posters declaring 'The two coolest spots in Enfield: Granada and the Swimming Pool' were put up, a little feebly, all round the neighbourhood during one particular heat wave. At the Granada in Walthamstow the manager introduced bagatelle tables with rubber wheels so that they could be rolled up and down the queues to entertain people as they waited.

As for taste in films, the manager of the Willesden Granada reported that Mae West had actually disgusted some members of the audience in *I'm No Angel*. 'Nobody in this district will be much concerned if they never see or hear of Mae West again. Her novelty value has meant money, but she should now be allowed to rest peacefully in her deserved place in history, alongside the Loch Ness Monster.'

On 26 November 1936 Sidney and Zoë were married. Sidney was thirty-seven; Zoë twenty-four. The ceremony took place at ten o'clock in the morning, in a registry office, in complete secrecy. Cecil and Myra were present, as well as his mother, David Blairman and Ewart Hodgson. Afterwards the party went off to lunch at the Grosvenor Hotel, before Sidney and Zoë caught a plane to Paris and the Ritz. That night they dined with Otto Katz.

The marriage would certainly have taken place earlier had it not been for Sidney's apprehensions about his mother's disapproval that Zoë was not Jewish. In fact, Mrs Bernstein, formidable as she could be, was very fond of Zoë, and had soundly snubbed the local rabbi's wife who had come to commiserate with her by declaring herself delighted with Sidney's choice. To please her, Zoë had started lessons towards converting to the Jewish faith.

Sidney and Zoë were in Cairo the day King Edward VIII abdicated, in the middle of December, looking at Tutankhamun's treasures, dug up by Howard Carter and Lord Carnarvon in 1922. *The Times* correspondent to Egypt had advised them to visit a particular collection and as Sidney was deliberating over a piece of carved stone, wondering whether to buy it, a voice behind him said: 'If I were you, I would.' It was Howard Carter. Sidney bought it. (A couple of years later, he sent it to the British Museum for further identification, and forgot all about it, until one day he saw a catalogue with a photograph of the stele and a note 'presented by Sidney Bernstein'. The British Museum had assumed it was a gift.)

Sidney and Zoë returned to London to find a pile of letters from their friends, many of them expressing some astonishment at the suddenness and silence of their marriage. Sidney, many people assumed, would marry, if at all, an established, fashionable Society figure, someone with tastes and opinions as committed and formed as his own. This elegant and laughing young journalist was a quite surprising choice, though Sidney's friends had already seen a certain amount of her down at Long Barn, where she seemed, always, to play a rather shadowy role, dominated by Sidney's wishes. Laz Aaronson wrote them a charming letter.

I do sincerely want to give you both my best wishes: and though that sounds trite it's good to be able to say it to some people who can snatch, even for a space, happiness out of our present time. I remember once (I wonder if you, Sidney, remember) how we walked, Sidney and David and I out of Hyères one evening when we were all close and unselfconscious and quietly talkative. It was evening and we walked along a narrow neck of land past gleaming saltpans like new snow and saw Toulon's first lights and the island of the Blot go down in the darkness, and we talked about marriage and Sidney said that marriage once it came would be for him a final thing and would fill his life with meaning. I hope it *will* be so (and why shouldn't it?) I wish it will be so. My love to you both. Good luck. Laz.

Sidney was clearly very happy, and a new, jaunty note was creeping into his letters. 'My wife's implicit charges are unfounded', he wrote to Christiansen, presumably in response to some lighthearted accusation, 'I did *not* bang doors, jog my feet, twiddle my fingers. I was *not* clumsy, useless or bored.' He signed himself: 'Zoë Farmer's husband.' At the same time he sent the Christiansens two live geese as a rather improbable present.

Not long after their return from Cairo, where both he and Zoë had fallen ill with 'Egyptian fever', the two went off to ski in Kitzbuhel and Sidney wrote to Komisarjevsky, 'Zoe and I are lazy people (I only give a show of great energy and this only in bouts) and we rose late in the morning, slept before dinner and ate too much most of the day.'

Before getting married, Sidney had bought a farm in Kent with cottages that could be turned into a pleasant house, an oasthouse, and fields that sloped gently across a long valley. The place was called Coppings; it consisted of some hundred and seventy acres of indifferent farming land. About this time Sidney was given a dog, an Irish setter, and he asked O'Casey what to call it. After some months a postcard arrived with one word – 'Red', signed 'Sean'. Sidney settled for that.

In March, Coppings was ready, and the weekend gatherings that were such a pleasure in Sidney's life began again. Peggy Ashcroft, by now divorced from Komisarjevsky and doing a London theatre season with John Gielgud, came down, as did Cedric Belfrage and Molly Castle, who had married not long after his world tour. The weekends were still full of excellent food and games of tennis on the new court, but now the talk was nearly always political, anxious forebodings of war. Koteliansky had introduced Sidney to the painter Mark Gertler, who became a frequent visitor, a slight, pale, remarkably fine-looking man, rather formal and withdrawn in the company of strangers, but delightfully humorous and an excellent mimic with his friends. Gertler was an unhappy figure, given to alternating moods of terrible depression and often on the edge of total poverty. Sidney, characteristically, commissioned him to paint a portrait of his mother, and paid the bills when he had to spend some time in a sanatorium in Norfolk. Gertler, in return, gathered Sidney into his own world, and introduced him to Carrington (with whom he had been much in love) and to Lady Ottoline Morrell.

At this time Sidney had also become much involved with the Spanish Civil War. He never went to Spain himself, but he travelled backwards and forwards between London and Paris, where Otto Katz (who by now was sometimes using the name André Simon), Ellen Wilkinson and others interviewed refugees fleeing from Franco and co-ordinated ways of sending money and supplies across the border. In the spring of 1937 he agreed to allocate a portion of the takings from his Sunday cinema openings – a part of which, since 1930, when they became legal, went to charity – to the Joint Committee for Spanish Relief, and to provide money for its chairman, the Duchess of Atholl, MP, to go to Spain with Otto Katz as guide. Ian Mikardo had, by now, become a friend, and Sidney's secretary remembers the two of them closeted together in the office for hours talking about Spain. Sidney was also a subscriber to the Left Book Club, founded in 1936 by Victor Gollancz, and which became something of a centre for support of the Spanish Republic. Hemingway and the Dutch documentary film-maker Joris Ivens were working on a film about the civil war, *Spanish Earth*, and Sidney went to considerable lengths to ensure that it got a proper showing in London. (Not always an easy feat; the British Board of Film Censors remained as intransigent as they had been earlier on the question of anti-Nazi films. *Professor Mamlock*, a Soviet film made in 1938 about the Jews in Germany, was banned by the LCC: Sidney had it put on at the Academy in Oxford Street.)

He was also drawn into the campaign to get Arthur Koestler released from the Seville Jail where he had been condemned to death on the charge of espionage. Koestler had been sent to Lisbon and Seville for the *News Chronicle* and when Málaga had fallen to the rebels, had been taken prisoner. Sir Peter Chalmers-Mitchell, the English scientist with whom he had stayed, had been released after the British Navy intervened, but Koestler, as a Hungarian citizen, was not. Topsy O'Flaherty, who was helping Koestler's wife Dorothy bring what pressure she could on people with influence, wrote to ask Sidney whether he could find a right-wing Conservative to take up the cause. Sidney arranged for a meeting between Dorothy and Harold Nicolson.

Dorothy's efforts in fact resulted in hundreds of telegrams and letters of protest – fifty-eight signed by British MPs – being sent to Franco, and on 14 May Koestler was exchanged for a Nationalist hostage held by the Government.

In the summer of 1938 Sidney and David Blairman set off to walk in the Tatra mountains in Czechoslovakia. Sidney's voyages abroad went on just as they always had. It was to be Sidney and Blairman's last walk, and as they wandered through the tranquil country villages, with the farmers getting in the harvests, they knew it. There was a feeling of war. Even before they left London, Frederick Voigt had slipped a note under Sidney's door, warning him against the journey. In a Bierstube up in the mountains, a waiter came over and placed a little Union Jack on the table so that everyone would know that they were British.

After that, it just seemed a question of waiting. Anti-Semitism, everywhere, appeared on the increase, even in England, where the gardens of the semi-detached houses in Sidney's childhood district of Ilford were found one morning full of cards saying: 'Britons, do not allow Jews to tamper with white girls'. The film business, in particular, seemed vulnerable to attack: a placard pasted on to the wall opposite one Empire read: 'Cinema for sale. Apply to the nearest synagogue.'

Late in 1936 there had been fears among shareholders that the Ostrer brothers, who controlled the £14 million Gaumont British Corporation, would be 'attacked as aliens, foreigners and Jews' at a forthcoming annual general meeting. It might not have had the horrendous violence of the continent, but it was there none the less. There seemed to float in the air a general acceptance that England was being drawn into the European war on behalf of the Jews. Sidney fought it where he could: he gave funds to John Marchbank of the National Union of Railwaymen to help him pay for his defence in a slander action brought by Mosley; he gave money to the refugees, by now arriving across Europe in thousands to get away from Germany, and he helped, when he could, to find jobs for them; he discussed the setting up of a Jewish state with people who wrote to him about it – but it was anti-Nazism, not the question of a free Zionist state, that concerned him.

In June, Mark Gertler committed suicide. It was a Saturday, the day he was due down at Coppings for the weekend. He had tried to kill himself before. His death increased everyone's feelings of desolation and impending doom. The blazing hot summer went on, with talk now always of war, with the left tending to be anti-war and anti-Chamberlain, and those favouring appeasement accusing the anti-Munich faction of pushing Hitler into a war that he didn't want.

For Sidney, even though he knew that he and his family were on the

Gestapo's *Sonderfahndungsliste Grossbritannien*, the black list of those known for their anti-Nazi work, there was really now no choice. There was nothing left but to fight. He wrote gloomily to Komisarjevsky in Switzerland: 'Everything seems dead; here we are as flat as pancakes. At the present moment I am looking forward to a nice long sleep; everybody else is waiting for something to happen.'

By September a new crisis had been reached. After the annexation of Austria in the spring, Czechoslovakia had become Hitler's next target; on 15 September Chamberlain flew, to general applause, to see Hitler. When the mission of appeasement failed, Chamberlain flew to see him again. Parliament gathered on the 28th, to hear the Prime Minister describe his attempts to secure peace.

That day, Sidney went to the Strangers' Gallery in the House of Commons and watched as Margesson, the Government Chief Whip, came in after Chamberlain had been speaking for about an hour and handed him a piece of paper. 'Ah,' said Chamberlain, turning back to face the House, 'I have now been informed by Herr Hitler that he invites me to meet him at Munich tomorrow morning.' Sidney listened sadly as the cheers went up.

On the steps outside he met Noël Coward. 'Isn't this wonderful?' said Coward. 'We'll have no war.'

'No,' replied Sidney, 'I think it's absolutely terrible. We will have war.'

6

Hollywood at War

3 SEPTEMBER 1939 was a Sunday. The British ultimatum to Hitler expired at 11 a.m. Sidney and Zoë were at Coppings with friends when Chamberlain's edgy, slightly grating voice came on the radio to announce that his latest move for peace had come to nothing. Nobody at Coppings heard the radio. They were all busy discussing whether or not there would be war. Within days, Sidney sat down to write to friends about getting a wartime job. To Basil Dean, director of ENSA, the Entertainments National Service Association, he wrote: 'Can I help you in organising entertainment for troops? I am 41 in January, so don't expect to be called up for some time.' Members of Parliament like James Frederick Emery, Harold Nicolson and Dick Plummer were sounded out about possible positions in the newly formed Ministry of Information. As Sidney explained in a letter to Ellen Wilkinson:

> You know my contacts among writers and artists and the press, in America and most parts of Europe, and I thought perhaps you might be able to suggest how I should set about getting in touch with powers that be. I don't want – if I can help it – to go through the Conservative Party Propaganda Department!!

Her answer was not altogether encouraging:

> The Ministry of Information is in chaos. Perth has been refusing to let anyone do anything, ably supported in this by Admiral Osborne. The place is stuffed (rather than staffed) by Everyone's relations ...

I am just going North to try and sort out the evacuation mess in my area . . . then I will arrange for you to have lunch with whoever seems best able to help . . . My one idea is to keep as many of the worthwhile men alive till the end of this war, as well as getting the live wires like you into places where they can help. Otherwise the prospect is grim.

Too impatient to wait, Sidney now put in for the Royal Air Force Volunteer Reserve, listing his occupations since leaving school as 'engineering, building, construction, general organisation, business control', and his special skills as 'general knowledge of internal combustion engines and accountancy'. He added that he was now Chairman and Managing Director of Granada Theatres, with a staff of 1,200, and that he had flown many miles as a passenger.

While waiting for answers to his applications, Sidney turned to some of the many matters that required his attention. First, barely nine days after the outbreak of war, he wrote off to *The Times*, voicing his extreme concern that the war should not be allowed to arrest British film production or, by going back on the recent quota Act, dissipate the 'technical and creative talents which have been developed in the past few years'. 'There is', he wrote, 'labour and talent in this country for the making of good films . . . not necessarily amongst the tired and elderly film producers and financiers, but amongst the younger and more inventive of our film workmen.' This labour, he made it clear, must be spared from war work.

On the administrative side there was the Film Society to wind up. Its last performance, the 108th, had been on 23 April, when Eisenstein's *Alexander Nevski* had been shown. The next season was due to start in October. Over the telephone and by letter, Sidney now advised members that there would be no Society for the duration of the war. (After it was over, the Film Society did start up again, but in a slightly different form, as the New London Film Society. Sidney played no part in it.)

Then there was his own chain of thirty-nine cinemas to attend to. The day war was declared all British cinemas had been officially shut down in anticipation of an immediate series of bombing raids. Cinema managers had been expecting the order, having received circulars in August about closure together with lengthy instructions about sandbags, bandages and candles.

On Monday 4 September, therefore, with nothing else to do, the staff settled down to intensive spring cleaning of the cinemas, got out their first-aid boxes and practised fire drills. At the Granada Edmonton the usherettes played bowls in the aisles. Soon the spirit of the war took over: members of staff were sent out to forage for secondhand bicycles while those who stayed behind were issued with safety pins and bandages.

As the days passed and no bombs fell, cinema owners began to protest against the order. On 6 September, a deputation from the CEA, led by its Chairman, Deputy Chairman and Secretary, went to call on Herbert Morrison, by then Chairman of the LCC. They found him in his dressing-gown, perched on a makeshift bed in his office. Whatever they told him was persuasive, for on the 9th instructions were issued for the cinemas in the outer London areas to reopen.

The audiences flocked loyally back to their locals, but found very altered theatres. Gone were the flashing lights and neon signs, the publicity stunts and handouts and the potted plants. Black paint and black curtains were everywhere, the staff were parading in gas masks, and soon, as paper-control orders took effect, posters grew smaller and smaller, and finally vanished altogether. None of this had any effect at all on the attendances. On the contrary the public seemed to crave the cinema more than ever, and particularly escapist films: *Gunga Din*, *Wuthering Heights*, *Beau Geste*, *Destry Rides Again* and *Jamaica Inn* all ran to packed houses. It was as if people were looking for some kind of release from the tensions outside, and they came to find it among the gangsters and the cowboys.

Sidney was at his desk in Golden Square one day when John Betjeman called to see him with a message from Sir Kenneth Clark, the Surveyor of the King's pictures. Clark had been told that he would shortly be put in charge of the Films Section at the Ministry of Information and wanted to ask Sidney's advice. 'What', said Betjeman, 'should the Government be doing about film and propaganda?' It was a satisfying moment for Sidney. He reached down, opened a drawer in his desk and drew out a prepared typed document: 'British Film Production and Propaganda by Film'. He had occupied some of the days before war was declared by mapping out his thoughts on how films could be used in case of war. 'The first thing which the Films Section ... must do is to determine its policy ... It is submitted that to be effective ... propaganda must be completely concealed behind a screen of real entertainment.' Newsreel, he had written, was essential and must be given full facilities and proper distribution, and for this, as for the distribution of all film material, good relations with the big American companies were crucial. The paper went on to deal with quotas, feature films, financing and the need for a Film Bank. It was coherent, detailed planning, but a long time was to pass before such coherence found a place in MoI thinking. Sidney now passed the document over to Betjeman, who was gratifyingly astonished. Not long afterwards came an invitation from Clark to join the Ministry. Despite his earlier application, Sidney refused: not while Chamberlain was in power.

One other invitation soon came his way, and this he was eager to accept. Leigh Ashton and Michael Stewart, both of whom had worked for the Victoria and Albert Museum and were now in charge of the Spanish desk in the Foreign Office, came to ask Sidney what could be done about the money made by British film companies in Spain and now frozen there, following the suspension of all import permits. The Spanish Government, more interested in the starvation that was now facing the country than in matters like entertainment, had quite simply put a ban on all foreign film arrangements. Sidney had contacts of his own in Spain. A friend called George Thomson, who was representing the advertising agency J. Walter Thompson, had informed Sidney of what was happening by letter. Sidney now contacted him and between them they came up with a proposal to put to the Spanish Government. It amounted to an agreement whereby the British could import ten films into Spain, in return for co-operating in the making of one Spanish film, on Spanish soil, and then exporting it. Sidney had a few ideas of his own for the type of film most appropriate for Spain. One was the adaptation of A. J. Cronin's *The Stars Look Down* which concerned a strike in a coal-mine, just the sort of thing he believed should be shown in a fascist country where striking was forbidden. Instantly there came a message from the Foreign Office: would Sidney go to see them? They were anxious that such a film might prove seditious. That question resolved – Sidney won the argument – he now prepared to leave for Madrid, but before he had begun to pack an unexpected event prevented his departure: the British Government and MI5 mysteriously refused to let him leave the country. It was to be some months before he discovered why.

And so he stayed in London, chafing at his desk, waiting for wartime employment. He had been cheated of action of any kind in the First World War; now he began to fear the same thing was going to happen again. The phoney war dragged on. Autumn gave place to the coldest winter for forty-five years: even the Thames froze, for over eight unbroken miles. For Christmas, Sidney sent some of his friends presents of torches, and Campbell Dixon, of the *Daily Telegraph*, wrote to say that it was 'the most useful thing you could possibly have thought of, next to an usherette'.

It was no bad place to be, however, at this moment, sitting on the side lines. The Ministry of Information, on which Sidney still had his future ambitions firmly placed, was in a condition of irresolution and muddle, unable to decide what role propaganda should be playing in the war. The lack of direction was all the more absurd in that there had been a great deal of time in which to plan its function. Once the disarmament conference had failed, and Hitler had taken control of Germany, the British Cabinet had begun to plan for war, and by July 1935 a subcommittee had been set up to consider how best both to control and to issue news in time of war. Twelve months later in 1936, a report was produced, recommending the setting up of a Ministry of Information with five divisions – Administration, News, Control (Censorship), Publicity and Collecting (Intelligence) – whose role was to be that of distributing all information regarding the war and presenting the national case at home and abroad. No one doubted the importance of this machinery for propaganda – hadn't *The Times* written, at the end of the First World War: 'Good propaganda probably saved a year of war and this meant the saving of thousands of millions of money and probably of at least a million lives'? The question was of what exactly propaganda should consist (given that much of what had been put out in the 1914–18 war was now known to have been blatant lies), and how, once you had decided what it was, you dealt with it. The planners, in their deliberations, had somehow failed to take into account either the fact that communications, in all its forms, had grown vastly more sophisticated in twenty years, or that the Ministers in charge of different Government departments, especially the Foreign Office, were highly unlikely to agree, when the moment came, to relinquish all control over their publicity to another, centralised body.

When war was finally declared, then, the MoI had got off to a predictably disastrous start. Not one of the people appointed knew about the gathering or dissemination of news, the censors were inexperienced and were receiving contradictory instructions, and the posters hastily issued by the MoI with slogans like 'Your courage, your cheerfulness, your resolution will bring us victory' were obviously designed for widespread air raids and not the prevailing uneasy tranquillity. By September 1939, Lord Macmillan, the Minister who had been put in charge of the MoI, reported to his colleagues that the 'Press were in a state of revolt against what seemed like arbitrary but blanket censorship of much of the news'.

The Films Division, which had been made a separate department of the MoI, was not exempt from either the chaos or the public criticism. Like the rest of the Ministry it had been modelled on its First World War equivalent, in this case the Cinema Propaganda Department, only here even less attempt had been made to adapt it to the modern world. Though sensitive to the propaganda value of filmed material, they were confident that cinemas would stay closed for some time, and had therefore decided mistakenly to give serious planning for them a low priority. What was more, no one had paused to contemplate the technical complexities of sound films, with their far greater potential for propaganda subtleties, and for the need to employ people who knew something about them. Instead they had turned to the formula devised by Sir William Jury, the one-time fairground operator, who had decided during the First World War that the best way of handling film was not to form a specialist team inside the Ministry, but to go outside it, to commercial producers, and commission from them what film they needed.

While Lord Macmillan at the top of the Ministry of Information was grappling with the fury of other Ministers who now complained bitterly that they should be allowed to control their own information (which, in time, they were allowed to do), Sir Joseph Ball, highly successful film propagandist for the Conservative Party, and now appointed head of the Films Division, was fighting off a virulent and outraged attack from the Labour Party, who found his appointment tactless; from the artistic and literary world, who took him for a Philistine; and from the small independent documentary film-makers, who were furious at having been neglected. In his haste, and somewhat doubtful of their political allegiance, Ball had in fact decided to ignore the sixty or so film-makers belonging to John Grierson's documentary movement, who by 1939 had produced some two hundred films, many of them winners of prestigious international film prizes, and who now regarded themselves as 'propagandists with a social purpose'. Into this category came the GPO film unit, which started life in 1929 in the Empire Marketing Board, the various full-time documentary units already established within some of the large British companies, and a small number of individual companies, making films for industrial sponsors or Government agencies.

The first films to emerge from Ball's Division in the autumn of 1939 showed only too clearly the dangers of using undirected advertising commercial or newsreel companies. Some of the films were withdrawn without ever being shown; others had to be drastically re-edited. In the newspapers, particularly the left-wing literary magazines, critics deplored what they saw to be a wasteful combination of cliché and vulgarity, beneficial to no one, patronising and contemptible. In Germany, on the other hand, the film side of propaganda had got off to a magnificent start, and at one point British audiences were reduced to seeing the early days of the war on German footage, bought from the neutral countries.

Meanwhile throughout the MoI, as politicians and civil servants realised that propaganda was too serious a subject to be left to amateurs, key appointments changed hands. At the top, Lord Reith was brought in from the BBC and instantly planned a series of sensible improvements. In the Films Division, the highly unpopular Sir Joseph Ball was replaced first by Sir Kenneth Clark who, though well liked by the literary and political left, was still somewhat bemused by his appointment ('Was it because they muddled "pictures" with "films"?' he asked Sidney), and then by Jack Beddington of the Shell Film Unit, which was a far more inspired choice, since Beddington represented the most respected of the documentary units in industry, Shell, but also had links with Grierson's documentary film-makers. He brought with him to the MoI Film Division Sir Arthur Elton, next to Grierson one of the most outstanding figures in British documentaries. (Grierson had by now left for Canada, where he had been appointed Film Commissioner to the Canadian National Film Board.)

On 10 May 1940, Chamberlain resigned and Churchill became Prime Minister. Lord Reith, who loathed Churchill and referred to him as a 'horrid fellow', left the MoI and his place was taken by Duff Cooper. In June Duff Cooper, very aware of the importance of MoI links not only with every facet of the British film industry but with overseas and particularly American film companies and distributors, offered the job of Films Adviser to Sidney. As he was about to dispatch the letter of invitation, he received a visit from MI5, telling him that he couldn't employ Sidney. He asked why not, and was told that Sidney was known to visit the Russian Embassy every week. With this, they began to outline what amounted to a formal declaration that Sidney was a member of the Communist Party. (He had never set foot inside the Russian Embassy, nor voted for anything but the Labour Party and had never been a member of the Communist Party.) Duff Cooper, with his little moustache and rather petulant drawl, stated flatly: 'Bernstein is in.' The letter went off. But the slur remained. It explained, of course, why Sidney had not been allowed into Spain.

With Chamberlain gone, there was nothing to keep Sidney away from a job he had long coveted. He accepted, with considerably more pleasure than the dry tone of his letter to his friend Frederick Voigt suggests: 'They tell me it's a heart tearing, soul frustrating job, but who can refuse Mr Duff Cooper?' Before the end of the month, he had resigned from his directorships, stood down from Granada, leaving Cecil in charge, and written to the RAF telling them that he no longer wished to be put on their reserve list. It was the last of the Films Division's major changes. Though there were still to be a great number of problems, the section now settled down to a pattern that was to keep relatively constant throughout the rest of the war.

But first they had a policy to formulate, and into this Sidney threw himself with customary vigour, showering Beddington with memos, and joining others in the film world in signing proposals for different courses of action. It took him a while to adjust. 'I had left a world of overstatement for a world of understatement,' he was to write later of his sudden transition from businessman to civil servant.

On 13 June, together with Michael Balcon (one of the independent producers), George Archibald (Joint Managing Director of United Artists Corporation) and Basil Wright (documentary film-maker), he appealed for a better sense of direction and co-ordination in the Government's attitude towards film; for propaganda film to be 'prepared at the utmost speed'; for individual film directors to be assigned subjects; for a halt to 'the dispersal of valuable specialists and technicians into other branches of national service'; and for steps to be taken to ensure that, by repealing the 1938 Film Act, as the Government had said it intended to, it was not going to deal a death blow to the British film industry by abandoning the quota system. In time, almost all this advice was to become part of the Division's procedure.

Shortly after Sidney's appointment, the 13th Select Committee on National Expenditure, which had turned its attentions to the chaotic affairs of the MoI during the spring and early summer of 1940, produced a report on the Films Division. After much wrangling (for some of their suggestions, if implemented, would have led to widespread resignations) it was now agreed that the Division would produce documentaries, but not as many as they had hoped, that they would continue to try to establish audiences outside cinemas, using mobile projectors and school halls and factories, and that five-minute 'shorts', intended to put across essential messages concerning wartime Britain to really mass audiences, would be commissioned from commercial film-makers, as well as from the GPO film unit which had now been absorbed into the MoI and rechristened, on Sidney's suggestion, the Crown Film Unit. Ian Dalrymple was brought in to head the new unit, and this too was a good choice, for he combined exceptional skills of his own as a director with a real sympathy for the outside documentary movement.

In all these deliberations, Sidney was already playing the conciliatory role of his Film Society days. If it was one marked side of his character to be irascible, impatient and utterly demanding of others, it was another to be a peacemaker between warring factions. It is significant that it was to him, rather than to other more prominent members of the Films Division, that Michael Balcon wrote to voice his grievances:

> You know yourself, Sidney, that the whole tragedy of the film production business is that every Tom, Dick and Harry wants to play at making films . . . under the Films Division, producers like myself

have been reduced to the status of vendors of studio space . . . As you know, I am delighted that the Ministry has had the good sense to appoint you to the Films Division. I pray that you will be allowed to achieve the reforms there which are so necessary and which I know you have in mind.

Balcon was not the only man to appreciate Sidney's appointment. On 4 June the *Kinematograph Weekly* Screencomber column used an ironical note to mark its own relief:

The appointment is so revolutionary as to constitute a first class scandal . . . Bernstein, I understand, has been in the film business all his life and frankly acknowledges a complete understanding of films . . . This gives him an unfair advantage over those many members of the Films Section who have no knowledge whatsoever of pictures or of the Film Business. This may be someone or other's mistaken idea of efficiency, but it is not my idea of cricket.

The Films Division offices had been set up, together with most of the MoI departments, in Senate House in Malet Street, the tall, pale, grey-stone 1930s tower that had been requisitioned from London University. Ignoring Beddington's snide remarks, Sidney arrived with his own antique desk and high bookcase, and threw out the Government issue furniture. He hung his pictures on the walls. Since his job was honorary, there was nothing anyone could do. (The same was not true of John Betjeman who had been employed to write scripts and had decided that he was entitled to a carpet. One day he walked up the road to Heal's and ordered a fluffy white rug. The administrative officers at the MoI forced him to return it.)

The Films Division was a good place to be. It was full of people like Dallas Bower and John Betjeman who brought a great deal of laughter with them. Betjeman, in particular, had devised a way of intimidating those of the civil servants he found most pompous: he would wait until there was a lift full of people, then say in a very loud voice, picking on some unfortunate employee, cowering in one corner, 'It's not true, you know, that [X] is a Communist' (or German spy, or homosexual, or whatever he felt best suited the occasion). And the days were constantly enlivened by scriptwriters, commentators and advisers who kept passing through the office, people like Eric Ambler, Graham Greene or J. B. Priestley, come to discuss plans, show drafts or complain about bureaucratic difficulties.

The department and the film-makers liked Sidney. They admired his seemingly inexhaustible drive, what Dallas Bower remembers as a

'Churchillian sense of "Action this day"', and they found him approachable, with none of the stalling methods of the civil servants. They responded when he seemed enthusiastic and were grateful that he took care not to interfere in the actual making of the films, reserving his energy for the not inconsiderable battles he had to wage with the often very reluctant film industry to get it to put on the material the Government wished screened. But they did not find him cosy. He was grander, richer, busier and more detached than most of them, in his perfect dark-blue suit, his white shirts, his navy overcoat slung nonchalantly over his arms as he dashed down the corridors, heading for another appointment, another Ministry. He didn't often join the 'boys from Mini' as they set off on their lunchtime expeditions to the Rising Sun in Tottenham Court Road or to buy books in a secondhand bookshop in Store Street.

Betjeman conjured up that spirit of the place, with its camaraderie, its touch of whimsy and its absolute exclusion of all things bureaucratic, in his poem:

> I wish I were – I often think –
> Another Maurice Maeterlinck
> So I could write a play with ease
> About four little busy B's
> Who fly about and buzz and buzz
> And stay exactly as they wuzz
> And buzz about and fly and fly
> About the spacious MoI
> Then settle in the glittering sun
> Content with having nothing done.
> Sing,
> Beddington, Bernstein, Betjeman, Bower
> Sing,
> Winken, Blinken and Nod
> Sing,
> Shell, Granada, sing Norman Tower
> Make a five minute treatment of God.
>
>
> Take down this letter, dear Miss Broom,
> And send it – to you know whom
> Say that we've got a peculiar feeling
> There *was* an idea received from Ealing
> Last month – or was it the month before –
> We've lost it – but couldn't he send some more

Say that we're glad to have anything new, Sir
Make it amusing – write dear Producer.
There's the letter – now go and compile it
Get a reply and forget to file it –
Sing,
Beddington, Bernstein, Betjeman, Bower
Sing,
Ho! for the Treasure-ee
Sing,
Hey! for a Conference once an hour,
Sing,
Ho! for Victore-ee

Outside the Ministry, Sidney was also extremely busy. In 1938 he and Zoë had moved into two immense and very stylish flats across the front of Albany, in Piccadilly, 11a and 12. But they spent as much of their time as possible still at Coppings, from where, once the bombing raids started, they could watch the planes overhead on their route to London. In the summer of 1940, he wrote to some friends in Shrewsbury, asking them to find for him a house with a garden in their area to act as refuge for London friends and family needing a respite from the bombing. 'Rather fancy a square house,' he wrote, 'the old Cotswold or Georgian type, but we want it to be one that can be run by one servant.' By this time the Nazi blacklist was a serious issue in view of possible invasion and Sidney was planning to establish a meeting spot for members of his family and similarly threatened friends, where they could gather before proceeding to the Welsh coast. Jimmy Barber, a director of Granada, had a boat in readiness in which they intended to cross to Ireland.

In September, a year after the Government had predicted heavy aerial bombardments and closed the cinemas, the London Blitz began. For over two months, an average of 160 bombers dropped 200 tons of high explosives and 182 canisters of incendiaries every night. Nowhere, except possibly down at the very bottom of the Underground, could you escape the din. Theatres closed at once, but the Granada cinema circuit, like many other London cinemas, stayed open. While the Luftwaffe bombed London for ninety-one nights without a pause, Granada took to offering shelter and entertainment throughout the night for their clients, and those in the audiences sometimes sat through five feature films in succession, together with 'manager's own shows', with volunteer entertainers recruited from the audience. 'A priority air raid warning will be given to cinema managers when aircraft are sighted over the North Sea,' read one memo issued to managers. 'You will not on any account pass on this priority warning to your audience. You will merely give the warning "Red roses" to your staff so they will be prepared.' (The somewhat quaint phrase has lasted in Granada terminology: to this day it is the Company's fire code.)

People took to arriving with their blankets and pillows, but as staff succumbed to exhaustion, the all-night service ceased. Of Granada's London cinemas, one was destroyed, nine had to close down at some point, but the rest never missed a day. The only serious casualty came on the night of 12 November at the Granada in Wandsworth Road. At 8 p.m., with 500 people in the audience, a bomb fell on the roof and exploded in the auditorium: ten people were killed and thirty-five injured, some losing arms and legs.

Cecil was now entirely in charge of Granada Theatres. As soon as the war had broken out the Bernsteins had told their employees that their jobs would remain theirs, with pay, for the duration of the war, all the time they were away on service. (When Quentin Reynolds, an American journalist who was a friend of Sidney's, reported this fact in a column in *Variety* a judge called J. Goldstein wrote in with an excess of sentimental fervour: 'It would give any man pleasure to know that there are people like that still living.')

At weekends, despite the Blitz, the Bernsteins still tried to get to Coppings, where, as Sidney wrote to Elsa Laughton, 'we stand in the grounds watching our Spitfires bringing down the Germans ... we found it exciting – it was like watching a Roman sporting event.' The gay and social weekends had virtually stopped but a number of friends had been invited down to take refuge in the outlying cottages, and one of these was Len Lye, whose wife Janet gave birth to two children, Bix and Yancy, during their stay at Coppings. (Later, the Lyes returned to America where the animator designed cartoons to help American soldiers with the Japanese language.) During the week, Sidney and Zoë continued to live in Albany. Friends remember evenings with a lot of enjoyable conversation, until the sirens forced them down into the basement. By day, if in London, Sidney was occasionally to be found doing his quota of Home Guard sentry duty at the doors of the MoI, in his dark-blue suit, with a tin hat perched on his head, and clutching a rifle and bayonet. But he was enjoying it. It was quite unlike anything he had ever done before.

The war days threw up unexpected encounters. One night Sidney had been working very late at the Ministry and, as he left Senate House about midnight to walk home, a taxi-driver called out to him: 'Do you want a lift?' Sidney crossed the road and got in. The driver introduced himself: it was his cousin Max Gausten, whom Sidney dimly remembered from Ilford days. He said that he had been following Sidney about for an opportunity to speak to him about a personal matter: his fifteen-year-old son had falsified his age on the registration papers and run off to join the Merchant Navy. Could Sidney get him out? Sidney now recalled that somewhere in the Bernstein family history was another boy who had done precisely the same thing in the First World War. That was Max. The boy was doing only what his father had done. Just the same, Sidney did get him out, though the boy joined up again the instant he turned sixteen.

Sidney had also kept in touch with Ellen Wilkinson. When Herbert Morrison was made Minister of Home Security in place of John Anderson, Ellen Wilkinson became his parliamentary secretary. Ellen had long been trying to bring the two men together; it was no secret that Sidney was deeply suspicious of the energetic Morrison with his somewhat unscrupulous manner, a 'Tammany Hall man' as he called him. The day the appointment was announced the three were finally due to have lunch together at the Ivy restaurant. Sidney offered to postpone the meeting, but Morrison insisted that it go ahead. Over lunch Sidney asked Morrison if he had seen his files when he took over the department. Morrison replied that he had certainly asked to see the personal files they held on himself and Ellen, but that a civil servant had replied smoothly: 'Minister, they were destroyed yesterday.' Morrison cited this as an example of British probity; what amazed Sidney was that he actually seemed to believe the civil servant.

About this time, the Luftwaffe began to devote their attention to a systematic destruction of British aircraft factories. Towards the end of September the Bristol Aeroplane Company's works at Filton were destroyed; the next night it was the turn of Supermarine in Southampton.

In May, Beaverbrook had been brought in as Minister of Aircraft Production by his close and old friend Churchill, who was complaining bitterly at the slowness in turning out aircraft. He took the line that an independent Ministry of Aircraft Production was the solution, much the same way as in the First World War the Ministry of Munitions had been invented to overcome the chronic shortage of shells.

Now, with the heavy bombing of his factories, Beaverbrook started seizing every piece of suitable property he could lay his hands on. When protests were raised, he threatened to commandeer Winchester Cathedral as a store if nothing else could be found for him. By the end of October three hundred sites had been turned over to aircraft factories.

Not unnaturally, perhaps, Beaverbrook's eye soon fell on the film studios, ideally situated for the most part outside London, and of the right size and shape to meet his requirements. Cries of outrage were heard coming from film-makers, already desperately worried about loss of personnel and shortage of rawstock.

Sidney had promised to provide Churchill with feature films for weekends whenever he wanted them. In the middle of October he had an idea that was typical both of his relationship with Beaverbrook and his particular brand of irreverent humour. Both Churchill and Beaverbrook – an addict of films, who had installed projectors both at his London house and at Cherkely – were due to spend the weekend with Ronnie Tree, at Ditchley. Sidney now asked Granada's editors to insert two extra captions into the coming weekend's film programme.

LORD BEAVERBROOK

Your needs are urgent but we must have propaganda films too. Why invade every studio?

Dear Lord Beaverbrook, can't you spare us Denham?

Sidney L. Bernstein
Films Division
Ministry of Information

The second, in *London Can Take It*, said:

This film was made at Denham, one of the last studios left. Without properly equipped studios like Denham, there can be no propaganda films.
This film will be shown in 15,000 cinemas in the USA alone.
Will you lay off Denham, Lord Beaverbrook?

Churchill was not amused, but Beaverbrook was. On the Monday morning he sent for Sidney. Beaverbrook usually wore short boots with laces and Sidney remembers how he watched these stout feet walking across the room to meet him. The two men argued for some time, with Sidney explaining how the loss of any more studios would be disastrous for production, and finally Beaverbrook, whose interest in films included some technical understanding, said: 'All right. I won't take another studio without consulting you first.'

He kept his word. The Films Division did not hear from him again.

By the autumn of 1940, the Films Division was in fact producing what were arguably some of the best things to emerge from their efforts. One of these was *London Can Take It*, produced by Ian Dalrymple, by now head of the Crown Film Unit.

Sidney and Beddington had asked Movietone to supply them with footage of the Blitz, on the understanding that the newsreel company would then assemble a film. Harry Watt, an established film director now working with the Crown Film Unit, felt that specialists in documentary should be given the job of editing. Sidney sent him to argue the case with Sir Gordon Craig, head of Movietone. Watt came back with a deal. Movietone would sell their footage to the MoI, at £1 a foot, and Watt himself would make the film.

It took the Crown Film Unit a fortnight to complete, editing by day, shooting extra film by night. Sidney came to see the rushes. There was talk about who should be the commentator, and the feeling was that an American must be found since *London Can Take It* was destined largely for American audiences. Someone suggested Helen Kilpatrick of the *Chicago News*. Harry Watt wasn't very happy about using a woman's voice.

That weekend Quentin Reynolds, Sidney's American journalist friend from *Colliers Magazine*, a tall, portly, genial figure who had a great love for England, came down to stay at Coppings. On Saturday evening Sidney stood listening to him as he talked, leaning against the fireplace, rolling his sentences majestically in a full clear voice, and suddenly thought: 'That is the voice for *London Can Take It*.'

On Monday morning he sent Harry Watt to the Savoy to meet Reynolds, who agreed to try his voice out at the Denham studios. He was driven down and placed before a microphone. He had never spoken on the radio before. His voice boomed out. Watt asked him to speak more gently; it was not much better. Then he had an idea: he asked Reynolds to try sitting rather than standing at the microphone and to use a whisper. With that, the famous deep throaty growl, that went on to become 'Schickelgruber' and then to entrance the English-speaking world on a hundred radio talks, was born. After the dubbing was finished Reynolds took the film team to dinner at the Savoy. (Stewart McAllister, the man who had edited the entire film, had not been to bed for four nights; he collapsed into his lobster soup.)

Sidney himself was now becoming something of an authority within the Films Division, not least because the Division itself had the very substantial power of being the one agency within the film world that regulated supplies and rawstock, and ruled over exemption from military service. Sidney, as an organiser, was not only sympathetic and open minded, but he was not bound by civil service rules. In case of need, of any kind, people now came to him. His own cinemas, as well as his many film industry contacts, meant that he was also closely in touch with how the public actually felt about the shorts. Granada managers had been asked to report weekly to head office with criticisms from the public and lists eventually reached Sidney's desk every Monday with 'Well received' or 'Received with derisive laughter' alongside the different titles. (One short, entitled *We've got to get rid of the rats*, came back with the somewhat cryptic: 'It would have taken ten *Silly Symphonies* to make this film acceptable.')

Because of his wide circle of friends, he became the recipient of many letters of complaint from independent film-makers, who continued to feel rejected and bypassed. Frank Launder, writing on behalf of British screenwriters, protested that the MoI Film Department, 'far from being imaginative, was merely acting as a sort of medium through which the somewhat unimaginative spirits of the other Ministers manifest themselves . . .' In the spring of 1941, complaints poured in on Sidney from all sides, and no sooner had he placated one faction of the industry than another rose up in revolt. A typical confusion came when in March two Army cameramen went with the Air Force on a raid to the Lofoten Islands. The material they returned with was superb and the MoI decided to make it into a short. Distributors, taking up the cause of the newsreel companies who had not been allowed to go on the raid and now protested this was unfair, blacked the short. Sidney took hours to smooth over the ill-feeling.

Then came another threat of disruption to the MoI Films Division. A panel of inquiry set up by the Ministry of Labour suddenly ruled that the job of film technician would cease to be a reserved occupation, thereby making all those under twenty-five liable for call-up and jeopardising the jobs of 1,020 men in the film industry. This too led to long hours of consultation and an eventual compromise. To Edward Porter, training to be a bomber pilot in Torquay, Sidney wrote that 'the atmosphere is now a cross between a daily lecture by a school master, a revivalist meeting in Bloomsbury and the Burning of the Cross . . . I have seen Ministers, Directors, Generals and Deputy Directors and all, but we don't seem to get much forwarder, or perhaps we do, but not fast enough for me.' By mid-March 1941, in fact, he was beginning to contemplate resignation and, comparing his job to 'hitting cotton wool with a sledge hammer', drafted a letter:

> The position of Adviser becomes untenable . . . In the eight months I have been here I have managed to bring some order into the chaos . . . but anything which I have been able to do has taken more effort and time than was necessary because of the laborious explanations to people who do not understand films, and strangely enough, are not really interested in them . . . We get involved with disputes with the film trade and the newsreel companies because we have no policy; because in many cases we are not even sure of the matter we are discussing; and a great deal of the trouble is caused through the inability to make prompt decisions.

These were strong words, and they were in fact never sent. Sidney stayed where he was.

In any case, he had a personal problem to sort out. The previous summer, before the Blitz began, his sister Beryl Stone whose husband was in the army had taken her two children and a niece to America. Describing her affectionately to friends as 'my favourite sister' Sidney had written to Elsa and Charles Laughton and to Walter Hutchinson of 20th Century Fox to ask them whether they could lend him $1,000 for her for the duration of the war.

Early in 1941 he received a summons from the Treasury. Somewhat facetious wording in his letters, which had been censored, suggested that he intended to return the money within a year, thereby infringing the Finance Act. (Sidney, jocularly, had implied that the war itself would be over by that time.) The Treasury was not disposed to take the matter so lightly and the case came up in Bow Street, in what Sidney described to friends as the 'Pinero manner'. In the event, the presiding magistrate dismissed the case altogether, with ten guineas' costs, and 'not a stain on my character'. Sidney was not a little irritated at so much wasted time, and regarded the niggardly behaviour of the Treasury as ill considered, since, as he pointed out to the court through his lawyer, he had in fact lent more than £10,000 to the Treasury for the war and surrendered to them all his dollars and USA securities.

Within the entire MoI too the rows rumbled on, with those in charge complaining that they were nothing more than messenger boys for the other departments. Even Beaverbrook intervened at one point to object that the Ministry should either be given more power, or abolished altogether. In July 1941, after barely a year in charge, Duff Cooper resigned. 'When I appealed for support to the PM,' he wrote later in his memoirs, 'I seldom got it. He was not interested in the subject. He knew that propaganda was not going to win the war. Looking back, I think he was right.' He left to be Resident Minister in Singapore.

It had not been Duff Cooper's fault, but his departure marked a turn for the better in the tide of the MoI's affairs. In his place Churchill decided to appoint Brendan Bracken, the untidy red-haired Irishman with thick glasses and a reputation for unscrupulous behaviour and great rudeness. Bracken was a man people either liked and remained loyal to all their lives, or mistrusted so deeply that they could not bear to be long in his company. Churchill loved him. His standing with the Prime Minister, as well as his close friendship with Beaverbrook, now meant that the new Minister of Information was at last able to argue with some degree of effectiveness with more senior colleagues. As a former newspaper man – he had once owned the *Financial Times* – Bracken also knew just how newspapers worked. He was gifted with a quick wit, and had a canny understanding of how to pick the right man and then let him get on with his job.

There was one final change of cast, and then the MoI began to find a pace and voice of its own. Sir Walter Monckton, a charming barrister more suited to legal pleasantries than the dictatorship of high office, was now replaced as Director General by Sir Cyril Radcliffe, whose incisive nature was ideal for the post. Sidney later described him as having a steel-trap mind and unyielding logic. At last, the right team was in control: the two men at the top were determined to establish the principle that the only reason for suppressing a story was that it would give the enemy valuable new information, and concerned that the best way to sustain morale was to keep pouring out plenty of facts. There was to be the minimum of random censorship. It was a happy solution, and was now to last for the rest of the war. It was happy for Sidney too, in that both Radcliffe and Bracken were good friends (Sidney was one of the few people whom Bracken liked unequivocally), and that now at last the Films Division was going to be able to pursue a policy of making films and distributing them without incessant interruption and vacillation.

On 23 July, Sidney wrote to his new chief a token letter of resignation:

> It may be that you would like to make your own selection of advisers. Therefore, if in your plans you feel more free by having my resignation – well – I offer this as my act of hara-kiri as far as 'Mini' is concerned.

It was not accepted.

By now, the late spring of 1941, the real issue, as far as Sidney was concerned, was America. At home, the new Bracken-Radcliffe team was ensuring a definite smoothness of production. The MoI shorts were being churned out week after week, and by formal agreement with cinema exhibitors, largely forged by Sidney, getting regular showings throughout the country. Longer documentaries were being made, with co-operation from the different forces, though the question of access remained a prickly issue right up until the end of the war, as did that of rivalry between the forces and the newsreel companies. Newsreels were being viewed twice a week at the MoI, then going out on circulation: Sidney had been able to point out that in the interests of preserving an ever decreasing amount of rawstock, districts should share the same print, regardless of who the distributor was, and this had been agreed and was working. As for the non-theatrical side, that was not really in his hands; though he had some say in persuading Francis Meynell, working for Mather and Crowther Ltd and commissioned by Lord Woolton to make a film about home food produce and in particular a bumper crop of carrots, to cable Walt Disney for help: 'Will you ask Walt draw . . . figures illustrating Doctor Carrot, Clara Carrot and Carrotty George Stop urgently need Ministry of Food to make propaganda for consumption of record crop carrots.' This side of the MoI's work was in fact working well, with seventy-five mobile cinemas, each using a 16mm projector, transported in a small Ford car, criss-crossing the country from church hall to school, factory or farm building.

The film team was in fact finally being allowed to function as it should, even if Beddington and Sidney did not greatly care for one another personally. To their subordinates, at least, they shared a supreme virtue: both were leaders who possessed the gift of backing those who worked for them, always, almost regardless of circumstance. True, there were factions and strong partisanship within the department; some people markedly preferred Beddington to Sidney, and others favoured Sidney. Both men possessed very demanding characters. But no one denied that they complemented each other marvellously, Beddington with his wide-ranging friendships among the documentary directors and writers, and Sidney with his many contacts in the industry itself.

Growing more urgent every day, on the other hand, was the question of how to handle pro-British propaganda in America, how to attract assistance for the allies, without finally alienating the isolationists. It was a highly sensitive issue and had its roots in the aftermath of the First World War. Then, not long after the cessation of hostilities, a storm of protest had broken out in the USA from people claiming that the British had infiltrated the American press and had been so devious and effective in their propaganda that they had tricked America into coming into the war. Reports of British brilliance at intelligence had gained such currency that even German generals, reminiscing later, became prone to attribute the collapse of German morale in 1918 at least partially to British Propaganda efforts. Now, in the first year of the war in Europe, a poll of Americans showed that 40 per cent felt themselves to have been victims of British 'propaganda and selfish interests' and had no intention of being so duped again. Lord Lothian, British Ambassador to Washington, reported: 'The British are held to be great adepts at the subtlest arts of propaganda and capable of luring innocent Americans into their traps.'

It was a question of allaying these fears while ensuring American support for the war. The reports reaching the MoI from correspondents in America were not always reassuring, particularly because the British censorship, still acting quixotically when it came to relaying news of how England was bearing up, insisted on conveying a picture of a country largely able to fend for itself. In the American Midwest, in particular, the isolationists were fighting determinedly against what they called the 'risk of war'. David Wills, reporting for the *News Chronicle* from Chicago, noted that 'among the businessmen here the most vocal are either sincere appeasers of the pre-Munich Chamberlain school, or anti-semite, or even admirers of so called Nazi efficiency.' In New York, the newspapers continued to reflect the country's sense of confusion and disunity, with the *New York Post*, *Herald Tribune* and *New York Times* calling for intervention, and the *New York Daily News* remaining violently isolationist.

Hollywood was trying hard to avoid politics. In 1938 the Hays report on the film industry had announced piously that 'propaganda disguised as entertainment would be neither honest salesmanship nor honest showmanship' and for the most part the studios listened. Notable exceptions were the Warner brothers who, in 1939, had made *Confessions of a Nazi Spy*, the story of a former FBI man who had cracked a Nazi spy-ring within the ranks of the American German Bund, but so hostile were some Americans that a cinema showing it was burned to the ground in Milwaukee by enraged pro-Nazis. Not unnaturally other studios were deterred from repeating the experiment, especially when, in April 1940, news reached Hollywood that a Polish exhibitor in Warsaw had been hanged in his own cinema after a screening of *Confessions*. The Warner brothers kept up their crusade, however, not by making films, but by donating two Spitfires to Britain.

Then a number of things happened to shift American opinion. President Roosevelt, increasingly joining the interventionist side, was re-elected and went on to get the Lend-Lease Bill through Congress, which enabled him at last to give Britain virtually all the equipment it needed, on terms to be judged at his own discretion. At the same time, more realistic and less censored news from Britain gave the Americans the first real glimpse they had had so far of just how desperately badly the war was going. Hollywood responded by giving the Lend-Lease debates favourable newsreel coverage and settled down, tentatively, and in spite of loud accusations of war-mongering by Senator Burton Wheeler, to producing a series of muted but emotional pleas for involvement.

The other event that did something to influence American public opinion was the showing of Harry Watt's *London Can Take It* (arranged, by Sidney, through Harry Warner) which, as Sidney had predicted to Beaverbrook, had been shown at 12,000 cinemas within months of its arrival in America, to an estimated 60 million viewers. Quentin

Reynolds, riding the success for all it was worth, lecturing and fund-raising throughout America, reported that:

> David Selznick is slug nutty about *London Can Take It* ... He wants me to make a picture a month in England ... Pick the subjects, write, speak the commentary and in short run the thing. The pictures would be distributed by United Artists ... Hollywood would go to war tomorrow.
>
> It's the most enthusiastic place in the US. Guys like Douglas Fairbanks Jnr have done terrific jobs here for England, and that is all reflected in these parties. Parties are the only way Hollywood knows of expressing itself.

Even Edward Porter, temporarily posted to the Washington Embassy, wrote to tell Sidney that 'Lindbergh rates hisses when he appears on the screen' and that the newsreels had become markedly more pro-British.

The question was now: how to capitalise on such success and keep the momentum going? In the spring of 1941 Ian Dalrymple and Harry Watt started work on a feature-length documentary about an RAF bombing raid. It was to be called *Target for Tonight*. It had no great plot and very little glamour, but when it was completed those who saw it agreed that its aerial photography was superb and that the stark realism of its pace did nothing to detract from its impact. At the MoI the decision was made to send it over to America as a successor to *London Can Take It* and that this time every American film company of any standing should be pressed to launch it. When a candidate of sufficient stature to talk on equal terms with the heads of the American studios was sought, Sidney was the unanimous, obvious choice.

On 18 August 1941 Sidney left for America; he was to be away for five weeks. His journey was made in total secrecy: Sidney travelled in an American Liberator bomber from Prestwick to Newfoundland, huddled along a bomb rack. Having remembered his Russian literature, he had sensibly taken the precaution of wrapping himself in a layer of newspapers to keep out the intense cold. According to a brief diary he kept of the trip, he 'slept a night under canvas' in Newfoundland, then flew on to Washington, to talk to Lord Halifax, who had replaced Lord Lothian as British Ambassador in December, and then to New York. His sister Beryl came to meet him, and Hitchcock was there, and so was Iris Barry, by now Film Curator at the Museum of Modern Art and married to its director, Dick Abbott.

Sidney was extremely busy: he organised a lunch meeting at the St Regis for the heads of all the newsreel companies, gave a talk to the March of Time School of Journalism on wartime documentaries, and then laid on a viewing of *Target for Tonight*. The New York heads of the film studios all turned up, but their reaction was disappointingly muted: this bald tale of bombers, mumbled incomprehensibly in British voices, had nothing of the immediate appeal of *London Can Take It*. They dithered. Sidney realised that he had no choice but to take the film on to Hollywood where his closer friendships with people like Darryl F. Zanuck, David Selznick and the Warner brothers might have more sway.

That Saturday night he asked the British Embassy to arrange a flight to the West Coast only to be told that such a thing was impossible. Every plane was booked for many weeks ahead. So he walked down into the lobby of the St Regis – Sidney particularly liked the hotel because it was the one place you could still get kippers – and asked the porters, most of whom were Irish: 'Anyone want to help a limey?' There was much laughter and shouts of 'No'. A few hours later he had a passage for Los Angeles that night.

After the austerities of two years of war, the food rationing and the black-outs, Hollywood was lush beyond dreams. It was midsummer; the weather was tropical, the ocean brilliant and the colours overpowering. In Beverly Hills and Bel Air, where Sidney spent his time, there was a sort of forgotten innocence, a tranquillity and lack of flurry he had quite forgotten in two years. There was unlimited food and wine, parties every evening, while by day people swam up and down their pools in a leisurely way just as they had always done. It all made the war seem a long way away.

Hitchcock, who had flown on ahead, now met him at the airport with Victor Saville and took him back to stay at his house on St Cloud Road. Sidney phoned Harry Warner, and arranged to dine with him the following night, a Sunday, considering him to be the best hope for *Target*, and then went off to dine with the Hitchcocks at Romanov's. As he was describing events in England, a breathless figure appeared at their table: it was Irving Asher, one of the senior producers at MGM. 'Sidney, I have been searching Hollywood for you. Louis B. Mayer wants to see you. It's urgent.' Asher was standing directly behind Hitchcock's chair, and Sidney glanced across to see how he should react. Hitchcock nodded; Sidney agreed to lunch with Mayer the next day.

Louis B. Mayer was a tyrant and a legend in Hollywood: stubborn, sentimental, with an egomania excessive even in a city of people as self-obsessed as those who came to Hollywood to make their fortune. 'Mayer's-Ganze-Mispochen' was how people referred to MGM, 'Mayer's whole family', not only because it was filled with his relations but because all those who worked there were encouraged to keep up the myth of a great family with a Jewish patriarch at the top who loved obedience and order. Mayer was also a Republican. By the summer of 1941 MGM had done nothing for the allies in Europe.

The lunch took place at Mayer's home in Santa Monica on Sunday. Dozens of guests had been invited and after some hours of amiable generalities Sidney grew restless. Then Mayer appeared at his side and suggested that they go upstairs to his private room to talk. Mayer was at his most expansive: 'Sidney, what can we do for you British?'

Sidney had never greatly cared for Mayer. He found his style too despotic. 'Louis, you've never done a damned thing for us. Never. Not a thing all this time. Why now?'

'Well,' replied Mayer, 'I'm going to.' And he proceeded first to describe to Sidney the plot of a feature film based on a column that appeared in the London *Times*, called *Mrs Miniver*, and then, to Sidney's growing astonishment, though these antics of Mayer's were familiar to anyone who knew Hollywood well, to act out whole episodes of the movie, taking first one part and then another, bustling from side to side, his round, rather racoon-like face creased into expressions of disdain, anguish or fear.

While this was going on Asher walked in and stood watching. When the performance came to an end, to Sidney's even greater embarrassment Asher fell to his knees, clasped his hands together and, like a medieval supplicant, begged Mayer to let him direct the film.

The meeting lasted three hours. Sidney left with an agreement that MGM would make *Mrs Miniver*, the story of an English woman in wartime Britain, and that Greer Garson would star in it. Sidney had tried to persuade Mayer to make the film in England, arguing that it would help Britain greatly. This might have been possible but Greer Garson would not go home. (Irving Asher never got the job of directing it; that went to William Wyler.)

The same night, Sidney dined with Harry Warner and his family. An enormous fillet of beef had been laid on for his benefit, and Sidney, who had seen little good meat in two years, watched with pain as the laden dish emptied on its progress around the table towards him. As the last slice vanished, just before the butler reached him, Harry Warner caught sight of his expression and laughed. 'Don't worry, Sidney. We have a whole second fillet in the kitchen just for you.'

After dinner, Sidney went out to the car and fetched *Target for Tonight*. Harry Warner liked it, and suggested that it be properly screened for the whole studio the next morning. 'But now, Sidney, I'll show you something.' And he put on a new Warner Brothers film about a Presbyterian minister, reminding Sidney of the famous Hollywood lunch in 1936 at which he had castigated the Hollywood producers for using nothing but white and Catholic priests.

The screening of *Target for Tonight* for the department heads the next morning was again a disappointment. Their reaction was much the same as that of the New York film people. But one of Warner's top producers, Hal Wallis, came up with an idea: why not redub *Target* specifically for America, with an American rather than an English commentator? This was done. The department heads, who returned to see the new version, declared themselves delighted: the movie had been transformed. Now the American public would finally understand what was being said. *Target for Tonight* went out on the major circuits across America to considerable acclaim. And it set a precedent. From now on redubbing, and occasionally re-editing, of English material would become standard practice.

Sidney spent just under a week in Hollywood. Part of his brief had been to look into the position of the British residents in Hollywood, suffering, as he now found, from an intense sense of guilt at being out of England. On the outbreak of war nearly every able-bodied British man in Hollywood had volunteered but only David Niven had actually managed to get into the Army, and he only did so to the considerable anger of Samuel Goldwyn, to whom he was under contract.

The guilt of those who remained – Hitchcock, Victor Saville, Charles Bennett, Sir Cedric Hardwicke, Robert Stevenson, R. C. Sherriff, Laurence Olivier and many others, for by the the end of the 1930s a great number of British actors and film-makers had been lured to Hollywood by the promise of better parts and higher salaries – had been greatly increased by a particularly virulent campaign of abuse against them on both sides of the Atlantic. In May 1940 Sir Seymour Hicks had sneered that these expatriates were 'gallantly facing the footlights' and proposed a new film to be called *Gone With the Wind Up* starring Charles Laughton, Hitchcock and Herbert Marshall. Even the fact that Lord Lothian, and later Lord Halifax, had advised them to remain, on the grounds that they were far more useful exercising their influence in Hollywood, and that many donated generously from their salaries to war funds, had done little either to calm their anxiety or to appease their critics. Sidney now went round the various studios, adding his own conviction that they were far more valuable where they were as ambassadors to Hollywood: he likened their presence in America to that of the settler who had travelled on the 'pilgrim ship'. As he pointed out, if there were to be a reverse journey of the *Mayflower*, what work would there be back home for its passengers?

With one Englishman, Sidney had somewhat less of a success. He had first met Charlie Chaplin in 1930, and over subsequent visits the two men had become good friends. On arriving now in Hollywood,

Sidney had asked him, over dinner at the Hitchcock house, whether he could have, on behalf of the MoI, the rights to *The Great Dictator*, Chaplin's satire on Hitler and Mussolini. The Films Division wanted to show it in the Middle East, on their mobile 16mm projectors. No, said Chaplin, Sidney could not.

'You've got currency frozen in England,' said Sidney. 'If I get that out, will you then?'

'Perhaps,' replied Chaplin.

'What about if I guaranteed you a certain sum now for the film, would that do?'

'Perhaps.'

The conversation lasted all evening. Sidney was completely unable to understand the reason for Chaplin's reluctance. Finally, at two o'clock in the morning, sitting in the car parked outside the house, preparing to drive home, Chaplin explained. It was quite simple, he told Sidney. He didn't want to be seen on a small screen. He kept to his word; nothing was to persuade him. Sidney never did get the rights to *The Great Dictator*.

On the last day of August, Sidney returned to New York. It was a sweltering, humid day and he retreated inside the St Regis – the only hotel to possess air-conditioning – to spend Labour Day at work on an early script of *Mrs Miniver* that Louis B. Mayer had sent him to check that the details were authentically English. At lunchtime he tried to leave the building to go for a walk, but the blast of hot air from the streets pushed him back up to his room.

He had one more task to accomplish before leaving America. While in Washington a delighted Lord Halifax had informed him that Archibald McLeish, the poet, had managed, after considerable efforts, to persuade President Roosevelt to pass an order making the showing of British wartime shorts compulsory in every cinema in the country. On hearing this, Sidney had evidently looked downcast, for Lord Halifax asked: 'Isn't this what you wanted?' 'No sir,' replied Sidney. 'How do you think audiences will react when cinema managers come on stage to tell them that on the order of the president they have been obliged to show films about the war in Britain?'

Now, back in New York, and with the help of friends in the administration, he managed to get the order rescinded. He felt absolutely certain that coercion in America would be just as harmful as it would be back at home, and in England he had fought hard against it, preferring to reason with the exhibitors rather than bully them.

The diary for his last day in America gives some idea of how very hard he worked. 'Office morning – Warners. Campbells, Kastner. Lunched Sheila Hibben. Roberts. Office Again. Cocktails with Campbell. Dined Thomson and Dixie Barclay Room. Office again until 11.30. Train to

Washington 1.45 a.m.'

He returned to England the way he had come, by bomber, but this time the plane was insulated and the passengers were given special clothing and Mae Wests to wear. There was a pause in Montreal where the plane was grounded by freak ice for almost four days. Sidney spent time with Beaverbrook's brother, Allen Aitken, and his daughter Margaret. The trip had been, in every sense, a great personal success. On his return to the MoI, he was able to report that 'despite much confusion and muddle-headed thinking among the film people both about their duty to their own country and their desire to help Britain and her allies' MGM was set to make at least one major pro-British feature film, the Warner brothers were going to distribute *Target for Tonight* (which was an enormous success), Walter Wanger was going to go ahead with a film based on the RAF, *Eagle Squadron*, and that Zanuck, Schenck and Selznick were all viewing the idea of patriotic propaganda movies with increasing enthusiasm. His good contacts were beginning to pay off.

Sidney returned to London and to the MoI in the middle of September. Whenever he found a spare moment he renewed his crusade to organise a Film History of the war, an idea he had first proposed on joining the MoI in the late spring of 1940 and one that seemed more than usually thwarted by bureaucratic indifference and inertia. Sidney's point, and he made it frequently to all those who would listen to him, was that unless proper collation and indexing of war film material was carried out while it was being shot the war would end with no film record, and a unique form of contemporary archive would be lost. Sidney's plea for a 'controlling authority', possibly under the aegis of the Historical Section of the Cabinet, but not under that of the Imperial War Museum, which had neither the money nor the facilities for it, finally reached the Cabinet, which, like everyone else, stalled. Memos, letters, papers all accumulated in a large pink folder. One day, however, Sidney received instructions to discuss the matter with the Head of the Historical Section. He was delighted, believing that at last someone was taking his project seriously.

The man in charge was particularly welcoming. 'Bernstein, this is a brilliant idea. It's come at the right time because I've just finished work on the West African campaign.'

Sidney felt some sense of confusion. 'I didn't know we had one.'

'No, no, of course we haven't *now*. I'm talking about the First World War.' It turned out that, after all, no one was envisaging a *modern* film record. Sidney, defeated, gave up.

In October came an invitation from the Department of National

Service Entertainment for him to go out to the Middle East to take charge of all cinema activities. He was offered a rank of Major. Sidney refused as it was rapidly becoming plain that there was something wrong with his health.

He had woken one morning in Arlington House to find that he was coughing blood. The height of the war was not the best moment to find a doctor in central London, Zoë was away from London working on an article, and the porter had returned from a rather hasty search leading a tall, emaciated man who looked somewhat like Boris Karloff, and whose method of diagnosis turned out to be a pellet of lead suspended from a piece of string which he swung over Sidney's chest like a pendulum. 'You are very ill,' Boris Karloff finally pronounced in lugubrious tones, and left. Sidney languished in bed. Finally he had the sense to phone his friend David Blairman, who instantly sent round his own doctor to take X-rays. These revealed an acute form of tuberculosis, probably aggravated by the unpressurised flight out to America on the bomber. Specialists recommended a year in a clinic in Switzerland, which they could arrange. Sidney was appalled. Eventually they reached a compromise: three months, never leaving his bed, somewhere by the sea.

On 14 November Sidney, Zoë, Yvonne, the maid from Coppings, and a full-time nurse moved into a flat at Marine Gate in Brighton. To help pass the time, for Sidney was predictably the most restless of invalids (his health had always been excellent and an illness of this kind seemed to him absurd), he decided to become an expert on the collapse of Germany after the First World War and began ordering books from as far afield as the Huntingdon Library in Los Angeles, to be transported across the Atlantic by US Air Force friends.

It was not a bad time. Sidney could receive visitors, providing they left by nine o'clock; those who came did their best to bring him smoked salmon and caviar. When he grew stronger, he took to going to the movies in Brighton in the afternoon, where he discovered that many of the 'B' pictures he had attacked so ferociously for their mediocrity before the war were in fact rather better than the feature films.

Sidney was still at Marine Gate in December and it was there, on the 7th, that they heard over the radio of the attack on Pearl Harbor. Sidney's reaction was immediate and predictably euphoric: now, at last, there would be no more American vacillation about the war in Europe. Unable to travel, he spent hours on the telephone to the MoI in London, discussing how the Japanese attack would affect the work of the Ministry.

There was one cause for immediate relief within the film world both in London and Hollywood. In October the American Senate, pushed by the American First Committee, which had been growing increasingly uneasy about the effects of pro-British films, fearing that they would undermine their isolationist stance, had passed a resolution proposing a congressional subcommittee to investigate 'any propaganda disseminated by motion pictures ... to influence public sentiment in the direction of participation by the US in the European war'. The motion had been moved by Senators Gerald Nye and D. Worth Clark, and warmly supported by the German Consul in Los Angeles and the German Ambassador in Washington, as well as by Joseph Kennedy, the tall, red-haired Bostonian, Ambassador to London in 1938, who had attempted to sway the USA in the direction of Hitler. Apart from being an isolationist, Nye was also an anti-Semite: Sidney had been in America that summer when the Senator had made a widely reported racist speech in St Louis.

By early December both Harry Warner and Darryl F. Zanuck had appeared before the committee. The next on the list was Sir Alexander Korda, who had been subpoenaed to appear on the 12th, and was dreading the possibility that, as the most visible and prominent British film-maker in Hollywood, he was liable to be made a scapegoat for the industry. Sidney had been much involved with the hearings, having spent considerable time in Hollywood trying to instil a sense of aggression, rather than guilt, in those liable to be called up, and having been at least partly responsible for the appointment of the remarkable lawyer Wendell Wilkie as their defence counsel. Pearl Harbor brought the hearings to an abrupt close.

In the late spring of 1942, sufficiently recovered to resume normal working life, Sidney was asked to go to America once again, this time to liaise between the MoI and the American Government propaganda agencies, and to establish a British Films Division within the British Information Services. Now that America had entered the war a far more sophisticated system of propaganda between the two countries was clearly called for and again Sidney, with his experience and contacts, was the natural choice. Before accepting the job, he asked to be allowed to take $1,000 a month allowance for entertainment, arguing that he could not possibly continue to depend on the hospitality of the Americans, and that it was harmful for mutual relations that he should do so. His request led to a tangle of uneasy bureaucratic rulings – despite the fact that he was asking to be allowed to take his own money – but eventually Treasury permission was given.

The month before he left Sidney was asked by Brendan Bracken to call on John Winant, newly arrived American Ambassador, who was concerned that the British were receiving not only too little information about the American way of life, but information of totally the wrong kind. Since this was a theme that preoccupied Sidney greatly – he had argued at length while in America before that the Hollywood movies were only managing to project an image of a prosperous, glossy, rather vainglorious country – he was eager to help.

Winant was a shy, self-effacing man, who looked a little like Abraham Lincoln and was much loved by people who knew him well. He and Sidney took to each other, especially as Winant started outlining his plans for a British Division, to be set up in London precisely in order to convey a more accurate picture of America to the British. Winant knew that Sidney was shortly to leave for America, and now asked him whether he couldn't persuade his Hollywood studio friends to help.

Sidney agreed but suggested that at the same time the person to approach was really Darryl F. Zanuck, the head of 20th Century Fox, who, after Pearl Harbor, had joined the American Film Unit and was currently in England. (Sidney had just had a curious meeting with him. Zanuck had arrived in England demanding to talk with a high-ranking British figure. Sidney had been detailed for the job, which he had agreed to take only on condition that he be given the largest office in the building in which to receive the movie mogul. He was given Brendan Bracken's. Zanuck arrived in riding breeches, switching a crop against his gleaming boots. The gist of the message was that Halifax, British Ambassador to Washington, would have to go: Hollywood didn't like him. Sidney, somewhat surprised, said he would report the request.)

Winant rang for his secretary and asked Sidney to dictate to her the exact spelling of Zanuck's full name (Winant was no movie buff). To Zanuck's surprise, he was now invited to accompany the Ambassador wherever he went, while Winant tried to get across to him the importance of finding ways of getting the British to understand America. Whether or not Sidney's scheme paid off was never very clear.

Sidney left for America by seaplane from Poole Harbour, on 19 May 1942. The plane was full of men in dressing-gowns and pyjamas who turned out to be ferry pilots returning home from bringing over a consignment of Spitfires to Britain, and now on their way, at short notice, to collect more. The journey took twenty-eight hours. Sidney spent part of the time playing poker with the ferry pilots.

He could not have arrived at a more interesting moment. After months of indecision caused partly by the memories of First World War propaganda, the Federal Government had finally launched a new department to help fight at least this side of the war. The Office of War Information, as it was called, was to be the dominant agency in their campaign.

By the time Sidney reached America he had already had a number of dealings with the key figures who were now in charge at the OWI, and two men in particular, Archibald MacLeish (who had helped to rescind Halifax's arrangement to make the showing of British shorts compulsory) and the playwright Robert Sherwood, had become good friends. The mutual sympathy between the three men was understandable. All shared a hatred for fascism and strong feelings about the role propaganda could play. In earlier conversations they had agreed that in a democracy propaganda had to be based on the 'strategy of truth' and this meant putting out honest accounts of what was happening and leaving the public to make up its own mind.

For MacLeish, who had become Librarian of Congress in 1939, victory could only come if American opinion could be harnessed firmly behind the war. His concern was mainly with domestic matters and how to establish an open and frank network with press and media. He was made assistant director in charge of OWI's Policy Development Branch. Robert Sherwood, the gaunt, somewhat mournful-looking 6 ft 7 in. playwright whom a secretary had once nicknamed affectionately the 'walking coffin', shared the same forthright approach, but was more interested in overseas propaganda. He had worked as a speechwriter for President Roosevelt during the 1940 campaign and was now made head of OWI's Overseas Branch. Elmer Davis, the popular radio commentator and journalist, was appointed Director.

The cast looked promising, but already, even as the executive order establishing OWI was being passed, it was clear that trouble lay ahead. Like MoI, the OWI was going to suffer from the fact that it was not going to be a central agency handling all information, but only a co-ordinator of the various activities of the federal departments, each of which possessed its own information unit. Nor was any one very clear about the direction the new agency was to pursue, since Roosevelt, so positive in spelling out the need for 'four essential human freedoms' (of speech and expression, of worship, from want and from fear), had managed to avoid including guidance as to the actual aims of the struggle.

And so now, at their meetings in New York and Washington, Sidney, MacLeish and Sherwood discussed endlessly the crucial question of what exactly the nature of propaganda was in a democratic society at war. What, they asked each other, *were* the duties of bodies like the MoI or OWI: to boost support for it? or simply to follow the administration's lead?

There were no easy answers, particularly at this stage of the war, and Sidney set about performing some of the more specific tasks he had been sent to America to perform. Howard Dietz, head of MGM Publicity and a well-known lyricist, invited Sidney to give a talk to a lunch of 250 leading people in the film world at the Eddison Hotel – he had expected a gathering of six friends and was so appalled on looking round the door that he had retired to the bar for a Fernet Branca first – in which he repeated Winant's message that films giving a realistic picture of American life were now desperately needed. 'We don't get enough films that show how the ordinary American lives,' he told the audience, standing behind his table on the raised platform. 'We get a steady stream of glamour boys and girls, and of spies, of crooks and millionaires ... but do these films show the brave, energetic, pioneering spirit of America now, rising proudly and joining us in the fight?' Sidney was never a good speaker, sounding strangely awkward and strained for all his enthusiasm and convictions, and what was more he had the misfortune of following Zero Mostel the comedian, who gave impersonations of Hitler and Mussolini. But still he was wildly cheered. These were things the Americans now wanted to hear.

Most of June was spent on the East Coast, negotiating with OWI, setting up a Films Division to co-ordinate the British film and propaganda work, travelling between New York and Washington. To London he wrote:

> It is difficult to rest in Washington. Appointments start at 9.00 am and sometimes finished at 1.30 am. Hotels are bad, some dirty, all uncomfortable, that is, if you can get a room. Restaurants are crowded, expensive, food badly cooked ... Have seen Iris, who hasn't changed much, except looks smarter ... Hitchcock who came to New York for the weekend to see me and is as fat as ever ... 21 is busier than ever ... In retrospect and in the quietness of a dull boring hotel bedroom at 82 in the shade I realise we made a pretty good team.

At the peak of the heat wave he caught the *Chief* to Chicago to try to reason with Colonel McCormick of the *Tribune*, who had been printing a series of articles enormously hostile to Britain. He took with him some of the MoI films and won from him a grudging agreement that McCormick would at least mute the tone of some of his more outrageous attacks.

At the beginning of June *Mrs Miniver* opened at the Radio City Music Hall in New York. It was an instant, overwhelming success. Within ten weeks this soft and sentimental film about the tribulations of an English woman in wartime had been seen by one and a half million Americans. *Mrs Miniver* took four of the five top Academy Awards. Roosevelt himself told Wyler that he believed the film had lessened the problems of awarding increased aid to Britain. Sidney was just savouring the success when he was summoned to Washington to see

Lord Halifax. The Embassy, he was informed, was appalled by the film: all those who had seen it thought it gave a shocking and distorted picture of Britain.

Sidney was dismayed but also disbelieving. He rang Dr Gallup of the newly popular Gallup Polls and asked him to carry out a survey. Dr Gallup, who was immediately friendly and insisted on giving his services free, came to New York from Boston and arranged to monitor the attitudes towards Britain of those who had seen *Mrs Miniver* and two other pro-British movies (*Eagle Squadron* and *This Above All*), and compare them to those of people who hadn't. By October, Dr Gallup was able to report that those who had seen the British movies were 17 per cent more favourable towards Britain in their feelings than those who had not, a result he considered 'remarkable'.

The days were not wholly devoted to work. Isaiah Berlin, then working in Washington and writing the regular Embassy round-ups for London, rang him one day from the Gotham Hotel – Sidney was staying at the St Regis opposite – and asked him to come round to see him as he was feeling very ill. Sidney rushed over and found Berlin in an obviously bad way, but impeccably turned out in a pale, grey flannel boiler suit, with a waiter bringing in twenty-four oysters. Next day Sidney managed to find a bed for him in the Presbyterian hospital, and whenever he was in New York visited him daily. Berlin insisted on playing a game he had invented called 'Who would be the Quislings of England?', and visitors had to prove their case to his satisfaction.

Orson Welles was in New York and one Saturday the two of them set off to spend the weekend with Dorothy and Bill Paley of CBS who had a house on Long Island. In high spirits they caught a horse and carriage to Penn Station, then went to eat oysters and drink champagne at the bar. They missed their train. When they finally got to Long Island they found a house-party in full swing: Tyrone Power was there, and Fay Wray and Robert Riskin who were shortly to marry. Sidney knew most of the guests from previous visits and was made much of since he brought recent news of Europe and the war. Orson Welles told a story about the woman who had such a mania about cleanliness that she got her maid to wash her paper money every day and hang it on a line across the room to dry. It was a memorably pleasurable weekend and a rare break in Sidney's frenetic round of meetings.

In August Sidney went to Hollywood. One off-shoot of the OWI of special relevance to Sidney had been the creation of a Motion Picture Bureau under Lowell Mellett, and Nelson Pointer had been appointed in California to advise the studios on official war policy. By the time Sidney got there, directors like Frank Capra, William Wyler, John Huston and John Ford were already hard at work making documentaries of the kind being turned out in England for the MoI. (Capra had once referred to them disparagingly as 'ash can films made by crooks with long hair'). The whole mood of the place was entirely different from that of his previous visit barely six months before. Gone was the reluctance and uncertainty. Sidney now had no trouble in getting the leading studios to distribute both British feature films and shorts. If anything, as he reported to London, matters had now gone so far that there was a new danger: the American Government was so anxious to play up its own part in the war that it was investing a great deal of money in the film industry, with the result that the American war effort might soon appear on the screens in such a way that the British cause was entirely dwarfed.

One of Sidney's jobs was to find a British director who would be nominated by the British Government to interpret the American scene for British audiences. At first sight Sir Alexander Korda, the man who had given the British film industry such a boost with *Henry VIII* and who had spent the previous three years making frankly pro-British movies in Hollywood (*Lady Hamilton* was considered so illustrative of the Anglo-American bond that when Churchill and Roosevelt met in Newfoundland to formulate the Atlantic Charter, they had watched the movie after dinner), seemed the ideal choice. But Sidney had his doubts. He knew Korda, who had dazzled London with his charm and his extravagance, of old. He also knew something of his financial chaos. Early on in the war Brendan Bracken and the Prudential had asked him to look into the director's money matters, British Lion, his film company, having been loaned £3 million by the Government. Sidney had unearthed quite unbelievable confusion. (Sidney was with Korda one day in London when he received a letter from his bank manager stating that his overdraft had reached enormous proportions. In the car, on their way to see Merle Oberon, whom Korda was about to marry, he asked his chauffeur to stop the Rolls outside Cartier's. He emerged a few minutes later with a priceless necklace. 'You don't have to worry about the bank, Sidney,' he had said as he climbed back into the car, 'as long as you owe them *enough*.')

'In my view,' Sidney now wrote to London, 'his talents for the grandiose will not be required in a film designed to show the common man's way of living ... If we want an English director ... he should be one who has simpler tastes than Alex.' He added a comic footnote: 'Personal note: Korda in Hollywood was rather like this:

Dear Sidney
Please advise me.
Shall I work in Hollywood?

143

Shall I work in England?
I am tired of films
Shall I work with Louis B. Mayer?
He wants me to be a Vice President of MGM.
Shall I work for Political Warfare in England?
I am still tired of films.
If I work for MGM will the British industry
say I have sold out to an American company?
Shall I make 'War and Peace' in England?
Shall I make 'War and Peace' in America?
Shall I make 'War and Peace' for Metro in Hollywood?
Shall I make 'War and Peace' for Columbia in England?
Shall I make 'War and Peace'?
I want to go back to England
It's your duty (meaning me) to stay in the US
and have rank of Colonel.
People don't like me in England.
People do like me in England.

I then went for a swim in his pool.'

Sidney was back in Washington by the end of August, planning to fly up to Ottawa to meet John Grierson, with whom the MoI had been having increasingly difficult dealings. In December, six months earlier, Grierson had sent the Films Division a cable in which he criticised the British shorts as lacking all journalistic and theatrical impact and being 'slow, diffuse and parochial in theme' and added that British documentary units had failed to grasp proper editorial techniques.

There was, of course, some truth in what he said, and Sidney himself had witnessed how ill-suited some British film material was for North American audiences. But Grierson's words were hardly tactful. Nor had he endeared himself to anyone by coming to London and announcing over dinner with a gathering of film people at L'Étoile that 'London is finished. It won't be the capital of the British Empire any more. That's going to be in Canada.'

By the summer of 1942, furthermore, he had taken steps of his own to use and re-edit the British documentaries that came his way. Taking the material sent to him by the MoI he recut it in such a way that the heroes of the day appeared to be all Canadians. As Sidney was preparing to leave for Canada he had an embarrassed call from the Embassy. 'You can't go to Canada, I'm sorry. We ought to tell you. You're persona non grata. Grierson doesn't want anyone coming to upset his film production.'

It didn't take Sidney long to work out how best to deal with this. He called on his friends in the American film companies and arranged that from then on all British material would be distributed in Canada, not by Grierson, but directly by the major American companies.

By the end of October, Sidney's mission had come to an end. He was anxious to get back to London. Distribution for British films was ensured with the major companies; close relations had been set up with the OWI, and a Films Division under George Archibald and a Scot called Thomas Baird had now been established, with a staff of twelve, to promote British films. Lord Halifax cabled home ahead of him that Sidney had 'overcome great difficulties with considerable skill'. Sidney had every reason to be pleased with what he had achieved.

7

The Propaganda War

DURING THE WEEKS that followed his return to London, Sidney drew up a report of his American journey and pointed to some conclusions for the British film industry. Foremost among them was an issue that had plagued British documentary-makers – and indeed had been the basis of the row with John Grierson – since the beginning of the war. The American public, wrote Sidney, was now, six months after Pearl Harbor, not merely ready to learn about their new ally, but exceedingly anxious to feel a sense of partnership with it. The film distributors had also formally agreed to show any British material sent across the Atlantic. The trouble was simply, as Grierson had pointed out, that there was so little available that had any relevance at all to Americans. 'To force the American to digest our home consumption films', Sidney concluded, 'is a well nigh impossible task. Our imperative need is for films to suit *their* tastes, films which will command equal attention with the best American films.'

It was not exactly anyone's fault – after all why should film-makers be geared to the idiosyncrasies of other countries? – but for the first time it really mattered. Other forces now came to join the controversy. A film man called W. Matvyn Wright, whom Sidney referred to as 'our travelling fireman', wrote from America to say that the English voices in the documentaries that were reaching New York were 'muffled, fast and plummy' and that the average American viewer really '*likes, loves* and *devours* the sounds (real) of falling bombs, crashing walls, men shouting, etc. Can't you make them *louder* and knock them off their seats?'

146

The Propaganda War

In London, C. A. Lejeune, the film critic, wrote in the *Financial Times*: 'What has the average American gathered from our films about us? Beyond a dim impression of laconic bravery, beyond the fact that we smoke pipes, talk about cricket and stood up well to the London blitz, practically nothing.'

From New York, not long after Sidney's return, came a long letter from Thomas Baird, now the second-in-command of the Film Division Sidney had set up at the British Information Services. Baird had been to discuss with Samuel Spewack, the energetic playwright in charge of the OWI's film section, the unsatisfactory image of Britain that was crossing the Atlantic. 'There is a continual play on the theme that England is the country of tradition and America the country of ideas,' he wrote to Sidney, 'that we are hidebound and they are progressive; that we lean on the past and the Americans look to the future ... as a nation (it is generally felt) we have no political sense, and the nation is misled by its upper classes.'

What was needed now, Sidney argued with his colleagues at the Ministry, was a new, more robust approach to propaganda, with emphasis on the fact that the Britons 'not only know how to die but know how to win'. It was no longer a question of wooing allies; they had already been wooed. Film-makers had to cajole them into a state of mutual understanding.

Accordingly, and falling back once again on his network of friends among the Hollywood movie moguls, Sidney sent off a print of the most recent and popular of current documentaries, *Next of Kin*, to David Selznick for a full American analysis. The cable he received in reply came as an unpleasant shock, even to those expecting to be criticised. It ran to four typed pages and was absolutely blunt in its condemnation. The words were all the harder to take in that Thorold Dickinson's film about the dangers of careless talk, originally made for Army audiences but then put out commercially, had been widely praised in England, where C. A. Lejeune had called it 'the perfect spy story'. *Next of Kin* invented the seedy, ineffectual little hero, later to become the key figure in so many spy stories.

David Selznick had invited Ernst Lubitsch, the Paramount producer, and the screenwriter Nunnally Johnson to the viewing. On behalf of them all, Selznick cabled to Sidney:

Release in this country of the film in anything like the present version would be dreadful error from the standpoint of British American relations ... All the English officers are portrayed as stupid, careless and derelict ... calculated to increase the fears of Americans and mothers especially, that the British are simply muddling along, and

that their sons will die because of British incompetence. This is
aggravated by contrast with portrayal of brilliance and complete
efficiency of German intelligence ... This latter point is felt so
strongly that all here believe the film could be more profitably
run in German for home consumption and for building German
morale ...

Perhaps even worse, is the portrayal of so many British civilians as
informers and spies, giving the impression that England is overrun
by traitors ... So strong was the feeling that no attempt should be
made even to salvage the film, that I had difficulty in forcing rational
discussion.

Selznick continued, in the same vein, for several paragraphs, then
outlined an alternative synopsis of a story which would 'show that all of
England is on its toes and is keeping its mouth shut' but that this
'devotion to duty' is negated 'when one fine English boy innocently, but
imprudently, speaks to one fine English girl with whom he is in love'.
Then followed a tale of guilelessness, suspense and ultimate tragedy.
'Warmest regards', concluded Selznick, 'from your Hollywood
correspondent and heckler.'

The *Next of Kin* demolition was in itself intensely interesting. It
showed just how great was the gap between English and American
film-makers, just how unbridgeable that between their two styles. It
boded ill for the propaganda alliance. Conflicts of this nature were
precisely the sort of thing that made Sidney's job seem, at times, so
unrewarding. For when he relayed Selznick's comments to Thorold
Dickinson, the English director was not surprisingly very offended.
The version that eventually went out in America, though not reshot to
Selznick's specifications, was cut by almost a third and so tampered
with that it did much to reduce the sympathy British film-makers felt
towards their new allies. Sidney himself did not emerge too well from
the exchange. Inevitably, but unfairly, in the eyes of the British he
became contaminated by the sentimentality and trivia of the American
demands, and years after the war, some of the documentary
film-makers still blamed him for what they saw as unnecessary watering
down of their films.

While he was in America, Sidney's task of providing films for the Prime
Minister, who wanted them for weekends, had fallen to his secretary
Miss Wilkinson, herself a passionate film enthusiast. One weekend
Churchill asked for a recently finished naval film called *San Demetrio
London*. She saw no reason not to send it. The choice almost cost her
her job.

What Miss Wilkinson did not know was that it was not a subject or a film liable to please Churchill and that the Films Division had already gone to some lengths to keep it away from him. On the Monday morning the print was returned, together with one of Churchill's famous long slips of paper, bearing the words: 'Pray who is responsible for this dastardly film? It must be stopped.'

By the time the matter reached Sidney, the department was in uproar. Sidney had a friend in the navy called Anthony Kimmins. Through him, he arranged to have *San Demetrio London* shown to the First Sea Lord, Sir Dudley Pound. There was an anxious moment while the Films Division waited: a great deal of time and money had, after all, been spent on this venture. Then came a note for Churchill. 'I think', wrote Sir Dudley, 'that the British navy can take this. And a great deal more.'

Sidney was also called in to arbitrate over Coward's rendering of Mountbatten on the doomed destroyer *Torrin*. *In Which We Serve* had a prickly history. The previous year Brendan Bracken had called on Sidney to intervene in a dispute he was having with Mountbatten, who wanted Noël Coward to direct a full-length feature film about the navy and the *Torrin*, and which would inevitably tie up much of the scarce resources of the diminished British film industry. Sidney had been detailed to take Noël Coward out to lunch and talk him out of it.

They had gone to eat at the Savoy. 'I know what you want to see me about, Sidney,' said Coward, as they sat down. Sidney paused for a moment, then tried to deflect him. 'Do you really believe that you could play the part of Mountbatten?' Coward looked astonished. 'Of course I could. Aren't I an actor?' Somehow by the time lunch had come to an end, Coward had persuaded Sidney to let him go ahead, and Sidney returned to the MoI to report his defeat. *In Which We Serve* was finished in record time, with Noël Coward not only producing, co-directing, and writing the script and the music, but also giving an impressive performance as the captain of the crippled destroyer. The film, released in 1942, was greeted as the first really important film of the Second World War and won a special Academy Award.

In December, Sidney's mother Jane was seventy. The demands of his job kept him for weeks on end from paying her visits, but he phoned her constantly and Zoë, of whom she was particularly fond, went to see her when she could. Much of Sidney's limited family correspondence of those days concerned her welfare. Now, to celebrate her birthday, Sidney was determined to provide the best occasion he could summon up in London, by taking a family party to the Trocadero to dine. It was a diminished group, with Beryl in America and most of the other children scattered by the war. Sidney took these events seriously, just as he did Christmas, conscientiously sending Miss Wilkinson off to buy presents for all the children, god-children and others, under twenty-one, to whom he felt in any way bound. Zoë was still in London, and was building up a substantial reputation of her own as a journalist. Even Beaverbrook had mellowed towards her, summoning her to his desk one day after a story of hers (on Russian artillery) had appeared in the *Daily Express*, with the words: 'Zoë Farmer. You are a journalist. I salute you.'

The Bernsteins, by the winter of 1943, were living in a flat in Arlington House, the vast stone building by the Ritz, their Albany flat having been damaged by a bomb while Sidney was in North Africa. Coppings was still used for weekends, and the cottages continued to be lent to homeless friends. The local Agricultural office had agreed to look after the farm as he was often away, and they had turned it over to wartime production: flax grew in brilliant yellow crops all over the dipping valley. Weekends had become sober and solitary occasions, though friends on leave came down when they could. By this time Sidney had installed his own film projector in the hall, where guests sat in comfort after dinner. On Sundays, they played tennis, or walked across to a nearby farm owned by Jack Freeman who was teaching Sidney how to shoot with a .22. There was still a lot of talk, but the guests were tired, more anxious.

By now, Sidney no longer had time for his sudden and explosive visits to the cinemas: their management was entirely in Cecil's hands. The war had brought more women into the business and Granada was now training girls as 'operettes'. The company was also increasing the catering side of the cinemas, as women doing war work took to eating out at nights, with the unfortunate result that, as the rationing of china was brought in, an epidemic of pilfering broke out with twenty thousand pieces disappearing in a single year. A travelling 'cold sweet' chef was appointed to work miracles with jelly, ice cream having finally succumbed to rationing.

Earlier, in the spring of 1943 discussions had begun at the MoI about the need for someone to visit North Africa, where the allies had taken Morocco and Algeria, to report on the highly confused state of the cinemas, and to co-ordinate some kind of propaganda policy with the Army Film Unit, stationed near the front. Brendan Bracken was at the meeting, as were Foreign Office officials and several of the senior MoI figures. By common consent, they all turned to Sidney: '*You* go.' Sidney was delighted to do so. His job in the Films Division had reached a point where it could look after itself for a few weeks, and he had long wanted to visit a war front and get some feeling of the fighting

More than that, he wished to see for himself exactly how, in practice, he allies were merging their propaganda efforts. He prepared to leave.

However, almost immediately, there was consternation among the Americans to whom his mission had been announced. Sidney, they made it plain, was not an acceptable choice. At the MoI, the news was greeted with amazement. The mystery took some days to clear up. One morning, a call came to Sir Cyril Radcliffe from General Eisenhower. They were bothered, said Eisenhower, by these rumours that kept reaching them that Sidney was a member of the Communist Party. Was that in fact true? Once again, Sir Cyril Radcliffe had to vouch for him: Sidney, he told him, had never been a member of the Communist Party. The ban was lifted. Sidney was given an honorary rank of Lieutenant Colonel, and issued with a uniform; on 17 March he caught a plane for Lisbon.

On 8 November 1942 when the allies had landed troops in Morocco and Algeria, 'psychological warriors' had landed with them, members of the newly formed Psychological Warfare Branch, an amalgam of OWI and the American strategic services, and MoI and its British propaganda arm, the Psychological Warfare Executive, brought together by General Eisenhower, who had been persuaded by the American war propagandists to include it as a tactic in his campaign. 'I don't know much about psychological warfare,' Eisenhower had said, but I want to give it every chance.' He had, however, insisted that it come under military control, and the new unit had been placed under a willing but slightly sceptical cavalry officer called Colonel Hazeltine. He, too, professed himself ignorant but enthusiastic on the subject of propaganda.

After their arrival in North Africa the PWB men had set about securing such facilities as could be used for publicity – newspaper plants, radio stations and cinemas. Immediately, they ran into ideological trouble. The PWB had thought to bring with them several hundred thousand leaflets attacking Admiral Jean François Darlan and he other Vichy representatives in North Africa, since it had been assumed by the allies that Henri Giraud, a celebrated French general recently escaped from a German prison, would persuade the North African French to cease resistance. When Giraud proved unhelpful, Eisenhower had turned instead to Darlan, commander-in-chief of the French Armed Forces, a known Nazi sympathiser and collaborator. In return for a relatively bloodless ceasefire, they had assured Darlan that they would not interfere with French control in North Africa, however repressive that might be.

The PWB men, most of them moulded in the liberal OWI mark of Sherwood and MacLeish, were appalled by the deal. They now had the frustrating and humiliating task of destroying their anti-Darlan leaflets and turning over the radio stations to the French.

It was into this propaganda chaos that Sidney fell when he reached Algiers. Films, he found, had been put under 'E' section and the control of a screenwriter called Oliver Garrett whom Sidney had known for years and greatly respected, but who had been as yet unable to establish any working system for the distribution of allied films. This, as Sidney immediately reported back to London, was due mainly to a hitch in newsreel agreements. During the Vichy regime, by Government decree, *France Actualité* had been compulsorily booked to all cinemas. On entering Algiers, the PWB had signed an unfortunate agreement with Cinemaroc, a pro-Vichy organisation, which effectively biased news against the allies. When they realised their mistake, PWB cancelled the agreement, and now, at about the time Sidney reached Algiers, a new deal was taking shape, whereby the allies were going to produce and distribute their own newsreel, a joint Anglo-American-French enterprise. It had taken weeks to arrange. When the first newsreels were shown, the public queued for several blocks to see them; for many, it was their first view of the free world for over two years, the Vichy Government having ordered the elimination of all film material post-1937 to make more room for recent German propaganda.

The way was now open for Sidney to set up a commercial distribution of British films, working closely with PWB and the Americans; the job was made more pleasurable by the presence in North Africa of Robert Sherwood. 'The general position is one of complete disorganisation,' he wrote to London, 'but there is no problem here that a good organiser can't cure ... There is, in the propaganda sense, a profitable field that is ours for the plucking or ploughing.'

Within a few days of his arrival he had called a meeting of all film distributors and set about getting only those films shown that had first been approved by the allies; he had reopened the cinemas that had been closed; he had set up a means of censorship; and he had sifted through the individual distributors themselves, separating pro-allies from pro-Vichy. Whenever he came across them, he impounded all Axis films, in the hope that they would yield invaluable pictures of collaborators and prominent German generals.

None of it was easy. Some of the more canny pro-Nazi cinema owners took the simple evasive tactic of declaring that their cinemas were fully booked to old French movies, thereby avoiding having to show allied documentaries. Furthermore, the Americans were already ahead in that ill-defined but nevertheless real game of rivalry between two allies, and while forty-five American features (including *Yankie Doodle Dandy Dumbo* and *Tarzan and His Mate*) were ready for distribution, already subtitled in French, not one British film had reached North Africa.

Outside Algiers, film matters were in a still greater muddle. In towns where electricity had been cut off cinemas were boarded up and closed, and cinema owners had vanished. Sidney complained crossly to Beddington that he had no typewriter, no stenographer, no chairs, and a lot of willing but uselessly inexperienced volunteers. But he persisted, and by the end of April was able to report that British newsreels, shorts and documentaries were now being distributed free to commercial companies and that he was giving *Desert Victory*, Roy Boulting's highly praised film of the Egypt-Libya campaign, a gala première in every major Algerian and Moroccan town. 'Even Peyrouton turned up with a Senegalese guard of honour,' he wrote to London, the showman's voice coming through. 'The Lambeth Walk, which we included in the programme, was an outstanding hit, as was also the Royal Marine Band which [we] borrowed from a cruiser to play the overture and national anthems.' One can't help wondering what the French made of it all.

Sidney had been billeted in a small hotel. He found Algiers, with its nightly air raids and anti-aircraft guns and its cockerels crowing from every terrace, extremely noisy, and recorded in his diary: 'Army rations, no milk, oranges; whisky, gin; noise of shutters opening in the morning; Casablanca palm and date country like Hollywood.'

Towards the end of April, having established a working procedure for films, Sidney left to visit Hugh Stewart, head of the British Army Film Unit stationed at Teboursouk near the front. Before the war Stewart had worked as a film editor for Alexander Korda and Victor Saville. Sidney knew him well. He found the unit comfortably installed in a requisitioned hotel called L'Hôtel du Phoenix opposite the police station, ten miles from the front; since there was typhus in the area, the town was virtually deserted. There were two officers and fifteen sergeants, all cameramen trained at the film school started early in the war at Pinewood studios. Sidney was intensely interested in everything, and insisted, Hugh Stewart remembers, on being told exactly how the system worked, stage by stage, from initial filming to getting the reels to London and the MoI. He stayed four days, and talked wistfully once again to Stewart about his hopes of gathering material for a real film history of the war.

At the beginning of May it became clear that the final move towards Tunis had begun. While Montgomery and the Eighth Army had been driving the Germans along the coast road from Alamein to Mareth, General Anderson and the First Army had been fighting their way from Algiers to meet him. Sidney was determined to be part of the forces entering the city.

Early on the morning of 7 May he had the fortune to fall in with

Alexander Clifford of the *Daily Mail* and Christopher Buckley of the
Telegraph, two friends from Fleet Street. At about 2.30 in the afternoon
their jeep managed to get behind an armoured division that was clearing
the way into Tunis, in such a way that theirs was one of the first vehicles
to enter the city, driving behind ten armoured cars.

Sidney wrote in his diary:

> Passed the sign of Tunis at 4.30 then a few hundred yards on, 3 or was
> it 4, roads converge on to the St Cyprien road. The road facing the
> left had a stationary lorry in the centre and behind the lorry, lying on
> his stomach, the dead driver, a German, his face turned sideways and
> his eyes wide open. His map case still hanging from his shoulder lay
> beside him. All along the road we followed for the next half hour
> Germans were coming out from all sides to surrender. I was
> embarrassed at them offering themselves to me. I was also
> embarrassed by the welcome from the civilians.

The welcome was indeed moving; a sort of hysteria seemed to grip the
city as the allied troops advanced, with people crying and shouting
rushing forwards to kiss the troops and throw flowers over their cars. In
the centre of the town, German soldiers, not knowing the allied arrival
was imminent, were still sitting drinking in the cafés. Sidney wrote
affectionately to Zoë, obviously overwhelmed by all he had seen, saying
how embarrassed he had been at the warmth with which he was
received, since he was no fighting soldier. It was very characteristic of
him to say so.

Sidney's role in North Africa was now over. He had been there nearly
ten weeks. By three o'clock on the 8th he had already met the leading
Tunisian film people and supervised the arrival of allied films; he spent
the following day impounding over 50,000 feet of Axis propaganda
films and newsreels and dispatched them immediately to London. After
much wrangling he had managed to appoint Lieutenant Fredman as
Films Officer, and he now left in his hands the task of ensuring a regular
distribution of feature and documentary films throughout North
Africa. Fredman, he reported to Beddington, was 'tough enough for the
local film sharks'.

Once again he had every reason to be pleased with what he had
accomplished. He had instituted order where previously there had been
chaos, he had secured a reasonable showing for British films, and, most
importantly perhaps, he had laid down a model for allied film
distribution for the campaigns to come.

Sidney reached London late in May, returning the way he had come
through Lisbon. He stayed with Michael Stewart, now press attaché at

the British Embassy, and ran unexpectedly into his sister Beryl, on her way home from America and briefly marooned in Portugal awaiting transport to England. They were delighted to meet and exchange news: apart from his mother and Cecil, Beryl was the member of his family to whom he felt closest, the one perhaps most like him, with her energy and considerable, if at times rather brisk, charm.

In his absence a number of meetings had been held at the MoI to discuss films for liberated Europe, and propaganda policy in general with regard to the reoccupied countries. They were the first of what were to be dozens of committees and mountains of paperwork on the subject. In June, for example, an entire conference, with representatives from Belgium, Czechoslovakia, France, Greece, Norway, Poland, the USSR and Yugoslavia, was convened by the Foreign Office and the MoI to debate not only such technical questions as how to re-equip cinemas, but the more intangible ones of policy. How, the organisers asked, were the allies to avoid imposing a rigid pattern of reconstruction upon the liberated peoples who had shown proof of their own democratic traditions and policies?

Sidney, fresh from his North African experiences, felt strongly that film had a vital psychological role to play and he now put forward his plan that documentary films should be prepared that had been specifically geared to the needs of each European country, including material appropriate to its own past and its own experience of the war. These would include newsreel coverage of the various campaigns, some sort of commentary on the causes of war, and dubbed shorts and features. The work, he argued, should be divided between the OWI and the MoI and handled by the PWB country by country as the allied troops went in.

But first there was the Italian campaign to consider. In July, the allied forces had landed in Sicily, and Richard Crossman, at the Political Intelligence Department in London, suggested to Kenneth Grubb of the MoI that Sidney should be sent to Italy, since what was needed was a man of his stature to ensure that British film propaganda was put on an equal footing with the American one.

In the event, Sidney paid only one brief visit to Rome, after it fell, preferring to conduct film matters through an extremely energetic ex-Granada man called Vernon Jarratt, a huge, bluff figure with a great orange moustache, whose passion in life was speed and films. Jarrett now criss-crossed Italy on a roaring motor-cycle, pushing British films. It was something of a challenge since Robert Riskin, head of OWI's Overseas Film Bureau, had already prepared forty Hollywood movies, complete with Italian subtitles, ready for instant distribution, 'stressing entertainment rather than propaganda, with the idea being first to get the Italians patronising the theatre and friendly, and then insert propaganda by means of shorts'. The British, for their part, having spent the early summer months mulling over, in some confusion, their attitude towards the Italians, were not so eager to please, as Beddington wrote in a letter to Arthur Calder-Marshall, who had been brought into the MoI. 'The main thing to bear in mind at the moment about the Italian people as I see it, is not that they possess comic, endearing, treacherous or affectionate characteristics, but that they have been fighting for three years and are still committed to doing so. They are therefore enemies ...'

It was not so much that the Americans and the British differed in their objectives, but the fact remained that for all Sidney's hard work, nothing could mitigate the acute difference in their two styles. (That Sidney kept pushing for mutual understanding is shown in a letter he wrote not long after the landings to a friend with the Eighth Army, Geoffrey Keating: 'There has been very little American material, which we always need, so when you have cameramen to spare and they're in the US army zone send them over to take some scenes of what the Yanks are doing – or what you think the British public should think they're doing.')

By the summer of 1943 the Anglo-American film remittance agreement, whereby only a percentage of money earned in Britain by American movies was allowed to leave the country, had come to an end. Sidney had been much involved in drafting the agreement, and was now equally caught up in negotiating a new system of reciprocal understandings, which would take its place, morally if not financially. Each country, for example, had the right to veto the films of the other, and consultations frequently went on during the shooting of films destined for export. In the original version of Darryl F. Zanuck's *A Yank in the RAF* Tyrone Power was destined to die. The MoI, through Sidney, got 20th Century Fox to keep him alive on the grounds that they didn't want the American public to see an American dying for the British cause. Equally, when Walter Wanger wanted to put a woman air controller in *Eagle Squadron* Sidney was able to persuade him not to, arguing that it would be quite false, since the RAF had no women air controllers, and that it would be giving an inaccurate picture of Britain to suggest that women ran the RAF.

For all this, disputes between the two allies on matters of film kept recurring. At the end of the North African fighting the MoI asked Hugh Stewart to make a film documentary of the campaign, modelled on the highly successful *Desert Victory*, which had been really the first war film to show human details of campaign life. It was to be the first allied co-production and before beginning editing Stewart asked the

Americans for all their footage of the campaign. Frank Capra, the Hollywood director and now a Colonel in the Army, was assigned to head the American side.

There was no reply to Stewart's request. As the weeks passed and no American appeared, he and Roy Boulting decided to go ahead and start making the film. By the summer of 1943 it was virtually ready. At that point, Colonel Capra turned up, summoned Stewart to the Grosvenor Hotel and presented him with the American script and the American rushes of the film. Stewart, appalled, explained that he was just completing a version, and the two men agreed to see what the other had prepared. What Capra thought is not known, but Stewart was both impressed and dismayed. The American version had been largely reshot in the Californian desert, using one of the cameras out of focus. The film looked good, but it had little to do with the North African campaign.

Eventually the two teams came to an agreement that they would merge each other's material, using Pinewood studios outside London, that they would call their film *Tunisian Victory* (and not *Africa Freed* as Stewart had planned), and that Stewart would accompany Capra back to America with the finished version ('in the capacity of a watchdog', as he later put it). The British were not particularly pleased, but at least, as Stewart says, 'it was a joint allied film, it did have Eisenhower to introduce it, and the Americans were forced to take notice that the British had played their part, and lost more lives, in North Africa.' When the *Daily Express* complained that Capra had put into the film fictitious American scenes, 'added Tchaikovsky's Piano Concerto No. 1 in B Flat Minor for background music and added a fine overtone of emotional purpose to the whole', Sidney, to whom Anglo-American film problems all made their way in the end, was able to reply firmly that Hugh Stewart and Roy Boulting had been in control at Pinewood.

Anglo-American rivalries and bitterness in the world of film were to reach their peak with a movie called *Objective Burma*, starring Errol Flynn, and produced by the most liberal of the Hollywood studios, Warner Brothers. *Objective Burma* was conceived of as a rather typical war movie of jungle combat featuring a small group of American paratroopers sent behind enemy lines to perform a crucial mission. No slight to the British was apparently intended. However the script singularly failed to show the British operation in Burma, making the entire campaign appear to be an all-American victory, and after it had played for a week in London in 1945, Warner Brothers withdrew the film in response to the tirade of fury that had broken out in the English press. What was revealing was how very passionately people cared.

During the autumn Ed Murrow and his wife Janet became close

friends of Sidney and Zoë. Of Sidney's enormous range of acquaintances these were two with whom Zoë felt particularly at ease. By then Murrow was already something of a legend in broadcasting, a man who was gifted not just with a natural rhythm to his speech, and a natural style, but who possessed that unique ability of being able to convey something happening in one part of the world to people many thousands of miles away, who couldn't see what was going on, and knew nothing about the place in which it was happening. *This is England*, Murrow's weekly broadcast to America, had been going out every Sunday since 1941. Murrow, like Sherwood and MacLeish, felt strong ties to Europe, and had his own version of how things should be. He had first met Sidney some time before the war in New York, with Dorothy and William Paley, and after arriving in England had done some recording for Sidney's MoI shorts, as had his wife Janet, all part of Sidney's quest for pleasing North American voices best able to convey Britain to the Americans.

In London the Bernsteins and the Murrows met occasionally to dine at L'Étoile, the Ivy or the Connaught, or simply to talk or drink at the Savoy, for many of the war years the gathering place for journalists. As the winter of 1943 drew in, Sidney asked them down for a quiet weekend at Coppings. Over Saturday lunch Murrow asked what had become of Long Barn, and Sidney explained that it had been taken over for a spell by Lindbergh. After breakfast on Sunday, they walked over to look at the house. They found it full of children's cots, and were told that the Nicolsons had lent it to the Royal Society for the Prevention of Cruelty to Children for the duration of the war, and that it was now filled with evacuees from London.

The following week, when Murrow came to do his broadcast he read out over the air to many millions of Americans: 'At the weekend I visited the house which gave refuge to Charles Lindbergh. I thought you would be interested to know that the house is now giving refuge to the children who have had to leave London because of the bombs dropped by Lindbergh's friends.'

By December, a reformed Psychological Warfare Division, attached to Supreme Headquarters Allied Expeditionary Force, began to take shape at Norfolk House in London. It had a new head, General McClure, and the same two civilian advisers who had worked with PWB, Richard Crossman and Charles Douglas Jackson of *Time* Magazine. It had also become an increasingly military operation, far from the original dreams of OWI's early philosophers who had long since lost their influence (Archibald MacLeish, defeated in his dreams for the Domestic branch by conservative congressmen and the military, had by now given up and returned to the Library of Congress). But in keeping with its new prestige, acquired through the North African and Italian campaigns, it had been awarded more power and more resources.

By the spring of 1944 the men at Norfolk House were able to call on a reservoir of military and civilian manpower, a training camp and bombers and were preparing to carry their leaflet messages into Europe. The OWI side of the operation alone was expanding its London base to 1,600 people. Propaganda may not have gone the way the pioneers envisaged, but at least it had acquired a role and a respect that few had anticipated.

On 11 April, C. D. Jackson, deputy director of the G6 Division of PWD, wrote to offer Sidney the job of head of its cinema section, with Laudy Lawrence, an American wheeler-dealer, in charge of field operations. Sidney himself was to have control of policy and production. Sidney considered the proposal carefully, then turned it down. More precisely, he turned it down officially. As he explained to Jackson, given Anglo-American rivalries in the world of films, such a job, entrusted to an Englishman, could not fail to be highly contentious. In practice, he agreed to take it on, with no title. For the rest of the war, he supervised all film operations for PWD – anonymously.

On the morning of D-Day, 6 June 1944, twenty-seven million propaganda leaflets, prepared by PWD in London, were dropped along the coast between Brittany and the Zuider Zee, and a PWD team of three men went ashore in Normandy. The first film officer landed at Omaha beach near the mouth of the river Vire on the 26th and travelled to Cherbourg, hoping to find the stockpile of allied films, already dubbed and subtitled, waiting for him. They had not arrived. Using his initiative, he questioned the intelligence officers and heard that a first mobile film unit had already landed further down the coast and that they were carrying a print of *Desert Victory*. He borrowed it and put it on in Cherbourg on 6 July. There was no electricity, so he requisitioned a generator: the queues were as long as those on Broadway. His deputy, finding communications at the beachhead slow and confused, made his way to Bayeux, and set up a distribution centre for film. Eleven days after the Omaha landings the main stockpile of films was put ashore at Cherbourg.

Following the allied breakthrough, film officers, appointed by Sidney, travelled slowly behind the advancing armies, opening cinemas wherever they found electricity. One of them reached Rennes the day it was liberated and entered the town ahead of the civil affairs officers. He had the good fortune to come across an old British truck, captured by the Germans in 1940, and now abandoned in a shed. He requisitioned it and filled it with films.

When the liberation of Paris seemed imminent, the films officer gathered together enough films to supply each first-run cinema in the capital, and set off for Paris, until he was stopped by fighting on the road between Rambouillet and Trappes. Two days later, hearing that the Orléans–Paris road had been cleared, he entered Paris. Within twenty-four hours he had contacted the French representatives of the film industry who had been sympathetic to the allied cause to plan future distribution. The reopening of the Paris cinemas had to wait however until early in October, when the electricity was fully reconnected, but meanwhile a film exchange was set up to service the regions.

In the early days the French public was desperate to see anything: what one journalist called 'a genuine film hunger' seemed to grip the country. The mobile units, operating in villages which had no cinemas, set up their projectors in châteaux, barns, halls, even, on occasion, in monasteries. People walked to them for miles from the surrounding countryside. The money collected was given to the Mayor for charity.

But as time went by, the French began to demand more home-produced films, and started to complain that they were not receiving the latest films from abroad, and that some, like *Gone With the Wind*, *The Great Dictator* and Disney cartoons were being kept from them altogether. (Sidney had still not made any progress with Chaplin.)

The task facing Sidney and the PWD film unit was a formidable one. They knew from advance intelligence that there were some 4,500 cinemas in France and that these needed reopening as soon as possible. To do so they had to find not just technical expertise, but sufficient prints, and of the right kind. The question, as with North Africa and Italy, was: what exactly constituted the right kind of film? The Americans opted for escapism, and their first batch of features included *Fantasia*, *Flesh and Fantasy* and *It Started with Eve*. The British, arguing that people who had lived through four years of war were still passionately interested in it, sent films that gave them a picture of the war as lived in the allied countries: *Desert Victory*, *In Which We Serve* and *Coastal Command*. The argument between the two allies as to who was providing the better diet of films rumbled on for the remaining months of the war.

There was still a great deal of talk about making films geared specifically to the war history and needs of each country, Sidney's old argument. 'We must fill the gap of history which exists between occupation and liberation,' wrote Arthur Elton in an MoI memorandum, 'and we must explain ourselves and our culture ... we should look on each of our films, not as an entity in itself, but as part of a pattern, and we should use every available technique at our disposal ... It will remain the job of the commercial film industry to entertain and amuse, though their films can and must do a propaganda job at the same time.'

One way the planners had envisaged of putting across both their picture of the past and the messages they wished understood for the future was with newsreel. In early discussions PWD members had relied on a period after the Vichy newsreel *France Actualité* had been stopped when there would be a gap before a new French one got going; this they intended to fill, as they had in North Africa, with their own, using the time carefully to feed French hunger for news after four years of deprivation, while portraying the magnitude of the allied war effort. As it turned out, the French film industry was considerably better prepared than anyone had expected and Vichy newsreels gave way to the Gaullist *Actualité Française* with barely a pause. By 2 November, *Le Monde Libre*, the allies' hopeful contribution prepared in London, was off French screens altogether.

The organisation behind the film programme lay with Sidney who, shortly after his film officer Lacey Kastner had reached Paris, began commuting between his office in London and rooms in a requisitioned hotel in Rue St Honoré, from where he complained once again to London that there was no secretary, no furniture and no car for William Fenn, the British film officer who replaced Kastner in Paris. It was not, he wrote, a question of lack of courtesy, simply the same old 'form of inertia, inferiority complex and lack of understanding of the complex problems involved'.

Shortly after his appointment, Sidney had been presented by Eisenhower with a high-ranking SHAEF pass, which authorised him to carry out all psychological warfare duties, including 'interrogation of civilian population, and prisoners of war, photography, radio, leaflet production and distribution, news and press and poster display'. At times, he now found, his duties also ran to censorship, and any letters with references to film that sounded suspect were sent to him to vet. He also discovered that he was responsible for captured enemy film.

Given the enormous size of the job, the actual staff handling PWD films work remained incredibly small. Sidney appointed one assistant, Richard Wainwright, and three specialists, and among the five of them, and their secretaries, with their headquarters at the MoI in London, they dealt with the entire volume of production, language versions, liaison with the different ministries and with SHAEF headquarters. As each European country was liberated Sidney appointed a new films officer and an assistant to take charge of reopening the cinemas, getting in touch with local film distributors, and trying to return the film world as rapidly as possible to a normal state of commercial distribution, while ensuring that all films that came on were acceptably pro-allies.

There was a brief contretemps in the late summer when an embarrassed and apologetic Arthur Calder Marshall wrote a long memo to Sidney on the question of whether or not Jews should be appointed as film officers on the continent.

> The high percentage of Jews connected with the film business does mean that the reactionary forces, who may in certain cases be liquidated, but in most cases will be driven underground, will fix on the reinstatement of Jewish control as proof of the nazi proposition ... if a film officer makes a mistake, it will be a more serious mistake if he is a Jew than if he is an Aryan ... the political capital which the underground anti-semitic forces will be able to make out of these incidents, will reflect dangerously on our position.

Sidney's answer was terse: 'I consider that regardless of personal and racial prejudice, we must pass no "rule" which will at any time give an excuse for the elimination of the candidate best equipped for any particular job.' And there the matter ended.

In the autumn of 1944 Sidney had the idea of inviting Hitchcock over from Hollywood to make two films for the PWD about the French resistance, as a tribute to their work. Hitchcock spoke good French. Selznick, to whom Hitchcock was under contract, complained but eventually released him and the English director duly arrived by boat (there had been no room on any plane) to make *Bon Voyage* and *Adventure Malgache* (which was never released, since it failed to show the Free French, so the story went, in the truly heroic light in which they wished to be seen).

Sidney was now working harder than ever, rarely leaving his office except to go home and sleep. As the allies kept moving forward, so the size of the operation grew, with more exile governments and more films having to be dubbed and subtitled and sent forward, and more problems of co-ordination with new distributors cropping up.

Though based in London, Sidney was constantly travelling. Early in the spring of 1945 he flew to Oslo with the RAF; the Germans had just moved out, the British were moving in. Sidney went to call on the Mayor, who asked him to come and have dinner with the city councillors.

There was wine to drink, the Mayor having taken the precaution early in the war of hiding bottles in the loch. But there was only fish to eat. Sidney had an RAF aide whom he now asked if he could find some bread among the supplies brought in by the British. A number of loaves were produced and Sidney ceremoniously presented them to the Mayor. During dinner, Sidney asked what single item he had most missed during the many months of austerity. 'Cigars and cigarettes,' the Mayor and the councillors agreed. At that moment Sidney remembered that up in his room was a box of twenty-five Havana cigars, sent to him by Hitchcock. He went to collect it. There were almost, he says, tears in the men's eyes when it appeared on the table.

These were amusing interludes, but it was not a happy time in Sidney's life. The war had been taking its toll of friends, and in the late summer Sidney received news that Edward Porter, the companion of his American travels, who had recently spent a long-weekend's leave at Coppings, was missing. In reply to a letter, Commander Sharp of Porter's base wrote to tell him:

On the night that he was missing Porter was on a mining operation in the Stettin Canal. His job was to drop a line of flame floats in the canal from a low altitude. His aircraft must have been hit during this stage or shortly after as he was heard to say on the R/T 'I'm afraid I've had it and will have to bale out'. His Deputy, who was also working with him at low altitude, at once wished him the best of luck, to which Porter replied: 'Thank you'.

I understand that he sounded very calm in his conversation and appeared to be taking his time. This is substantiated by the fact that his W/T Operator was still sending messages several minutes later, and it was not until eight minutes later that he sent out his final message to the Main Force. No more was heard from the aircraft after this.

For a few more weeks, Sidney and Porter's other friends hoped to hear that he had been captured. By the autumn they gave up hoping.

Early in March 1945, the Americans crossed the Rhine. There had long been a state of awe among the allies at the efficiency and determination of the German propaganda machine under Goebbels. Top secret documents had been circulated discussing the highly centralised control of the German film industry. A special tripartite Anglo-American-Russian team had been envisaged to monitor and re-establish the film industry during the period of occupation. Censorship of existing material was to be very strict, as was that of the future German film industry that the allies pictured growing from the ashes of the old. Unlike the liberated countries, there were to be no specially produced films for Germany, both because the right German-speaking actors could not be found and because it was felt that it would be wrong to use British and American currency in return for a revenue of marks. Feature films to be shown, therefore, were going to have to be pre-1939 German films, or allied films dubbed, after the occupation, in Germany.

In the event, arriving in Germany, Sidney found that a larger number of opera houses, cinemas, concert and music halls had been destroyed than anyone had expected. He also learnt that there had been no live theatrical production in Germany for many months, since Dr Goebbels had closed all theatres, operas and cabarets, disbanded all orchestras, and suspended all artistic production in schools and universities. One result was that only a shell of an organisation now remained and at SHAEF it was felt highly unlikely that there would be much German effort at revival during the period of allied responsibility. Sidney, none the less, followed his by now established routine and started moving through the country with his film officers, getting in touch with cinema owners and distributors who did not appear to be too tainted by Nazism.

At the end of April 1945 the allies entered Buchenwald. Next day, towards the end of the afternoon, they reached Belsen. The following morning, on 22 April, Sidney came to the concentration camp. He stayed all day. That night he visited the nearest journalists' camp and persuaded an old friend, Alan Moorehead, of the *Express*, to go in and write about what he had seen. Then he drank an entire bottle of whisky; it had, friends remembered later, no effect on him at all.

Next day, he started preparing for a film on the Nazi concentration camps. It was not a totally new idea. As early as February, Sidney, George Archibald and Sergei Nolbandov, an old friend of Sidney's who had been working as a film editor for the MoI, had been discussing ways of making a film to show the Nazi atrocities that had been committed around the world, an 'objective report, almost like a criminal investigation report', Nolbandov wrote in a letter to Archibald, 'which would demonstrate the terror method used by the Germans in occupied Europe, Russia, etc.'

That was long before the liberation of the camps. Now, as reports started reaching Sidney of the enormous scale of the German extermination programme, he made plans for a 'German Special Film', an Anglo-American co-production, to be made for SHAEF and intended primarily for showing within Germany, with a second English version for distribution around the world. Sidney was absolutely clear about what he was trying to do: he wanted the Germans to see for themselves, in such a way that they could never refute it, what had been happening on German soil, and he wanted a record of the atrocities for the whole world to witness. His paper for SHAEF ran to nine pages. The psychological warfare purposes of such a film would come, he explained,

a) by showing the German people specific crimes committed by the Nazis in their name, to arouse them against the National Socialist Party and to cause them to oppose its attempts to organise terrorist or guerrilla activity under Allied occupation

b) by reminding the German people of their past acquiesence in the perpetration of such crimes, to make them aware that they cannot escape sharing the responsibility for them, and thus to promote German acceptance of the justice of Allied occupation measures.

Almost immediately, he ran into difficulties. As the footage shot by army film units throughout Germany began to reach England, horrified film people inside the MoI expressed their fear that unless the concentration camp film was wholly convincing, 'it might have a boomerang effect since the public might query its authenticity'. Not one of these observers doubted the truth of what they were seeing – the Film Censor Cecil Matthews called the material the 'most damning and incontrovertible evidence it has been my lot to view' – but it was almost too strong: how could anyone believe it?

Sidney was utterly determined to produce a documentary record of the camps. Feeling that he needed authenticating evidence for every single step he wrote to Paul Wyland, the cameraman of Movietone News who had covered the Italian camps, and asked him to take sound interviews as well as filmed records of the British officers and German SS men at Belsen itself. On 7 May he wrote to all SHAEF films people: 'Cameramen should photograph any material which will show the connection between German industry and concentration camps – e.g. name plates or incinerators, gas chambers or other equipment ... in particular attempts should be made to establish the firm which built the camp ... the makers of the tattooing and/or branding machines used for numbering prisoners.' He requested that German generals should be taken through Dachau and photographed, that local mayors be at the areas where bodies were being burned, and that all places where 'scientific experiments' had taken place should be filmed. Wherever possible, the name and address of every person who appeared on screen should be recorded and anyone speaking on camera should give his or her name, rank and war record.

'It is of extreme importance that German audiences see the faces of the individuals directly responsible, and be given opportunity to study them carefully as representative types of the Nazi elite ... The film', he wrote, 'should therefore take the form of a prosecuting counsel stating his case.' There were few better placed than Sidney to understand just how horrifying the case was.

By May 1945, some of his zeal for the project had spread around the Films Division of the MoI. Anyone going into Germany was asked to search out authentic Nazi film and archive material. But all this was taking time and by the end of the month a certain note of anxiety was appearing in Sidney's letters. He was forty-six, and had long since perfected his public persona, that of a wry, cool, humorous and understanding man: but here, as nowhere else, the tension showed. He cared deeply about what he had seen personally at Belsen, and now witnessed as the reels of film poured into his office from the other concentration camps. Indeed, it is possible that the German programme of extermination affected him more profoundly than any other single episode of his life. Not prepared to discuss these feelings, he took the one course of action open to him: he fought, with a tenacity that was at times astonishing, to produce his own contribution.

The longer the production of the film took, however, the more the authorities urged on Sidney even greater efforts at authentication. Davidson Taylor, Chief of Theatre at SHAEF, wrote to Sidney saying that he was finding within Germany that a mood of dissociation from the atrocities was fast spreading through the German people. He suggested that any film should include such horrifying footage as that of the barn in Gelsenkirchen where a thousand people had been herded into a hayrick soaked in petrol and set fire to. This, he said, might 'help rouse the personal consciences of the Germans who have allowed these cruelties to multiply within their midst'.

By early June Sidney was urging speed, but he was still writing to all his contacts for more facts, evidence, maps, names, letters, logs and lists. He had come to the conclusion that the film needed the best film-makers he could recruit, so he now summoned Hitchcock from across the Atlantic to direct it, asked Colin Wills of the *News Chronicle* to write a first outline, and appointed Solly Zuckerman to be medical and scientific adviser. Richard Crossman agreed to work on the treatment. Stewart MacAllister and Peter Tanner were to be the editors. And his film editor friend, Sergei Nolbandov – of whom Sidney once said that if ever he wanted a piece of film of elephants crossing the Alps, it would be to him that he would go – was co-ordinating the efforts of the team. It was a great tribute to Sidney that Hitchcock agreed to come. Hitchcock was fastidious to the point of obsession and hated, with what amounted to a kind of terror, the idea of sharing a cabin or a bathroom. Sidney tried, but failed, to get him a passage on a bomber. In the event, Hitchcock agreed to take the ship and had to sleep in a dormitory with thirty other people.

By the beginning of July the film ran into a new snag: OWI decided to back out. In the preceding months they had gone ahead with a newsreel compilation of the atrocities of their own and were proposing to start screening it in Germany. However the British team went ahead, and by the 24th Crossman had delivered his treatment and Hitchcock was at work in London assembling and cutting 800,000 feet of impounded and allied film material.

Today, six reels of the proposed seven reel film still exist. They are kept at the Imperial War Museum in London. Hitchcock's film opens with Hitler and the cheering crowds, and follows the allies as they move through neat and tidy orchards, and well stocked farms, into the Belsen camp, with its living skeletons, piles of bodies and staring guards. Then comes the job of cleaning up the camp. The film runs for about an hour; eleven Nazi concentration camps appear.

When it was ready Sidney had it put on for a number of Government officials in London. They were very impressed, they told Sidney. But it had all become rather awkward. In the months it had taken to prepare the film, relations with Germany had changed. To show such material, now, might make matters more difficult. Sidney had suspected there would be trouble. Donald McLachlan, of the Political Intelligence Department of the Foreign Office, had written to him in early August:

> . . . policy at the moment in Germany is entirely in the direction of encouraging, stimulating and interesting the Germans out of their apathy . . . there may therefore be no hurry for it, and rawstock and technical personnel could perhaps for the moment be spared from it for the needs which the C-in-C has stated as urgent . . .

The German atrocities film has never been shown. All the papers relating to it are kept in the Public Record Office in Kew. There is a faded buff-coloured file, Number F 3080, which includes official letters, Sidney's notes and memos, exchanges between SHAEF and the MoI. The correspondence peters out at the end of July 1945. There are references to two further files. These have vanished. The catalogue has no record of them. No one, perhaps, will ever know who took the final decision to shelve the film, nor when it became finally certain that no German was going to have to witness an incontrovertible record of the Nazis' final solution.

Sidney and Zoë were in London when the news of Germany's unconditional surrender was picked up from the German radio at lunchtime on 7 May. Even before the official announcement that the 8th would be a national holiday, Londoners poured into the streets and

Sidney and Zoë, Cecil and his wife Myra, joined the crowds in Piccadilly and Trafalgar Square. 'Isn't it wonderful?' Sidney wrote to his cousin Sidney Wolberg in America. 'Peace is divine, as the coloured Father used to say in Harlem . . . Many of the public buildings were illuminated and it was very, very exciting.' He and Zoë spent the evening of VE day alone, celebrating the victory.

He was exhausted. Now he longed to return to Coppings, to the weekend gatherings and to those of his friends who had survived the war.

Some time before the concentration camp film was nearly finished Sidney wrote to Cyril Radcliffe asking for release from the MoI. He could justifiably argue that his job was done. In the year that had passed since the allies first landed in Normandy he had supervised the setting up of production and dubbing studios in London, Paris, Brussels, Rome and Cairo; he had arranged for the showing of over a quarter of a million copies of allied film, in seventeen different languages and dialects, throughout Europe. Many millions of people, every week, whether in cinemas or at mobile units, were now watching feature films and newsreels of the free world.

When news of his departure became known, tributes to his work flocked into the MoI. From Brigadier General McClure, Chief of the Information Control Division of the US forces, came a warm letter of thanks:

> Your untiring and unselfish efforts, your sound business judgement and objective view of Anglo-American relations have made the Films Section an outstanding success. No one of our activities was more fraught with dangers or filled with greater potential frictions. The way that you handled the Film Section allowed me to breathe rather freely and left me with a feeling that the job was being done fairly and efficiently.

Sir Cyril Radcliffe added his own praise: 'I do not know what would have become of the British interest if it had not been for you and the small band of skilled people that you were able to recruit.'

Sidney wrote some letters of praise and thanks himself, mainly to people in the Hollywood film industry, and to Robert Riskin at the OWI. Just before leaving the Ministry he gave a party for a hundred wartime friends and colleagues. He and Zoë were planning to take a holiday; Sidney was dreaming, he wrote to a friend, of 'a haircut when I want it – stay in bed as long as I like – and I hope to enjoy the pleasure of refusing to answer the telephone when it rings'. He had been working without pause for just over five years.

When the war was over, General Eisenhower wrote to the Psychological Warfare Division:

> I am convinced that the expenditure of men and money in wielding the spoken and written word was an important contributing factor in undermining the enemy's will to resist and supporting the fighting morale of our potential allies in the occupied countries.

As a weapon of war British and American propaganda had turned out to be a highly efficient instrument, proving again and again that it had its role to play in demoralising the German armed forces, raising morale among resistance movements, and winning the support of people behind the allied fronts, even if the early hopeful idealism of Sidney and the founders of OWI had come to little. There had been little place for propaganda for democracy in a war being fought so expressly for military victory.

But this had not really been Sidney's business. His job had been to provide first the allies, then the occupied countries as they were liberated, with such documentary record of the war as they wanted, and films to make them forget; the balance of film propaganda had been in his hands. And this he had done, despite jealousies, rivalries, bureaucratic inertia and technical difficulties that seemed at times insurmountable. His one regret was that apart from the newsreels the contribution he cared most about, the war atrocities film, had come too late.

8

With Hitchcock in Hollywood

IN THE LATE spring of 1945, while Alfred Hitchcock was at work in London on the final rushes of the German atrocities film, Sidney invited him to Coppings for the weekend. The two of them had spent many weekends in Kent together just before and during the war, when Hitchcock was in England. For all their outward physical differences – Sidney tall, and slightly intimidating, Hitchcock short, overweight, with the look of an anxious hamster – they were in many ways amazingly alike: both of them shy and fastidious, both formal in dress and manner, both Englishmen from the East End of London (Hitchcock had been born in Leytonstone, five miles from Ilford, in 1899, the same year as Sidney), both nostalgic about music hall, and both with yearnings for the ebullience of Hollywood. They shared a love of paintings: Hitchcock was also an early collector of Paul Klee. They shared, too, a love of good wine and fine food, though Hitchcock, unlike Sidney, was an excellent cook.

Now, as the allies in Europe were beginning their final push on Berlin, Hitchcock talked to Sidney about the difficulties of being a director in Hollywood, without independent backing, always beholden to the big studios. Though already something of a name in the American film world, with *Rebecca*, *The Man Who Knew Too Much*, *The Thirty-Nine Steps* and *Jamaica Inn* behind him, he was still, as he explained to Sidney, obliged to work with people like David Selznick constantly supervising his every shot. On the Saturday night, as they finished their drink in front of the fire at Coppings, Hitchock suddenly asked Sidney whether he would consider coming in with him, as a

170

partner. No, said Sidney, he wouldn't. He didn't want to live in California and he had not yet decided what he was going to do once the war ended.

During the night, Sidney thought more about Hitchcock's suggestion. Had there perhaps been a cry for help hidden behind his invitation? After all, Hitchcock had never in his life been in a position of financial independence, able to make movies precisely as he wanted to. And wasn't it perhaps also a solution to his own dilemma of what he would do after the war? Five years at the MoI, working on a scale far more challenging and powerful than anything he had been involved with before, had given him a definite longing for expansion, something he knew the ownership of a chain of cinemas would never again satisfy. He didn't want to own a newspaper. Politics, for a variety of reasons, was out. It was too late for architecture. What else was left? Over breakfast he said cautiously to Hitchcock: 'I've been thinking. I could come in with you, set everything up, on the side, as a friend, not a partner.'

Greatly to his surprise, Hitchcock turned down the offer immediately. 'That isn't what I meant at all. I meant I was looking for someone to work with. For me, Sidney, what counts is who you work with every day.' It was a very flattering offer, a genuine testimonial of friendship from a man as wary and solitary as Hitchcock. 'All right,' Sidney said at last. 'We'll be partners.' So began a venture that was to occupy him for the larger part of the next five years, and that was to move his life and his friendships almost entirely to California.

That Sidney should now go into production was not really surprising. A lot of offers had come his way during the closing years of the war, but none had quite the same appeal. There had been, for instance, Ellen Wilkinson's suggestion that he should take over the Arts Council from Maynard Keynes, who had died. Sidney had refused: he felt he possessed neither the breadth of knowledge nor the intellectual understanding to follow the distinguished economist. Then the BBC had asked him whether he would join with his old friend Charles Cochran to set up a London Symphony Orchestra, modelled on the great American ones. Here he had been more tempted. But all initial efforts had come to nothing, thwarted largely by bureaucracy, and the project was shelved. Predictably Sidney's later reaction was to say of the failure: 'We didn't fight hard enough.' Failure is not something that he has ever readily accepted: to fail is not to have tried hard enough.

Recently, too, he had been putting out some feelers of his own. As early as September 1944, he had sent a telegram to David Selznick in Hollywood: 'Supposing my participating in film production after the war would be interested to know whether there will be any basis for discussion with you and your colleagues for granting partnership share in United Artists . . . alternating production here and in America preferably with you . . . ' Selznick's reply, characteristically running to four pages, put an end to all dreams of going in with United Artists: he told Sidney that they had already turned down other British offers. Instead, he had put forward the suggestion of a British producing unit of which he and Sidney would be joint owners. ' . . . if you will forgive my saying so probably need you less than you need me stop on the other hand think you are an extraordinary bright boy and believe we could do some interesting things together . . . ' That plan too had come to nothing.

Before it was clear that the war was coming to an end Sidney had also proposed to the Treasury a series of filmed plays, shot on stage and using an entire battery of cameras, featuring the best English actors and the masterpieces of British drama, largely as a propaganda exercise and to capture some of the excellent productions that John Gielgud was then staging at Stratford. Sir Cyril Radcliffe, to whom he had put the idea, had sent him to talk to Sir Edward Playfair, at the Treasury, who, somewhat to his surprise, agreed to allocate nearly £1 million for the project. As it was, the war finished and Sidney backed out: he needed something more demanding, more exotic, to take his mind off the years of war.

The fact that he now proposed to go into partnership with Hitchcock and accepted that he would be spending a great deal of his life in Hollywood, says something about the increasingly strong pull he felt coming from the Californian studios. He was, as he frequently said, a showman, for all the modesty and the reticence, and for a showman Hollywood was the right place to be. There was something about that world, with its flamboyancy and toughness, its showiness and energy, that acted like a charm on this most unlikely of moguls. It was all on a different plane: larger, louder, glossier and more demanding. After six years of wartime England, where the greyness seemed to be lingering on indefinitely, the image of such brightness was too much to turn down.

No sooner had Sir Cyril Radcliffe released him from the MoI than Sidney applied for a three to six months' visa for America to 'discuss possible joint film undertakings' now that the Americans and the British were no longer sharing interests as they had under SHAEF. He proposed, he told the Home Office, to give a series of lectures at Yale, Columbia and Carnegie Technical College on the subject of 'Films as weapons of warfare and instruments of education' and he gave as his sponsors the American Ambassador, Averell Harriman, William Paley, President of CBC, David Selznick and Quentin Reynolds. In a long letter to A. G. White at the Board of Trade Sidney asked for some sort of guidance as to plans for the official future of the British film industry. 'I do not want to commit myself definitely to embark on a production career', he wrote, 'until I know what writers, technicians, studios, etc. are available.' The Board of Trade's reply was not encouraging. New studios, in Britain, he was told, 'look like being a very difficult proposition for a considerable time to come'. Sidney had always envisaged production being split between England and America; in view of these words, it seemed sensible to start off in America.

Early in September, Zoë left for America to write a series of pieces on post-war America for the *News Chronicle*, which she had joined in 1944 at the invitation of its new editor, Sir Gerald Barry. She had intended to go sooner in fact, and had got as far as Holland in the late spring, only to have to turn back with severe pleurisy and go, much as Sidney had done in 1941, to recuperate in Hove. Now she flew to New York, feasting on a breakfast of orange juice and eggs and bacon, arranged for her by Hitchcock, when the plane came down to refuel in Newfoundland. In New York she took a room at the St Regis, on the mezzanine floor; she hated heights.

Before leaving to join her Sidney spent some weeks trying to gather suitable material for his lecture tour. He wrote to the heads of the British studios for 'amusing or educative' stories of the appalling difficulties of wartime production. He also had a comic exchange of cables – Sidney, like Selznick, was fast becoming addicted to the memo and the cable – with Hitchcock over a possible subject for their first film. Hitchcock was chafing at Sidney's delay and in the late summer dispatched a nine-page cable asking for his views on a film he described as 'Sidney Bernstein presents Cary Grant as Alfred Hitchcock's Hamlet a modern thriller by William Shakespeare'. This modern *Hamlet*, he informed Sidney, was to be a psychological melodrama. Cary Grant was enthusiastic; Dan O'Shea, executive vice-president of David O. Selznick Productions, had said it would be a 'terrific piece of showmanship'. Would Sidney like to find a Professor of English to do a modern language version? 'Naturally', he concluded, 'I am concerned about maintaining secrecy on this because the idea is in public domain and could easily be stolen.' Sidney, evidently, did not take the suggestion altogether seriously.

... as I see Hamlet he was a neurotic adolescent and therefore suggest you consider whether Cary's mother might outreach age sexually attractive which appears essential William Shakespeare play stop also end sequences require consideration unless you make them Japanese family but this is one heck of subject to cable about stop meantime consulting professionally friend who authority Shakespeare but understanding popular audience appeal.

As promised, he set about finding a suitable English scholar and turned to his friend Jock Dent who agreed to write him a full analysis of the various versions of *Hamlet*.

On 21 October, Sidney set sail on the *Queen Elizabeth*. He left behind him appalling gales and torrential rain, with heavy seas washing up mines along the coast of southern England. In the hold was a cabin trunk, a wardrobe trunk and two suitcases, containing the clothes he thought a long stay in America would demand: ski trousers, jodhpurs, nine suits and three overcoats. Between Halifax and New York the trunk was lost and with it six of the suits, leaving him sartorially ill-equipped, a position made all the more unfortunate by the fact that he had used all the coupons from his wartime clothes rationing for the first wardrobe and had none left over.

In New York, Sidney met Zoë and the two set off on different trips. Zoë went to Denver, Salt Lake City and San Francisco to write her articles for the *News Chronicle*; she had taught herself to tell a story well and was acquiring something of a reputation as a journalist: furthermore, she now had the luck to be present at some of the early McCarthy hearings. It is revealing of how close Zoë had become to Sidney's family that Mrs Bernstein, his mother, wrote to her from England about them. Sidney divided his time between his lecturing assignments and the West Coast.

When he reached Hollywood, Sidney settled down with Hitchcock to formulate the precise and final details of their new company. Cary Grant, who was to have joined them, was persuaded not to, Hitchcock having taken against the idea of him as partner. *Hamlet* was also put to one side, not least because an American writer, hearing of their plans, had issued a writ against them for plagiarism, pointing to a modern *Hamlet* that he had recently published and of which no one had ever heard. The case threatened to become serious. Sidney managed to dodge the summons, as did Cary Grant, still at this stage involved with them. Eventually, Hitchcock hired a lawyer and the matter was settled out of court.

In the months that they had been apart, however, Hitchcock had been thinking carefully about Sidney's old proposal to the Treasury for filming stage plays as they took place. When they now sat down to discuss the subject and nature of their first film, Hitchcock suggested to Sidney that they experiment with the technique of filming and try using single long shots, each of them the length of a full reel, but applied not to a stage play, but to a thriller. The story that he now put forward was the theme of a play that had enjoyed a successful run in the West End of London, called *Rope*, by Patrick Hamilton, based on a famous American case in which two young boys, Leopold and Loeb, murdered a third in order to prove that they were exceptionally intelligent. Hitchcock wanted James Stewart to star as the philosophy professor who taught the two boys, and later solves the crime. Sidney, who had seen the play and liked it, and felt that the decision on the content of the films really lay with Hitchcock, agreed. He was much encouraged, too, by Hitchcock's assurance that the film would be inexpensive and the shooting period – given the long single takes – very short. Given the precarious position of the British film industry, they agreed that their first film at least would be shot in America.

Warner Brothers, like every Hollywood studio on the lookout for ideas, had been watching the progress of the new partnership closely, and now stepped in with an offer to take over the production. Hitchcock and Sidney refused an outright deal but after discussion, agreed, for a share of the profits, to use Warner Brothers' studios, and an office on the site, and to let Warner's handle the distribution of *Rope*. For the rest of the backing Sidney went to Sloane Colt and Alex Ardrey of the Bankers' Trust where, to his great surprise, he was refused help. The bankers told him that they did not consider James Stewart a sound financial investment, since his ratings with the public had fallen drastically over the past six years: a recent poll had placed him thirty-sixth in popularity among male stars. 'But that was because he was in the Air Force,' Sidney protested. The bankers shrugged. Disconcerted, Sidney told Stewart what had happened: he instantly agreed to waive a fee in exchange for a percentage of the film's returns (and so made, in the end, three times as much).

Early in February, the deeds of Transatlantic Picture Corporation, as the company had been named, were signed, and Sidney decided to return to England. He flew to the East Coast, pausing briefly in Sainte Marguerite in Quebec to ski, before going to spend a few days in New York with Quentin Reynolds on Riverside Drive. Before his departure Hitchcock had ceremoniously presented him with a marble clock inscribed 'From all at Transatlantic Pictures': there was no one else in the company apart from the two of them. In reply to a cable from Cecil in London telling him that the *News Chronicle* had published a story about his partnership with Hitchcock, he now issued a short statement to the press.

The morning he was due to board the Clipper Service across the Atlantic, he woke with a high temperature. Doctors were called, then day nurses and night nurses; streptococcic throat was diagnosed. After a few weeks, he was allowed to go to Atlantic City to convalesce. There he developed gingivitis and shingles: the aftermath of the tension of the war years. When he asked the dentist who had cured him how much he owed him the man refused to take any money, saying that he had had a son in England during the war, and that everyone had been extremely kind to him.

Before he returned to England, Sidney learnt that Orson Welles was in London and phoned Zoë to ask her to look after him. (Since both Bernsteins travelled constantly, mainly on work of their own, it was not unusual to find them on different sides of the Atlantic.) She reported somewhat wryly to Olive Gardiner, Sidney's current secretary and one of several staunch and affectionate ladies who worked for him, that she was to 'lay on everything for him ... he wants 6 bottles of champagne and a bottle of Whisky and one Gin sent to him, also flowers and for you to call him (or write a note) saying that we can lend him a secretary if required ... and arrange about a car for him if he wants one (can we???) ... Also I am to arrange with Cyril Connolly and you to give a cocktail party for him ... Thank God they will only be here 3 days so if we give them the flower and egg treatment that will probably suffice.' Just of what the 'egg' treatment consisted is not clear.

In January a room in Sidney's office in Wardour Street had been set aside for Hitchcock and Transatlantic; here readers settled down to scripts. Sidney wrote to a friend, 'the problem as always is the writer. I have read the work of a great number recommended here but they are not very high quality.'

As he was beginning to find, the process of turning *Rope* from a play into a film script was not an easy one. Patrick Hamilton, the author, lived in London, and Sidney had agreed that they would work together on turning out a suitable script. Every free morning therefore Hamilton arrived at Arlington House and the two discussed the film script for *Rope*. Neither Sidney nor Hamilton could see a way of transforming one of the clues, a ticket for the theatre, which on stage could be handled in conversation, into a realistic shot on camera. At the end of three months the script was at a standstill. It was only sorted out when Sidney paid a fleeting visit to New York and went one night to see the opening of Arthur Laurents's *Heartsong*, produced by Irene Selznick, in Newhaven and later met the young author and engaged him to do a new filmscript for *Rope*. Laurents, who was subsequently to become famous for his *West Side Story*, turned in a satisfactory solution to their problem.

Though the first, and most advanced, *Rope* was not the only idea under discussion. At the end of July the historian Hugh Trevor-Roper, who was the British Intelligence Officer who had investigated Hitler's death, had sent Sidney the page proofs of his book, *The Last Days of*

Hitler. As a possible subject for a film, the idea continued to fascinate Sidney and he wrote and told Trevor-Roper so, adding that only one problem continued to perplex him, and that was how, on film, to avoid turning Hitler into a hero? 'If he is acted as the proverbial stage or cinema villain the film itself would have no value,' he wrote. 'And if the part is played to reflect his hysteria the audience would laugh in the wrong places.' Trevor-Roper replied at some length.

My suggestion is that it would be historically wrong to make Hitler a figure of fun ... What I would like an audience to think to themselves as they left such a film would be: here was, clearly, a 'great man' – a man of no ordinary stature or power, and one whose greatness is sufficiently apparent to us to enable us to see, in some measure, why he achieved such power. On the other hand, we have seen the cost at which this greatness was achieved and expressed. Every gesture of superhuman power is made at the expense of humanity, until finally the gestures which have some heroic quality, by their mere exorbitancy, when seen simply as scenes in the Bunker, are seen also as meaningless rhodomontade to which a very real value, and the future of Germany, is sacrificed ... I would not try to caricature Hitler's real stature; but I would emphasize the fatal price which was necessary to exhibit it. The bombed cities, the concentration camps, the blown bridges and factories, and the defeated and conquered people, are the conditions upon which the heroics of the Bunker depend; and in this context, Hitler is not a ridiculous but a terrible figure, a warning that abstract qualities like 'greatness', 'heroism', 'faith', etc, which it is so easy uncritically to admire, can really only be judged by descending to earth and examining their application, their direction and their cost ...

Sidney, deliberating how best to proceed, took the precaution of registering the title and now commissioned the Audience Research Company in Hollywood to carry out a public survey of the idea as the subject matter for a film. The report, when it arrived, was not encouraging. Most of the men who had been questioned welcomed the subject, but the women were almost unanimous in their disapproval. Sidney consulted Hitchcock again, then asked Rank in Britain whether they might be interested in coming in on the film as a co-production. Rank declined, and the idea was put on one side, and later dropped altogether.

Meanwhile, Transatlantic Pictures was attracting considerable outside interest. Not long after his return to London Sidney was approached by Frank Launder and Sidney Gilliat, two former screenwriters turned director-producers who had worked earlier with Hitchcock on *The Lady Vanishes* and now wanted to join the company, acting as quasi-independent directors under the company banner. In one of their regular Sunday-morning telephone conversations across the Atlantic – Sidney and Hitchcock spoke regularly every week when not in the same country – Sidney told him about the offer and Hitchcock seemed enthusiastic, agreeing that it should be up to Sidney to work out the details. Just before the contract was due to be signed, Frank Launder asked Sidney who had the final say in the company. 'I do,' replied Sidney.

'Well, who has the final say between you and Hitchcock?'

'I do,' said Sidney. 'I have to, because otherwise we could find ourselves in a situation where nothing got done. But I'm well aware of the fact that the moment I exercise it, it's the end of our partnership.' The clarity and business sense was typical of Sidney, but it did not please Launder and Gilliat, who withdrew from the deal.

As the company began to take shape more and more outsiders hovered, eager to join them, yet uncertain about what they really wanted to do in the confusion that followed the war. Even before *Rope* was cast, Hitchcock and Sidney had already gone ahead with plans for a second production, *Under Capricorn*, a melodrama set in Australia at the time of penal settlements, to be filmed in England. Ingrid Bergman, who had starred in the highly successful *Notorious* for Hitchcock, had agreed to play the female lead. James Mason, currently undecided about whether to move to Hollywood or wait for the revival of the British film industry, invited Sidney to lunch at his house in Hertfordshire to discuss the possibility of starring opposite her. There were two main parts for men, and Mason followed up the lunch with a letter to Sidney: 'You remember that I said of Capricorn that I was slightly alarmed that the other man's part seemed perhaps more important than the one you suggested I should play ... ' Sidney liked Mason, but this was his first encounter as a producer with the susceptibility of stars. Talks with Mason came to nothing, though the actor later became a friend of his.

During the summer of 1946 the weekends at Coppings resumed. Little had been altered by six years of war, except that perhaps the cast was somewhat different. Film people were beginning to come more often; journalists and academics, who once had filled the house with their anxieties about fascism and the rise of the right, less. Sidney's world was changing. Edward Porter was dead; Komisarjevsky had remarried and gone to live in America; there had been a falling out with Voigt over the Berlin correspondent's seemingly rapid move from left to right (Cedric Belfrage had accused him in the *News Chronicle* of

20 Cecil Bernstein, Sidney's brother

above 21 Sidney with Quentin Reynolds, the day before Granada went on the air, 2 May 1956

left 22 Sean O'Casey

opposite above left 23 Victor Peers

opposite above right 24 Herbert Fontaine

opposite below left 25 Denis Forman

opposite below right 26 Joe Warton

27 Alex and Sidney Bernstein with Denis Forman and their pilot on their way to Granada Television Centre, Manchester, 1973

28 Sidney with Teddy Kollek, Mayor of Jerusalem since 1965, at a London dinner, 1979

being anti-patriotic and Voigt had sued and won the case: there was some feeling in Voigt's mind that the plot had been hatched at Coppings, though he later asked Sidney to be godfather to his daughter Evelyn); and Cedric and Molly Belfrage, who had gone to America in 1936, had now settled permanently in New York. There was more drink, and more talk of movies, and when Burgess Meredith brought Paulette Goddard for the weekend she wore a crimson evening dress so exotic that two visiting godchildren were unable to eat their ice creams. Zoë, who found the film world somewhat daunting and missed the cosiness of her Fleet Street friends, went on a jaunt with Beryl Stone and an American cousin of Sidney's to Paris, and wrote wistfully to Rufus and Philip Jordan, friends now working at the British Embassy in Washington:

> It's a mackintosh summer and everyone over twenty five is suffering those aches we try to wash away with whisky if you have it ... But me, I must admit to be struggling through the phase known as putting your back into it: I dream of Arizona and steaks and charming morons who laugh a lot and talk a lot for no other reason than they are full of food and enjoy good dentistry.

Early in May Sidney had put in a request to the military authorities that he be allowed to attend the final days of the Nuremberg Trials. He had received a cautious letter of acceptance in return in which it had been pointed out to him that the authorities were above all eager to get across two points to the world at large: one was that every criminal, however bad, gets a hearing, and the other that every man, however great, is brought to justice. As the date of the trials' conclusion grew nearer, however, the press for space in the courtroom grew so great that it was only Sidney's contact with Sir Norman Birkett that finally earned him a place. On 20 September, he flew to Berlin and wandered around the streets, flattened and no longer familiar, in search of remembered landmarks, then travelled on next day by American plane to Nuremberg.

The city was packed. Sidney found himself billeted in a room with the *Express*'s Beverley Baxter, who kept talking about the way the war had been won by the Conservative Party. Sidney found it all very unreal. He was in the courtroom as each of the sentences was read out, and he marked them down carefully in a notebook, the verdicts alongside the names: all twenty-one who had stood trial, whether present or in absentia, guilty; all, except for six, to die by hanging. He was there when Goering, found guilty on all four counts of the indictment – conspiracy, waging of aggressive war, commission of war crimes and commission of crimes against humanity – was sentenced to

179

hang, but failed to hear the sentence not once but three times, because his headphones were not working, so that a young American corporal had to vault over the barrier and adjust his set. Sidney felt no pity. He listened to the conversations about the legality of the trial, evening after evening among the journalists he knew who were covering the proceedings, but he couldn't forget Belsen. He wrote to William Fenn, his former films officer in Paris, after one session in the courtroom: 'Nuremberg was very satisfying in a strange way although seeing eleven people sentenced to death wants a little stomaching. But I think the Tribunal has been worthwhile and I have hopes of its effect upon man.' It was somehow very like him that, faced with events that genuinely distressed and affected him, he put them aside, and for public consumption added a note of black humour: 'On judgment day,' he told Fenn, 'the attraction at the local cinema was a film called "Swing Parade of 1946".'

Sidney returned to England in time to attend a dinner given in his honour by the British Film Producers Association at the Dorchester Hotel, in which he spoke of himself unequivocally and for the first time as a 'producer'. The days of being an 'exhibitor' were over.

There was nothing now to keep him in London any longer, and he set about planning what was to be a long stay in California while *Rope*, finally scripted and cast, was shot. The Bernsteins had taken a house in a suburb of Los Angeles, Bel Air with its tropical splendour and brilliance, and Miss Goodwin, their white-haired housekeeper at Arlington House, to go with them.

Hollywood had been altered remarkably little by the war. In 1947 the great changes that were eventually to hit the world of the movie moguls, and obliterate for ever their power and their fiefs, had not yet arrived, though there was an intimation on the horizon. The old colony was still more or less complete and the refugees from Hitler who had so enriched the studios during the war years had not yet returned to Europe. Hollywood, the Bernsteins discovered, as they settled into their rented house at Palm Drive, with Miss Goodwin and a black maid, was very comfortable, very lively and full of friends.

Apart from Hitchcock, his wife Alma and daughter Pat, who, after some years of uncertainty, had decided to put down serious roots in America and had bought a house on Bellagio Road, overlooking the golf course at Bel Air, as well as a weekend retreat near Santa Cruz, there were the Chaplins, Victor Saville, Peter Lorre (who had lived with Sidney in Albermarle Street in the 1930s after Sidney got him out of Germany), and Bertolt Brecht and Charles Laughton, hard at work on a first production of *Galileo* for John Houseman's Coronet Theatre. It was the age of the musical and the productions that were to make MGM famous were bringing people like Adolph Green and Betty Comden to Hollywood and a lot of fun and music to the parties to which Sidney and Zoë found themselves invited. Ira and George Gershwin were friends. At their house on North Rocksbury Drive a light was left on late into the night to show friends that they would be welcome; after dinner Ira Gershwin would sit at the piano and play songs from his early shows. Sidney found that he was thought of as an authority on old Hollywood and was amused when young newcomers sat at his feet to hear tales of the fabulous early days. To many, he seemed very different from the usual type of Hollywood producer: slightly withdrawn, even forbidding, with considerable subdued energy, but none of the bonhomie of the true Californian.

Zoë, who looked so charming and so elegant, was and remained a little anxious in this very different world, all the more so as there really was nothing much for her to do. Sidney, on the other hand, blossomed and it was in these early post-war years that he began to make friends with many people whose company he valued and who were to become completely devoted to him. Adolph Green and Betty Comden, close friends to this day, remember with fondness the occasion of their first proper meeting. They had been introduced briefly at a party and liked each other. Soon afterwards a chauffeur-driven car purred softly up behind them as they were walking along a street in Beverly Hills and stopped. It was Sidney: they were instantly delighted and amazed at the informality and friendliness of so formal-seeming a man. They, in return, made him laugh. Friends like these, made in America – Moss and Kitty Hart, Marietta Peabody, later Mrs Ronald Tree, the Murrows, the Reynolds – have been a lasting and extremely agreeable ingredient of his life.

The Bernsteins had arrived in Hollywood shortly before Hitchcock was to start shooting. From the first, the two men, in their impeccable dark suits and white shirts (Sidney, during his entire life, has never abandoned his own particular style of formal dress) in vivid contrast to Cecil B. de Mille's jodhpurs, or the more usual West Coast polo shirt and slacks, settled into a routine. Sidney spent every day on the set, watching the shooting, but taking care not to interfere. Hitchcock had finally decided in favour of their earlier idea of making *Rope*, not using the conventional five- to fifteen-second 'takes', but in long, continuous shots lasting ten minutes, the entire film roll in the camera magazine. It was to be the first time that such a technique had been tried out and what appealed to Hitchcock was the challenge of seeing whether such a thing was in fact possible on film, whether it could introduce some of the tension of the live stage performance. It was also his first colour film. Sidney, the observer, was fascinated: he shared with Hitchcock an intense interest in the practicalities of the job. What was more, he was curious, as he had been all his life, about every detail going on around him.

In the evening, he went back with Hitchcock to watch the rushes and discuss the day's shooting. Alma, who was herself a scriptwriter, would join in the talk, usually over dinner, either cooked by Hitchcock, who spent what free time he had lovingly at work in the kitchen, or at one of his chosen Hollywood restaurants. Alma, who like Hitchcock preferred an unpretentious and unfussy life, also cooked and shared his taste for determinedly English surroundings: chintz curtains and armchairs and heavy polished oak furniture. They were a close and very dependent couple and both devoted to their only child, Pat.

Hitchcock, always fat, was constantly worrying about dieting. He kept rigidly to black coffee for breakfast, a steak and beans or broccoli for lunch. Over dinner, he would try to tempt Sidney with a soufflé. When Sidney succumbed, Hitchcock would eat half of it, and next morning complain bitterly that his diet had been broken. Stories of Hitchcock's gastronomic passions were becoming legendary. By the time Sidney reached Hollywood in the late 1940s, Hitchcock had already made an agreement with friends in New York, Los Angeles and England by which a supply of frozen sole and plaice reached him regularly. He showed Sidney how to thaw the fish carefully in cold water.

They never quarrelled, though Hitchcock was in many ways and for many people a difficult man, uneasy, vulnerable yet very intimidating, with his practical jokes and his acute shyness. That was possibly because Sidney had such a strong sense of his own role in the partnership and was scrupulous about keeping to his side of it, and because he was rapidly taking over full control of all business matters, a chore Hitchcock had always loathed. It was, too, because Sidney never actually quarrelled with anyone. The word doesn't apply to him. He may be furious, obstinate, even dictatorial, but he is not argumentative. With friends, if he disagrees, he seems to withdraw, though not to capitulate.

After two days of filming in technicolour they decided they would like to see the rushes, not in the usual black and white, but in technicolour. The laboratories were reluctant and said that they had never had such a request before but finally, under Sidney's insistence, yielded. It was as well that they did, because it turned out that the cameraman had failed to follow Hitchcock's instructions about the lighting, and the New York skyline, when it came to sunset, was bathed in an improbable orange colour, rather as if the city were on fire. Five reels had to be shot again adding nine days to the schedule. Left to himself, Hitchcock, who hated confrontations, would merely have asked the same cameraman to do the job again. Sidney was not prepared to. He discussed the technical side of it with the cameraman, concluded that he was not going to be able to adapt to what they wanted, and asked for his resignation.

The English side of the company had been run from London by Victor Peers, a studio manager for Gaumont British whom Hitchcock had known in the 1930s. Victor Peers and Sidney had met once, during the war. When Sidney was looking for the right man to run the Crown Film Unit for the MoI he was told about Peers, who was in the Air Force. Sidney asked for him to be found and sent to see him. Twenty-four hours later Peers arrived in his office. Sidney put to him what was clearly a very inviting offer. Peers explained that he preferred to stay in the services since he had served in the RAF in the First World War, and his son was serving in it now. 'But', he concluded somewhat bitterly, 'with your authority I'm sure you can order me to join you.' Sidney got to his feet. 'Thank you, Mr Peers, perhaps we'll meet again after the war.' Peers now crossed the Atlantic to join them in California, a modest, cautious man, much liked by all those who met him, with an absolutely clear instinct for the complexities of the film business.

The three men, for they took on no one else, had a great deal of fun. They worked either from a room in Hitchcock's house, or at the Warner Brothers studios. When Sidney was told by an employee that Jack Warner, the more tycoon-like and aggressive of the brothers, with his small moustache and dapper appearance, received a copy of every Western Union telegram dispatched from his studios, he and Hitchcock started inventing joke ones calculated to perplex and tease him.

In the evenings they sometimes went to Hitchcock's regular restaurants, Chasens or Romanov's, where Hitchcock would be served with his invariable steak, and they would watch the other diners and talk about film life. Hitchcock, who never wrote letters, was a famous raconteur, talking hour after hour in that slow, deadpan voice, with its traces of Cockney, rarely smiling, always extremely funny. They seldom invited anyone else to join them. Hitchcock would never ask anyone to dinner until he felt he knew the person well. There were no unplanned engagements, no casual visitors. It suited Sidney very well: he liked the ease and the domesticity of the household and it was here that he spent some of his happiest times in Hollywood. However, to outsiders, the seclusion, in a city that fed on publicity and exuberance, was incomprehensible, and Sidney came to be touched by Hitchcock's reputation for being a little odd, defiantly English. Neither went much to parties; neither had affairs with film stars. Of the two Hitchcock was regarded as by far the more eccentric, with his habit of falling sound asleep after dinner, wherever he was.

One night, Evelyn Waugh, who had a ferocious and inexplicable hatred for Hitchcock, came into the Bel Air Hotel while the two friends were there. Sidney turned to Hitchcock: 'Let's pretend we're having a really funny time. Whatever I say, you laugh, and I'll do the same.' They started laughing. Soon they couldn't stop. From across the aisle, Evelyn Waugh, his face purple with loathing, sat glaring at them, in silence.

Another evening, while Sidney was staying in the Hitchcocks' house in Bel Air with its chintzes and polished brass, there was an earthquake. Sidney, Alma and Hitchcock stood in their dressing-gowns in the main corridor as the walls creaked, the pictures swayed and the furniture rattled. Next day at the studio all the talk was of the event. That night, Sidney was dining with the Chaplins. They came to collect him and Sidney had barely climbed into the car when Oona described to him their own experience of the earthquake. Charlie, she said, had rushed into her room saying urgently: 'Come on, come on, hurry, get out.' 'But what about the children?' she had replied. 'To hell with the children,' Chaplin had declared. Oona told the story affectionately, for Chaplin was devoted to his children. It was simply, Sidney reflected, that he loved her more than anybody else.

There was something about this way of life that delighted Sidney, though Zoë increasingly found the exuberance oppressive. It wasn't just the energy and the enthusiasm. But there was a sort of openness in the way the movie people behaved towards each other that had been totally lacking in everything that he had known in England. Not long after reaching Hollywood John Huston had called on him to see whether he could be of help by reading any of the proposed Transatlantic scripts. When one was ready he picked it up, studied it at length, and discussed it. Sidney found this sense of easy, unambivalent camaraderie exhilarating, so different from the studio atmosphere in England.

1947 was a year of extraordinary activity for Sidney. It was as if, released from the war and the directives and orders of others, his energy had to flow everywhere at once. There was almost no film matter, on either side of the Atlantic, on which his advice was not sought. In the British film world there was a growing anxiety about the promised new Cinematograph Act. As Sidney wrote to Harold Wilson and Sir Stafford Cripps at the Board of Trade, small independent circuits like Granada were being discriminated against by the power of the two large combines, who had formed second booking groups of their own, in such a way that the major films, instead of being available after a first run to the independents, were now effectively taken up by the second circuits. In his letters he asked for legislation to restrict this practice. Meanwhile, in America, he became much involved in the frantic discussions that broke out in the studios when Hugh Dalton, the British Chancellor of the Exchequer, suddenly announced Customs Duty of 75 per cent to be prepaid on the value of all films imported into England. The measure had been introduced, as usual, to protect the once again ailing British industry, but it had devastating effects. Led by Nicholas Schenck of MGM in Hollywood the studios passed a resolution to suspend indefinitely all shipments of film to Britain. After a great deal of talk on both sides of the ocean, and a great number of letters and meetings, the order was rescinded. It had become apparent that the British public, by now addicted to their American diet, were extremely reluctant to give up the Hollywood epics for long. Dalton agreed to withdraw the Customs Duty, while raising the quota of British-made movies to be seen on British screens from 20 per cent to 45 per cent.

1947 was also the year that Sidney's sixth cinema questionnaire was published, and while much of the actual work was in the hands of Ewart Hodgson at Granada, some of it inevitably concerned Sidney. The questionnaires had now been running for some twenty years, at considerable cost, since 120,000 forms were issued each time, but also to considerable and by now worldwide acclaim. By 1947 there was the added interest that there were five samples with which to compare the new questionnaire, and the fact that ten years had elapsed since the last. The results reached Sidney in Hollywood by telegram. Given his new venture, they could hardly have been more pleasing. Alfred Hitchcock was leading the field as the most popular director on the British screen, with Sir Alexander Korda, Orson Welles and Noël Coward some way behind. It was a pity however that discussions with James Mason had come to nothing: he topped the male actors' poll.

Once again, 2,000 of the questionnaires went out to 'prominent' people, some of them personal friends of Sidney's. Almost the first back came from Bernard Shaw, who wrote: 'Bless you, I haven't seen a film for years. I'm too old for play and picture going. GBS.'

In the course of the year the Bernstein brothers, communicating largely by cable, decided to extend the questionnaire to children, partly in response to a battle that had broken out in the newspapers over the suitability of the films shown in Children's Matinees, not just at the Granadas, but also in the Odeons and Gaumonts. Some of the films shown, critics suggested, were too violent; others not educational enough. Cecil, in Sidney's absence, asked their child psychologist friend, Dr Emmanuel Miller, to comment on the Granada matinees. Dr Miller reported that he had found the Westerns 'emotionally quite innocuous', but that the newsreel had seemed 'singularly uninstructive' and that pictures in which either children or animals were mistreated should be 'rigidly excluded'. Later, Dr Miller helped draw up a questionnaire designed for children. Characteristically, the Bernsteins had been quicker off the mark than the other circuits. Their questionnaire lent them an immediately authoritative voice to allay the wild parental fears that had broken out, particularly as Dr Miller was able to conclude from his researches that 'it can be said with certain reservations that these children's performances do not provoke any alarming responses'.

The controversy was not quite dead however. In May 1950, in the week that the Government brought out a report by the Departmental Committee on Children and the Cinema, *Picture Post* sent a photographer with an infra-red camera to a children's matinee to catch the expressions of the children as they watched. Their reactions were indeed startling: alarm, fear, shock, disbelief.

Rope opened in New York in September 1948 at the Globe Theatre. Earlier, Sidney had cabled to Cecil that the 'one and only preview enormous success and Warners very confident will be big hit'. They were slightly over-optimistic. *Rope* received cautiously good reviews. *Time and Tide* called Hitchcock's techniques 'brilliant, exciting and stimulating' but the subject came in for a good deal of attack. In London, when it opened in November, the *New Statesman* deplored the new mania for violence, saying that the film was as good as any Hitchcock had made but that it fascinated 'by an eel-like passage through actuality'.

As *Rope* began to be sold abroad, there were a number of setbacks. Both the French and the Italian censors banned it, on the grounds of excessive violence and 'sadism'. (From South Africa came word that the film was doing well: just before *Rope* opened in Johannesburg two young Jewish boys had been arrested for murdering a girl.) The English reviews were, on the whole, tepid, and history has given *Rope* a low place among Hitchcock's films. The long, continuous shot as invented by Hitchcock and Sidney, which demanded incredibly complicated technical innovations – a whole special floor, mobile clouds dangling from wires, furniture mounted on rollers – is thought neither to have justified its expense (one and a half million dollars) nor to have added anything to film technique, other than a sense of experiment. 'I undertook *Rope* as a stunt,' Hitchcock told François Truffaut in 1965. 'That's the only way that I can describe it. I really don't know how I came to indulge in it.'

Long before *Rope* opened, however, Transatlantic was well advanced with the second film, *Under Capricorn*. The final cast included Joseph Cotten and Michael Wilding, as well as Ingrid Bergman, with whom Sidney now formed a close and lasting friendship. There had been a long and confused quest for scriptwriters during which dozens of possible people, both English and American, had been considered. Some had been rejected; others had rejected themselves. Rodney Ackland was considered too busy; J. B. Williams too pedestrian; Peter Ustinov too expensive; Enid Bagnold too difficult to work with.

The decision had been made to shoot the film in England, and while Sidney returned to London, in the spring of 1948, to set up the production, Hitchcock remained in Hollywood shooting a trailer for *Rope*. He arrived at Pinewood studios to find a great array of problems. Within days of starting work the electricians walked out on strike, after two of their members were sacked for coming to work late two days running. Though their case was against MGM and not Transatlantic, it cost the company £2,000. As Ingrid Bergman reported to a friend in Hollywood: 'It is a hostile feeling on the set that just kills you. People hardly look or speak to you.'

Then Ingrid Bergman herself hated Hitchcock's new technique of continuous long shots that he insisted on using again, complaining that the system of rehearsing one day and shooting the next made everyone nervous. There were arguments. Sidney did not interfere. He stood, silently, on the edge of the set, watching.

After one particularly bitter altercation, when Ingrid Bergman protested that an eleven-minute continuous shot, in which the camera followed her around the house, was an impossible demand, Hitchcock agreed to play the scene two ways: his way, and the more conventional method of breaking it up into small takes. Viewing the rushes that night, Ingrid Bergman agreed that Hitchcock's method gave the finer result. 'Some of these damned long scenes work out very well,' she wrote to her friend Ruth. After that, peace was restored. Perhaps to soothe frayed tempers, Sidney gave an enormous party for Ingrid Bergman at the Savoy.

But *Under Capricorn* did not go well. Michael Wilding's voice came out indistinct and garbled and Sidney had to find a voice specialist to coach him over the weekends. He got pleurisy and fell behind in his schedules.

The culminating blow came when Hitchcock returned to Hollywood to shoot the exteriors and the weather was so bad that filming was delayed for two weeks, by which time the Warner Brothers lot was booked for another production. When the film was completed, the colour was found to be faulty, and the film itself too long, and too slow to get started. Frantic cables, with suggested cuts, flashed backwards and forwards across the Atlantic between Hitchcock and Sidney. 'Continuity, 6000 miles away,' reported Sidney pathetically in a letter to Victor Peers, 'appears to be a little difficult to control.'

Under Capricorn opened in New York at the Radio City Music Hall on 8 September 1949. Sidney cabled Harold Wilson at the Board of Trade to ask him to get all the publicity for it that he could as it was the first British movie to receive its première in America. Early reviews were unexpectedly good, with Louella Parsons, the doyenne of the columnists, awarding Michael Wilding the laurel of best supporting actor. Some called it Ingrid Bergman's finest performance. Walter Winchell wrote: 'Bergman – they clap her and love her.'

The voices of praise did not last. Some time in the previous year Ingrid Bergman had gone to see Roberto Rossellini's *Open City*. She had been immensely impressed, and wrote to tell the Italian director so, asking whether he might be able to find a part for her in one of his films. Rossellini had been flattered and later that year had come to pay her a visit in California; what had started as a simple business interest turned into a love affair. Ingrid Bergman was married at the time to a Swedish neurosurgeon called Petter Lindstrom. Rossellini was with Anna Magnani.

Just before *Under Capricorn* was released, Ingrid Bergman took off to join Rossellini in Stromboli where they were to make a film together. Before leaving, she promised Hitchcock and Sidney that she would take no action of any kind to publicise what she was doing until *Capricorn* had been showing for two months. The Hays Code was still virulently in force in America and a scandal could have a ruinous effect on the box-office returns of a film.

Shortly after the opening night in New York the scandal broke. Ingrid Bergman had not behaved with the greatest discretion in Stromboli and Rossellini, in such financial straits that his creditors were trying to impound the film, had persuaded Ingrid Bergman to issue a statement on the grounds that it would pacify them. Michael Wilson, who worked for RKO, backers of the film, wrote to warn Sidney: 'She is completely infatuated all over again now that the film is virtually ended.' The day the story appeared in the American papers Sidney was in New York. He went to Radio City Music Hall and questioned the long queues winding around the block outside: 'What do you think about Miss Bergman's escapades?' Most of them had no view. They hadn't read the papers. When they did, the queues began to fade away. The Catholic organisations in America banned the film, and gradually, as they watched and remembered the moral strictures of the times, even the cinema owners began to turn against it.

Sidney was as worried about Ingrid Bergman as he was about the success of his film. He wrote to her in Stromboli, giving her news of the good early reviews and urging her to come over for the London opening on 6 October. Ingrid Bergman hesitated, then refused. 'I don't intend ever again of my own free will to see the press and answer questions,' she replied. 'I really believe this will be the end of me. I am perfectly willing to pay for my own faults – but I also have to pay for the mistakes of others, for their ambition, for their pride and their eagerness to talk for me. I don't need a bridge to America, Sidney, for I don't intend to go back.'

Sidney's closeness to Ingrid Bergman at this stage mystified Hitchcock: although he was extremely fond of her, treating her, as he did all his leading ladies, with a mixture of edginess and geniality, he couldn't understand her behaviour in running off, so publicly and at such a time, with Rossellini, nor why Sidney defended her. She had a certain position to keep up, he would say to Sidney; what she was doing simply wasn't right.

Later, when Ingrid Bergman did come to England, Sidney did all he could to help in the fight she and Lindstrom waged over custody of their only daughter, Pia. Coppings became a centre for family meetings. 'Sidney', Ingrid Bergman said many years later, 'was the most generous and thoughtful of friends. It was a mark of his character that he was in fact the only person I know to have made friends with all three of my husbands.' (And, she added, the only producer she had worked with not to have made a pass at her.)

When *Under Capricorn* opened in London, Sidney acted as host to Sir Stafford Cripps and twenty members of the Cabinet. The film, greeted indifferently by the British critics, did not last long on the circuits and was something of an economic disaster for Transatlantic though the losses were eventually covered by the sale of the television rights. In the end the bank that had financed it reclaimed the picture. Only in recent years has it become a cult of the French cinema.

If Sidney was particularly sympathetic to Ingrid Bergman, it may in part have been because he was having problems with his own marriage. Hollywood had not worked out well for Zoë: she was fond of their closer friends, but found the larger world of the studios with their intrigues and their brashness too much for her. Increasingly, over the years of Sidney's involvement with Hollywood, she had found excuses to leave earlier and go home ahead of him when he made trips back to Europe. When the moment came to return, she delayed, wanting to spend time with her family and her own close friends, like Brenda Christiansen,

Molly Belfrage or John Rayner, Fleet Street people whose style of life she greatly preferred to the grandeur of Sidney's. Inevitably, there had been rows: friends in America noticed how rarely she accompanied him to parties. Long before Sidney was ready to leave America for good, she returned to London.

Perhaps because Sidney was so intensely caught up in business activities more demanding than any in which he had previously been involved, or perhaps, as he says himself, because he and Hitchcock were Englishmen, the political witch-hunts in Hollywood that began in 1947 touched him personally, and Transatlantic in general, very little. It was not until the small, rednecked insurance broker J. Parnell Thomas, head of the House of Representatives Un-American Activities Committee, was well into his mission to 'expose and ferret out' communist sympathisers in Hollywood that Sidney really took in what was happening.

The Un-American Activities Committee had been in existence since the 1930s but all previous attempts to investigate Hollywood had been met with derision. Now, as the Cold War spread, the Hollywood villains stopped being Nazis and turned into communists. The early investigation of 'friendly witnesses', endlessly filmed and photographed, were like scenes from the movies; even the evidence tended to sound like a script. Then came the stand of the 'unfriendly' ten, who decided to take the Fifth Amendment rather than be sucked further into proceedings that had degenerated into brawls and shouting matches.

The world most under attack in Hollywood was the world Sidney knew best: it included the liberal writers and actors and directors whose sympathies and interests lay closest to his own. Among them were people like Burgess Meredith, interrogated early in the year, Brecht, who left the country, and Lillian Hellman, who ceased to get commissions for scripts. Sidney was in Hollywood and following the proceedings carefully when in October the Washington hearings opened and planeloads of stars flew to the capital in support of the 'unfriendly' witnesses, led by Humphrey Bogart and Lauren Bacall, a close and good friend of Sidney's. He was in Hollywood for the fund-raising parties of those blacklisted and subpoenaed and gave generously when he could. But he was never touched by the proceedings himself, though he did put up a fight to employ Ben Shan to design Transatlantic Pictures' posters and publicity. He lost it. Ben Shan was on Warner Brothers' blacklist and by the time Sidney wanted to use him the small type on studio contracts included a clause banning 'communists'. The witch-hunts, with their hysteria, their idiocy and their cowardice, probably affected him, as they did many others, only as it became clear that they were all part of the dissolution of Hollywood, in stripping the studios of all intellectual confidence for more than a decade to come.

Sidney, in any case, had a battle of his own to fight, on the other side of the Atlantic. It stemmed, ironically, from a perceptive and altruistic campaign of his own, in the war, to conserve dwindling British reserves of film rawstock.

In 1943, the Board of Trade, in response to a suggestion of Sidney's, had passed the Cinematograph Film Order Control, under which neighbouring cinemas, instead of receiving individual copies of newsreels, would 'cross over' and share a single copy. The agreement, issued under the Emergency Powers Act, was to remain in force for as long as the Order lasted.

By the late spring of 1947 Sidney was complaining that the order should be rescinded as it was now being used to save dollars, not rawstock. The quality of the newsreels allocated to cinemas under the agreement had fallen so drastically that only by reintroducing a sense of competition could any sort of improvement be achieved. Prompted by Sidney, John Foster asked questions in the House of Commons. Sidney himself wrote Sir Stafford Cripps, and later Harold Wilson, at the Board of Trade long and reproachful letters.

Finally, since no action was forthcoming, he chose one of his cinemas in Aylesbury, belonging to his London and District Cinemas group, and gave four weeks' notice that he was going to terminate the contract and stop taking the newsreels from 20th Century Fox and Movietone. Sidney was in New York at the time of his decision. He rang Victor Peers, by then back in London, and asked him to produce a newsreel for Granada Theatres, to be ready in two weeks' time. Victor Peers was appalled. 'What with?' he asked frantically down the telephone. 'Well,' replied Sidney, reassuringly from five thousand miles away, 'go round to all the Embassies and see what they can give you. I have already arranged for you to have the rights to a World Newsreel produced here. Let's call it International Newsreel.' By the time the official contract had come to an end, Granada's own newsreel was ready.

For a while, the newsreel companies did nothing. Then Movietone, owned half by 20th Century Fox and half by Lord Rothermere, sued. Sidney hastily commissioned an analysis of the contents of Movietone newsreels and was able to show in court that sport was their staple item, commanding seventy-six items for every fourteen for military parades, eleven for disasters, sixteen for world affairs, two for elections, three for trade union matters and fifty-three for Royalty.

Nevertheless, at the first hearing Mr Justice Slade decided in Movietone's favour, declaring that Granada was still bound by its contract.* Sidney, ever litigious, took it to the Court of Appeal, despite a message from his friend Sir Cyril Radcliffe to save his money as he had no chance of succeeding. However, there Lord Justice Denning on behalf of the three judges reversed the decision, saying that 'the words of a contract should not be allowed to become tyrannical masters'. Movietone immediately asked for, and were granted, leave to carry it to the House of Lords.

In the House of Lords, Sidney lost. As he was leaving the court he met Sir Gordon Craig, head of Movietone, strolling past the Law Courts. 'Ah well, Sidney,' he said smugly, 'that settles that.'

'Oh no, it doesn't,' replied Sidney smartly. 'That was a case for only one cinema. We have another thirty-eight. We shall take the case up for each one of them.'

Before anyone had a chance to act, the matter was solved. Nobody will ever know whether Sidney would actually have carried out his threat. On 1 October 1950 Harold Wilson managed to pass a Bill revoking the Film Control Order of 1943. Cinemas were now able to enter into whatever arrangement they chose with the newsreel companies.

The third Transatlantic film was *I Confess*, an adaptation of a French story called 'Redemption' by Louis Verneuil, which itself had been based on a play by Paul Anthelme, *Nos deux Consciences*, first produced in Paris in 1902. The plot revolved around a priest who is convicted of a murder committed by a man who has confessed the crime to him in the confessional – perfect in every sense for that element of tortured suspense so loved by Hitchcock. *I Confess* was to be shot in French Canada, the closest Hitchcock and Sidney could get to the original setting.

Like *Under Capricorn*, *I Confess* was fated to suffer disasters: only in this case they started far earlier. Long before casting even began, Olive Gardiner, Sidney's secretary, was warning that the outline, prepared by Lesley Storm, was likely to be 'classified as both anti-social and amoral by all the Associations, Societies, Borough and County Council and hospital after-care welfare workers'. Several more scriptwriters were brought in.

There were also a number of difficulties inherent in the story itself, not least of them the problem of making it plausible when reset in the context of Canada. Sidney asked Stuart Legg, Grierson's assistant and former film-maker with the GPO, now a producer in Canada, to

---

* The British Movietone *v.* London and District Cinemas Ltd became a test case for the law on Contract.

comment on whether such a priest would in fact be convicted under Canadian law. Legg took the problem to the Archbishop of Ottawa, Monsignor Vachon, who declared himself delighted with the script. '*Ça,*' he commented, '*c'est du cinema.*' His approval was endorsed by the sterner figure of Father Guay, Canada's chief church censor, a man Legg reported as being a 'stickler for orthodoxy'. Father Guay added, however, that he was bothered by the implication in the story that the priest reveals something that he can only logically have learnt through hearing confession. At one point Sidney himself joined in the religious debate. When on a trip to Quebec he went to call on the Cardinal. He had been told that he would have to kiss his ring. On arriving in his office, he asked: 'Sir, I am a Jew. Do I have to kiss your ring?' 'Of course not,' replied the Cardinal courteously. The two got on very well, and the Cardinal promised to help with the film in any way he could.

These legal and religious discussions took time. And as the weeks passed, so Sidney became ever more obsessed with the authenticity of the research. 'Is a notice posted outside the prison at Montreal when a man is executed?' he wrote anxiously to Louis Paré of the Quebec Municipal Tourist Office. 'Is a prisoner under sentence of death isolated when he is in Quebec?' At one point, an exhausted Victor Peers wrote to Olive Gardiner that 'even earthquakes have not accelerated the ponderous preparation of *I Confess*'.

In December 1950 came a new problem. A Mr Jack de Witt had sold a similar plot to Stanley Bergerman and Leslie Fenton who now announced plans to start filming in Mexico. Ways of keeping the two films different now had to be found.

Then Sidney, his natural litigiousness carrying him this time into new waters, decided to sue Warner Brothers for having held advertising rebates that should have come to Transatlantic from their distribution of *Rope* and *Under Capricorn*. Hitchcock was appalled. For Sidney, who continued to meet Jack Warner at parties when in Hollywood, it was all part of a game.

At last, early in 1951, casting began. Montgomery Clift agreed to play the part of the condemned priest. The role of the Quebec Society woman who has had an affair with the priest before he was ordained was far more difficult to fill. Various agencies were consulted because Hitchcock wanted to find someone with a European accent, preferably unknown to North American audiences. Sidney then remembered a Swedish actress called Anita Bjork whom he had seen and admired as Miss Julie in Alf Sjoberg's film of the Strindberg play. He cabled Cecil in London, asking him to visit the actress in Sweden to report on her English, and find out whether she would be willing to take the part. She was, and the contract was signed.

Anita Bjork arrived in New York on her way to join the company. She was met at the airport by Kay Brown, an old friend of Hitchcock's and now a member of the prestigious agency MCA, who had agreed to look after the actress on her way through. Kay Brown was appalled to discover that Anita Bjork had brought with her not just her lover, an eminent Swedish dramatist, but an illegitimate baby. She wired Hitchcock and Sidney to warn them. In 1951 film stars could not behave so freely. The Hays Code was still in force, and *Under Capricorn* had scarcely enjoyed a smooth path.

Her fears were more than justified. When Warner Brothers heard what was happening they panicked. Jack Warner spoke to Sidney and said to him: 'You simply can't do this. Not again. Not with *another* Swedish girl.' Sidney hesitated. Warner then suggested that Anita Bjork might fly over the border to Mexico, get a divorce from her former husband, and marry the child's father. Not surprisingly, Anita Bjork refused. She flew back to Sweden, with Sidney's help.

Sidney now resigned from the film. He felt that there were too many compromises involved. In fact there was not much left for him to do. Anne Baxter had agreed to take over Anita Bjork's role and Hitchcock was ready to start filming. Sidney removed his name from the film's production list, and amicably parted company with Transatlantic leaving Hitchcock, by now far too deeply committed to the film to pull out, to carry on without him.

Back in Hollywood, packing up, Sidney learnt that his friend Walter Wanger had been arrested for shooting his wife's lover in a car park. The man was severely injured but not dead. It hadn't been long since Sidney had seen Wanger and given an enormous lunch party for him at Claridge's to celebrate his appointment as President of the Academy of Motion Picture Arts and Sciences. Some time later, Wanger was sent for trial and found guilty, but his sentence was deferred to allow him time to complete a film. During this time Wanger was persona non grata in Hollywood, but Sidney had pressed him to ring whenever he wanted to talk, and instructed his office staff always to put him through. One day, while in an important meeting, his phone rang. He picked it up and found it was Wanger. Distracted, he said: 'Walter, I can't talk now. I've got a lot of people here. Can you ring me when you're free?' It was only later that he saw from the headlines how unfortunate his choice of words had been: Wanger had just been sentenced to go to prison.

I Confess got mixed reviews. There was widespread praise for the shots of Quebec, and some critics called the film 'the Hitchcock touch' at its best: 'powerful, masterly, full of suspense'. The British film censors labelled it sadistic as they had *Rope*, but it had a surprisingly good reception with the Catholic Church.

This film marked the end of Transatlantic and the end of Sidney's direct involvement in the Hollywood movie world. He continued to advise Hitchcock, who rapidly made a new deal with Universal and started work on *Rear Window*; but only as a friend. Some of the scripts, like *To Catch a Thief*, which he had bought for Transatlantic one day over lunch with the head of Random House, Bennett Cert, or *Dark Duty*, or *Dial M for Murder*, which he and Hitchcock had spent many long evenings discussing, were eventually made into films. By then, Sidney had left.

Hollywood, as he had begun to realise, was not for him. In the five years since he and Hitchcock had first become partners, the world of the American film-makers had changed beyond recognition. A combination of the anti-trust laws, which had during the closing years of the 1940s severed for ever that cosy symbiosis of production company and cinema circuit which had ensured an automatic distribution for all studio films, the emasculating effects of the political witch-hunts and the fast-growing tentacles of television had effectively broken the glory of Hollywood. Briefly, Sidney considered either setting up on his own, or accepting an invitation from Charlie Chaplin to work as co-producer on *Limelight*. But Hollywood, without Hitchcock, felt wrong. He was not, he decided, the stuff of which moguls are made. And the age of the mogul was over.

9

The Television Franchise

HAD IT NOT been for television, Sidney's return to England might have
been bleak indeed. His forays into film production had proved
entertaining, but financially and critically unremarkable – two
indifferent films and a resignation over a third – and whatever dreams
he may have had of working permanently in films in California had
vanished along with Hollywood's own rapidly diminishing powers. His
marriage to Zoë was over: there was no patching up a difference of style
and taste as basic as theirs.

Then several close friends had died: Alexander Clifford, the
much-loved and respected war correspondent with whom Sidney had
entered Tunis in 1943, died early in 1952 of Parkinson's Disease, after a
number of sad and fond last weekends at Coppings; and both Philip
Jordan, another journalist, and Koteliansky were dead. Even his
London home had gone: when they parted, Sidney left Zoë in Arlington
House and moved himself into a rented flat in Mount Street.

In time, Zoë moved into a house in Vincent Square, in Westminster,
where she learnt to play the piano. He kept in touch, remembering
birthdays with telegrams. In 1959 she married again, Robin Barry, Iris
Barry's son by Wyndham Lewis, whom Sidney had looked after in the
1930s and who remembered her as the kind and lively young visitor to
Long Barn he had admired so long before. Zoë died in 1972.

By the early 1950s, there was television, and its commercial possibilities
were becoming a force no one could afford to ignore. The absolute
monopoly enjoyed by the BBC since 1936 was being threatened from all

sides. With hindsight, there seems something absolutely inevitable about its arrival, and something just as inevitable about Sidney's eventual involvement in it. He had long abandoned all thought of a career in politics. Politics, he frequently says, demands too many compromises. He had never desired to join that particular fraternity of Fleet Street proprietors (Gaitskell had pressed him, as he did many others, to buy the *Daily Herald*; Sidney declined). Business, the world of straight finance, had never had much lure for him, though he had proved, and was to do so again, that he was exceptionally able at making money. Television, on the other hand, had everything: the novelty he craved, a challenge that verged on the impossible, and that sense of newness and risk he seemed to need so acutely.

In 1948, long before any real talk of commercial television, Sidney and Cecil had applied to the Postmaster-General for a licence to operate a closed television system in their own cinemas. Their plan had been to televise plays on the last night of their West End or Stratford-upon-Avon runs, and then show them, for one night only, on the large screens of the Granadas, in such a way that country towns like Shrewsbury and Maidstone would have the chance to see first-class drama. It was a precise and possible scheme, and it bore all the Bernstein hallmarks: a new form of entertainment, designed to provide something of quality for people who might not otherwise have access to it.

The Postmaster-General had turned it down. But from then on, at every hint of progress, Sidney and Cecil had submitted a new application. Each time, they had received the same formal and stalling reply. To the Beveridge Committee, set up in 1949 to inquire into the future of all broadcasting, both radio and television, before what was becoming the increasingly contentious question of the renewal of the BBC's Charter, due in 1951, they had explained the reasoning behind their original proposal.

> While the right of access to the domestic sound and television receivers of millions of people carries with it such great propaganda power that it cannot be entrusted to any person or bodies other than a public corporation or a number of public corporations ... this public monopoly of broadcasting to the home should not be artificially shielded from the competition of forms of entertainment which are made available outside the home.

These were perhaps the first intimations that Sidney and Cecil were very conscious indeed of the enormous inroads television was going to make into the film industry, which, as Sidney declared, 'had a right to expect that it shall not be required to fight this duel with a shorter sword than its opponents'.

Not that the Bernsteins' proposals were made entirely without misgivings. Personally, Sidney was against commercial television. During his film production years in America he and Victor Peers had gone to some lengths to learn all the technicalities of the medium, and at one point NBC had invited him to produce films for television with Hitchcock. What he had seen there had made him wary of the dangers of advertising. He was also a close and old friend of Sir Cyril Radcliffe (named to chair the Committee of Inquiry, but then made a Law Lord before it opened), who was a passionate opponent of commercial television and said so, very forcefully and at extreme length – in an almost unprecedentedly long letter of 164 lines to *The Times*. Also, Sidney had long been an admirer of the BBC for its standards and its probity, even if he sometimes found its scope cramping – he once declared that Reith cast a 'restrictive shadow' – and its customs foolish. (He could never forget his talk on the cinema for Lionel Fielden in 1929, when the man who welcomed him to the BBC recording studio had been pointedly appalled that Sidney had come in a grey suit rather than a dinner jacket.) What he was thinking of during these early years, he later explained, was some kind of non-profit-making organisation, running parallel to the BBC, so that if people working in television lost their BBC jobs there would be another place for them to go. If it all sounds a little naïve now, it was unquestionably something Sidney felt strongly at the time. The gamekeeper had not turned poacher yet.

While observing and waiting, Sidney turned his restless attentions back to his own company. Privately he may have been thinking that now was the moment to build up Granada in such a way that it had the financial resources and the public prestige to back any future applications in the field of television. He didn't say so, but, putting America and all that went with it behind him, he got down to one of his customary blitzes of intense work. It was at this point that he began to rely on the team of people who came together to build the Granada empire into a solid and prosperous enterprise, and later formed the backbone of his television company. They seemed, on the surface, surprising choices. But all were extraordinarily loyal to him, and he trusted their abilities and their judgment in a way that he trusted almost no one else's. It is certainly arguable that without them the business would have taken a very different shape. There was, first of all, Sidney's brother Cecil, an altogether calmer figure, but sharing Sidney's old-fashioned courtesy and formality of manner: he was very knowledgeable about the minutiae of the film industry and had good friends among its members. (Neither Max nor Albert ever held top jobs in the organisation.) There was Herbert Fontaine, a former booking manager who was gifted to the point of extraordinary intuition when it came to movie matters: he simply knew what would be popular. (Fontaine was also a pianist and highly eccentric, given to clog dancing when thinking through problems.) There was Victor Peers, his associate from Transatlantic, a canny, wholly reliable man of whom it was often remarked that he had been schooled by the Jesuits. There was Denis Forman, who came to join Sidney from the British Film Institute. And there was Joe Warton, the accountant – who first came into Sidney's life when he was working as clerk to his father's accountant, E. G. Bygrave – a thick-set, redfaced man, usually puffing on the largest of all possible cigars, who looked a bit stolid until he smiled. A Granada employee once sat next to him for the then five-hour train journey from Manchester to London. For the entire time Warton sat, staring straight ahead, saying nothing. As they pulled into Euston the man could bear it no longer: 'Joe, what in God's name have you been thinking about?'

'Ah,' replied Warton, shaking himself as from a coma, 'I've just done this year's company accounts.'

It was these five, who spent almost their entire working lives with Sidney, who were the people he listened to. Later, of course, came others: Tim Hewat, Barrie Heads, David Plowright and Derek Granger.

The war had seen the last great public age of the film. Never before had so many people – over thirty million a week in England alone – gone to the movies. The return to peacetime, the reopening of pubs and restaurants, the development of television, all combined to lure people away from those havens of emotional and physical safety in which they had sought refuge from the bombs. Between 1946 and 1951 attendances fell by five million people. Sidney now fought this decline, just as earlier he had ridden the success.

The Granada circuit, when he returned to work on it, was prosperous, if dilapidated. Shortage of paint and restrictions that lasted well into the post-war years forbade fundamental redecoration and prevented building so that all expansion had to be done by buying existing theatres and converting them. Some of the buildings were derelict. When Granada bought the Metropolitan in the Edgware Road, sixteen pantechnicons were needed to clear away the rubbish. During the war years the Bernsteins had acquired fifteen cinemas from owners who, for one reason or another, wanted to get out of them. To these, Sidney added cinemas in Kennington, Thornton Heath and Deptford from a man who was emigrating to South Africa; the Medway group of theatres at Grantham, Norwood, Dartford and Sydenham and a company with existing cinemas at Chichester, Epsom and Clapham Junction. Remembering the success of the MoI's mobile film units, he bought and equipped a number of vans to visit villages in the South of England where there were no cinemas.

In July 1946 the capital of the company had been reorganised and increased to £2,100,000 (divided into 100,000 $4\frac{1}{2}$ per cent Redeemable Cumulative Preference Shares of £1 each, 600,000 6 per cent Cumulative Second Preference Shares of £1 each and 2,000,000 ordinary shares of 5*s*. each. Of the $4\frac{1}{2}$ per cent Preference Shares, 800,000 were offered to the public at 20/6 as well as about 250,000 of the 6 per cent at 24/6. The prospectus was oversubscribed eight times. With the money raised Cecil and Sidney paid off all the accumulated loans).

Where they owned two cinemas in the same town or district, or where a new cinema lacked the style of a Granada, the more modest of the two was given the name Century. But everywhere the old Bernstein standards prevailed. Managers were groomed through the system and even if all the old employees were automatically welcomed back after war service, it was made absolutely plain that everyone was going to have to work very hard indeed.

In these post-war years the famous surprise Bernstein visits started up again. A dark car would draw up in front of a cinema, the door would be flung open and Sidney would charge, always a little brusque, always in a hurry, always perfectly dressed, up the stairs and into the foyer. 'How's business? What is this week's publicity?'

Sidney liked managers who stood up to him, who kept their nerve and didn't apologise. He preferred, recalls one former employee, for them to be tall and impressive men, but tolerated shorter ones if they dressed well and, as he put it, had a 'bright eye'. Invariably his visits would be followed by terse and exhortatory memos: 'No serious attempt has been made to pick paper up from the floor.' 'The flag was flying after sunset.' 'Could service in the kiosk be speeded up?' 'Staff were flashing torches from the bottom of the stalls. Can we improve upon our staff directional work?' As another Granada man, who spent many years himself in the theatres, explained: 'People used to ask us: why doesn't the Granada circuit grow bigger? The answer was that then it wouldn't have been Sidney's. He wouldn't have been able to concern himself personally with every detail. It was *his* fief. People not only had to be good when they worked for Granada: they had to please *him*.'

Some of the managers left, intimidated by this intense scrutiny, and unable to forge the sort of relationship with Sidney that would breach it. Most stayed. They liked the sense of pride and responsibility that went with a Bernstein job: Sidney always said that a cinema manager should have the same status as a bank manager, with a good office and a decent drink allowance, so that he could entertain, if need be, the Mayor. They appreciated the worth of a Granada training, by the 1950s an automatic passport to a job in any of the other cinema circuits. And so these fifty or so men, with their fifty or so undermanagers, in their grey suits before 6 pm and their dinner jackets for the evening, threw themselves into administering a hierarchical system of extraordinary rigidity. It had been an amazing spectacle in the 1930s; after the war its days were obviously numbered, but no one clung on to its customs more strongly than Sidney. Up to the 1960s Granada managers carried out a daily inspection of their troops assembled on the stage in their Roxy-style blue and gold uniforms, with pill-box hats and capes and red piping; usherettes' stockings were scrutinised for ladders, ushers' white gloves for total whiteness.

On Sundays, managers came in early to write up their weekly reports for Sidney. If it all seemed very exacting, at least they knew that the Bernstein brothers were working as hard as they were. On holidays, Sidney insisted that the senior executives, himself included, show themselves in the theatres. He was also fair-minded, even if the form it took was as individual as everything else about him. When, one Christmas Eve, part of the ceiling at the Granada in Tooting fell down, he instructed the Jewish members of staff to turn out and help, pointing out that these were celebrations for Christians and that they were given the Jewish holidays.

Some Thursdays, the managers were summoned to executive meetings at Golden Square to discuss posters and publicity. These gatherings were events of some importance: Sidney was a fanatic about publicity stunts and had instituted a system whereby winning ideas won bonuses for those who dreamt them up. Afterwards, there might be dinner at the Café Royal.

Sidney loved these stunts. Well into the 1950s he seemed to retain a sort of boyish eagerness for the new and the exotic, often deluging managers with his own ideas, farfetched and absurdly elaborate schemes for clues and passwords, with all the pleasure of a small boy who had just pulled off a superb practical joke. He was not above adding jocularly to his memos: 'Don't ask any of the elderly and tired people of Golden Square. They'd only file it.' It was a game, but it never lost its charm. That was what made Sidney so perplexing to those who met him: here was, clearly, an imposing intellectual presence, as well as the most obstinate and exacting of businessmen. So how did you explain the sudden charm, the flights of frivolity? To many, the pieces never seemed to fit together.

There was, of course, an increasing need for gimmicks, anything to ginger up the steadily diminishing numbers of cinema-goers. For most theatres, the war had spelt an end to the variety act: managers felt it safer and more reliable to book films than search the country for turns that grew less interesting and more expensive with the years. But Sidney, who loved the spectacle, and remembered better than anyone the trumpeting elephants, the jugglers and the singers, made one last effort, in the face of considerable reluctance from his colleagues, to bring back acts to the Granada circuit. As he wrote to Herbert Fontaine in 1952:

> I think one of the answers for some theatres . . . is occasionally to put on stage shows which even though not staggeringly profitable will do the theatre more good than showing the indifferent film . . . If Granada theatres have live showmen, energetic, virile, aggressive men (and maybe women), who will go after whatever business is around, they will not only survive, but will remain an important independent group.

And so they tried, but they were not very successful. A first collection of acts put on at the Granada, Walthamstow, was packed out, and the show moved on to Clapham Junction. Sidney was delighted. But there it performed to exactly the same number of people in a week that it had in a night at Walthamstow. Within a few months Sidney had concluded reluctantly that there was an unmistakable pattern in all this. An audience for variety did, indeed, still exist. But it was a one-night audience, and no matter what the draw, no theatre could be filled satisfactorily for any longer. The touring weekly Granada shows were dropped; in their place came occasional one-night bookings for performers; increasingly, as the 1960s drew nearer, a pop star.

There were still, however, individual triumphs. Not long after his return from America, Sidney, who loved ballet and had a stubborn belief in the value of taking cultural events to places where they never usually went, had the idea of inviting the entire Royal Ballet complete with stars, Corps de Ballet and orchestra to his suburban theatres. He asked Moira Shearer to appear at the Granada in Woolwich, and with her came a less known ballerina, Margot Fonteyn. To his surprise, it was Fonteyn, rather than the more famous star of *Red Shoes*, who packed the greater audience. One night, he drove down to see the show. Afterwards, he waited outside in his car to give the two dancers a lift home. When they stepped through the stage door, he let the moment pass, and feeling unable to break into their intimacy watched them, deep in conversation, set off down the road for the nearest railway station. Remembering the adulation of the Russian public for their ballerinas, he marvelled at the ordinariness of their lives.

Sidney was not alone in trying to keep the cinema from oblivion. The film industry itself was engaged in an almost hysterical search for a gimmick of such dazzling originality and charm that all the old audiences would flock back. Month after month, Hollywood dreamt up and turned out ever more complicated technical novelties, heralded by the industry as the most startling and exciting new developments and greeted by film critics with groans and calls for a return to serious production. There were 3-D, which gave spectators bewildering experiences of width, depth and stereophonic sound, and Cinerama, which seemed to hurtle viewers into infinity. As Sidney wrote to a friend in New York: 'We are all involved here in 3-D, Cinemascope, Wide Screen and Narrow Screen and what you will ... So far the results appear to be exploited at a level of culture somewhere below the depths of degradation.' An anonymous poem, written at the time, did the rounds of the Granada employees:

> 3-D or not 3-D – that is the question –
> Whether 'tis wiser at this moment to install
> A plastic screen in glitt'ring silver sprayed,
> Or bide awhile and let things take their course,
> Standardisation-wise? ...

As many of his letters to Hitchcock show, Sidney was following the developments with more than casual or joking interest. The two men exchanged views weekly on the technical innovations of the new systems as well as on their likely appeal to the public. Then, in 1953, Granada saw a chance to act.

One of the most lasting of the technical improvements to come out of Hollywood, it seemed to Cecil and to Victor Peers who was by now in charge of the maintenance division of Granada Theatres, was panoramic film, a system using a special lens, invented by a Frenchman called Henri Chrétien, that fitted on to an ordinary 35mm camera and took wide-angle shots. The resulting film was then projected on to a screen not only very much larger than its predecessors, but longer and thinner. As in the early days of the talkies, there was fierce competition in California to capture the market. Cinemascope led the field, and with the exception of Paramount, was soon adopted by all the major American film companies. Sidney reported his first taste of the new screen in a letter to Hitchcock:

The demonstration itself was farcical. Held at the Odeon, Tottenham Court Road ... All the Big Boys were there including Skouras. Arc Lamps and what you will. They then unfurled the enormous screen ... All the films were interrupted by different people speaking through the mike saying what a wonderful, brilliant, great industrialist was Mister Skouras for having discovered this wonderful, wonderful invention which was going to save us from unfair attacks by television ... After that Skouras spoke, but must admit was difficult to understand him or anyone else because the sound was so abominable ... Anyhow they don't say how much films will cost. Won't say when the equipment will be ready. So exhibitors are wary.

Victor Peers was less wary than most. He pressed Cecil to experiment with large screens and extra sound, and though the first showing was disappointing in that not one of the fourteen people he had carefully selected (a bank manager, a gardener and so on) even noticed the difference, he continued to believe in its future.

His chance came as a result of a row between 20th Century Fox and the Rank Organisation which normally showed Fox films. It proved an extraordinary coup for Granada. The disagreement concerned the sound system to be used. Fox insisted on the installation of special stereophonic sound equipment. Rank objected. Fox's first Cinemascope film was *The Robe*, which had its European première at Rank's Odeon in Leicester Square on 19 November 1953. After this pre-release run, with packed audiences that reminded exhibitors pleasurably of the early days of *The Jazz Singer*, Rank refused to screen *The Robe* anywhere else.

Granada was ready. Following the developing row closely, Victor Peers had lined up every manufacturer they would need to install Cinemascope in a hurry. He also ordered three screens, costing several hundred pounds each, in readiness. As the days passed, and there seemed no easy resolution to the Fox row, his spirits sank. What happened next has become one of the legends that make up Granada lore.

One morning Cecil rang Peers and asked him to come to his office. When he got there he learnt that a deal had just been signed with 20th Century Fox, allowing Granada full and sole rights to Cinemascope. For all his mockery of Spyros Skouras, Sidney was an old friend of 20th Century Fox's president (who had in fact received a special Academy Award in recognition of the company's 'imagination, showmanship and foresight' in setting up Cinemascope). Furthermore, three weeks before *The Robe* opened, he had received a cable from Hitchcock telling him that Jack Warner had just informed him in confidence that he was abandoning his own panoramic system – WarnerSuperscope – and turning over to Fox's Cinemascope. Its success now seemed assured.

The only problem, as Cecil explained to Peers, was time: how to install the equipment fast enough not to lose the momentum generated by *The Robe*'s success in the West End? It was Peers's great moment. He told Cecil that the theatres were ready for Cinemascope. Eleven days later, *The Robe* opened at the Granada in Harrow and week by week, as the Bernstein theatres were converted to Cinemascope, they put on *The Robe*, and broke all their own previous box-office records. Had Sidney been actively looking for ways to prove Granada's financial stability and pioneering spirit he could not have found anything more ingenious.

These were good times for him in the film world. He seemed to be everywhere at once, arranging a new questionnaire, becoming one of the main crusaders leading the industry's attack on the Entertainment Tax – the first charge on takings – which he declared to be exorbitant and ill-placed, and becoming the exhibitor who first made the decision to break the general release pattern. The custom in the early 1950s was to play each film for one week in each cinema, however great its popularity. When *The King and I* looked set to be an immense box-office success, Granada made a deal with its distributors, once again 20th Century Fox, to let it run in selected cinemas until the demand for it was exhausted. Some of the exhibitors who had previously run their films concurrently with Granada complained bitterly when their schedules were upset, but the public, who didn't have to follow *The King and I* all over Greater London, were delighted.

Sidney was also endlessly casting around for ways of bringing more serious material to British screens. When on a visit to New York, he went one day to call on Ed Murrow and learned that CBS were about to show two twenty-six-minute documentaries the American broadcaster Howard K. Smith had just completed about racial discrimination in South Africa. Sidney decided to buy them and put them on at selected Granadas. 'The British public', he wrote in a note to Cecil and Peers, 'should know what America is saying about one of our Dominions. It will obviously be a controversial subject matter, but on that I will take a chance.'

The South African films were followed by another Ed Murrow documentary, this time an interview with the American atomic scientist Oppenheimer. (Sidney invited all the prominent British scientists to a showing at Golden Square, among them Sir Alexander Todd, Professor Lindstead, Sir William Slater, Sir John Cockcroft and Solly Zuckerman. As the party was dispersing, one came up to Sidney and said: 'Do you realise that if there had been an accident, you would have killed off all the British scientists who matter?') The films may not have been immense popular successes in Walthamstow and East Ham, or caused quite the intellectual stir that Sidney had hoped for, but they were proof of a spirit of social responsibility no one could ignore.

Not that Sidney was above having fun in the temperamental world of film deals. Some time after he finally returned to England he received a plaintive telegram from Jack Warner about the case he and Hitchcock had brought against Warner Brothers for withholding reimbursements on advertising for *Rope* and *Under Capricorn*. Hitchcock had advised Sidney to drop it, but Sidney, as always when faced with the prospect of some enjoyable litigation, had refused. 'In my opinion', cabled Jack Warner, 'this procedure one of unwarranted harassment ... I do not see why you ... persist in suing. For years have heard people say you were a difficult man to do business with I have always said opposite therefore my surprise you taking this action and feel you should call off lawsuit and lets be friends.' Hitchcock followed this up with 'Jack Warner has personally requested me to remove you from his neck.' Sidney was enjoying himself. 'Tell Jack Warner', he cabled in reply, 'he has only to pay us what he owes us and we can all live happily ever afterwards.' In due course, Warner paid.

While waiting for further news from television, and fearing he might not find the time again, Sidney made a plan to travel to the Far East. He had never been outside Europe or North and South America. In January 1953 he announced that he would be making a 'fact finding trip' on behalf of Transatlantic Pictures Corporation (for all other purposes virtually defunct) to the Far East 'and anywhere else that promises colour and excitement for the screen' with a view to filming 'the vast panorama of the East in a modern sort of John Buchan story but with special regard for cinema suspense which the world knows as the "Hitchcock touch".' It is very unlikely that he really envisaged a fourth collaboration with Hitchcock, who was by then deeply involved in a whole series of films for Warner's, but on 26 January 1953 Sidney caught a plane for Bombay. On board were Vivien Leigh and Edwina Mountbatten. Before leaving he wrote to a friend: 'Been reviewing my past ... My life has been simple enough. Just too many people, too many theatres, too many films, too much reading ... too much work and too much Christmas.' He left behind him heavy storms and torrential rain.

The Far East was all that Sidney had hoped for and more: hotter, stranger, more beautiful, and full of absurd and memorable remnants of colonial days. He travelled with a friend, Alan Moorehead, and the two journeyed from Bombay to the Ajunta and Allora Caves, then to Calcutta, by train, taking their food with them. Everywhere they went they found invitations to dinner and a pleasant, formal, old-fashioned life. Sidney, who had equipped himself with introductions to the Indian film world, did the minimum of work; instead he spent hours taking photographs with a primitive Brownie camera, which kept going wrong, so that he would seek out local film people not to discuss their work, but for help in mending his Brownie.

From India they moved on to Burma, Singapore and Sarawak, where Sidney's friend from Ministry of Information days, founder of Mass Observation Tom Harrisson, now working for the British Government in the Far East, had arranged a trip up the river to see the Dyaks, shooting the rapids in a dug-out and staying in the traditional long houses. It was a world very distant from that of Government House and colonial administrators playing Gilbert and Sullivan on creaking gramophones. The first morning upriver Sidney woke in agonising pain. The sciatica that had been bothering him ever since the start of the trip now threatened to bring it to an abrupt end. Unable to bear the idea of flying straight home he took a great quantity of pain-killers and the two travellers moved on again, this time to Thailand and up to near the Chinese border at Chung Mi, where they stayed in an enormous British Consulate with a statue of Queen Victoria the size of a small room, and where a visiting doctor cured Sidney's sciatica with an injection into the nerve. After a visit to Ankar Watt they came close to heavy fighting and had to be escorted out by a French convoy.

Sidney was away for nearly three months. The trip was slightly marred by one of his court cases, provoked this time by a bad-tempered captain on board the *Glenartney*, between Hong Kong and Singapore.

Sidney had booked, long in advance, a stateroom. When he came on board, he found he had been moved to a smaller, inferior, cabin. He protested; his friends had been put into the cabins they had booked. The captain refused to intervene. Later that day, the captain invited the Mooreheads to sit at his table – but not Sidney. The three friends decided to eat together, at a table of their own.

While they were having lunch, the Captain sent a steward to summon Sidney to his cabin. Sidney sent back a message to say that he would come after he had finished eating.

By the time Sidney reached his cabin, the Captain had worked himself up into an immense rage. 'You would like me to turn my ship back to Hong Kong, wouldn't you?' he shouted at Sidney.

'Yes,' replied Sidney calmly. 'I wouldn't mind that a bit. Let's see you turn it round.'

By now the Captain was too angry to be reasonable. He ordered

Sidney to take his meals with the crew. For the rest of the trip, therefore, he and the Mooreheads ate lunch at 11.30 am and dinner at 6 pm, putting their clocks back in such a way that the days made sense. Sidney retaliated by sending long wireless messages over the ship's open radio to his solicitors in London asking them what legal action was possible by a passenger against a Ship's Captain.

Months later, back in England, Sidney did indeed bring a lawsuit, having summoned to his aid an impressive collection of British legal minds. The case was settled out of court, in October, while Sidney was away in Margate at the Labour Party Conference. He was instructed to pay half the costs. On the surface, the reason given was always that of the switched cabin, which made little sense, even with a man as litigious as Sidney. In fact, the case was more complicated. Sidney, a Jew, had not been invited to sit at the Captain's table. He was not a man to let anti-Semitism pass unchallenged. (In a minor way, he had suffered this type of racial prejudice before. In the mid-1940s Sir Gerald Barry and Vernon Bartlett, the writer, had put Sidney up for the Travellers' Club. A member of the committee suggested that they remove his name as he might not be accepted. Barry and Bartlett did so and resigned.)

1954 was an *annus mirabilis* for Sidney. As in 1947, when he had seemed to be on both sides of the Atlantic at once, making films, advising on film industry matters, travelling and directing his own business, now, again, there was no brake to his enthusiasms or to his energy. In well under a year he flew to America to give evidence on behalf of his friend Quentin Reynolds in a major lawsuit, played a part in formulating a section of the Television Bill, prepared and submitted an application for one of the independent television contracts, won it, diversified into business interests in Canada, and got married. He was fifty-five.

The Quentin Reynolds lawsuit had been a long time in coming. In November 1949 the Hearst columnist Westbrook Pegler had written a piece describing Reynolds as a man with 'a yellow streak', a 'mangy hide' and 'a protuberant belly filled with something other than guts'. The respected *Colliers* reporter, broadcaster about Britain during the war, sued. Among other things, he claimed loss of income: he had written 311 articles for *Colliers* before the attack, but none had been taken since.

As the trial grew nearer, Reynolds found that he had a formidable galaxy of international supporters willing to testify on behalf of his courage and probity. But these were McCarthy days and he was nervous. Sidney volunteered to speak on his wartime work in London, though Sir Cyril Radcliffe urgently advised him not to, saying that a socialist of his standing would be crucified in an American court.

Sidney consulted his solicitor, Sir Edwin Herbert, and asked him to describe the position to Reynolds's lawyer, Louis Nizer, over the telephone. He had made his promise, he told friends, and he was going. Reynolds, with his jovial and at times rather overpowering manner, his drinking and exuberance, was an old friend, and Sidney felt England owed him something.

On reaching New York, Sidney went to call on Nizer. He found the celebrated lawyer in an immense, lofty office, seated on a raised platform, a spotlight playing on him and acolytes grouped round the podium. The room was lined with bound volumes of law books.

Nizer thanked Sidney for coming, and Sidney explained his anxiety that he might in fact be doing more harm than good by testifying for Reynolds, given his known socialist views. Nizer asked: 'Mr Bernstein: may I put a few questions to you? Are you Chairman of Granada Theatres Ltd? Were you Chairman of the Transatlantic Pictures Corporation? Do you own these outside business interests which I will list? After hearing of *your* involvements, Mr Bernstein, *nobody* in the United States will believe that you are a socialist.'

The trial lasted eight weeks. Its high point came when Nizer cross-examined Pegler and made him admit 130 contradictions of testimony, then got him to brand as pro-communist a statement read out in court that Pegler himself had actually written. Sidney, in the witness box, gave a dignified and collected testimonial and Pegler's lawyer, Charles Henry, was unable to deflect him from an admiring portrait of Reynolds among the London bombs, or from describing to the jury how one night he, Ed Murrow and Reynolds had been driving home, during the Blitz, and Reynolds had stopped the car, climbed out holding a newspaper and said to the others: 'I bet £1 that I can read the paper by the light of the anti-aircraft fire and bombs.' Hardly, as Sidney pointed out, the act of a coward.

Sidney, who had been staying in George Backer's apartment, above Truman Capote, with whom he discussed the trial's progress day by day, could not stay for the verdict. The Jury were out for eleven hours. When they came back in they told a courtroom, still crowded at one o'clock in the morning, that Reynolds had been awarded $175,000, the highest damages in the history of American libel. Reynolds wrote to Sidney: 'It's still hard to believe that it happened. It is so seldom stories like ours have a happy ending, and believe me, you played a great part in having it end as it did.'

By the early summer of 1954 Sidney was totally absorbed in the passing of the Television Bill. It is worth examining those years in some detail if only to understand the extraordinary passions provoked by the spectre of a broadcasting station sponsored by advertisers. Today, when advertising has become so accepted as to be commonplace, it is impossible to comprehend the strength and depth of the hostility to independent television clung to by its early opponents. There was outrage, a sense of fury that seemed, often, to verge on hysteria. To many, it seemed to bode the end of all decent broadcasting.

The first television service in the world was begun by the BBC at Alexandra Palace in 1936. From then until the war, when it shut down completely for seven years, sober, slightly unctuous broadcasters put out a selection of light entertainment, drama, cartoons and popular music.

The high spots of the service were the outside broadcasts, feats of technical genius, which brought the Lord Mayor's show and the Oxford and Cambridge boat race to the screens. By the time war broke out there were twenty thousand television sets in and around London, the only area in the country able to receive the service.

In the weeks that followed the Labour Party's electoral victory in 1945 there were some Conservatives who felt that the BBC had contributed to its result by their pro-Labour attitudes. Remembering the success of the propaganda forces during the war, and the BBC's role as an instrument of the Government, they now feared that the new Labour politicians, bent on social revolution, would use it to perpetuate Labour rule. They demanded that an inquiry be held into the whole subject of broadcasting before the BBC's Charter, due to expire at the end of 1946, was renewed.

After considerable hedging, a temporary renewal of the Charter, and a White Paper on broadcasting policy which did no more than temporise, the Government finally announced, in January 1949, that it was going to set up a committee of inquiry. In June, its chairman was appointed, in the form of Lord Beveridge. The Committee of Inquiry was the fourth to be held since regular broadcasting began in Britain at the end of 1922: not one of its predecessors had actively recommended a BBC monopoly, though in practice its special role had always been upheld.

The Committee of Inquiry was really all about this question of monopoly. Should the BBC, proven custodians of high standards and moral responsibility, be allowed to continue to guide the taste of the British public, or should the people henceforth be exposed unprotected to a corrupting new world of consumption and competition?

When Beveridge reported, he came down firmly on the side of monopoly. The BBC was not to be challenged. Broadcasting in Britain was to remain in the hands of a single, independent, but Government-financed, corporation. A lone dissenting voice was heard

29 Noël Coward with Oona and Charlie Chaplin, Vevey, 1970

30 Sandra Bernstein with David and Jane

31 Ed Murrow, David Bernstein and Charles Laughton at Coppings, 1957

32 Coppings Farm, Leigh, Kent, the house Sidney bought in 1936

33 Lady Bernstein

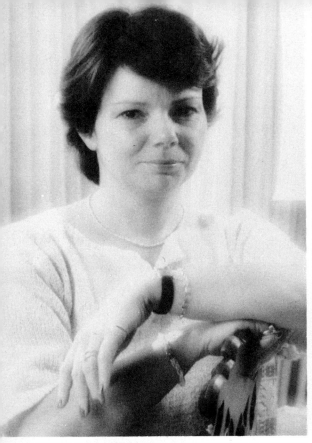

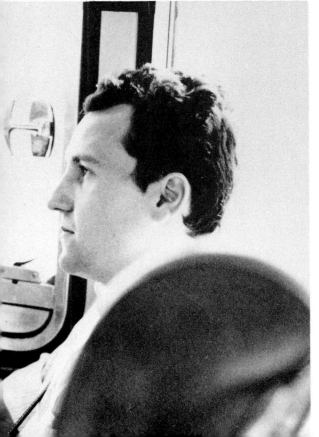

above left 34 Charlotte
above right 35 Jane
below left 36 David

from Selwyn Lloyd, Conservative member of the committee who had been to America, observed its broadcasting systems, considered its drawbacks and dangers and now recommended a dual system, commercial radio and television alongside public service broadcasting.

Between the formation of the Beveridge Committee in the summer of 1949, and the presentation of its report to Parliament in January 1951, however, there was a marked upheaval in British politics. At the 1950 General Election, Attlee's majority had been reduced to six. What was more, some of the leading members of his Government had been politically crippled by ill health. Ernest Bevin, made responsible for broadcasting after illness forced him to hand over the more arduous Foreign Office to Herbert Morrison, died in April 1950 without having laid down any firm guidelines. With his death, responsibility for broadcasting passed to Patrick Gordon-Walker, who carried far less weight in Cabinet.

These political turmoils came at a critical time for broadcasting. The BBC's Charter was once again due to end, in December 1951. And in July, the Government had published a highly controversial White Paper, which upheld the BBC's monopoly, but at the same time proposed to put the control of regional broadcasting into the hands of local government councillors.

When the Conservative Party came to power in the autumn of 1951 – Attlee having called an election and lost it to an overall Conservative majority of sixteen – they decided to buy themselves some time before pronouncing on what was by now the extremely contentious subject of broadcasting. Earl de la Warr, Postmaster-General, announced that the BBC's licence would be extended for another six months.

Now began a period of unprecedentedly frantic and contradictory debate, made all the more acute by Labour's declaration that if the Conservative Party broke the BBC monopoly, they would restore it the moment they got back into power. The two camps lined up. Against monopoly, and in favour of some kind of commercial television, were the Conservative backbench study group, with supporters in the Cabinet and at Party headquarters, some of the advertising and radio industries, and a private company, set up precisely so as to become the first commercial television consortium, called the Associated Broadcasting Development Company. In favour of the BBC monopoly, and opposing all change, were the Labour Party (largely undivided except for Anthony Wedgwood Benn, who had proposed a compromise in the shape of 'the reorganisation of the BBC in such a way as to avoid many of the monopoly dangers'), a mixed group of Conservative MPs, some high-ranking civil servants, Lord Reith, the BBC's first Director-General and the figure most hallowed in British broadcasting, the BBC itself, and all those who saw themselves as defending the 'decencies of life', as well as an organisation called the National Television Council, set up by the Labour MP Christopher Mayhew expressly to fight commercial television.

Beyond politics, passions ran no less high. Gallup polls of 1952 and 1953 show the country slightly biased in favour of commercial television. Two out of three people canvassed by the *Daily Express* said they would welcome it. More than any other single event perhaps the Coronation in June 1953 won the public over to television, but it also intensified the public debate. The conflict of views is perfectly summarised in two newspaper leaders. On 4 June, the *Daily Express*, admitting reluctantly that the BBC's excellent coverage of the event would serve to bolster the cause of monopoly, concluded: 'Be sure that the achievements of the BBC ... would have been more pronounced still if there had been some competition.' The *Daily Sketch*, on the other hand, declared: 'The lesson is that once sponsored radio and TV are admitted nothing is sacred. After yesterday's wonderful feat, the people will say: "No sponsoring at any price".' Sidney himself watched the event on the television set at the RAC club. He admired what he saw, but must have felt a certain conflict of interests when he learnt that a film of the Coronation, *A Queen is Crowned*, broke all Granada cinema records.

The advent of commercial television was now growing closer day by day, though the debate continued as fiercely as ever. In May 1952 a Government White Paper had contained at least a form of acceptance of the idea of broadcasting competition, and that had been approved in the House of Commons, in principle, by 297 votes to 269. In July 1953 the Postmaster-General's Television Advisory Committee reported that an independent television service was now technically possible. And on 3 November 1953, in the Queen's Speech at the Opening of Parliament, the Government announced that legislation for the establishment of independent television would come before Parliament in the forthcoming session. Ten days later, a second White Paper appeared, announcing that a public corporation would be set up which would own and control the transmitters and then lease out television facilities to programme contractors. The spectre had arrived.

Now came the final battle. Despite clear signs of defeat, the hard core anti-commercial television advocates refused to give up. The debates in the House of Lords and the Commons were exceptionally well attended, but also exceptionally bitter. Lord Hailsham, speaking against the Government's proposals, compared sponsored broadcasting to 'small pox, bubonic plague and the Black Death'.

On 4 March 1954 the Television Bill was introduced. Its opponents fought it line by line, sometimes word by word. They insisted on the use of the word 'commercial' so that the new service would carry the same pejorative stigma as a 'commercial' hotel. They made plain their disgust at the idea that money-making was going to enter the sacred circles of broadcasting. They did their best to remove all programmes containing matters of taste – education, religion, news and coverage of Royal occasions – from the contamination of advertisers. And in the end, after a debate of over eighty hours in the Commons alone, they lost by 302 votes to 280. The depth of their fears was part of a spirit of animosity and mistrust that was to surround the new service for many of its early years.

The Television Bill received the Royal Assent on 30 July 1954. It contained twenty sections and three schedules, a hotchpotch of clauses and subclauses so emasculated by debate and often so imprecise that Denis Lloyd, Quain Professor of Jurisprudence at London University, immediately dubbed it 'a collection of vague and ill defined duties'. There were pronouncements about advertisers and their possible influence; about the content and type of programmes; about religious, political and educational coverage; about how to award the contracts. But sometimes it was very hard indeed to understand just what was being said.

In the drafting of one of these sections, Sidney played an important part. In the original Bill, paragraph (a) of sub-section 1 insisted 'that the tone and style of the programmes are predominantly British'. This was an unmistakable reference to the fear of many that commercial television, unless properly protected, would become a junior brother to American television, just as, in the pre-quota days, the British film industry had been entirely dominated by Hollywood.

In the debates, amendments were put forward seeking to introduce a fixed quota for British productions. The strongest argument against – that such a quota would be inflexible, would have to apply also to the BBC and would run the risk of retaliation by other countries – was put by Viscount Swinton, who, as Sir Philip Cunliffe-Lister, President of the Board of Trade, had introduced the film quota in the 1927 Cinematograph Films Act.

Outside Parliament, fourteen organisations combined to put forward the case for the entertainment profession, with Gordon Sandison, Secretary of the British Actors' Equity Association, announcing that in their united view, no less than 80 per cent of the programmes transmitted by any television station should be British. This suggestion was not just anathema to Lord Swinton and to the defenders of the Bill, who had argued, over every amendment, for a spirit of flexibility, but to many outsiders as well.

Sidney, who had campaigned actively in the 1920s for a film quota, understood the issues better than anyone. He feared, among other things, that too rigid a policy would lead only to trickeries and subterfuge. He invited Gordon Sandison of Equity, George Elvin of the ACT and representatives of the Musicians' Union and other unions involved to a series of lunches at his offices in Golden Square, and persuaded them to support his view that the proportion of British to foreign material should be largely left to the discretion of the controlling authority, and guided by mutual understandings and agreements. His scheme became known as the Gentleman's Agreement. It was never published, but its general guidelines included a resolution that no more than seven hours of foreign material should be shown in an average week. The notion was accepted, though discussions lasted almost up until ITV came on the air, and was to govern the early principles of what became known as 'proper proportions'.

Within a few days of the Royal Assent to the Television Bill, the body that was to control the new machinery came into being. An Independent Television Authority was set up under the chairmanship of Sir Kenneth Clark, who had filled in the years since his spell at the MoI by becoming Chairman of the Arts Council, with nine other members, and the imprecise but extraordinarily demanding job of having to plan a network of television transmitting stations and select companies to provide programmes for them. Three hundred and thirty-two people applied for the job of the Authority's first Director-General. After brief deliberations – for a spirit of haste had now replaced the procrastinations of years – it went to Sir Robert Fraser, an Australian journalist and Director-General of the Central Office of Information. Sir Gerald Barry, former director of the highly successful Festival of Britain, the only other serious contender, was not considered tough enough for the job. On 25 August, less than two months after the Royal Assent, the long awaited advertisement finally appeared in the newspapers:

> The Independent Television Authority invites applications from those interested in becoming programme contractors in accordance with the provisions of the Television Act. Applicants should give a broad picture of the type of programme they would provide, their proposals for network or local broadcasting of their programmes, some indication of their financial resources and the length of contract they would desire.

The first areas to be provided with the new service were to be those most densely populated: London, the Midlands and the North. The move had been made: but no one yet knew quite what would happen next.

Granada had in effect been applying for the job for years. Ever since their first 1948 inquiry, the Bernsteins had been keeping up a regular if one-sided correspondence with the Postmaster-General's office. As early as June 1950 Sidney had invited Ian Mikardo, head of a research organisation and a friend from the 1930s, to help prepare Granada's case for presentation to the Beveridge Committee. As White Paper followed White Paper, and events seemed to be marching towards commercial television, Mikardo had continued to help, putting out feelers in the House of Commons and formulating approaches best suited to securing a contract.

That a firm approach would be made by Granada, when the right day came, was made absolutely plain by the early summer of 1953, a year before the Bill was passed. *The Times* of 18 June carried a large, boxed advertisement. At the top was a bust of Barnum, Sidney's old showman hero. Underneath were the words:

Show business is as old as Barnum, as new as television. The Granada Theatres Limited has an unbroken record of success in what is happily called 'show business' ... With this record behind it Granada Theatres Limited has applied to the Postmaster-General for a licence to operate a commercial television station.

That same month Sidney had written to Herbert Morrison, after the Labour defeat of November 1951 an ordinary MP once again, but one whose views of commercial television remained as hostile as before. Sidney's letter summed up his position beautifully.

I think you should know that my company have applied to the Postmaster-General for a licence to operate a Commercial Television Station.

This does not indicate any change of feelings about commercial or sponsored television; I still think the country would be better off without it.

However, if there is to be commercial television in this country, we think we should be in, and this may very well be useful one day.

I have told Morgan Phillips [General Secretary of the Labour Party] of our application, and my views.

Morrison's reply was brief. 'With you,' he wrote, 'I hope that nobody gets a chance.'

When that chance came, however, Granada was one of the first groups to act. The decision had really been Sidney's. There had been no one moment during the preceding years when the top Granada men – Cecil, Victor Peers, Joe Warton and Sidney himself – had sat down and planned to apply. The feeling had simply evolved. If it rested ultimately with Sidney it was because it was his enthusiasm and nerve that had to carry the day and because that had always been his role in Granada: the man who had ideas and took decisions, while the others deliberated, reasoned with him, voiced their fears and doubts and in the end interpreted what had been decided to the outside world. Later, Sidney was to justify his seeming volte-face from being a declared opponent of commercial television to becoming chairman of one of the first applying bidders by saying simply that once the 'big boys' were in the race, he had felt he had no alternative but to enter it himself. (It is interesting to remember that of the four winning groups, three had earlier announced their opposition to independent television.)

On 20 September Granada wrote to the ITA:

> We wish to become exclusive programme contractors for the Manchester/Liverpool station for seven days a week. We also desire that for two consecutive week days the programmes we put out from this station should be televised from all other stations operated under your Authority.
>
> We appreciate that there may be interests in the Manchester/Liverpool area who would wish to be associated and, should we be appointed, we would welcome their proposals.
>
> It would be our purpose, equipped with our experience in presenting ballet, symphony concerts, opera, stage plays, pantomimes, variety shows and, of course, films, to provide programmes of high quality and wide scope which would attract the public at all levels ...

Some time afterwards he was to explain in a speech to the Manchester Publicity Association why he chose to go north.

> People have asked me why I applied for the Northern region. I have answered that London is full of displaced persons. The North is a close-knit, indigenous, industrial society, a homogeneous, cultured group with a record for music, theatre, literature and newspapers not found elsewhere.
>
> These reasons are true. But I am now going to tell you how I really came to the decision.
>
> It was brought about by two maps: a population map of Great

Britain and a rainfall map. Any sensible person, after studying these two maps for a few minutes, would realise that if commercial TV is going to be a success anywhere in the world, it would be in the industrial North of England.

Granada's application was one of ninety-eight. Most of these soon vanished, simply withdrawing their requests. Twenty-six remained with some hope of success. Interviews began on 28 September. On 14 October Granada was called to the Arts Council in St James's Square where the ITA was temporarily lodged. Sidney came accompanied by Cecil, Victor Peers and Joe Warton, and the four men spent the hour allocated to them in reassuring the Authority as to their financial viability (they stated that they had £3 million), their experience and their readiness. It was an informal gathering and the Granada group sensed it had gone well. When they filed out, in their ordinary business suits, they were astonished to see that the consortium that were to be interviewed after them, the ex-BBC man Norman Collins and the Associated Broadcasting Development Group, were sitting waiting in formal morning coats and top hats.

A week later, Granada learnt that the contract for the North was theirs. The Bernsteins hadn't got all they had asked for – five days rather than seven, and no agreements as yet about networking – but that hardly mattered. The excitement at Golden Square was enormous. Telegrams of congratulations poured in. To Francis Meynell's 'Hurrah. Well done', Sidney replied: 'Thank you. Now the fun and troubles begin.' To Ed Murrow, he wrote, in an unusually cheerful mood: 'We have lost our virginity ... Where commercial television will lead us I don't know, but we're certainly on our way ...'

In making its choice the Authority said that it had been 'helped by no precedent'. It took as 'its main criterion of choice the ability of the various applicants, so far as this could be judged, to produce as a long term and continuing operation balanced programmes of high quality.' Though they may not have spelt it out very fully, financial considerations were clearly paramount in their deliberations. The expenses of setting up a television service from scratch were undoubtedly going to be enormous – no one, yet, knew quite how big – and it would be many months before anyone would learn how the advertisers, those despised sponsors who were the linchpin of the system, were going to respond.

That Granada should have been one of the first selected was entirely to be expected. While the precise reasons behind the ITA Board's decisions were never published, it was soon known that they had had very few doubts about the Company's suitability. Granada's record, after all, was impressive. It had wide experience of all the different areas of the entertainment world. It had recently, with its far-sighted leap into Cinemascope, proved itself capable of a quick and inspired sense of business. There was little doubt about its financial soundness. Furthermore, Sidney's own record was good: the Film Society, the Ministry of Information, Psychological Warfare, the Transatlantic Pictures Corporation, all guarantees of reliability and the ability to meet challenges.

Sidney himself was not particularly surprised at the decision, though he was later gratified to learn from Lord Hinchcliffe, a member of the Authority, that they had been impressed by the fact that while the other interested groups had lobbied actively to secure a contract, Granada alone had kept itself aloof from all such machinations. What he did not know, or discover for many years, was that there had been a last-minute wavering at the Authority over Sidney's reputed early membership of the Communist Party; that doubt had been raised again. 'Government circles', as Kenneth Clark was to write in *The Other Half* (John Murray, 1977), the first volume of his autobiography, 'put a good deal of pressure on the ITA to turn down Granada's application'. However Clark knew Sidney well from the MoI days, had made inquiries of MI5, and been reassured that Sidney was not a Party member. He threatened to resign if Granada was not given the contract. Objections were withdrawn.

Three other contracts had been awarded, each of an approximately similar value, assessed in terms of population density and time on the air, in such a way that none could dominate. London, Monday to Friday, went to Broadcast Relay Services/Associated Newspapers (later Associated-Rediffusion), an amalgam of newspaper backers and a company already operating broadcasting stations in Canada. London, Saturday and Sunday, and the Midlands, Monday to Friday, were offered to Associated Broadcasting Development Group, the first Independent Television consortium. The Kemsley Press/Maurice Winnick Group, an alliance of television and newspaper interests, settled for the Midlands, Saturday and Sunday, and the North, Saturday and Sunday. Fraser later described the process of allocating to these companies their portion, and persuading them to accept it, as 'a delicate and laborious task'.

As soon as the appointments became known, a fresh row broke out in Parliament. There were cries of political partiality. The presence of newspaper proprietors among the contractors, in particular, infuriated the Labour Party, who accused the Government of supporting their own, in the form of the marked Conservative interests of Lord Kemsley and Lord Rothermere. (No one mentioned Sidney's forty-year affiliation to the Labour Party.) On 23 November, Herbert Morrison moved 'That this House expresses its alarm at the manner in which the Television Act is operating; and requests Her Majesty's Government to bring forward legislation to amend or repeal the Act.' Though the motion went to a division and was defeated by 300 votes to 268, it showed that the animosities were all still there.

The newspapers were, of course, much obsessed with this new enterprise, spending many hours trying to gauge how far commercial television would threaten their profits. They also felt, with some justification, that newspaper experience was an excellent preparation for television. Cecil King, proprietor of the *Daily Mirror*, was one of the newspaper men who watched the alliances most closely. In August, a fortnight before the ITA advertisement appeared in the newspaper, King had invited Sidney to lunch at his office off Fleet Street.

Sidney had never been there before. In the hall he had found a corpulent commissionaire crouched inside a minute cubby hole, positioned under a large steel engraving of Lord Northcliffe. He had been ushered into a hydraulic lift and borne up to a fine room at the top, with a fire burning in the grate, and another immense picture of Lord Northcliffe, this time in oils, hanging above the fireplace. Standing beneath it had been Cecil King, in the same position and wearing much the same suit as his uncle and mentor.

Over lunch, King had suggested that he might become a partner in the Granada application. Sidney had not hesitated before replying. He felt about partners much as he had felt when people had approached him and Hitchcock in Hollywood. 'We could only have a partner whom we respected, and whom we were prepared to listen to,' he had said to King. 'Our position at the moment is that we have so many different and curious schemes and we don't think any outsider would find them acceptable. We have decided to have no partners.' King had tried to persuade him, not on the grounds of money, since he had made it plain that he assumed Sidney's financial resources were sufficient, but in terms of the expertise a daily newspaper could bring to the deal. But Sidney had been adamant. The two men had parted amicably.

Months later, when the *Mirror* seemed to be waging a particularly unbending war against the independent companies, Sidney met King at a party given to celebrate the opening of the Richard Buckle Diaghilev exhibition in Halkin Street. 'Well,' said King, 'we're having a lot of fun with criticising television.'

'I'm not sure I am,' replied Sidney.

'Don't worry, Bernstein,' King said consolingly, laying his arm around Sidney's shoulders, 'we'll look after you.' To Sidney, it all seemed suddenly rather reminiscent of the Tammany Hall labour bosses in New York.

King was not the only newspaper man to make an advance. A more unexpected approach came from Beaverbrook, a long and openly declared enemy of commercial television. In October, Arthur Christiansen, an old friend of Sidney's and Editor of the Daily Express, rang to ask whether he and Max Aitken could call on him. They appeared shortly afterwards at Mount Street for a drink. To Sidney's absolute astonishment Christiansen told him that they had come to buy a share in Granada Television. 'What about the old man?' asked Sidney. 'I know that he's against it.'

'Not if it's with you,' was the reply, a further mark of the extraordinarily ambivalent relationship between Sidney and Beaverbrook. Sidney, however, declined.

Aitken then asked for the promise of a first option, should Granada ever change its mind. 'No,' said Sidney. 'I don't see why I should give you an option. I can't think of a single good reason why.'

Had Granada been short of money, it is possible that Sidney might have viewed these overtures more favourably. As it was, he had just had an extremely flattering demonstration of the City's confidence in Granada. One morning a senior director of Barclays Bank had been shown into his office in Golden Square. Sidney greeted the man with some misgivings, assuming that he had come to voice his doubts about Granada's application.

'I have come to tell you', said the director, 'that we have today placed an extra half-million pounds at your company's credit. We hear that you are going into television and we wish to support you all we can.'

Question nine of the preliminary form for applicants had mentioned August 1955 as a possible starting date for the new service. Few bidders had taken it seriously. How could anyone be expected to launch an entirely new venture, complete with a wholly different technology, an as yet unfound site, and an immense staff of people as yet unrecruited and inexperienced, in under a year? To their dismay, when Fraser gathered the four winning contractors together for a first meeting, he repeated that August 1955 was indeed the date at which the Authority was aiming.

The reason for such speed was simple. The passing of the Act had done nothing to dispel the hostility of its opponents. Attlee's words, that he would reverse the decision on Labour regaining power, still rang unpleasantly in people's ears. On the other hand, if ITV had already been on the air, with what the Authority calculated to be some six million licence holders, for over a year before the general election, due to take place in October 1956 at the latest, then Labour would find it very hard to dismantle it. The Authority had given itself a year to set up independent television.

Sidney was fifty-five and about to embark on the hardest, most demanding and most perilous working year of his life. Before setting out on it, he got married. On 11 December, in New York, he married Sandra Malone, a calm, shy Canadian girl with straight heavy dark-red hair and a wide and smiling face. He had met her in Los Angeles, during his years with Hitchcock, when she had arrived in California with a friend. In the Far East with Alan Moorehead, in 1953, he had received a letter from her: reading it, he had realised how much he had liked her, and had invited her to visit him in London, making her his guest at the Dorchester Hotel. It was there that they decided to get married.

Sandra was thirty-one, with a nine-year-old daughter called Charlotte. The wedding took place in a New York registry office, in equal secrecy to his first. Few of Sidney's friends were even aware of Sandra's existence: even in California there was surprise at the news.

It was not, his friends soon agreed, in any way unexpected that Sidney should marry again. Indeed, they had been awaiting the event for some years. But Sidney had now done much as he had done with Zoë: married a considerably younger, less obviously worldly figure than most of his women friends, among whom were not only Hollywood actresses – Ingrid Bergman, Lauren Bacall, Claudette Colbert – but writers, political hostesses, women long established in professional working careers of their own. What no one appeared to have seen was that Sidney longed for family life and for children. With Sandra, he suddenly found that it was still all possible.

His English friends, however, were left in ignorance of the event until long after the ceremony had taken place. It was not until 19 January, 1955, over a month later, that the announcement appeared in the Marriages column of the *Daily Telegraph*.

10

Coming on the Air

THOUGH IT WAS to be some months before the final contracts with the ITA were drawn up, Cecil and Sidney now set about forming a wholly owned subsidiary company to run the television side. They began by calling it Granada Television Ltd, then switched to Granada TV Network Ltd; the two brothers were named as directors and Joe Warton became company secretary. Long before the deeds were signed, however, a northern site had to be found, cleared and plans for a television centre commissioned, for, with the announcement of the contract winners had come the news that the ITA had rejected the idea, put forward during the debates in the House of Commons, and supported by some of the bidders, of operating the network centrally from London.

Sidney, Cecil, Joe Warton and Victor Peers set off on a tour of the North. They started in Liverpool, where they were conducted round possible sites by the city's public relations officer, Jim Phoenix. Nothing suitable was seen, but Sidney was so impressed by Phoenix that he later offered him the job of Granada's northern representative.

An estate agent in Manchester called Phillip Sutton had been given the job of searching out five acres of land as close as possible to the Blackfriars Telephone Exchange; the nearer it was, the shorter the distance for the Post Office to install sound and vision circuits between the studios and the terminus for the links to other regions. He came up with a plot near Didsbury, and two warehouses in Salford by the Irwell, behind a railway yard, both instantly rejected. There was also a plot of four and three-quarter acres of semi-derelict land in the heart of the city, covered in small businesses working out of little huts and workshops, with ten rent-controlled cottages, a petrol station and a man with a horse and cart. The site belonged to the Manchester Ship Canal Company and below ground level there was still a tunnel running towards Central Station, a quarter of a mile away. The front of the site opened on to Quay Street, Water Street, Atherton Street and Grape Street. The back was overlooked by two enormous fine brick warehouses and a stretch of the Liverpool to Manchester railway, the very place where William Huskison, the Cabinet Minister, was killed by the *Rocket* on the day of the inaugural celebrations in September 1830 before the horrified gaze of the Prime Minister, the Duke of Wellington.

Sidney came to Manchester for a final tour of inspection. He was taken first to Salford, which he pronounced disappointing: he found the surroundings depressing and feared for the effect on visitors. He walked back to the Midland Hotel past the Quay Street site, with its 'For Sale' sign hanging from a post. Peers explained why he had rejected it; it was under offer to the Manchester Corporation for an exhibition hall. Sidney, standing at the kerb, said, 'This is it. This is the place we must have.'

There was no time to waste. In matters of this kind, Sidney was extremely obstinate. He rang the agents, who told him that the site had been sold. Sidney pointed out that it still had a 'for sale' sign up. 'Either you get in touch with the Manchester Ship Canal Company or I do. If I do, you get no commission.' He got his way. Eighty thousand pounds were handed over to Manchester Ship Canal Company. Cottage and workshop tenants were speedily rehoused, and the horse and cart man moved elsewhere. Only the garage was allowed to stay.

In all their deliberations two major problems faced the Bernsteins, adding greatly to their uncertainty about how much speed was actually necessary. The first was how much television material, how many programmes, in fact, Granada was going to need to produce before the opening night: the competing companies had agreed that in principle there would be a certain amount of sharing – 'networking' – of programmes. But no one, it now turned out, had any clear idea at all of what this involved.

The second question concerned the transmitter and the date by which it would be ready; it was the more crucial of the two. It had been suggested that the ITA might share the BBC's masts, and in all the early discussions the BBC appeared willing to let the independent stations use their facilities at Sutton Coldfield (the Midlands transmitting station), at Holme Moss, on the Pennines, which covered both Lancashire and Yorkshire, and at Crystal Palace, the new station the BBC was currently building for the London area. At that point the scheme ran into difficulties. The BBC announced that Crystal Palace would not after all be ready until 1956 – well beyond the ITA's politically dictated target for opening. Then the BBC masts turned out to be technically different from those needed to take the Authority's types of aerial and transmission line. But it was not until the spring of 1955 that the idea of sharing the BBC's transmitters at Sutton Coldfield and Holme Moss was finally abandoned.

All this had an important bearing on Granada's timing. If Holme Moss was used, then Granada would be able to cover its whole area, coast to coast. If the BBC transmitter was rejected, and a similar one built by the ITA within five miles of Holme Moss, the position located by the engineers as the best to give coverage of both Yorkshire and Lancashire, then Granada would still be able to cover its area. The problem, once again, was political. The ITA's engineers had decided that they would need at least eighteen months to construct a single transmitter powerful enough to cover the whole region, particularly because of the appalling working conditions in the Pennines during the winter months. The ITA did not have eighteen months to lose.

And so, on 25 February 1955, the ITA announced that it would be putting up two transmitters for the North, one at Winter Hill and one at Emley Moor and that the Lancashire area, at least, would be ready for transmission some time early in 1956. This would have the further advantage, they explained, of allowing Lancashire and Yorkshire to be 'treated in such a way that their respective regional interests could receive expression in the programmes'.

What they did not add publicly was that by erecting two transmitters they left open the possibility that they might one day split the contract for the North into two – which they were indeed to do, though not for another thirteen years. Sidney was well aware of what was going on. On 24 January he had had a telephone discussion with Sir Robert Fraser. From notes taken at the time it is absolutely clear that the ITA was wondering whether it would not be better to allocate the whole of Lancashire to one contractor and the whole of Yorkshire to another. Sir Robert also understood, as he conveyed to Sidney, that this idea would not go down well, and was therefore still disposed towards 'throwing in' Yorkshire with Lancashire.

From the first Sidney objected strongly to any suggestion that his territory be cut in two, or in any way considered separately. In a series of increasingly acrimonious letters to the Authority he expressed his disappointment at being deprived of a service he had been led to expect, namely the means of coming on to the air at the same time as the other stations and to the whole of his 'constituency' at once. For, it soon became clear, not using the BBC transmitter, and building two instead of one, was going to mean that he could now open only with Lancashire. Yorkshire would have to wait another six months. On 17 March he wrote to Sir Robert Fraser:

> Instead of starting commercial transmissions with an audience potential of 12 millions, we are now being asked to go into business with a potential of 6 millions.
>
> We cannot escape the impression that we are being asked to pay a very high price indeed to hasten the inauguration of ITA service elsewhere. We have always reiterated our belief that starting commercial television in one region is extremely hazardous, and flouts the obvious foundation of good programming . . .
>
> The economic base of all our planning has been continuously chipped away.

If the dates for coming on the air were at least now settled – May 1956 for Lancashire, November for Yorkshire – they had a further disadvantage. Both were bad moments at which to try to lure business from very sceptical advertisers. Reg Hammans, the senior engineer Sidney had recruited to direct the technical side of his new station, came down firmly in agreement with him, arguing that the Authority's technicians had been unduly alarmist, and that it would be perfectly possible to complete a single, powerful transmitter in that time.

Sir Robert and the Authority remained adamant. Sidney had no choice but to comply, but the exchange lent a somewhat bitter note to their early relationship.

At least Granada now had more time to prepare its site. Sidney's dream was to erect a model television centre, the first of its kind in Britain to be designed and built from the ground up, 'as if we were men from Mars'. Ralph Tubbs had been the architect of the Dome of Discovery at the 1951 Festival of Britain. Sidney now rang him up and introduced himself. He was in one of his genial, exuberant moods. 'Mr Tubbs? I want to put an idea to you. Are you standing up or sitting down?' He failed to notice the air of surprise from the other end of the line.

'I'm standing up.'

'Well, would you mind sitting down? Would you design a television centre for me?'

'I'm glad you asked me to sit down,' remarked Tubbs, drily. What Sidney did not know, and later learnt to his extreme embarrassment, was that Tubbs had lost a leg in the war.

Ralph Tubbs took the job. While he, Reg Hammans and Sol Cornberg, an NBC consultant loaned to Granada, now settled down to producing a master plan of interrelated studios, offices, dressing-rooms and stores, Sidney, Cecil and Victor Peers embarked on a series of meetings in London with the ITA and the three other contractors to establish exactly how the new service was going to run. In these, Granada played a key role. They were, quite simply, more experienced than the others, particularly in the area of entertainment. Associated-Rediffusion, for instance, had no one on its board at all with any background of show business. (The ITA's own lack of experience in entertainment had in fact so daunted Sir Kenneth Clark that he set up an entertainment sub-committee from outside to advise him. In the event, it never met.)

The other area where Granada played a strong part was news. It was a subject Sidney cared about deeply. In his original application he had spoken of a weekly round-up from America by Ed Murrow. He was absolutely determined to get away from the unimaginative and stuffy BBC presentation of the current events. When the companies met first to discuss the issue they quickly agreed that news should be put into the hands of a special body under their control. Sidney, in particular, came down strongly in favour of a jointly owned and managed co-operative. Despite some objections by members of the ITA, who preferred the idea of handing over the whole job to PA and Reuters, the subsidiary specialist company scheme won the day, but not without countless meetings, at which the whole concept of a new kind of news service was hatched out, involving presenters with strong personalities rather than the characterless newscasters of the BBC. Later, Victor Peers was to say that without Sidney a very different sort of service might have emerged.

Sidney was, and remained, somewhat ambivalent about presenters. He liked them to possess recognisable identities but he did not want them turned into stars. Even Ed Murrow's particular kind of approach – articulate, factual, but unmistakably personal – seemed to him too committed and too bound up with individual personalities.

Like everything else to do with the new television, the news was born out of many meetings and in a great deal of confusion, caused not least by its premises. The A-R building in Kingsway where ITN started was so inefficiently organised for a news service, with a newsroom on the second floor, a studio on the eighth and a catastrophically unreliable lift, that there were frequently minor mutinies among the staff. After visiting the building one day, Sidney set about arranging for improvements. (There is an apocryphal story that he urged the staff to strike.)

Where Granada seemed to lack the expertise of the other companies was over the highly charged question of advertising. While Associated-Rediffusion, for example, had a deputy chairman with a wide knowledge of the subject, D.F.S. McClean of Associated Newspapers, Granada had no one at all. Staff who attended the company meetings on the subject simply tended to listen to what the others said. It was not until October 1955 that Granada found its own voice in the form of the former marketing director of Quaker Oats, Alex Anson, whom Sidney brought in as Director of Sales.

There was another area in which Granada failed and this was to have serious implications for the whole service. When the original contract with the bidders was drawn up, minimum and maximum broadcasting hours were laid down by the ITA. Four hours a day, or twenty a week, had been decided as the least the new service should provide; eight and thirty-five respectively as the most. From the first moment he learnt of them, Sidney, who personally would have gone for two hours a day in the early months, pleaded with the others to accept the minimum. Associated-Rediffusion disagreed; they argued that the prestige of independent television would suffer unless they were seen to be filling their whole quota. Sidney pointed out that since they were to go on the air first, Associated-Rediffusion were in fact only making things very difficult for themselves. No one else was convinced. What was more, ATV (a newly constituted consortium, bringing in the show business triumvirate of Prince Littler, Val Parnell and Lew Grade, in the wake of a reshuffle) were also pushing hard for the maximum hours. Granada was overruled. And so, as each company went on the air, it had to work to the maximum, with the very difficulties that Sidney had foreseen. No company, in those first days, had the backing, the expertise or the imagination to produce eight hours of fresh, live entertainment every day. As Sidney had warned, they had to fall back on films.

During the months of ceaseless decision and discussion, when the senior members of the four companies were everywhere at once, debating everything from how to equip a television studio to what fee to pay an entertainer, Sidney found time to take a few brief moments' holiday. Early in the year he was in St Moritz skiing with Sandra and Charlotte: these winter holidays, most often taken in Suvretta House just outside the town, were to become an agreeable ritual in the Bernsteins' life. This year, it was something of a film world reunion. The Hitchcocks, Sir Alexander Korda and Carol Reed were all staying near by. The Bernsteins returned to Coppings to thick ice and heavy snowfalls and the house was cut off from the outside world for four days. 'Sandra is well,' Sidney reported to Hitchcock, 'Charlotte happy at day school and all Coppings is gay.' Charlotte and Sidney had taken warmly to each other, Charlotte requesting, from the first, to take the name Bernstein.

In February, Sidney wrote to Sean and Eileen O'Casey, inviting them to be his guests at the first night of O'Casey's play *The Bishop's Bonfire* which Tyrone Guthrie was producing in Dublin, with Cyril Cusack and Seamus Kavanagh. It was a thoughtful gesture to make at such a moment of intense personal preoccupation, but Sidney well knew that O'Casey had not been back to Ireland for many years and very probably could not afford to do so now. Eileen wrote gratefully back, explaining that O'Casey felt 'he would sooner go to Ireland, if the play made good and he had the money, in the summer, quietly and unnoticed; at least not as much.' In the end, the O'Casey daughter, Shivaun, went in his place with her mother, and Sandra bought her a red-flannel skirt and embroidered Irish blouse for the occasion.

The party reached Dublin in time for the dress rehearsal; Sidney, Eileen O'Casey recalled in her book *Sean*, was 'particularly nervous over the shooting scene in the third act'. He was right to be apprehensive. On the first night there was much applause but also booing and hostile shouts in Gaelic. It was all a little like the reception given in the 1920s to *The Plough and the Stars* when the audience of the Abbey Theatre rose up in a near riot of protest against O'Casey's play, and W. B. Yeats took to the stage to declare: 'Is this going to be a recurring celebration of Irish genius? Synge first, and then O'Casey. Dublin has once more rocked the cradle of a reputation.'

The morning after the first night of *The Bishop's Bonfire* the critics, who had been very hard on the play, and who were staying like the Bernstein party at the Shelbourne Hotel, tried to avoid Mrs O'Casey's glance. She was grateful for Sidney's upright and solid presence at her side, with the kind of dignity that seemed to belittle the attacks.

Sidney remained a valued friend of O'Casey's until his death in 1964. One day, shortly before the playwright died, Sidney hired a small plane to take him to Torquay, where O'Casey lived. They were a slightly unlikely pair, but Mrs O'Casey today can recall no moment of silence between the two men when they met. They talked, most of the time, about the theatre.

By April, it had become clear that the political pressure that had dogged the early months of the Authority's life was over. On the 6th, Eden succeeded Churchill as Prime Minister. He called a General Election for 26 May, at which the Conservative majority was increased from seventeen to sixty. The independent television companies were safe. But by this time plans for the opening in London by Associated-Rediffusion on 22 September were so far advanced that no one could seriously consider relaxing the pressure. Sidney wrote wryly to friends: 'Attlee and company came to Golden Square to see the

Labour Party TV Films and have asked me to join them in an inquest thereon. As a New Yorker character would say: "Now they ask me!" '

Jane Bernstein, Sidney's mother, died in March. She was eighty-three. Sidney had stayed close to her, retaining until the end his admiration and respect for the strength with which she had conducted her life. He had been extremely fond of her and now felt her loss sharply. The Bernsteins decided to spend the summer in England. Sidney was too caught up in work to leave. 'I attend meeting after meeting about TV,' he wrote to Charlie Chaplin in Geneva. 'But the meetings alas are not televised. They would be very very funny.' Sandra was pregnant and the baby expected for 'early Autumn release'. While Coppings was being extended to cope with the growing numbers of inhabitants, the family moved for a couple of weeks into Bailiffscourt Hotel in Climping near Littlehampton, 'a Tudor residence, con- structed stone by stone, oak beam by oak beam, lead light by lead light by a mad Guinness in 1934.' It was a very hot summer, almost too hot to work. From the windows of his office in Golden Square Sidney could see the Italians preparing for a summer festival in the street. 'Poor, poor sad Italians from Soho,' he wrote. 'It's all rather like an amateur performance at Herne Bay.'

In July 1955 Orson Welles married his third wife, Paola. After the ceremony, in a register office in London, they drove down to lunch at Coppings, making a frenzied and largely successful effort to escape from reporters. It was to have been a lunch party only, but the Welleses stayed on. 'There were high-powered telephone calls to London, Paris, Rome,' Sidney described the scene, 'train reservations for Paris by the midnight ferry from Dover ... Welcome enough but a little exhausting.'

The months leading up to the opening of the new service were made more frantic by last-minute changes of cast. By early 1955 it had become clear that Norman Collins's original consortium, the Associated Broadcasting Development Group, was not going to get on to the air at all without fresh backing, and that the ITA was highly reluctant to accept its proposal to bring in further Conservative newspaper interests in the form of the *News of the World* or the *Daily Express*. Eventually, in March, a solution had been reached that pleased all sides. Incorporated Television Co. Ltd, a group of largely entertainment interests composed of Moss Empires Ltd, Howard and Wyndham Ltd, the Grade organisation and the merchant bankers Warburg and Co. Ltd, who had earlier bid for a contract and lost it on the grounds that they did not possess the breadth of interests that ITA thought their winning contractors should possess, now merged with ABC to produce a new and powerful grouping, Associated Television. To ATV went ABC's original patch, London, Saturday and Sunday, and the Midlands, Monday to Friday. Lew Grade had entered television.

More dramatic perhaps, because the original group had appeared so promising, was the defection of the Kemsley-Winnick partnership. After some months of confusion, Lord Kemsley announced that he was going to withdraw altogether from television. But that was not until the end of June 1955. The consortium foundered. The day before Associated-Rediffusion went on the air, in September, ABC Television, under a former BBC radio and Pathé film man called Howard Thomas, who had originally applied and been turned down, was allocated the gap left by Kemsley-Winnick: the Midlands and the North, Saturday and Sunday. The main network was at last complete.

At 7.15 p.m. on Thursday, 22 September 1955, in an atmosphere of solemnity and pomp, to the sounds of Elgar's *Cockaigne* from Sir John Barbirolli and the Hallé Orchestra, Associated-Rediffusion came on the air. The ceremony took place in London's Guildhall before a banquet for five hundred and accompanied by smoked salmon, turtle soup, lobster in Chablis, roast grouse or partridge, pear melba and dessert. To drink there was white Burgundy, punch, Madeira, Rhine wine, champagne, claret, port and brandy. After the arrival of the guests came the National Anthem and speeches by the Lord Mayor of London, Sir Seymour Howard, and Sir Kenneth Clark, the chairman of the ITA. A hearty address was delivered by Dr Hill, Postmaster-General: 'There are some people who regret that television was ever invented ... But television is here and an immensely powerful, evergrowing medium it is ...'

This mildly sanctimonious tone vanished when Hughie Green came on screen to announce the first cash quiz, 'Double Your Money', and Christopher Chataway, better known to the British public as a runner, told viewers, in his guise as the first ITN newscaster, about an Old Bailey criminal trial. An hour after transmission started, a tube of toothpaste frozen inside a block of ice heralded the first commercial break. For all those who had fought so hard against the evil and morally corrupting powers of independent television, it was a bit of an anticlimax.

Sidney had been invited to the Guildhall to sit among the dignitaries and eat his roast grouse. He refused, not having a taste for such occasions and deploring the decision to turn a service intended for the public into an exclusive, white tie, ceremony. He was also able to plead family priorities, for Sandra was expected to give birth at any moment. (The baby, David, was born next day.) What Sidney did instead however was use the occasion for a bit of publicity of his own. Early on in his planning Sidney had announced the intention of setting up teams for Outside Broadcasts, 'Travelling Eyes' as he called them, who would circle the area, fully equipped as mobile control rooms, and bring outside events live to the screen. By September the Granada vans were not technically equipped, but considerable thought had gone into the design of these visible pale-blue vehicles and from the outside, at least, they appeared ready. As Associated-Rediffusion began to broadcast, Sidney sent them out to drive around London, particularly through the City and streets surrounding the Guildhall. 'Keep your eyes on Granada,' read the slogans painted on the sides. (He also had posters with the same words printed and stuck to the windows of some Granada offices in Warwick Street, which overlooked the offices of ABC, until the infuriated chairman, Sir Philip Warter, begged him to take them down.)

In the eyes of the critics, next morning, independent television had got off to a pale and timid start. 'It was BAD showmanship', complained Clifford Davis of the *Daily Mirror*, 'to waste so much time instead of getting on with the job that ITV has been brought in to do: ENTERTAIN.' Bernard Levin captured the mood perfectly in the *Manchester Guardian*, in a piece that mocked the terrors of those who had championed the BBC and morality. 'I feel neither uplifted nor depraved by what I have seen. But perhaps the deeper moral effects will make themselves felt only over a period of years.'

What viewers did not know was the combination of luck, planning and extraordinarily hard work that had gone into the launching of the new service. Right up to the last minute there was a strong possibility that the opening would have to be postponed. Associated-Rediffusion had appointed as general manager a retired naval officer called Captain Tom Brownrigg who had been overseeing the building of Bracknell New Town. Brownrigg hired 20th Century Fox studios in Wembley for the production of A-R's programmes and set about issuing orders and directives. The trouble was that Wembley was not a battleship and the unions did not care for his tone. The Association of Cine and Allied Technicians (ACT), later to become the Association of Cine and Television Technicians (ACTT) threatened industrial action. Their attitude was not softened by the fact that A-R's managing director, Paul Adorian, was pushing for the Municipal and General Workers' Union as the television union, or by the preference of some of those involved for the Association of Broadcasting Staffs. Granada's preferred union was the ACT. The day before A-R was to go on the air, the ACT announced that it was going to withdraw all its technicians.

Victor Peers had been a founder member of the ACT. He was honest and the union representatives respected him. When A-R came, in despair, to ask Sidney's advice about how to avert the threatened closure, Sidney proposed Peers as arbitrator. The suggestion mollified the ACT, who trusted Peers when he gave them his word that their complaints would be settled as soon as a meeting could be arranged. The strike was called off.

In the late summer of 1955, just as A-R was planning its opening night, the Manchester site was finally ready for the development of Granada's television centre. The job of constructing Phase 1, complete with one studio, telecine rooms, technical maintenance and rehearsal rooms, the conversion of a number of old buildings into property stores and offices, had gone to J. Gerrard and Sons Ltd of Swindon who had a good reputation for working to tight schedules. There was a great deal to be done: to lay the foundations alone, the contractors found they had to drill through fifteen feet down to bedrock, some of it rubble and the wrecks of old barges. Speed was still being urged on everybody, though Sidney had not given up his battle with Fraser to keep Granada off the air until both transmitters were ready.

In the middle of October Jim Phoenix, Sidney's northern representative, arrived on the site, installed himself in a wooden hut, and took charge. He had a typewriter, a secretary and a lamp, but nothing else. It became his job to help the operations of fourteen separate sub-contractors, arrange the installation of floodlights, so that work could continue long after the winter dusk had descended on the site, and sift through growing numbers of visitors in search of jobs. January 1956 was an exceptionally cold month. Anti-freeze had to be mixed into the concrete, and gas-powered heaters were brought to dry the plaster.

Ralph Tubbs, the master architect, and Sidney had formed an excellent working relationship, which was fortunate, given Sidney's never really articulated yearnings for architecture, what friends describe as the 'architect manqué' in him. The Phoenix Theatre and the super-cinemas of the 1920s and 1930s had partially satisfied that need – but not quite. Here, finally, was a chance to create an entire, enormous building of his own, a television centre the like of which had never been seen before, and to make it perfect. He could have been impossible, overbearing. As it was, he liked and admired Tubbs, and over most things he deferred to him. Sidney, as Tubbs soon discovered, had a passionate, almost obsessive interest not just in the broader sweeps of his new building, but in every single detail of its execution. The two men had spent six days 'locked up together, doing nothing else but formulate our plan', remembers Tubbs. It was a vast, splendid, ambitious plan, consisting of phases of construction, with a cautious start, building up, area by area, over time. (It has worked out much as the two men dreamt it.) After that, Sidney left him alone. 'He wanted to be told about everything, right down to the thickness of the floor screens, but he did not come and hang over me at site meetings. He said it was wrong for the client to be there. I considered that a nice gesture, as I knew perfectly well he was bursting to come.'

Sidney was not always so restrained. As with his theatres he wanted to know not only what was going on, but to lay down for himself exactly how and when it should be done. His overwhelming curiosity, which made him such an alert and enchanting friend, could be a burden for employees. He never really liked other people making decisions. The trouble was that there wasn't much time for ritual deliberations. Reg Hammans, a normally placid man, but now driven close to despair by the sheer psychological pressures of getting the service on to the air, had endlessly to decide between making a minor decision on his own, risking Sidney's displeasure, or postponing it altogether until Sidney returned from London to Manchester. It never lessened Hammans's respect for Sidney – to this day the engineer who laid Granada's technical foundations maintains that without Sidney the station would never have been launched – but it did increase the strain. And among the men who witnessed the process by which Sidney's decisions were made – 'Wait a minute: why have this?', 'Would something else not be cheaper?', 'Is there nothing better?' – was born the feeling that here was a man with an almost maniacal obsession with detail, a visionary who couldn't stick to his visions.

It was a difficult time for Sidney. Though now the decision to become a television company was made, and Cecil, Joe Warton and Victor Peers had declared themselves closely behind him, he continued to feel, rightly, a sense of personal responsibility. If Granada Television foundered, it would be his fault. After all, it was *his* life that had been insured, for £750,000, when the contract was signed. It was hardly surprising, then, that as the months passed, and the expenses mounted far beyond the original budget, Sidney fretted. No one, of course, could have said in advance precisely what it was all going to cost. But Sidney, when it came to money, was by nature and experience a man who believed that everything could be done better and more cheaply if you were rigorous enough in your standards and your practices. He had proved it before: why not now? Neither was the news from elsewhere good: both Associated-Rediffusion and ATV were losing money fast.

Money, therefore, became an increasingly delicate subject at Granada, with Sidney setting an example of frugality by travelling about Manchester in a small, slightly battered rented car. No employee, however senior, was permitted to spend more than £20 without the approval of a senior member of the Board. Technically this led to economies Hammans found frightening. The engineer had pressed for an additional source of power in the form of extra generators in case the mains failed. Sidney refused. Unlike all other stations, Granada had nothing to fall back on. The saving was enormous, but had the power failed it would have been catastrophic. As it happened the power never did fail. Later people were to say: 'Sidney's contribution, above all else, was that he kept his nerve.' Sidney himself accepts this.

And he could at times be accommodating. If he took decisions, sometimes in the face of all logical reasoning, he was also prepared to reverse them, if a good enough case was made. Silvio Narizzano was a Canadian television director, recruited by Sidney from CBC. He arrived at the sprouting television centre one day to find that Sidney had accepted Sol Cornberg's idea that the control room of the studio should have only monitors and no window at all. The window was in the process of being blocked up. Narizzano felt passionately that this was wrong: as a director he knew that he had to be able to see for himself everything that was going on in the studio and not just what the camera was picking up. He sensed too that actors needed that window and the contact it gave them with the director.

Sidney was in London that day. When he got back to Manchester he found an indignant Narizzano waiting for him. Together, and surrounded by some thirty interested members of the staff, they went to inspect the contested window. Narizzano made a speech about umbilical cords between actor and director. The technicians said it was ridiculous. Suddenly Sidney spoke up. 'If you want the window, Narizzano, you shall have it. From now on, it will be known as Narizzano's window.' He left.

While the building was going up, Granada was busy recruiting staff. It meant a great deal of work and a lot of commuting between London and Manchester. 'All well and some winter sunshine today,' Sidney wrote to Chaplin, telling him that at eight weeks the baby David already weighed 14 lb. 13 ozs and adding: 'TV is a bugger.' Recruiting is a lengthy process anywhere, but in the case of Granada it was further extended by a tradition that Sidney had insisted on bringing in from the theatres. Every potential employee had to be interviewed not just by the Bernstein brothers, but by every one of any standing in the company. What counted was not only experience and talent but, perhaps more important than either, the ability to get on with everyone else. As the appointments multiplied, so did the numbers of interviews and vettings. 'Sidney', says one early employee, 'was an excellent judge of people. Nearly all those he was wary of to start with left. He could detect that little bit of grit at a first interview.'

One of the problems about finding staff was where, given that no one knew precisely what would be needed in the way of skills, you looked for them. The BBC had staved off poaching as hard as it could – Reg Hammans was in fact one of the very few BBC men to go over to Granada – and Sidney had decided early on to turn to North America for help. Apart from the Canadian director Silvio Narizzano, there was Robert Heller, refugee from McCarthyism and an expert in programming, and Sol Cornberg, the technical genius borrowed from NBC.

In England, old film friends came to join the team; like Harry Watt, who had made *London Can Take It*, except that he left almost at once to study television production in America with Ed Murrow, begging Sidney in a long and detailed letter not to spend time and money on putting up the most splendid television centre in the world – another Granada Tooting? – if it was at the expense of recruiting talented people on to the staff (Sidney, some people complained, tended to go only for those he already knew). Denis Forman, former director of the British Film Institute, was now inveigled away by Sidney from an advertising agency. Forman's first job was as informal personnel officer and he set about recruiting a young team of journalists. Soon he moved to programme planning. A third crucial English arrival was Eddie Pola, a theatre director who had spent some time in America and who now came to take charge of variety entertainment.

Recruiting the sixty or so engineers the company thought they needed was particularly difficult. There was no such thing available as television experience. Granada engineers thus came from radar, from industry and from electrical engineering: only one in five had ever been inside a television studio before.

There were other problems. A-R's insistence on going for the maximum hours of transmission immediately meant that a complete contingent of staff had to be taken on at once, rather than building one up slowly. Then, by coming on the air last, Granada was also last in its search for staff, and some promising candidates went to the other stations. Finally, there was the vexed question of Manchester. From the earliest days Sidney had declared his credo for the North, sworn his allegiance to an area and to a channel: Granada was going to belong to the North, and there was to be nothing token about that commitment. Granada employees were going to have to live in Manchester, not commute.

Not all the Granada founding planners were altogether convinced by this pledge of Sidney's. Harry Watt, writing from America, urged that the main studio be built in London. Granada, he said, should have a 'Northern flavour' certainly, but it couldn't afford to do without the 'stars' or resources that could only be found in the capital. Neither, it now turned out, was every would-be television employee overjoyed at the idea of moving to Manchester. Usually Sidney, who could not be persuaded that his course of action was not the best one, was honest. For many, he paid the fares for reconnaissance trips and provided help with houses and finding schools. Sometimes though he chose to evade the issue. There were early recruits, like Silvio Narizzano, who later protested that they would never have joined Granada at all if someone had actually told them that it meant Manchester.

It was during these first, hard, confused months that Sidney and Cecil began to lay down a pattern of shared work that was to last until Cecil died in 1981. The two brothers had always been close; Sidney was less involved with either Max or Albert and could be irritable in their company. Now, as decisions piled up that needed to be taken, Cecil and Sidney spent a considerable amount of time every day on the telephone to each other, describing progress, reaching agreement. Sometimes it was Cecil who had the greater expertise and insisted on a certain course of action; more often it was Sidney who had been fired by some new scheme and was anxious to push it through. To some measure, these calls replaced meetings. Sidney, Cecil and their families met surprisingly little, though it also became true that a complete separation of work from friendship became something of Granada's style, at least at the top of the company. Sidney admired and liked the people who came to work for Granada; but not many felt sure they ever became true friends. Sidney's old dislike of the pack behaviour of the film world made him determined to keep his distance.

For some of the newcomers their first introduction to Sidney at work was when he came to lecture at the Viking Studios, in Kensington, fitted up by Marconi as a mock TV centre and hired by Granada to train production staff. Here in nine weeks they learnt everything from the technical skills of a vision mixer to how to produce a panel game or co-ordinate a musical. Sidney's role was to reassure them about the business and to describe his ideas about how drama should be filmed. He was an uneasy teacher, but his friendship with Eisenstein and his partnership with Hitchcock had had a marked effect on his thinking. The recruits were impressed by this tall, elegant figure, more scholarly than business-like, perched up on some scaffolding to address them.

At the end of February the eight or nine directors and assistants who seemed best suited to the job were sent up to Manchester to train on Sidney's Travelling Eyes. These two units, control rooms on wheels, with their mobile power generators, were immensely important to Granada. They were not only going to have to supplement the single Manchester studio but simply by being so visible they acted as superb publicity stunts for Granada. The sight of these luminous pale-blue vehicles with their distinctive lettering and aura of technical expertise, as they carried out their dummy run closed-circuit broadcasts at Stockport County's football match, or visited a boxing match at the Manchester YMCA, gave Northerners immense confidence in what was coming.

Their presence was particularly effective in that Granada appeared to be keeping almost totally silent about its plans for production. During the final months only two projects were announced to the public. One was that Sidney had invited Sir Solly Zuckerman, Secretary of the Zoological Society, to pioneer a completely new kind of film coverage of animal life. He wanted, as he put it, to get away from the 'buns to elephants' style of programme. It wasn't his first approach to the Zoo. Some years before, in 1952, he and Victor Rothschild had put money into a joint project with Julian Huxley, then the Society's Secretary, to produce films of the animals. At every stage, and for many reasons, these films had not turned out well. The difference now was that the proposal was on a different scale altogether. A special film unit was to be built at the Zoo, which would turn out regular programmes about animals, with continuity from generation to generation, and there were to be sponsored film wildlife expeditions abroad. A young zoologist called Desmond Morris was brought down from Oxford to introduce the programmes.

Granada's only other definite pronouncement concerned music. Sidney had never professed to know much about music, but he had a vast admiration for Sir Thomas Beecham, whose family he had known slightly for years. 'He was rare,' he now says about the conductor, using one of the highest words of praise in his particular private language, ranking only slightly below someone who 'has quality'. 'He was witty, gay, sporty, our sort of man.' The Beecham Pills Manchester background also gave him a local credential. In the early summer of 1955, through Denis Forman who was, by contrast to Sidney, very musical, Granada invited Sir Thomas to become musical consultant to the company. Sidney had had the idea, among other things, of filming the conductor at various stages of preparation for a concert, building up to the performance itself. Sir Thomas replied to the Granada proposal at some length. He looked upon television, he wrote, 'very much as a miniature or intimate version of the motion picture'. To satisfy the pictorial requirements of the medium he now suggested programmes that ranged from one-act operas to short ballets and the much neglected *tableaux vivants* of composers like Sibelius. At the end of his letter he proposed a yearly fee of £12,000. Granada accepted.

Sir Thomas Beecham's relationship with Granada was a good one.

Not long after Granada came on the air, the Temple Bar Music Association asked Sir Thomas to conduct a concert for them and invited the BBC to televise it. Sir Thomas, faithful to his promise, refused, saying that he would have no part in it unless Granada were the station to take full television rights. The Temple Bar Association clearly belonged to those who were suspicious of commercial television. Finally, with extreme reluctance, they agreed, but stipulated that no advertisements were to be shown at any time during the concert. Sidney refused. He had had no intention of breaking a performance with advertisements, but profoundly disliked this kind of bullying, superior interference. It was Sir Thomas who intervened and the concert went ahead.

Sidney and he became lifelong friends. When Sir Thomas was already in his seventies Sidney made one effort to put an end to a state of financial affairs in the conductor's life that seemed to be plaguing him. Sir Thomas was, and had long been, extremely, obsessively, anxious about the tax authorities, and, in order to minimise the time he spent in England, chose frequently to leave the country by night train for Paris the moment a concert ended. One day Sidney went to call on Sir Edward Playfair at the Treasury. He told him that he thought that it was disgraceful to harass such an old and distinguished man. Sir Edward offered to look into the matter.

A few weeks later he informed Sidney that there was some mistake. Sir Thomas was not being pursued for tax. He was in fact perfectly free to come and go as he pleased. No one was after him. Sidney was delighted and went round to tell Sir Thomas the news. But the conductor could not bring himself to believe it and he continued to hurry from the country the moment his concerts were over.

Granada's reticence about plans was not entirely intentional. One of the early recruits to Granada's staff had been Bob Heller, recommended by Ed Murrow, who had been running a sports station in Mexico after McCarthy had forced him out of America. Heller was intelligent, charming and exuded a certain forcefulness, but he was not decisive. Sidney put him in charge of programmes. As the months went by, no programmes materialised. Instead, a puppet called Jolly Good appeared, and Heller talked lovingly about the day when there would be a Jolly Good puppet show, with Jolly Good T-shirts and Jolly Good lemon squash. The model puppet sat displayed on his desk. Questioned about programmes he would say reassuringly: 'Television is an instantaneous medium. Wait till it starts. Then you'll make good programmes.'

Towards the end of March it became obvious that there was a real shortage of programmes, apart from the light entertainment that Cecil was supervising. Nor were there going to be any, unless someone acted quickly. Sidney himself had taken over the planning for opening night but beyond that there was a terrible void. Forman was the first to take in what was happening and he went in despair to Sidney, who called an urgent meeting of all senior producers and sketched out a series of ideas which were immediately put into effect. Heller had retired to his bed. He didn't reappear until just before Granada went on the air; shortly afterwards he left the company.

One effect of the hiatus was that in the absence of all pronouncements Granada was acquiring a reputation for high-mindedness and serious programmes. No one could quite say where the feeling came from. It may have been inspired by Granada's own application, in which it spoke of its experience of ballet, symphony concerts, opera and plays. It may simply have been a natural response to the attacks now being levelled against the commercial companies already on the air that their programmes were too trivial. Whatever the reason, people began to look to Granada for culture, and it was not until many months after the opening that the Bernsteins were able to persuade viewers that they were in fact a perfectly balanced station.

The last weeks before the opening were not very happy ones for the Bernsteins. Independent television was not proving a success. The critics did not like what they saw and were saying so, loudly. They complained that there was not enough contrast with the BBC. They said that the picture was poor. They described the quiz programmes as being of a very low standard. Public figures like the Archbishop of Canterbury and Christopher Mayhew were still venting their disapproval of the existence of the service altogether. What was more, the advertisers did not seem to care for it either. When the London audience turned out to be smaller than had been expected, advertisers began to pull out. On 31 March 1956, just weeks before Granada expected to go on the air, the *Daily Mail* quoted Sir Robert Fraser as saying that losses by the independent companies in the first six months were in the order of £600,000 to £700,000. None of this was reassuring. The others appeared to be failing: why should Granada succeed?

Against this gloomy background Granada now prepared to come on the air. On 20 April, while the building in Manchester was still full of carpenters and electricians, and much remained to be painted, it was suddenly announced that the opening would be Thursday 3 May, for the Lancashire station alone. Sidney had lost his battle to open with his entire territory. There were thirteen days to go.

A month before, Sidney had written to Sir Robert Fraser to tell him of his ideas for the opening programmes. 'This is an opportune time', he wrote, 'for saying that we are much opposed to the "white-tie civic" ceremonies such as were held in London and Birmingham.' What he proposed, he explained, was to launch Granada Television precisely as Granada had always launched their new theatres: by introducing, one by one, all the people from the foreman upwards who had combined to get the new service on the air. After this, he said, there would be 'one of our normal programmes'.

It fell to Victor Peers to do the actual launching. He, Sidney felt, had been the figure most responsible for co-ordinating the entire operation. Peers was nervous but delighted at the honour. At 7.30 on 3 May the screens of those viewers in the North who had had their television sets converted to receive Granada lit up to show Peers sitting at a desk. 'From the North, this is Granada – on Channel 9,' he announced in a clear, slightly unsteady voice. 'A year ago Granada was a blueprint, a promise. Tonight the North has a new television service created by the devotion and hard work of thousands of Northerners and friends from all over the world ... '

Quentin Reynolds had never really recovered his former prestige after the Pegler trial. In appreciation of his past work, and also because he admired him greatly as a broadcaster, Sidney had invited him to come to Manchester to act as introducer of 'Meet the People' on Granada's opening night. It was very nearly a disaster.

Reynolds had always been a heavy drinker. At the dress rehearsal, on the 2nd, he had turned up drunk, charming but swaying and incoherent. Sidney, appalled but realising that it was too late for a change, had led him back to the Midland Hotel; on the way Reynolds kept moaning: 'Sidney, I've let you down. I've let you down.'

However on the night of the 3rd he was sober. One by one, as they came to join him, in the centre of the stage, he introduced, in clear, friendly tones, Ralph Tubbs, Jack Caine, the twenty-stone builders' foreman, Harry Hunter who climbed the 450 foot mast at Winter Hill, the Lord Mayor of Manchester, Alderman Tom Regan, and his daughter, the Lady Mayoress and Sir Kenneth Clark.

The introductions over, Arthur Askey sang some impromptu songs as part of 'London Salutes Lancashire'; one of those saluting was Gracie Fields, old Granada and Bernstein friend, not in person, but filmed from Texas, wearing a ten-gallon hat. Then came an outside broadcast of a featherweight boxing contest from Liverpool, the first of a series called 'Blue Murder', presented by Douglas Fairbanks, and the news. The evening ended with a gesture absolutely typical of Sidney: a tribute to the BBC, compered by Aidan Crawley (the first head of independent news, who later resigned from ITN) in which the stars and founders of the rival service were honoured. It included a filmed talk, with Sidney himself, perched on the edge of a desk, giving a few words of introduction; no natural performer, he looked benign but decidedly nervous.

For most of those watching, the programmes were good, and set a right note, but they were not in themselves something radically new. The advertisements on the other hand were, and Granada was not a company to let an opportunity pass. Even here, something typical of the whole Bernstein ethos, that blend of high standards and strict economy, sounded out: 'Wise spending', an announcer told the viewers, 'eventually saves money. And savings can help deal with one aspect of our country's economic problems. So before we shop let us say to ourselves: "Is it essential?" If it is let us buy the best we can afford; if it is not essential, can we save?' It might have been Sidney talking.

Sidney himself spent the opening hours of transmission mostly by himself, watching the programmes on a television set in his office. He preferred to be alone. That morning he had received a cable from Vernon Jarratt, his mustachioed friend from the Italian campaign: 'Lighting a candle for you'. To which he had replied, since Jarratt was that same day opening a restaurant in Rome, 'Lighting a candelabra for you'. After it was all over, after it was clear that the evening had worked, the transmission had been clear, the picture good, the presentation serious but entertaining, Sidney and Sandra went to the Midland Hotel to see what was happening at the two small parties Granada was holding for the opening. One was for Granada staff and their wives. The other was for advertisers. Standing outside the door, Sidney overheard a Manchester voice exclaim crossly: 'Typical: that's for the toffs – not for the likes of us!' Any such festivity, the implication was, could only be for Londoners. The suggestion was all that Sidney had tried to avoid. What was more, it was wrong. Had friends not been there to lead Sidney away, the two men might have come to blows.

11

The Creation of Granada

AT FIRST, IT seemed to some of those most involved with Granada that while an immense amount of energy had gone into launching the television station, not a great deal had been kept back to formulate a policy for its programmes. The sheer physical and mental challenge of bringing a new independent service into existence appeared to have spent their forces: who was to shape the product?

True, the Bernsteins had always made it clear that theirs would be a responsible, ambitious, Northern-minded company which would talk to ordinary people in language they would understand; true, they had spoken splendidly of great dramas and highly professional light entertainment. But where was all this to come from? In the early months of the ITA's existence, Sir Robert Fraser had shown foresight when he said: 'The Authority has one moment of supreme and lasting influence over programmes: when it decides who will produce them and who will not.' After that, he seemed to imply, the Authority was not going to be left with all that much to say. Granada, under Sidney's very individual touch, now set about proving that far from being shapeless, it had clear ideas of where it was going, and furthermore, that it was going to be an institution unlike the other companies and very loath indeed to be shaped by any outside influence at all, whatever its title or its standing.

Granada came on the air, in the first week of May 1956, with its quota of foreign films, its much-publicised outside broadcasts conducted from the pale-blue vans, a great deal of material exchanged or 'networked' from the other companies, and four indigenous programmes all destined to long runs. There was 'Youth Is Asking', in which young people questioned a public figure, a panel game called 'My Wildest Dream', a quiz 'Spot the Tune', and 'Zoo Time'.

'Zoo Time' was an instant success. The public seemed to appreciate Sidney's desire to get away from buns and elephants and a cult soon formed around the affable figure of Desmond Morris, who had suggested having a special studio built at the zoo, and now was able to accustom the animal performers to a constant setting. 'Zoo Time' produced its mascots, in the shape of Nikki, a bear cub presented to the Queen by Bulganin and Khrushchev, and later, and more permanently, a chimpanzee called Congo, who took to painting, became a celebrated artist, and died young when, grown too large and dangerous for the programme, he was parted from the human beings to whom he had grown accustomed, and returned to the chimpanzee society he had never known.

The very fact that 'Zoo Time' – like every other programme at the time – was live, gave an edge to the performances, particularly since animals were so unpredictable. Not long after Congo joined the unit, Morris placed the monkey on the floor while he presented another animal to viewers from the top of a table. As he was describing the new beast's characteristics, his face contorted into what seemed to be a series of strange facial tics which caused his mouth and lips to twist in a very unattractive manner. When the show ended, Sidney rang the producer: Desmond Morris was indeed a competent and articulate presenter, but could he possibly learn to control his unfortunate affliction? It was then that it was revealed that Congo, hidden by the table, kept sinking his sharp little teeth into Morris's ankle and hanging on until he was kicked off, only to wait to find a fresh spot to attack. Another 'Zoo Time' was given over to watching a marmot climb out of its hole. The marmot refused to do so. Desmond Morris spent the half-hour improvising on the fascinating and diverse features of marmot behaviour, from time to time returning to peer hopefully at the empty hole, rather, as he later put it, 'like going back to Lords to see if the pitch was still covered'.

'Zoo Time' lasted for 331 programmes and formed only the first of a growing number of highly successful animal programmes put out by Granada. Sidney, who knew nothing at all about animals, encouraged the series, pleased that his first hunch about popular taste had proved so accurate. Some time later he discovered that a Giant Panda had been brought out of China destined for a zoo in America but that it had been stopped in Berlin and denied an entry visa into America on account of its communist origins. He asked a very surprised and disconcerted Joe Warton to accompany an expert from the London Zoo to Berlin, where they duly put in a bid for the animal and secured it, for £7,000.

The real attractions of Granada's early days, however, were its outside broadcasts. They were not only an essential technical addition, since Granada's studio facilities in Manchester were still very limited, but they provided the station with an immediate Northern credential. During one of the first weeks on the air, the two Travelling Eyes did eight outside broadcasts in five days: they talked to L. S. Lowry; they visited art galleries and old people's homes and exhibitions; they photographed Lancashire's main traffic bottlenecks. On Monday 7 May, three nights after Granada opened, they pulled off a scoop by covering, with a bare six hours' warning, the triumphant return home of the winning Manchester City soccer team, bearing their cup from Wembley.

Five vehicles were allocated to the job of transporting all movable equipment, and in an operation worthy of a small military action, cameras were carried up to windows overlooking the route, hundreds of yards of wire and cable were unrolled and connected, and the driver of a Manchester Corporation line maintenance lorry was cajoled into bearing the sound cable on his elevated platform across the crowds and traffic to a microphone in front of the Town Hall. Half an hour before the winning team showed up, Granada was ready for them. 'We haven't been so thrilled since the Coronation,' said the *News Chronicle*, the following morning. It had been the perfect test for the system and it had paid off. What was more, it was fun. It gave those who were involved, and those who had spent so long planning, an extraordinary sense of the as yet untried powers of the new medium.

There were, of course, appalling disasters: the weather was a perpetual gamble, the technical back-up of such ambitious transmission was still far from perfect, would-be performers turned out to be camera shy and timing bedevilled the organisers. Many of the early fiascos have become legends in Granada history, like the day a Travelling Eye spent half an hour with its cameras trained on Barton Bridge to watch it open for the ocean-going ships, and the bridge never opened; or the occasion when the two unions at Liverpool docks refused to participate in a programme twenty minutes before it went on the air, and the frantic interviewer had to latch on to a particularly inarticulate Ship's Captain, the only person he could find on the docks, and resort to questions like, 'Captain, is that a blue jersey you are wearing?'; or, perhaps most catastrophic of all, the day an Outside Broadcast visited the Reg Harris Cycle Stadium to cover a bicycle race, only to find that rain had caused it to be cancelled, so that the two presenters spent thirty minutes in the deserted stands talking to each other about bicycles as the rain poured down on their heads. But these were all part of the myth, the bravura of live television. Even Sidney, normally so utterly demanding of perfection, sympathised and laughed. There was nothing bogus about what was happening. What was more, it had a freshness that could only belong to television, and there was no mistaking the impact it was having on the public. 'People thought: this is amazing,' Sir Denis Forman once described the feeling. 'Here are people actually out in the open air taking motion pictures, and we can see them in our homes. It was as simple as that. It was as impressive as the early Lumière Brothers' films were, *and* it was in the North.'

And so, in these first few months at Granada, the programme-makers thrived, as they experimented with the seemingly limitless potential of their new toy. The contractors themselves, however, were not having such a good time. By the summer of 1956 it was clear that independent television had run into difficulties; it was far from certain that they were going to be resolved. Total financial collapse seemed imminent. The advertisers had not taken to the new medium as they had been expected to, and the costs of running an independent television station, let alone those of equipping it, were turning out to be far higher than anyone had calculated. Associated-Rediffusion was reported to be losing about £300 an hour, and had apparently been doing so since it went on the air the previous September. ATV's losses were smaller, but still disconcerting.

Granada was in a particularly unfortunate position. They had been obliged to start broadcasting when only one of their two transmitters was ready, and only two-thirds of their possible audience able to receive their programmes; there was very little chance indeed of their being able to break even, let alone make a profit, until their Yorkshire transmitter at Emley Moor started functioning towards the end of the year. Sidney's letters to the Authority and Sir Robert Fraser had by now become decidedly bitter. On 18 June, he wrote pointing out that, as he had feared and warned, his advertising revenue had been dramatically hit by having to open in summer. What was more, ABC Television, which had opened its weekday service in the Midlands in February, had scooped Granada by offering both areas to advertisers at a reduced rate for when its weekend Northern service opened. 'Our losses are staggering,' Sidney told the ITA. 'But not as a result of any extravagance on capital expenditure or operational costs.'

Over and above their day-to-day losses all four companies were having to find the money to pay the ITA the agreed rental – fixed at around two shillings per head of population in any given area – to cover their own running costs. When John Spencer Wills, the chairman of Associated-Rediffusion, spoke at the annual meeting he was voicing the anxieties of them all when he declared:

Never in all the thirty-five years I have been in the business have I come across a case in which the task of the entrepreneur has been made more difficult. A limited security of tenure from the Conservative Government, a threat of extinction from the Labour opposition, an excessively high annual payment to the ITA, an obligation to put on 'minority' programmes of small advertising value, a host of restrictions imposed by statute and licence, threats of additional competition from the BBC – all these must daunt the wildest optimist.

Presumably the former enemies of commercial television, whose hostility must have been inflamed at least partly by the prospect of so much money to be made, now felt some sort of grim satisfaction at what was happening.

At Granada, where losses were averaging £20,000 a week, Sidney and Cecil were faced with two possibilities for cutting costs. They could reduce the budgets for their productions, but these had already been reduced to the bare minimum, in keeping with the whole Granada ethos about waste and good housekeeping; or they could increase their revenue. It was with this latter choice in mind that, shortly after Granada came on the air, Sidney embarked on a series of visits to major Northern company chairmen who were big advertisers in newspapers with a view to drumming up custom in the summer months, traditionally the least propitious for advertising. Everywhere, he says, he was greeted with great courtesy. He came to these sceptical Northern businessmen with a very clear proposal. What he was asking for, he told them, was help – there was no disguising it – in these early months of his television service. In return for generous help now, in the form of booked advertising slots, he would help them later. What was more, if the programmes failed to meet a certain stipulated minimum number of viewers, he would credit the advertisers with a refund – rather on the model of the American newspapers, over which he had had his disagreement with Warner's.

A great many of these chairmen listened to him: Sidney could be very persuasive with his immense restrained charm, and that stillness of manner that comes with a certain kind of power. Before long, Beecham's, Lever Brothers and Colgate had agreed to lend their support. Meanwhile, Alex Anson was doing a similar sort of round of the smaller companies. His trawls brought in Leyland Paints, Guhl Laboratories and Rothstones, a gentleman's outfitters.

All of this, however, was still not nearly enough. The losses kept mounting. The only way out of what threatened now to be a genuine crisis seemed to be to share production costs with other weekday companies, not on the casual basis which had operated since the beginning of independent television, but according to a fixed, and carefully costed, formula.

Stories now started appearing in the newspapers saying that Granada had agreed to exchange more programmes with ATV, but that they were having some disagreements with A-R about networking. Two weeks later, Granada sold their first show, 'Spot the Tune', to the London and Midland companies. On 25 June, the *Manchester Guardian* reported 'hard bargaining and disagreement over which programmes are networked'. A-R was demanding high fees for its top light entertainment shows, and refusing some of Granada's more serious programmes on the grounds that they were 'parochial'.

It was at this point that Sidney made a financial deal that was to alter, immediately and unequivocally, the fortunes of Granada. The nature of this agreement was, for many years, surrounded in mystery. Few of its ramifications were committed to paper, only the companies concerned were aware of its existence, and the ITA itself chose to stand back from its details. The agreement was not in fact made public until 1972, when Peter Black wrote about it in his book on the television companies, *Mirror in the Corner* (Hutchinson, 1972).

To this day the deal retains an aura of secrecy. To my letter asking whether he would describe to me his side of the bargain, Sir John Spencer Wills, the main figure involved, replied with a polite refusal.

The facts appear to be these. When Granada first thought of applying for a television licence they considered the possibility of asking for the London station. It was there, they agreed, that lay the main fields of interest and influence: Parliament, the City, the main daily newspapers and big business. Sidney, however, argued against it. He knew about Associated-Rediffusion, and didn't believe that the Granada Group could possibly hope to compete with them. What was more, if they applied for London and were turned down, they would lose all chance of a television station anywhere. So Granada applied for the North.

But Sidney never forgot about the desirability of London. And even as he was building up 'Granadaland', as his region was fast becoming known, he looked forward to the day when he might get at least his 'window' on to London. Now, as financial difficulties pressed in on him, he suddenly saw a way of preserving his television company precisely as he had conceived it, and at the same time bringing in by now urgently needed money.

Sidney went to call on John Spencer Wills. He proposed to him that they enter into a private arrangement, for a limited period of time, whereby, in return for a percentage of the net revenue from advertising in the North (which was currently meagre, with no immediate signs of picking up), Associated-Rediffusion would pay Granada the total costs of producing all the programmes that were networked between them. The percentages of this net revenue were high: up until 1958, 90 per cent of the first £1 million, 87 per cent of the next £3 million and 85 per cent of everything above £4 million, but production costs were of course offset against them. What Associated-Rediffusion stood to gain were programmes, reliable and popular programmes, of which they were by now acutely in need. In return, Granada was to be made safe: the Bernsteins, with a single stroke of the pen, were to be protected from having to bring in partners, raise loans, or part with any corner of family control. (The spectre of partnership was, after all, something that hung over all the independent companies, and Sidney felt about it precisely as he had felt when he turned down would-be associates in the early days. Cecil King, the newspaper proprietor who had made advances to Granada, had announced that he would come into commercial television 'after the second bankruptcy' and had recently bought his way into ATV with a fresh injection of much-needed capital.)

Just who, precisely, was informed of the Granada deal is unknown. Certainly the secretaries of the two companies, Joe Warton of Granada and Arthur Groocock of A-R, knew what was going on, as did their legal advisers and the boards. At the ITA, Sir Kenneth Clark and Sir Robert Fraser were undoubtedly given some account of the proposed exchange but probably preferred, with the current financial position of the independent companies, not to ask too many questions. They knew both Sidney and Spencer Wills of old and were confident that neither of them was a man likely to behave in breach of the Act; they also had every confidence in Sir Edwin Herbert, who was in effect the author of the document.

So little was said by anyone. It was not until April 1959 that Sir Ivone Kirkpatrick, the new chairman of the ITA, asked to see a copy of the contract, and that was thought to be in response to speculation in the newspapers about the size of the Granada profits in comparison to those of the other television contractors.

Whether Sidney would actually have signed such a deal, or anyway precisely the same deal, had he suspected how imminent and how vast were to be the profits of commercial television, is impossible to say. For when the fortunes of the contractors sharply turned and picked up, never to fall again, almost within weeks of the contract being signed, and Roy Thompson was able to make his immortal remark that independent television was 'just like having a licence to print money', Granada was forced to part with a considerable sum of money to

Associated-Rediffusion. According to Peter Black, the figure was £8,044,238 in the four years that the deal lasted.

Sidney himself says that he does not regret the decision. It has become fashionable to say that, without the agreement with A-R, Granada might have been in acute financial trouble: rumours have circulated for years about a possible bankruptcy that first summer and about the Fridays that came and went without the Bernsteins being able to pay all the bills and all the wages. He denies this, as do most people who understand the details of the company's financial standing. Granada might have needed to look for help, but that help would have been forthcoming from Barclays Bank, who had supported them before and had evident trust in their soundness.

For Sidney, the point about the deal with A-R, then as now, was that it guaranteed Granada its 'window' on to London. From the day it was signed, he knew that many of the programmes made by his company about which he cared most would be seen not just in the North but where he wanted them to be seen, in the capital. 'It is important to emphasise that we actually got our window,' he says now. 'I had got what I wanted. Whether I paid too much or too little doesn't now matter.' Bernard Sendall, then assistant at the ITA to Sir Robert Fraser, and author of *Independent Television in Britain*, agrees. He calls the deal a 'brilliant achievement on the part of Sidney' and one that turned out to be 'as successful for one company as it was for the other ... The money Granada gave to Associated Rediffusion was well worth parting with in exchange for what Granada actually got,' he says. 'And you have to remember: of the original four, it is the only one to have survived to this day entirely intact.'

The contract secret but signed, Cecil and Sidney renewed their campaign to formulate a viable networking agreement with all the companies for a given number of hours and slots each week. It was Cecil who now became one of the chief architects of a strategy that lasted largely unchanged for the next twelve years.

First of all, a full and not very effective Network Committee came into being on which sat representatives not just from the original contractors, but from the newly formed Scottish Television Ltd and the Welsh TWW, as well as members of the ITA. This large and unwieldy body spawned a smaller and more significant one, on which sat Cecil for Granada, Lew Grade for ATV, Tom Brownrigg, the naval captain, for A-R, and Howard Thomas for ABC. It was here that the decisions were really made and here too that the personalities of those involved emerged most conclusively. According to various people who at one time or another were allowed into this inner sanctum the meetings were lively, informal affairs at which Lew Grade, being the loudest and funniest of those present, would barter unashamedly for his company and his programmes, Tom Brownrigg would speak in clipped navalese and tend to treat the others as junior ratings, while Cecil was polite and infinitely shrewd. Much of the actual politicking went on outside meetings, over the telephone, and it was during these talks, particularly between Cecil and Lew Grade, old sparring partners from the days when Lew Grade was an agent and Cecil was trying to hammer out the smallest possible performers' fees for the Granada Theatres, that the bones of the networking agreement were laid. The conversations were made all the easier because of the very real regard felt by the Bernstein brothers for the Grades' business acumen and their integrity.

A notional value was fixed for every programme, which was then traded with the other companies on the principle that everything was exchanged, not paid for, that everyone would watch everyone else very carefully, and that the London company equalled twice ATV in the Midlands and Granada in the North, because it reached twice their populations. No one was allowed a veto over anyone else's shows – but they could, and did, complain afterwards. It was horsetrading, at its most basic, with each trader out to see that his company didn't suffer; but when the deals were drawn up, they seemed to work, and they were respected.

It was perhaps only now that Sidney felt able at last to start putting his own stamp on to Granada. The company was safe. What was more the future prospects of independent television were suddenly beginning to look very good indeed. Before the first year was over, Granada Television seemed to be finding a clear voice of its own: alert, irreverent, a little brash sometimes, but always new. Some of this spirit came from Sidney personally, with his drive for perfection, his delight in showmanship – by now, a framed picture of his hero Barnum had been hung in every office – his admiration for his friend Ed Murrow's brand of inquiring television journalism, and for the acerbic and literary plays of the American theatre. Some of it came with the people he found, and brought in, like Tim Hewat, a rude and ebullient Australian, a former Beaverbrook man (who hesitated at first, fearing that Sidney might turn out to be worse to work for than Beaverbrook), Henry Kaplan, a forceful Canadian theatre director with thick, rather tangled hair, and an eager young reporter from the *Yorkshire Post* called Barrie Heads. In 1956 Granada was a lively place to be.

Within the first year on the air Granada had put on its programme of six young people cross-questioning a figure of public interest – 'Youth

Is Asking'. It was not the first, but it was the most powerful, of what were to be dozens of programmes designed to probe, elucidate, inquire. This was Sidney's commitment to accountability: the public, he said to everyone who came to Granada, deserve to know. We must tell them. The journalists who had been sceptical of television were very relieved. And to the early and not enormously successful 'A Case to Answer', in which two 'advocates' – Robin Day and Kenneth Harris – debated the case for and against certain social issues, were now added a number of one-off documentaries, attempts, as Denis Forman explained, to 'speed up certain processes of social reform'.

The first of these was a forty-five-minute programme on euthanasia, called 'Thou Shalt Not Kill?'. The issues were presented clearly, without ambiguity. The initial reaction, from press and public, was one of amazement. It was not just that the question itself had never been debated on television before, but that no one had ever thought to consider television as a medium in which such subjects could be aired at all. After euthanasia came homosexuality, with a characteristic Sidney intervention. 'I don't think', said Sidney at an early meeting to discuss the programme, 'that the audience is going to understand what this means.'

'What?' said Denis Forman, disbelievingly, 'What?'

'Well,' said Sidney, 'how many people really know what buggery is?'

'Good Lord,' said Forman, *everybody* knows what buggery is.'

Sidney flung open the door to his secretaries' office. 'What's buggery? Who can give me a definition of buggery?' The secretaries looked embarrassed. Denis Forman and Silvio Narizzano, who was in on the meeting, were now dispatched down the corridor. Narizzano remembers Forman bursting into people's offices, puffing on a cigarette holder and saying to the secretaries: 'Definition of buggery, please. Definition of buggery.'

'Homosexuality and the Law' was timed to coincide with the publication of the Wolfenden Report (Forman stayed up all night when it was released, in order to précis it and lose no time for the programme); after that came programmes on AID, coloured immigrants, mental illness, venereal disease and the Pill. 'Sidney gave us the feeling that there should be no area of public interest that was closed to the public,' says Barrie Heads, today Managing Director of Granada International. 'If we wavered he was always the one who said: "Give it a go. Why take no for an answer?"' To the journalists who had joined, Sidney now seemed to possess the energy and the courage of the great pioneering liberal reformers. 'We considered ourselves in competition not with the other television companies, but with national newspapers,' says David Plowright, who at twenty-six had come from the *Yorkshire Post* to take over the New Department. He well remembers the day when Granada was the first to give the news of Kennedy's assassination, long before the regular ITV news, by breaking into the middle of a programme, something of personal triumph for Barrie Heads, who was on the phone to New York when the news came through and kept the line open, while at the same time co-ordinating Granada's reaction to the event. (The regulations were later amended so that it would have been impossible for them to do so again.) 'It was a form of arrogance and he supported it.'

In time, the social documentaries acquired a regular slot and a form and were given a name, 'Searchlight', which Hewat once described as guided by the statement 'This is wrong; put it right', and of which he said: 'There will be a strong flavour of "I accuse" in our treatment.'

Alongside these documentaries was now running another series of programmes, different in presentation, but no less challenging to received wisdom and unquestioning patterns of thought. Towards the end of 1956, Sidney decided to start a short, critical programme about the content of British newspapers – highly characteristic of him, given his ambivalence about the press – based on A. J. Liebling's column in the *New Yorker* called 'Our Wayward Press'. Once again, it was to America that he was looking. 'What the Papers Say', hated, admired and feared, was to become one of the station's longest running programmes. For twelve and a half years, public figures were to challenge, over the network, the sanctity of the British press.

One of the ITA's earliest stipulations to the independent contractors had concerned the need to keep a balanced and impartial presentation. Unable to devise a way of making a single presenter impartial – to do so would have been to render the programme without meaning – Sidney came up with the idea of inviting three journalists to become presenters of the programme, rotated week by week, left, right and centre. Since no immediately identifiable Liberal could be found, 'What the Papers Say' went on the air in November, with Kingsley Martin, editor of the *New Statesman*, speaking for the left and Brian Inglis, assistant editor of the *Spectator*, for the right. The idea was for them to compare the way in which various newspapers treated the same stories in reporting them, and for them to add a personal comment of their own – no very difficult undertaking at a time when the popular papers were notoriously casual in their reporting of facts. (Brian Inglis remembers a day when six newspapers gave six different colours to the dress the Queen had worn the previous day.)

'What the Papers Say' started inauspiciously. Kingsley Martin had been delighted to appear, but was terrified of the mechanics of live television. He couldn't, he said, handle a teleprompter, peering at it recalls Brian Inglis, 'from under those great bushy eyebrows with a look of malevolence on this face'. Though begged to try, he said he would prefer to memorise his script.

On the night, he arrived at the studio in a state of acute anxiety, looking grey. Denis Forman, who was producing the programme, feared he might have a heart attack. He rang Sister Ross, the studio nurse: 'We've got an old man in studio four who I think is pretty ill and he's due on the air in twenty minutes. Perhaps we should have a doctor along who might give him something to see him through.' Sister Ross was one of those old-fashioned battleaxe ladies. Ten minutes later she appeared in studio four, where Kingsley Martin was quaking miserably in a chair. 'Where's the old man who needs a doctor?' she bawled. Martin didn't realise that it was for him, but he was interested in the scene. He pulled himself together and was then sufficiently reassured to appear. But he was not then and nor was he designed to be a natural television broadcaster and before long his place had been taken by an MP called J. P. W. Mallalieu whose left-wing credentials came from contributions to the *New Statesman*.

There wasn't sensational news every week, but that did not prevent a perpetual state of battle and intrigue with the ITA, who continued to be terrified of possible bias. (Bernard Levin claims to hold the record with seventeen breaches of the Television Act in a fifteen-minute programme, the night a murderer was hanged.) The Authority itself was in the throes of its own quarrels with some of the newspapers and in particularly the *Daily Express*, which hounded it unmercifully (and, in revenge, fed Granada with material). It was the sort of battle Sidney much enjoyed, even when Lord Drogheda, Chairman of the Newspaper Publishing Association, rang him regularly each week to complain of bias. It also gave him a reputation, in fact not entirely justified, for pursuing some kind of personal vendetta against the newspapers. But it did him no harm. It all added to Granada's fast-growing reputation for bravado. And the public, who responded by inundating Granada week after week with examples worthy of inclusion, liked it.

In time, 'What the Papers Say' changed. How much influence it had had in lessening discrepancies in newspaper coverage, or rendering reporting more accurate, is hard to say. Certainly, during the early 1960s, the number of errors dropped, but that may have had nothing to do with Granada. On the programme there was seen to be a gradual erosion of the old Liebling idea of rooting out inconsistencies in favour of a far more searching scrutiny of Fleet Street itself.

The natural consequence of this mood of inquisitiveness was a close look at politics. Here Granada had to move carefully. The sanctity of the political apparatus was enshrined in British law, and upheld vigorously by the BBC which traditionally confined itself to official party political broadcasts and rigidly excluded from all programmes any material that could conceivably be thought to influence opinion on election issues. (Balance, as Anthony Wedgwood Benn wittily observed in the debate on the Television Bill, was observed to the point where 'a Liberal must never be allowed to talk about bee keeping without a Tory talking about fish'.)

As early as August 1955, almost a year before Granada came on the air, Sidney warned Sir Robert Fraser that his attitude to political reporting was to be very different. In a letter commenting on the absurdity of the fourteen-day rule – the ban of all discussions on television of public issues due for debate in Parliament within the next fourteen days – Sidney wrote:

> ... we would like to register our view, which is firmly held, that at some time in the future we shall wish to contest what appears to us to be an arbitrary check on our freedom and independence, and one which surely conflicts with our national traditions. It would be a strange situation, to say the least of it, if Britain, while continuing to boast of her freedom of speech and her free Press, had to admit to the world that of her two television services one was in some degree a State service and the other had to submit to a political embargo on the free discussion of public affairs.

The first opportunity Granada had to free television from its political chains came with the Rochdale by-election of 5 February 1958. The Government, the Representation of the People Act and the Television Act were all of the view that the best way to handle the event was to pretend that it was not happening. The Bernsteins, and in particular Denis Forman and the current affairs team, disagreed. This was one of the very rare chances, they declared, that the public ever had of taking decisive action, and it was the duty of television to stimulate interest, present the issues and show the candidates.

The actual programme on the election, when it appeared, was marked more by a note of extreme caution and even dullness than by any apparent crusading spirit. All it consisted of in the end was a short debate, in which the three Rochdale candidates, under an independent chairman, discussed the issues involved in the election. It was the fact that it had taken place – and that Granada was neither sued nor even censured – that mattered. True, the turnout of voters had been particularly high for a by-election: 80.2 per cent. True, Ludovic

Kennedy, ex-Independent Television newscaster standing for the Liberals, had put his party into a good second place. But no one could possibly say how much either of these two facts had been influenced by the television coverage, and no one suggested that Granada had been anything but sublimely impartial, despite a great deal of behind-the-scenes bickering and confusion among the parties beforehand. None the less, a revolution had taken place. Rochdale was one decided step in proving that television was about reporting and about news as it happened, that it was an instrument intended to show the public what the real world was like, however distasteful or contentious that might be.

Early in 1959 there were rumours that there would be a general election in May. Granada, chiefly in the form of Denis Forman, was waiting. Weeks of discussion – Cecil had opposed the programme as had the IBA – had resulted in a proposed programme, to be called 'Marathon', in which every candidate within Granadaland, constituency by constituency, would make a brief election address, without debate or discussion. Initial reactions from the parties were promising: Morgan Phillips, who had had some 'pretty tough' arguments with Denis Forman over Rochdale, said that he would raise no objection on the part of the Labour Party, and the Conservatives remained noncommittal but well disposed. Then an election date failed to be set.

Six months later, it was announced for October. By now Granada had consulted Sir Ivor Jennings, Master of Trinity Hall, Cambridge, one of the leading authorities on the Constitution, as to the legality of what they proposed to do, and been told that as long as every candidate within each constituency appeared the programme would not be infringing the Representation of the People Act. When the moment came, 229 candidates contesting 100 constituencies in the Granada area were presented to the electors in 'Marathon' in two sessions each day. Each had one minute to state his case and one minute to reply. They had been told to wear plain ties, light but coloured shirts, how to speak ('Project your talk to just one person – say a friend sitting at home') and how to behave ('RELAX . . . and be yourself'). Afterwards, there was no complaint of unfair treatment. Granada had kept rigidly to its stop watch and there was none of the wrangling over etiquette and legal niceties between local and national party political offices that had plagued Rochdale.

After it was all over, Granada commissioned a sample survey. 'Marathon', everyone involved agreed, had been exciting as an experiment, but it made remarkably boring television. The only star was a young Tory woman, fighting a hopeless seat outside Manchester, who had been allocated a slot at twenty-past five in the afternoon. No sooner had the floor manager given her the cue to begin talking than she said briskly: 'Now children, go and tell Mummy there's a lady here who wants to speak to her.'

Even while the elections were going on, Granada had been pioneering another kind of political reporting. In 1957, they had put on a single, half-hour, programme on the annual conference of the TUC, and in the years that followed there were programmes on the TUC and political party conferences whenever these took place on Granada territory. All these, however, were reports after the event. In 1962, for the first time since Granada had come into existence, all three party conferences, as well as the TUC conference, were taking place in Granadaland. Sidney and Denis Forman took the decision to televise them in full, as they happened.

At first there were furious objections. Some said that if the conferences were televised, delegates would speak only to camera; others complained that several hours of political broadcasting every day would be extremely boring. Enormous efforts were made to overcome their anxieties. Sidney, in particular, handled the TUC, by reminding the leaders that newspapers invariably portrayed their members every year at conference time as 'wild men', and that journalists would find it much harder to write pieces summoning up such a picture of the unions if the perfectly ordinary – he thought, but did not add, even dull, agreeing with Low's portrayal of them in his cartoons as carthorses – members were seen behaving perfectly ordinarily on the screen day after day.

When the conferences were filmed the cameras were found to be no more intrusive than the press. Many viewers at home switched off. But one amateur statistician calculated that on a single day in 1962 more people saw the TUC at work on television than had attended the conference as delegates throughout its entire history. 'Full marks for Sidney Bernstein,' commented Neville Randall in the *Daily Sketch*. 'Why are the other contractors – and the BBC – afraid to do it at all?' (When the BBC subsequently turned up to televise a party conference they found a neat placard placed alongside the Granada Travelling Eye. 'Granada at the Conference ... *Beware of imitations.*' It was the sort of cheek Granada much enjoyed.)

In 1963, as if to make up for many hours of unsensational viewing, came two dramatic moments in the history of political television. The TUC conference in Brighton was locked in a seemingly irresolvable bind. George Woodcock, the TUC General Secretary, and Frank Cousins, the General Secretary of the Transport and General Workers' Union, were unable to agree on a paragraph dealing with wage restraint. It was a fundamental difference of opinion, crucial to current trade unionism, and efforts were being made on all sides to break the deadlock. One the morning of 3 September, the Council held a depressing meeting: Woodcock was silent, Cousins despondent.

A little later the Council met in the red drawing-room of the Brighton Pavilion. Suddenly Cousins spoke up. He understood, he said, that the TUC staff would be able to prepare a statement to replace the offending paragraph 40. 'It doesn't have to be drafted' replied Woodcock. 'I've got it here.' And, like a conjurer, he plucked the white rabbit from his attaché case.

When the furore died down it transpired that agreement had come about as a result of an interview which Granada had set up in the Corn Exchange adjoining the Conference Hall. Just before the end of the interview, Woodcock had been asked whether it might be possible to rewrite the critical paragraph. In certain circumstances it might be both desirable and possible to do so, replied Woodcock, 'if anybody asked me. But no one has.' The interview ended. Woodcock went away to prepare his rabbit.

Shortly afterwards the American weekly *Variety* described the event. 'Granada TV', said its reporter, in words that must have pleased Sidney greatly, 'has illustrated anew the capabilities of TV in presenting the news ... and when there is no news, in its ability to make it.'

The second and more spectacular of Granada's political conjuring tricks occurred on 10 October, barely a month later, at the Conservative Party conference. This time it came about largely as the result of a courageous and last-minute decision by Barrie Heads, the producer, not to wind up, as planned, at five o'clock, but to keep on televising the conference on the off-chance that an 'announcement' signalled for some time later was in fact important, and not about a delegate's lost pipe or handbag.

At five, the rest of the network abandoned the conference to go over to 'Criss Cross Quiz'. Granada stuck with it alone. And so when, a few minutes later, Lord Home appeared unexpectedly on the platform to announce that Macmillan was tendering his resignation to the Queen, it was only Granada who carried it, and only Granada that had the exquisite pleasure of being so quick off the mark that they were able to plan a special discussion programme on the resignation for that same evening while the other companies were floundering around trying to sort out what to do first. 'We felt very strongly that we were doing things in politics that the other companies were not doing,' Barrie Heads recalls. 'We took the risks and we got the backing.'

Granada's incursion into politics had a far greater theoretical than practical effect. No one would maintain that it is always enjoyable to watch hour after hour of political coverage: but an important point had been established. Politics after this was no longer going to be the province simply of politicians and newspapers; as many members of the viewing public as possible were going to be involved. For bright young men like Jeremy Isaacs (later Chief Executive of Channel 4), casting around after university for a career, Granada's courage and imagination in breaking new ground was a determining factor in deciding where their future lay.

Not everyone was delighted by Granada's tactics. Sub-section 1 of the Television Act (that 'collection of vague and ill defined duties') had included the words: 'that the programmes maintain a proper balance in their subject matter ... that due impartiality is preserved on the part of the persons providing the programmes as respects matters of political or industrial controversy or relating to current public policy.' Almost from its first week on the air Granada was in trouble with the Authority.

The first and main offender against the Act's code of due impartiality was the 'Searchlight' series, which had been born out of a characteristic exchange one night between Tim Hewat and Sidney, as they were leaving the Granada building in Manchester. On the corner of the street stood a dairy which was clearly extremely dirty. 'That's what we ought to be doing,' said Sidney. 'We should have our OB units there showing the filth of the place. We should be doing exposés, like the American journalists do.' That conversation, in the able and inventive hands of Michael Wooller and Tim Hewat, had turned rapidly into 'Searchlight' and within weeks a programme on dirty food was on the air. Exposés were anathema to the ITA. Immediately, Sir Robert Fraser complained. 'What would you suggest I do,' Sidney replied. 'Restore the balance by doing a programme on clean food?'

It was clearly absurd, but it was the start of a long, exhausting, sometimes amusing, often acrimonious exchange between Granada and the ITA that continued well into the late 1960s. Sir Robert Fraser had undertaken to safeguard the balance of the contractors; Sidney believed such a balance to be wrongly enforced. What was more, he didn't really believe in impartiality. By letter and by meeting they fought, backwards and forwards, advancing one step, retreating the next. They fought about drunken driving, they fought about the monarchy, suicide and hire purchase. They fought, passionately, about 'What the Papers Say'. Jeremy Isaacs remembers Sir Robert Fraser coming to Granada and telling the assembled 'Searchlight' team that every single episode of the series had been a direct infringement of the Television Act in that it had expressed a single point of view. And when 'Searchlight' came to an end and 'World in Action' was born they fought about a naval prison in which a young man hanged himself (the programme was cancelled) and then they fought about a programme on defence expenditure (Sidney and Hewat cancelled that programme rather than cut it and gave some of their material to the BBC, which included it in a 'Panorama' programme). The point about Sidney, several of the early documentary-makers at Granada said to me, was that he had to be convinced that what had been put together was fair and well researched. Once persuaded, he would fight to the death. Denis Mitchell, one of the most talented of Granada's film-makers, made a documentary about the Northern workingmen's clubs. It included a scene showing girls doing a striptease. The ITA demanded that the passage be removed. Sidney refused. He felt the scene was important: it showed the degradation of the girls' lives. 'The Entertainers' was put on a shelf. A year later, Sidney asked the ITA to look at it again. This time the Authority couldn't see why they had objected in the first place. 'This is much better,' they said, believing that the programme had been altered. It now went out, uncut, as made. In all this Sidney was tenacious.

Very rarely indeed did Sidney censor anything himself. He took the view that he had employed people whose working methods and ideas he trusted. In the early years only two documentaries in the course of preparation failed to reach the screen. One was on freemasonry – Cecil was a freemason and felt so strongly that Sidney went to some lengths to keep it off the air. The other was an interview between Malcolm Muggeridge and Oswald Mosley: Sidney, with the full support of Denis Forman, took the view that he would not have the British Fascist leader on Granada Television. The record, for a man as clear in his own ideas, was impressive.

Usually, the ITA complaint came by letter; sometimes it was settled amicably, over lunch at the Ritz; very occasionally there was a summons to ITA headquarters. 'Cuba *Si*' was a four-part series on Cuba and Batista, produced by the ever-contentious Tim Hewat. Sidney had seen the programme, and approved it, though he felt that, paradoxically, Hewat, a conservative in politics, had actually gone too far in his attack on Batista. As soon as the first programme had gone out Sir Ivone Kirkpatrick, by then Chairman of the ITA, sent for Sidney. The ITA offices were reached by a very long, dimly lit corridor with a low ceiling. As Sidney walked down it towards what he knew was going to be an important confrontation – over all these exchanges hung the unspoken threat that Granada might fail to get its licence renewed – he cheered himself up by calling out to anyone he encountered: 'Have you read Kafka?' He emerged from the meeting with an official reprimand, too many of which could in theory have led to the Granada licence being queried, and then sent copies of *The Trial* to all those he had met along the corridor.

Then there was the affair of the quiz. In the month after Granada came on the air, two quiz shows were fed into the schedule on the same day, 'Make up your Mind' and 'Spot the Tune'. There was nothing unusual in this. Quiz programmes, having proved themselves immensely popular in America, were obvious items for British commercial television, and the first ones to appear were unashamedly derivative of their American counterparts.

But Granada had an unlucky experience with its quizzes. In July 1958 a general knowledge quiz, based on the card game of pontoon, and called 'Twenty One', came on the air. Two months later a competitor, Bernard Davies, won £5,580, the largest amount ever won on British television. Shortly afterwards another former competitor told a newspaper that there had been irregularities in the way the show was run and that the organisers were in fact helping competitors to answer the questions, by leaving useful information lying about on the desk in such a way that they could see it.

Sidney was appalled. It was precisely the sort of allegation that he most dreaded, and his first impulse, as he explained later, was to fire somebody who had been involved in the programme. Instead, probably after calming and persuasive conversations with the less irascible Cecil, he announced that there would be a public inquiry into the matter, and a former Attorney-General, Sir Lionel Heald, QC, was asked to investigate the allegations.

When Heald reported, in February, he ruled that Granada was guilty of no malpractice or collusion, but that the 'Twenty One' production team had been misled by excessive zeal into adopting 'highly imprudent' methods, in that, to make the game more enjoyable, contestants had been given some very general indication of the sort of question to come. The company however was declared blameless, and quizzes continued, with a fulsome apology from the *Daily Sketch* which had rashly suggested that Granada was continuing to run fixed programmes.

The case, however, had its repercussions. New rules were drawn up by Victor Peers for the conduct of quiz shows and were accepted, with only minor amendments, by the ITA. And the ITA itself announced that it would be keeping a closer eye on the affairs of the independent companies. For Peers at least, this was one depressing step in the direction of diminished company freedom.

Nor was it only the ITA which was objecting to some of the things that Granada was doing. The advertisers occasionally took to protesting too. It was once again 'Cuba *Si*' that came in for the most virulent attack from various American companies, who, outraged by the label of banana republic that Hewat had given to Cuba, now threatened to withdraw their advertising. 'Fine,' said Sidney, 'you have an eight-week contract and after that expires you can do what you like. But I shall draw up a list of every company that withdraws its custom as an example of multinational censorship.' The advertisers muttered, but retracted. A similar instance was the question of the National Anthem. Many years earlier Sidney had cancelled the performance of the National Anthem in his cinemas on the grounds that the public rarely stayed to listen. When Sidney wrote to the ITA asking whether he might leave it out at the end of the evening's television performance, they made no objection. Many others did, however. Questions were asked in the House of Commons and a number of advertisers threatened a boycott.

It was all, of course, a far more complicated affair than simply a question of balance. During the late 1950s, none of the passions that had so fired the opponents of commercial television had really yet evaporated and everyone kept watching for slips, for any misdemeanour that might contravene the Act. From the first, long before Granada even came on the air, the Bernstein station was widely regarded as left-wing. As one documentary followed another, attacking the Establishment and questioning current social conditions, so the impression spread. In the early summer of 1958 the *Daily Mail* started a campaign against Granada's 'socialism', plaguing Sidney's life by sending reporters round to Mount Street to lie in wait for him outside his flat. Soon complaints from the ITA, and protests from the advertisers, were joined by attacks from the Conservative Party.

Lord Hailsham had never liked commercial television. It was in a speech of his to the House of Commons that had appeared the memorable comparison of commercial television to 'smallpox, bubonic plague and the Black Death'. Early in June 1958 Hailsham, then leader of the Conservative Party in the Lords, asked whether he could call on Sidney. Sidney agreed. He knew perfectly well that he was going to be charged with political bias against the Tory Party.

At 11 am on 24 June, Hailsham appeared in Golden Square. When Sidney realised he hadn't come alone, he excused himself on the pretext of going to ask for coffee and hurried down the corridor in search of Victor Peers. He felt that a second witness was essential.

When the four men were seated, Lord Hailsham delivered his complaint. The Granada current affairs producers, he said, were plainly biased in their choice of speakers. Why was it that, every time they had politicians on television, they invariably selected the most unattractive and implausible of Conservatives? Sidney was in a delightful position. 'Lord Hailsham,' Victor Peers was able to reply with complete honesty, 'we put on only the speakers who are sent to us by Central Office.' It was a pleasant moment. The papers covered the visit fully. Later, Lord Hailsham's office sent round a proposed joint statement for publication. 'This morning Lord Hailsham and Mr. Sidney Bernstein had a frank and amicable discussion in which they reviewed problems of mutual interest and concern.' Sidney amended it. He cut out 'and concern'.

A couple of days later came a letter from Michael Foot:

> . . . I must say I think it is a bit thick. If you think at any time that there is something effective that we could do about this business, I hope you won't hesitate to get in touch with me. I think it is important myself to kick up a row so that these Tory MP's (or any other for that matter) don't get ideas above their station!

Sidney replied: 'If there is any change in the position, I will certainly let you know. It rather looks as if Lord Hailsham and his friends have stumbled into commonsense.'

Lord Hailsham himself had not quite finished. He followed up the visit by a long letter. In it he expressed pleasure at their exchange of views and his hope that they would meet for similar talks in the future. 'I was particularly gratified to learn that we are both of us trying to play by the same rules,' he wrote, and added that he felt it proper that he should be allowed, as Chairman of the Party in power, 'from time to time to represent to you that the entertainment aspect of particular programmes is militating against objective presentation'. 'I cannot but think', he went on, 'that you would gain a little from our Organisation in preliminary discussions relating to particular programmes since we have a good deal of political experience.'

Looked at today, the suggestion is extraordinary; but it is intensely revealing of the aura that still, after three years on the air, surrounded the independent television companies. Sidney's answer to Hailsham was courteous but absolutely firm. He assured him that his own political views 'are not involved in any Granada programme, and never have been' and that his staff tried always to be fair. 'We, as a company, cannot get involved in the vulnerability, or otherwise, of a particular party,' he wrote. 'It has always seemed to us both natural and healthy that the Opposition and the public generally should want to criticise the Government of the day. But it is important not to confuse criticism with bias.'

The newspapers had enjoyed the whole event enormously. As the *Guardian* summed up approvingly, Sidney was far too astute a man to give the Conservatives a genuine cause for complaint.

"Well, Mr Bernstein, if you think that Chessea At Eight could really _do_ with a bell-ringing act . . ."

Investigative journalism, as it came to be known, was immensely important to Sidney. He believed in it, as a service that ought to be offered to his viewers, just as he believed in the educational programmes for which Granada soon began to make a name for itself. But since he was not a journalist himself, he tended to see his role in these programmes as that of chairman and supporter, encouraging and enthusing others like Barrie Heads and Denis Forman, but rarely instigating programmes himself. It was very different with two other parts of Granada: in both of these areas he felt much more personally involved as they were matters he knew about himself, and in which he had confidence of his own ability. The first was publicity, and here his authority was born of his theatre past and his instinctive flair for what attracted the public, as well as his confident and successful touch with journalists. The other was drama; and that was his great intellectual passion.

At about the time Granada went on the air, Sidney took on a young designer called Alan Pinnock. It was an extremely happy choice. Between the two of them was devised most of Granada's famously muted and elegant publicity. While ABC, from the beginning, decided to go for rather spectacular publicity, and ATV and A-R chose to distribute a great many expensive publications, Sidney opted for a modest and studied audience. Since no one else at Granada was very interested in the publicity side, it was he who made the decision to advertise Granada programmes only in the quality papers, as he had once advertised Rugby Portland Cement, on Francis Meynell's advice, the first time such a thing had been done. The *Guardian* and the *New Statesman* carried advertisements describing forthcoming plays and documentaries. He also devised the idea of producing booklets (modest-looking, more like Government White Papers) on the more serious topics that came from Granada and these were then sent off to MPs complete with actual scripts and carefully selected lists of interested people. In publicity, as in all other departments, there was to be no waste.

J. Walter Thompson, the first company to handle Granada, proved a failure: they were too big, too remote. Sidney switched to a smaller company, called Papert, Koenig and Lois, based in New York. It was from this firm that emerged the most brilliant of the Granada advertisements, those addressed to prominent figures ('Mr Clore, why don't you know Miss Jones?') with the suggestion that Granada could, on the screen, effect the introduction. Later came the advertisements in *Variety* for Granada's plays, with 'Who else loves Arthur Miller?' under a picture of Marilyn Monroe to advertise a coming production of *Death of a Salesman*. By the standards of much advertising, the campaigns were not expensive, and people noticed them; they knew they were different, and they liked them.

In time, the Papert, Koenig and Lois contract came to an end and most publicity fell to Alan Pinnock, by now well schooled in Sidney's taste for plain, factual, elegant material, in his mania for fiddling with detail, and in his occasional aberrations, like a demand that the word Granada be written in ever larger type, or an unfortunate passion for the combination of red and yellow. They made an excellent pair: Sidney, quick to see possibilities, very astute when it came to publicising the company, though critics soon complained that he was even more effective than Lew Grade at making the company synonymous with himself; Pinnock, a very inventive designer, anxious, but not cowed when it came to fights, as it sometimes did. 'The great thing', says Pinnock, 'was that I never had to please a committee. As long as I pleased Sidney, that was enough.'

Drama was a more complicated issue: but it was no less marked by Sidney's own hand. A lifetime's pleasure in the theatre, the friendship of Eisenstein, Komisarjevsky and Hitchcock, the years in Hollywood, had provided Sidney with very clear ideas about plays and their place in television. Of all Granada's many facets, it was the drama department that was most his own.

As soon as Granada came on the air Sidney let it be known that while he had every intention of building up a strong drama department, it would not be at once. Plays were going to have to wait. They were too important to rush, and there were too many things to work out properly – studio space and networking, for instance – beforehand. But he had not reckoned with the enthusiasm of the new recruits, several of whom, like Silvio Narizzano and Henry Kaplan, had come from the theatre, and by October the first studio play was on the air. Its title was *Shooting Star* and it was a ninety-minute adaptation by Martin Worth from a novel by Basil Thomas about corruption in the football industry. It was not only Northern, and thus consistent with Sidney's dreams for Granada's cultural identity, but it had the strong social message Sidney liked in his plays.

Shooting Star was networked and received good reviews, but it was the second Granada play that really laid the basis of the company's future reputation. One night, shortly after the play had opened, Sidney and Sandra went to the Royal Court in London to see a first play by a young British playwright. It was *Look Back in Anger* by John Osborne. The reviews had not been very good – it was some time still before Kenneth Tynan was to call it 'the best young play of the decade' and launch it on an amazing path to success – but Sidney was instantly struck by it. Back in Manchester, he discovered that Silvio Narizzano and others had also been to the play and were now mulling over its television possibilities.

The BBC, it turned out, had already signed an agreement with Osborne to transmit a twenty-minute scene from the play, but had announced that the whole version 'is not suitable for television audiences'. Sidney declared this to be nonsense. While some senior Granada figures protested that to show the whole thing would be folly, Tony Richardson, the stage director, and the cast arrived in Manchester, and a ninety-minute version – filling the play 'slot' – went out on 28 November, with a short introduction by Denis Forman warning of its unsuitability for children. *Look Back in Anger* was seen by over a million and a quarter viewers. The newspapers, next morning, were almost unanimous in their praise for Granada, the exception being, as was to be expected, the *Daily Express*, who declared that they felt like 'looking back in anger' at their ruined evening and complained at having missed Monica Dickens 'At Home' on the BBC.

The drama department was now fully launched. From trips to America Sidney returned bearing scripts by the American playwrights, people like Arthur Miller and Lillian Hellman, boycotted during McCarthyism. These were the plays he loved: well made, full of passion and social content. What was more, no one in England had ever seen them before.

Into his play department Sidney now drew Philip Mackie, a playwright friend of Denis Forman's, who arrived after a characteristic exchange with Sidney, some months after initial disagreements over what might be a suitable salary. 'I see you are offering me the post of Head of Drama,' Mackie wrote when the details were settled. 'No,' replied Sidney sharply, 'I'm asking you to be in charge of plays.' As head of the Story Department came Frances Head, a former *Vogue* cover girl who looked like a beautiful Pekinese and had the reputation of being a ferocious agent, and Derek Granger.

Granger was the theatre critic on the *Brighton Argus*, reviewing the plays during their 'try-outs' at the Theatre Royal in Brighton. After some years he moved to the *Financial Times*. Sidney had always read his column and, missing it, set about tracking down its author. Lunching at the Garrick Club one day, he met John Gielgud who was a friend of Granger's and had originally put Sidney on to his reviews; Gielgud gave him the address. Subsequently, Sidney wrote to invite Granger to visit him. 'What we need is good writing,' he told the young critic. 'If everything is well written it will be good. We need clarity.'

'What should I do?' asked Granger.

'I don't know,' said Sidney.

Granger joined Granada, but like everyone else, only after he had been exhaustively vetted by a great number of people.

Granada employees had noticed by now that while Sidney tended to cling on to everything for as long as he possibly could, there always came a moment when sheer pressure of work obliged him to leave responsibility to others. It was not true of drama. With plays he never let go. He was in at the beginning, reading and approving every script taken on; he talked daily to producers and directors; he sat through the final rehearsal, in the studios Granada had hired at the Oval, ignoring pleas from his chauffeur to move on to engagements where he was expected, and he was there at post-mortems. It was in drama that he was most acute as an analyst, insisting always on scrutinising every background detail so as to be able to describe most accurately how people behave. 'What do you think that chauffeur's wages are?' he would ask. 'Only once you know that can you decide what his off-duty clothes should be.' What he did not do, however, was interfere with the actors, invariably applauding from a darkened corner of the room, though afterwards he might mutter to the director in the corridor: 'Clarity. We must have more clarity.'

Inevitably, there were clashes. Some men like Mackie, men with strong opinions of their own, found the hovering unbearable and begged him to leave them alone. (Then Sidney would ring and say: 'You see how well I'm leaving you alone?') Others jibbed at the endless quibbling over costs, the reminders that established directors like Hitchcock had saved money and time by using not a whole wall but only half a wall when that was all that would be seen in shot. However, most of these early directors remember Sidney with great fondness. For all his interference, they knew how much he cared. And under his enthusiasm the department blossomed, turning out one excellent play after another, performed live, in a sort of charmed blaze of intensely hard work and the certainty that things were going well. In time, as video did away with the live performances, and the other independent companies improved their own drama departments ('You don't oppose me enough,' complained Sidney once to Derek Granger who was lamenting the way ABC was stealing Granada's thunder) some of the impetus was lost, but no one had forgotten the glory of the early years.

If Sidney loved plays, he didn't feel quite so involved with the day-to-day content of light entertainment. But Cecil, who had a genius for it, did, and it was under his aegis that the music hall enjoyed one last, brief, televised renaissance. 'Chelsea at Nine', as the Granada variety show was called, was collaboration at its best: for the years it lasted it produced a weekly hour's pleasure more entertaining and more professional than any other variety show then or since.

Granada owned two of the great old music halls, the Metropolitan in the Edgware Road, soon to be demolished to make way for a police station and a wider road, and the Chelsea Palace (both part of Adney Payne's Syndicate Halls). Badly lacking sufficient studio space in Manchester, and realising that they were unlikely to lure every artist so far north, it was decided to make the Chelsea Palace into the setting for a real variety show, not the pale imitation that was currently filling the other channels. They wanted ventriloquists and jazz musicians, Yehudi Menuhin and Maria Callas, a return to the great days of Sir Oswald Stoll and the London Coliseum where, in one evening, on stage, you could see Ellen Terry in a scene from Shakespeare, George Robey and Melba, Harry Lauder and Caruso. These were the dreams from Edmonton, all over again. And in time, with the help of Denis Forman, who turned out to be skilled and knowledgeable, they got their stars. Billie Holiday, by then frail and emaciated and soon to die, came to sing 'Please don't talk about me when I'm gone' and 'Strange Fruit'; Liberace played on a specially constructed rostrum; a hundred and twenty guardsmen wheeled and trouped on parade manoeuvres. There were extracts from plays, from the ballet, from opera; there were jazz musicians, singers and comedians – but nothing was hackneyed. Perhaps because Chelsea Palace had been a music hall itself, perhaps because the show was live and rushed – the stage, used for other Granada programmes, was never dark – a sort of camaraderie built up in the theatre, which spread to the performers, and beyond them to the viewers.

There was a second area which Sidney preferred to leave to others: that of labour relations and the unions. But the decision to do so came about only slowly and in a way intensely revealing of his own character.

Sidney was, by belief and temperament, sympathetic to unions. It was all part of his political credo. In the 1930s, when ACT had got into difficulties over money, he had agreed to back an overdraft until they could be settled. At Pinewood, on the set of *Under Capricorn*, he had shown himself to be very understanding of negotiating positions. But when it came to television, it was all rather different.

Until Granada opened, the staff working in Manchester devoted extraordinarily long hours to their jobs. There was no talk of overtime. Even after the station came on the air, the question of overtime pay remained astonishingly arbitrary, so that employees never knew whether or not they would be given extra money or the extent to which they could hope to be reimbursed for expenses. It was not, explains Reg Hammans, the engineer who was there from the start, a policy on the part of Granada to be mean: simply that the fear of trade unionism in independent television so haunted the company that even Granada preferred not to confront the problem. It was this lack of early and coherent action on the part of all the contractors, thinks Hammans, that attracted such later toughness.

The point was that Sidney didn't really feel that Granada was like the other companies. It was much smaller (at one time Granada employed half the staff that Associated-Rediffusion did) because to employ too many people would have been wasteful. None of the early arrivals had job titles – it wasn't that sort of place. And since he knew them all he felt, and often said, that it was more like a family company. If people didn't leave, and go to higher salaries elsewhere, it was because of this good feeling around the place. (The democratic structure of Granada, dear to Sidney's beliefs, was also a subject of some humour. Sidney had stipulated that everyone working for the company, from cleaner to managing director, should be listed alphabetically. He, however, was never called anything but *Mr* Sidney, or, to those who knew him well, S. L. B. Later, after he received his peerage, he sent a memo round the office saying he would like to go on being called *Mr* Sidney. In the middle of an office lunch, to his considerable embarrassment, a commissionaire boomed out: 'My Lord . . .') Right up until 1958, by which time each of the three other major contractors had had union disputes, Granada had not had a single day's stoppage.

There had, of course, been disagreements. But they had been quickly solved by talking. Cecil, Sidney or Victor Peers had rung Tom O'Brien of NATKE or George Elvin of ACTT and they had simply discussed the problem and sorted things out.

But as the 1960s wore on, the company grew (from 345 people on the opening night to 1,009 four years later); technical demands became greater, and elsewhere, down in the South, labour relations were acquiring an ever-greater importance inside television, so things changed. Sidney went on being autocratic but generous in the way he had before, only now people started to notice. Two particular incidents stick in people's memories.

One summer Granada had planned to cover the flower show at Southport. The afternoon before the show the technical supervisor, David Burton, came to where Sidney and Denis Forman were having tea to discuss a technical matter.

On the day of the show itself, the rain never stopped. All the cameras but one were knocked out. David Burton performed miracles in getting the show transmitted at all. But Sidney saw it differently. After it was over, he appeared and, in front of the assembled unit, bawled the supervisor out for incompetence and then suspended him. The men standing around were startled and appalled; though Burton was almost immediately reinstated – the very term 'suspended' was then in itself inapplicable – the scene left an uncomfortable impression on them.

The other occasion has gone down in Granada history under the somewhat jocular nickname of the 'peasants' revolt'. A suicide had been written into a script for 'Coronation Street'. The producer read it, and decided the scene was in poor taste; the director, on the other hand, liked it, and insisted that it be kept in. A furious debate broke out, drawing in producers and directors from other departments and lining them up, one against the other. Sidney now intervened, but only to uphold Company policy: that the producer and not the director should have the final say. There was no strike, but there was a great deal of bad feeling. The directors got together and expressed a feeling that they were being undermined: for the first time some had – and voiced – their doubts about the system and the company. To men more sensitively tuned to the precariousness of these discussions, Sidney had appeared tone deaf, pushing his power in a way that could do nothing but antagonise. (Sidney, later, made light of the event, saying it had been grossly exaggerated.)

Compared with some of the labour relations disputes inside television that were to come, neither of these two incidents was dramatic. But they worried Sidney. And as he became more baffled about how to handle an area in which he had believed himself an expert, so he backed away from it, placing union affairs first in the hands of Victor Peers, who excelled at them, and later with Bernard Floud and later again Julian Aymes. The union leaders liked this delegation. They liked the way that Sidney after a while refused to intervene, and offered them a cup of tea instead. George Elvin of ACTT recalls how easy he found dealings in the early years with Granada, and people are quick to point out that it was Granada, through Victor Peers, who solved the month-long Equity strike at the end of 1961.

There was only one occasion, after the first couple of years, when Sidney actually chose to get involved. But even then, it was a predictable kind of intervention. In 1964 ACTT gave four weeks' notice of their intention to strike over an issue of flexible rostering. Since the dispute had appeared, until that moment, to be settled between Julian Aymes and ACTT, and Granada believed agreement had been reached, everyone was appalled. Sidney now took steps of his own. He called for every file and the minutes of every meeting covering the dispute and read them, sitting alone in his office, item by item. Then he read them all over again. When it seemed there was no more to learn, and he had been absolutely convinced of the fairness and probity of Granada's position in the matter, he sat back. There was nothing more, he said, that he could, or would, do. The ACTT members were out, and Granada off the air for a month. Then, they accepted that they had not honoured the original agreement and went back.

Long before the 1950s came to an end independent television was plainly an enormous success. Set against what is in 1983 twenty-nine years of history, the period of doubts and anxiety can be seen to have been extremely brief. Once the audience and the advertisers were hooked, there was no going back. The very early years were inevitably marked by a spirit of competition with the BBC, which, almost immediately after the independent stations had come on the air, had been forced to yield an enormous percentage of viewers to the sharper, faster, less reverent offerings of the commercial companies. In September 1957 Sir Kenneth Clark claimed a 79:21 preference for ITV. In time, the balance was to swing towards half and half.

More interesting, perhaps, is the history of independent television's vast, almost dauntingly large, financial success. And in this, Granada took part, even if, as we have seen, its profits were curtailed by the deal with Associated-Rediffusion for the first four years of its life. When it opened, its potential audience was 275,000 homes: a month later, 370,000. From then until October the figures rose slowly. Then, in the space of a few weeks, everything changed: there was a jump to 754,000, largely because the Emley Moor transmitter was to open on 3 November and viewers had started buying, renting or converting sets. To encourage them, Granada dispatched its entire fleet of OB vehicles to give closed-circuit demonstrations throughout Granadaland's new bailiwick. There is an apocryphal story within Granada that the man who really took in what was happening was Victor Peers. On 3 November Peers had a heart attack. The last he remembered was worrying about money. It was four weeks before he was allowed to receive visitors. One of the first was Sidney. 'Victor,' he said, 'our losses are over. Our profits are as big as our losses were.'

With prosperity, too, came the second stage of Granada's building programme. Under Tubbs's guidance new studios doubled, then tripled, the capacity to produce studio programmes. Telecine and video-tape demanded ever more room. The engineers, at Granada, were treated precisely the same way as everyone else: they were expected to see Granada as something special. Until 1963 Granada men designed and fabricated more of their own equipment than any other company.

There is, perhaps, no greater single success story within the history of Granada than the birth and growth of 'Coronation Street', which went on the air on 9 December 1960 and has been the longest-lasting drama series in the history of British television. It started life banned from the networks as being too 'parochial'.

The idea for what was first called Florizel Street came from a gangling young man called Tony Warren who had been a child actor and had the idea of writing about the Lancashire world in which he had grown up. He took it to Harry Elton, one of Granada's Canadian recruits, who had surprisingly taken immediately to the North and possessed an acute instinct for Northern lore and Northern taste. Elton knew this was a winner. Cecil read the script on the plane down to London and, more cautiously, agreed with him. From there, as Norman Frisby, now head of Granada's press office, remembers, it 'just crept on the air'.

From the first, Granada's viewers loved it. There was something about the street, with its collection of wry, resigned, doughty characters, that rang a chord in Northern hearts. Cecil was later to say that he believed it had taken off because from that first moment Granada gave the programme of its best: its best directors, its best writers, its closest attention. After six months, ATV looked at the ratings and took it for the Midlands. Area by area, the English public was seduced. Sidney never quite understood 'Coronation Street' but he appreciated that his company had given birth to something of a miracle. What was more, it was impeccably Northern; and it was cheap.

By the end of its first year 'Coronation Street' was in the top ten most popular programmes. The following year, it reached the number one position, with twenty million regular viewers. Since then, it has rarely been anywhere else, though a generation of directors, writers and producers have come and made their names, and gone. Derek Granger, who produced 'Coronation Street' between 1961 and 1962, remembers the moment he knew that its fortunes were made. An embossed card had come from the Mayor of Blackpool, asking if 'Coronation Street' would come to switch on the illuminations at Blackpool. Along the route, the bus carrying the cast found groups of people, waving their handkerchiefs. They couldn't get into Blackpool. Police came with sirens to clear a path through the crowds.

There were among the public, however, those who watched the growing success of the independent companies and wondered how they could benefit from it. They saw how, in the year 1957-8, ATV reported a growth of profits from £450,000 to £4,050,000. And they watched too as stories appeared in the papers saying that Granada's advertising revenue could well be reaching £10 million in a single year. In August 1958 Investment Registry, 'on behalf of clients', offered to buy Granada's Ordinary Shares. The offer was made, not to the Board, but direct to shareholders by letter.

The following day, Sidney made a public statement. He explained that the directors, their families and friends, who owned some 75 per cent of the shares, did not intend to sell. It was a warning to the original shareholders that they would be wrong to sell at the price offered.

In the event, in the space of three days, Granada shares nearly tripled to 41s. 3d., and Sidney appealed through his stockbrokers to the Council of the Stock Exchange to stop the dealings. The Council did so. And on 30 January, his sixtieth birthday, Sidney told shareholders assembled for the annual general meeting that 200,000 ordinary shares would be issued to Granada executives and staff.

When it was all over, and what Sidney called the 'hullabaloo' subsided, when it was plain that there would be no takeover and that Granada shareholders had remained loyal, Sidney was left with a sour taste. He minded the exposure; he hated the upheaval and the suggestion that somewhere in the company financial malpractice had been going on. It was with some surprise and anguish that he declared: 'Something is happening which we don't quite understand.'

These early years of television left Sidney with very little time for a private life. Meetings with old friends – Oliver Messel, Ingrid Bergman, Lauren Bacall, Cyril Radcliffe – grew more infrequent, and were often cut short by urgent meetings or telephone calls. Sidney minded the loss since so much of the pleasure of his life had come from the leisurely, lengthy conversations he had with friends, conducted over interminable meals and country walks. 'I don't see you *often* enough,' he would say sadly over the telephone.

He minded too the fact that it gave him so little time to be at home with the baby and with Sandra, who had adapted very skilfully to the set pattern of his life and to the immense selection of friends who could at times be intimidating. She handled it all with remarkable calm, an agreeably wry sense of humour, and an absolute refusal to be overawed by the new world in which she now found herself. For Sidney, returning late from meetings, discussions, decisions, the new Coppings was a place of peace.

In the autumn of 1957, when they had been married for nearly three years, Sidney and Sandra gave an enormous party at the Savoy for the première of Charlie Chaplin's *A King in New York*. Over the years Sidney's friendship with Chaplin had grown closer. The Chaplins had moved to Switzerland in 1953, to a house they had bought called the Manoir de Ban in Vevey – and Sidney had sent them a greetings present of grouse by special air delivery. They had just come through an intensely unhappy period, having broken with their past American life, hounded by the tax authorities and threatened by a paternity suit.

Chaplin had stayed at Coppings while Oona had made one last trip back to Hollywood to wind up their affairs. He had been exceedingly anxious about her, pacing up and down the garden exclaiming melodramatic-ally: 'Have I sent her to her death?' Nor had their arrival in Europe been very auspicious. *Limelight*, the film that Chaplin had invited Sidney to co-produce, and which had been extremely badly greeted in America, had opened in Rome to a minor riot by what turned out to be the former members of the Fascist Party. As Oona wrote to Sidney: 'What terrified Charlie was seeing *Limelight* dubbed in Italian – really awful and a great shock.'

Now, things were working better for them again and Chaplin, a strange, insecure figure, had become the recipient of Sidney's somewhat rare personal letters. *A King in New York*, made at Shepperton, was receiving its première in London. There was a touching scene at the Savoy party. Sidney was sitting at a table with Sandra and the Chaplins when T. S. Eliot came up and asked Chaplin for his autograph. Chaplin flushed with pleasure, and for a second looked quite unsure whether this was not in fact an elaborate practical joke.

In July 1958 Sandra gave birth to a second child, a red-haired daughter called Jane. 'Mister Granada presents Jane Bernstein,' Sidney cabled the Hitchcocks in Hollywood. If David, by now nearly two, showed a remarkable resemblance to his uncle Max as a child, with his square face, slightly pointed chin and a permanent rather eager smile, the new baby was unmistakably like her mother.

Granada and home were kept determinedly apart. Sandra, maternal, somewhat shy, with a slow, pleasing Canadian voice, had no taste for the role of the Chairman's wife. Early on she had mastered the art of handling public occasions but she continued to hate them, feeling intimidated by all flamboyance and obviously miserable when the limelight fell too strongly on her. Instead, she preferred to bring up the children at Coppings and Mount Street, seeing a great deal of her own family – her mother, sister and brother-in-law all followed her to England and settled, her mother coming to live at Coppings – while Sidney divided his time between Golden Square and the Television Centre in Manchester, catching the sleeper backwards and forwards between the two and walking home from Euston to Mount Street through the deserted dawn streets.

Sidney was turning into a concerned and devoted father, telling friends, even in the middle of letters largely devoted to business, details of his children's weight and progress, and if he sometimes brought to family relations some of the inquisitorial obsessions of his working life, there was no mistaking the depth of his affections. Friends remember Sidney, at sixty, work pushed to one side, a small child perched on either knee. Coppings, once rather formal, was now filled with tricycles and stuffed animals. Those who had known Sidney for many years were delighted to see him so obviously happy. The choice of godparents was a reflection however of the extent to which Sandra had adapted to his life, and put her own behind her: Peter Brook (who replied to the invitation with a picture of a man with a long white beard and the words 'Do you mean something like this?') and Halford Redish, a business friend from the 1930s, for David; Irene Selznick and Bernard Levin for Jane. (Compared with the others, Bernard Levin was a recent friend, made when Levin, reviewing television in the *Guardian*, had implied that the Granada bosses were interfering with the programmes and Sidney wrote a sharp letter of complaint: almost from that first day the two became the closest of friends.)

Even the travelling was forced to slow down, though Sidney continued to make business trips to America, adding on, when he could, brief moments of holiday in the sun in Jamaica or Barbados. In 1958 he arranged a journey to Russia with Denis Forman, to 'learn something of what is going on in the fields of Television and the Arts', while he dispatched others to America and Canada to learn and watch. He had an idea that it might be possible to exchange television material with the Russians, bringing perhaps music and ballet back to Granada screens. Wearing tall fur hats with flaps, Sidney and Denis Forman flew to Berlin, then caught a train across Poland to Moscow. They stayed at the National Hotel – Sidney was given Lenin's sitting-room – and there drew up a programme of events which they split down the middle between them: three theatres or shows of some kind for each of them every day. In the day-time, they visited Alexandrov, Eisenstein's old assistant and now a highly successful film producer in Russia in his own right, with a dacha in the country; they looked at paintings; they talked to journalists; and they visited a film studio where students were practising on the sound controls against the film of *Lady Hamilton* starring Laurence Olivier and Vivien Leigh. It was from *The Times* correspondent Ralph Parker, now married to a Russian ballerina, that Sidney learned more details of the death of his friend Otto Katz, the prime organiser of the Reichstag Fire London counter-trial, who had stayed with him so often in Albemarle Street. Sidney had last seen Katz in the late 1930s, in Hollywood, where he had been fund-raising. Parker now described to him how, when Katz had returned to Prague after the war, he had been among those arrested and subjected to the notorious Stalin show trials of the Czechoslovakian and Bulgarian leadership, and later, like all of them, hanged. Pressed to reveal the names of British secret agents he had chosen at random the most improbable: Noël Coward and Claud Cockburn. It was rather a sober return to London. Fog grounded all planes and Sidney and Denis Forman caught a boat from Harwich; they found Margot Fonteyn and Michael Soames on the boat, and after an enjoyable evening's drinking, politely turned their booked cabin over to her.

By now, there were few of the travelling sprees of the early days, though when he could Sidney and Sandra would catch a plane for Paris or New York, generally for first nights of friends. Granada Television had become Sidney's daily life. At times, it seemed to those around him that it was his character that steered the entire operation. True, his partnership with Cecil, a steadier, calmer, less imaginative figure with an absolutely reliable taste and understanding of his own, and the same courteous, slightly elaborate manners, was fundamental to the company, and the cabinet that ran Granada at the top proved to be a team whose strengths and passions dovetailed in an amazingly successful way. It was Sidney who dreamt up the brilliant schemes, or recognised their possibilities when others brought them to him. But it was Cecil and Joe Warton and Victor Peers who made them possible, braking when they seemed excessive, getting rid of those that could never have worked, interpreting those that might to a larger world. In money, only Cecil and Warton could control Sidney. There was also Denis Forman, who gave every appearance of steadiness and control and who lent scholarship and intellectual backing to projects which might otherwise have lacked them. Over content of programmes, Sidney listened to him. As important as any of this perhaps was the fact that the men who came beneath them liked each other and worked well together – the Bernstein selection system had ensured this – so that the Programme Committee, the steering hand behind Granada's output, became an exceptional institution, affectionately and admiringly remembered by those asked to attend as a properly informal gathering, where no one was afraid to put his or her views, and where for all the company hierarchy, conversations were absolutely equal. No one took formal notes at a Programme Committee; but what was said was remembered. There was no future at all for any idea that had not been ratified by that gathering.

Yet Sidney himself remained the boss. He was the man people wanted to please. There is a memo from Victor Peers, written in December 1960. It contains two revealing sentences:

> The sheer weight of one person's personality begins, sooner or later, to make everyone pause to consider if what is proposed to be done will meet with that person's approval.

In view of the success which Granada has achieved, one cannot say that this is altogether a bad thing, but it is true that only the few are able to overcome this desire to please by following the Company line – or what is thought to be the Company line.

From the start, Sidney had exercised a curious fascination over everyone he had anything to do with, and as he made a point of eating in the canteen at lunchtime, and inquiring into every facet of the business, from cleaning staff to junior technicians, there was almost no one with whom he was not in contact. Soon, he became a figure of legendary powers. Before there was tape, he read all the scripts. He asked to see still photographs of the sets so that he could compare them with what was seen on the screen and check that there had been no waste. There was even a rumour that he had bought himself a T-square with which to measure the lettering as it appeared and verify that it was all properly aligned. The message was not lost on anyone. When the staff stopped feeling persecuted, they realised that it was instilling in them a genuine awareness that the money they spent had to have been spent visibly. 'It was to his credit that he trained us in good housekeeping,' says David Plowright, who joined when he was twenty-five, and is now Managing Director of Television, 'even if, at the time, you would be very irritated that all he seemed to have noticed was an unnecessary piece of cornice'. Sidney rarely praised. He liked to believe that those working for Granada naturally performed well.

There was, of course, an infuriating side to the energy, to the way he seemed to merge his personality and his whims with the entire organisation. He had a mania for neatness and detail that would, on occasion, explode into irrational anger when he would stalk through the offices complaining that the telephone directories were in the wrong order, or that too much stationery was being hoarded. Students of his eccentricities declare that he hated dangling earrings and suede shoes and beards and enjoyed creating legends about his taste. He drove people mad by ringing them up all the time, not to criticise, but to find out, to have his own say about every matter, however trivial, to be convinced that a certain step was the wisest one, a certain expenditure absolutely necessary. He outraged them, by banning drink on the premises after an office party had got out of hand, as if they were naughty schoolchildren, and by a sort of puritanism that seemed to some too cautious, too petty, too mean. And those who left, as some did, when they could no longer take the scrutiny, departed with a bitter sense that he could be too ruthless and too unkind. Those who saw disfavour coming, who heard the tell-tale note of the forgotten Christian name, then the title 'Mr', regretted that he didn't sometimes choose to adopt a more gentle tone.

But even those who were quite frightened of him admired him, and nearly everyone felt affection. They liked the way he didn't kowtow to local dignitaries – or, indeed, to anyone. They felt grateful at the way he looked after those in trouble, and brought into the company people he felt had been undervalued or wrongly bypassed elsewhere, like Quentin Reynolds, or Malcolm Muggeridge after the BBC dropped him for an anti-monarchist speech, or Cecil McGivern, the Reithian perfectionist who shared with Sidney an absolute belief that the general public will always respond to excellence, but whose perfectionism was too uncompromising for the BBC. They felt that they were learning, and while they experimented and explored their ideas, they were being supported by someone with all the courage and energy of one of the great founding newspaper proprietors. 'Isn't this exciting?' Sidney would say to the people he met in the corridors of Granada as he flew past, blue suit immaculate, coat flung over his shoulders, on his way to another meeting, another rehearsal. They were charmed, and they believed him. It *was* exciting: and he had made it so.

'The Czar of Granada'

12

'A Most Distinguished Citizen'

IN 1961, SIDNEY became a publisher. Given his early friendships, his eclectic and intense reading, and a taste for personal collecting that went back to the 1920s when he and an accountant friend would meet once a week for a sandwich in a tea-room off Piccadilly and then wander around the book barrows in Holborn, the move from television and into the production of books was an absolutely natural step. Furthermore it was a sensible one. Granada had already started bringing out books – a collection of Granada plays and two books about television – and in each case they had to make deals with outside publishers. All that was surprising perhaps was that the development came so fast. It was a bare five years since Granada Television had come on the air, and the company, though already highly profitable, was still in a state of continual inner flux and expansion.

It was not Sidney, however, who made the first move. Howard Samuel was the chairman of MacGibbon & Kee, a small, well-respected firm, but which had long been struggling to make a profitable turnover. In the summer of 1961 Samuel went to Greece for a holiday: in the course of an unexplained accident, he drowned. The firm was left in the hands of his brother, its joint owner but not a man either interested in publishing or in running the company himself. He turned to his solicitor for help in finding a buyer.

By the beginning of the 1960s, Arnold Goodman, the solicitor, was already an influential force in deals of this kind. What was more, he knew Sidney and his rather restless sense of business curiosity. He rang to suggest that he should buy MacGibbon & Kee. Sidney pondered. He liked the sound of the company, not too big, but lacking in managerial expertise. The package also included a subsidiary company with a medical list, the Staples Press, and an educational firm called Arco. It was a good way to begin.

After that, there was no looking back. Allen Lane of Penguin Books – Sidney often referred to their introduction of cheap paperbacks as the most important landmark in the history of publishing – rang him one day not long afterwards to ask whether he would be interested in buying with him a half share of Jonathan Cape, a company controlled by Wren Howard and Jonathan Cape's executors. The first deal foundered but by the autumn of 1962 Sidney was able to report to his shareholders that Granada now had its half share in Cape, because he had come to an arrangement with Wren Howard to buy Jonathan Cape's half interest.

Then followed more publishing acquisitions. One day, as Sidney was preparing to leave for a holiday in Spain with Sandra, Charlotte, and Peter and Natasha Brook, Herbert Agar, an American director of Rupert Hart-Davis, phoned him in Manchester to tell him that he should be thinking of buying the firm, recently bought up by the American publishers Harcourt Brace and now about to be resold. Hart-Davis, kept on by the Americans to manage the company, had recently turned down, on grounds of morality, *The Group*, Mary McCarthy's outspoken novel about some Vassar girls growing up in the 1960s and arguably the best-selling book of the year. For Harcourt Brace, this unworldliness had been the breaking point: William Jovanovich, head of the firm, told Sidney that they blamed it all on the influence of Hart-Davis's old school – Eton. Herbert Agar said it was an excellent firm none the less, and Sidney would be foolish to let it go.

Sidney protested that he was leaving on holiday, then relented so far as to agree to a midnight meeting in Mount Street between his train to London and his flight on the next morning to Spain. The meeting took place; Sidney made detailed notes before leaving for the airport and left them for Joe Warton.

Two weeks later, as he sat at a table in a café in a square in a small Spanish town, he heard a boy calling out 'Bernstein, Bernstein'. It was a summons to the local phone. On the line was Warton, telling him that the Hart-Davis proposal was financially a very poor risk: they agreed to turn it down. Sidney returned to his holiday. Later, on his return to London, Lord Goodman telephoned. 'Sidney, you have to take Hart-Davis. They'll *give* it to you. Harcourt Brace are desperate and Rupert Hart-Davis, who has a veto, has turned down Max Aitken, the *Daily Express* and others. He wants *you*.'

Sidney had never met Hart-Davis. When the deal had been signed he rang him up. 'I think it's time we met. I'm coming to London and will be having my hair cut at Claridge's. Let's have lunch after that. Whoever gets there first orders two dry Martinis.'

Sidney was at the table first. He watched as a tall, rather elegant figure wearing a bow tie made his way towards him. The two men talked, warily, sounding each other out. Sidney was relieved when they hit on such a mutually congenial topic as theatre design, and spoke warmly and at length of his close and happy association with Komisarjevsky. 'Ah yes,' said Hart-Davis drily. It was then that Sidney remembered how he had first come to meet Peggy Ashcroft, Hart-Davis's wife, having pillow fights with her and Komisarjevsky at Long Barn in the early 1930s. Peggy Ashcroft had left Hart-Davis for Komisarjevsky.

After the Hart-Davis purchase came Panther Books, the first Granada step into paperback and the mass market, another personal tribute to Sidney in that Joseph Pacey, Panther's founder, chose to sell to him rather than to an American company who had offered more money. It was Sidney's inspection later of the warehouses Panther owned in Teddington, where the packers were so cold that they were working in their overcoats, that sparked off first an ultimatum to the company to improve their business, and later to a thorough overhaul of the entire Granada publishing venture. In time, all the main interests were gathered together on a single site at St Albans, which handled the accounts and publicity for each of the separate companies, while a computer was primed to deal with distribution, and the day came when the wholly Granada-owned subsidiaries were put out under a single imprint.

As new acquisitions in the publishing world were made, so they were seen to complement each other, so that Granada's list soon spread almost to encircle the entire available market. Their move into highbrow non-fiction, with Paladin Books, in 1970, prompted one of Sidney's renowned acts of generosity. He had found, and brought in, a young literary protégé called Tony Richardson to start and run it. It was a company rule that all Granada staff had to have a medical examination before being taken on. The company doctor saw him. Later he rang Sidney: 'That boy has a year to live.' Sidney went to the board and persuaded them to take Richardson on and say nothing. (More than that, when Richardson was dying, and knew it, Sidney provided him with a car and everything else he could think of so that he could lead as normal a life as possible.)

Helped by what became, half-laughingly, half-admiringly, known throughout the company as the 'Granada standard' – a slogan that seemed to embrace all Sidney's spirit of economy and perfection, carried at moments to peaks of absurdity – the Granada publishing ventures have flourished. In the early 1970s they hit a low point with a bare £15,000 profit; ten years later, with authors like Henry Miller, Norman Mailer, Germaine Greer, Hemingway and Ian Fleming on their lists as companies were absorbed, Granada sold their publishing company to Collins for £8.7 million with a recent annual profit of £780,000.

From the first, however, Sidney was scrupulous – in a way that he had never been with his television directors – about leaving the choice of authors and books and the actual process of editing in the hands of those who ran the publishing companies. Granada was there, he would say, to help, with advice and money, and it was up to them to make their own advances. But he came to a great number of their meetings and the editors present noted that he grew restless at the long recitation of financial affairs, and seemed to hurry the proceedings along to the moment when he could savour an actual discussion about books, about whom to take on, and the nature of recent bestsellers. As with his early film-makers, however, it was Sidney who, on these occasions, was always quick to press the point that more money and not less should be spent on bringing in good authors, and that they should constantly risk more than they felt they could.

It is perhaps as a publisher that Sidney has most successfully been able to merge the two most dominant and seemingly contradictory strains in his character: the disinterested patron and intellectual, and the committed and imaginative businessman. As one publisher put it, it was in the world of books and book-selling that the Medici and the Rockefeller within him finally rolled, without friction, into one.

Sidney's business side, say his friends, should never be underestimated. Sidney has always loved the transactions and the meetings, all the minutiae that go into seeing a gap, moving into it on the best conceivable terms and ensuring thereafter that it works. The pleasure has lain largely in the challenge, the excitement of the risk, as well as in a certainty that the business practices that he has imposed on those around him are the best. The money and the profits are, of course, important; but much of that importance stems from the fact that they are the visible signs of successful ventures.

Though no other business venture was to bring Sidney the enormous pleasures of publishing, the 1960s were the years of Granada's major expansions, into television rentals and motorway service-stations, into the leasing of office furniture and the setting up of a record company, into insurance and property and bingo. Sidney had his hand in all of them.

Since he could not possibly hope to run the various offshoots with the same degree of avuncular intensity that he brought to television, it was the initiation of the new enterprises that most appealed to him, that precise instant of choice and the taking of crucial decisions. But when he could, with a flash of the old pernickety obsessiveness, he would still tinker remorselessly with the details.

Granada's first motorway service-station was built at Toddington on the M1. It was a vastly ambitious project: restaurants and cafés for a thousand people, two shops and a petrol station with sixty-four pumps, to be open seven days a week, twenty-four hours a day. Sidney spent disquieting hours sorting out in his mind how you could feed six thousand people, should they all happen to be travelling to a football match by coach at the same time.

It was hardly surprising, remembering his sudden descents on the hapless and unprepared cinema managers in the 1930s, that Sidney should have decided early on in the construction of Toddington to pay weekly visits to the site. On one occasion he found the architect standing discussing the framework of the building that was to span the motorway.

'Why is the first floor so high?' inquired Sidney ingenuously.

'Because it has to balance the height below,' he was told.

'Well, how high is that?'

'Eighteen feet.'

'Why?'

The architect kept his patience. 'We have planned for eighteen feet because that gives us a bit of room. Lorries may not need eighteen-feet clearance now, but what about the future, what about juggernauts?'

It sounded plausible, but Sidney knew, with the instinct that made him such a good amateur architect, that there was something inherently wrong in the argument. He kept fretting away at it. Finally it came to him. 'What is the clearance of the motorway bridges?' he asked. There was a pause. The architect confessed that he had no idea. Sidney sent him out – immediately – to measure. When he came back, it was with the rather sheepish confession that the bridges stood sixteen feet and seven inches above the road. Sidney was delighted. 'You mean to tell me that we are building for lorries which will never be able to reach us?'

There were, of course, financial set-backs, but they were few and none caused much more than a ripple on company profits. There was a small venture, with others, into bowling alleys which Sidney pushed with considerable enthusiasm, but which foundered as the British turned out to be less charmed by the activity than the Americans. Then there was the fiasco of Granada Films, a production company that was to turn out full-length feature films and be part of the big revival of the British cinema. Granada Films started out perfectly reasonably with a plan to produce six films; at its head was put the former Granada Television drama man, Philip Mackie. The trouble was that Mackie and Sidney had never found working relations easy.

Soon, Sidney lost interest in it: he had made up his mind that the enterprise was doomed to mediocrity. Occasionally, when they met in the corridors and Mackie would explain that he was working on new ideas, Sidney would infuriate the younger man by saying: 'Take Hitch's advice. Hitch used to sit by the pool and brood. Why don't you?'

Mackie raged, and sometimes there were rows, but there was little he could do. Sidney had simply withdrawn his attentions and there was no bringing them back. One indifferent film, *All the Way Up* starring Warren Mitchell, was eventually made: then Granada Films sank with no further trace. Mackie went off to write a thinly disguised portrait of life at Granada, called *The Organisation* (the star of which is a charming tyrant of a Big Brother who terrorises everyone and exercises total whimsical power but never appears on the stage), which was later made into a series for Yorkshire Television.

But these were the exceptions. Elsewhere there seemed to be little but success: Sidney's old joke about being born with a silver screen in his mouth might easily have been extended to cover the business world. For even his cinemas, at a moment when the whole world began to desert the movies, were to have a new lease of life.

Right through the 1950s the Granadas, still referred to by the Bernsteins as 'theatres' rather than cinemas, kept their sparklingly clean Moorish and Rococo interiors and their teams of trained usherettes in blue and gold uniforms turning out for stocking and glove inspection. But the spirit in them was dying, a process that not even Sidney's enormous energy could halt, in that it was mostly being diverted elsewhere, into television and the new companies. The administration of the theatres continued as professionally as ever, in the hands of men modelled by Cecil and Sidney to be reliable and perfectionists in the Bernstein manner, but not to take fresh decisions of their own. And so, in so much as any Granada venture has ever been allowed to run down, the theatres ran down. A few, like the Élite at Kingston, were sold.

But then bingo came along. At first Sidney was wary. There was something a little seedy about it all, something slightly unsavoury about an activity, however profitable, that had to flourish only by virtue of a loophole discovered in the Gaming Act. Granada decided to wait. But when the new Gaming Act finally regularised bingo, Sidney agreed to try it out, and clubs, bingo and social, opened in the Edgware Road, in Coventry, Leytonstone and Shrewsbury. By the early 1980s Granada was controlling thirty-two Bingo Social Clubs, converted from the cinemas and as splendid in their way as the Granada Super-cinemas before the war. Tooting, once again, is a show piece. If it is sad today to see the interior of the pink and gold Sidney and Komisarjevsky dream filled with futuristic machinery, bright neon lighting and modern banks of seats, and hear the amplified jar of the voices as they call out the winning numbers over the loudspeaker, it is nevertheless remarkable that the building itself still stands, preserved and very little destroyed, its restoration having cost some three times the sum spent on its original creation and having been done with the same attention to detail that went into the first design.

More spectacular, in a business sense, and most successful of all the fields of business that Granada has entered, has been the one they tried out first, in a tentative way, before the end of the 1950s: television rental. In 1959, Granada bought a few shops around Manchester, characteristically putting their own engineers on to designing a set called Instant TV which would not suffer from the maddening afflic-tion of taking minutes to warm up. In 1961 they had twenty shops. In 1965 these had multiplied to over two hundred. But then Sidney, for whom the rental world had exercised a curious fascination, set his eyes on a bigger market. In 1968 Granada did a reverse take-over of Robinson Rentals, and somewhat later bought another rental company called Spectra, and found itself with nearly a million subscribers on its books. It was during these years, as one merchant banker put it, that the City, in its full conservatism, accepted that Sidney and Granada had 'arrived'. And the City magnates liked him: they admired his indifference to quick profits, just as they marvelled at what one man called his 'prescience' in business matters.

More predictably perhaps, as Granada Television grew and proved itself sound, so it turned to help other emerging television contractors. To the original four were soon added a further ten and when Granada could, or was asked to, it intervened, not in the shape of money, since that went against ITA regulations, but with advice about expenditure and costs, about what form applications should take and what guarantees to include, about how to set up outside broadcasts and the best kind of studio equipment to buy.

'We felt', says Sidney, 'that, as representatives of independent television, we were only as good as the sum of all the companies. Everyone had to be good. One bad one would pull us all down.' Sometimes he took an active personal hand: he persuaded Lawrence Scott of the *Manchester Guardian* to make a bid for Anglia Television, and the ITA that Scott's consortium was a viable one. He gave his help and his backing to the Black brothers, old showmen friends with experience of variety, who were after the Newcastle area. There was something in all this expansion that appealed to him: he had taken the risk, and it had worked well for him. He wanted others to do the same.

It was natural too that Granada should look abroad and take a hand in nascent television stations elsewhere. Stuart Griffiths was one of Sidney's early bright young men from Canada, brought home by Joe Warton after a trawl for North American expertise and soon installed by Sidney as programme controller. It wasn't one of his happiest appointments. Stuart Griffiths was to have inculcated what Sidney had decided was a necessary note of serious and reflective planning; but the problem with Griffiths was that he was too serious, and that seriousness was a very far cry from Sidney's ideas about what made good television. Griffiths was also one of those unfortunate people who got Sidney wrong. He understood that he had been made Controller of Programmes. In other companies that might indeed have been so. In Granada it wasn't. There was no such thing as a Controller of Programmes, and if there was one, it was Sidney himself.

And so a fractious and troubled relationship persisted until early in 1960, when the Canadian Conservative Party announced that it would allow CBC's monopoly to be broken and invited applications for commercial stations. Griffiths had long dreamt of his own channel: Sidney was willing to help.

The ideal station for which to apply would have been Toronto, but a Conservative newspaper man called John Bassett had a strong local team lined up. Ottawa seemed the next most attractive proposition, and Griffiths, with a group of Canadian businessmen and a 30 per cent financial stake from Granada – the maximum foreign money permitted under Canadian law – as well as two seats on the board, now applied for and won the contract for the CJOH station.

At first, the station prospered. But Griffiths was a man of dreams and these included a vision of cable. The day came when Sidney learned that, without consulting the Board, Griffiths had put in a £4 million bid for a studio in Montreal, a sum considered even by the people who owned it (and rang Sidney to alert him to what was happening) to be fantastic. On a very few occasions in his life, Sidney has resorted to the tactics of showman tycoonery. This was one of them. With Bob Carr and Joe Warton he caught a plane to Ottawa and attended a meeting of the shareholders. 'Granada has never sold anything before,' Sidney announced. 'But I have come here, to seven or eight feet of snow, leaving behind me England covered in daffodils, to warn you that the directors you are proposing to re-elect are megalomaniacs. If you keep them, we will sell our shares.' The men were re-elected. Granada sold out. Soon they learnt that the Ottawa station was in serious difficulties and was sold to a competitive company.

The Crown Agents then approached Granada for help in Nigeria, and early in the 1960s Sidney and Cecil agreed to become partners and overseers in a project to design and install a television system in conjunction with EMI, who were to do the technical side of the work. Granada stipulated, however, that theirs would be a non-profit-making arrangement. In the months that followed, Nigerians came to Granada to be trained and Granada staff flew out to Kaduna to advise on questions of administration and the setting up of a TV and radio station. When internal disputes brought in a new Government three Granada men happened to be in Nigeria at the time and were horrified to learn that the very people with whom they had been amicably discussing business the night before had just had their heads cut off.

More ambitious perhaps was a plan of Sidney's to help cement a project in the Caribbean for a political federation of the islands by setting up a parallel federation of telecommunications. Sidney's idea was that this might further unite a group of people and interests made more divided by the sheer difficulties of existing communication between the islands. The scheme was all the more interesting to him in that his friend Ronald Tree, the British-American former member of Parliament and close associate of Churchill's who, having sold his English house, Ditchley, had built a famous villa on Barbados, Heron Bay, modelled on the Palladian Villa Maser in Asola, and that Sidney and Sandra were now looking for land on which to build a house of their own. He left the island, as he wrote to Marietta, Ronald Tree's wife, after one visit, with a 'passionate desire to build the house on the beach and to have a "look out" site in the hills'.

The discussions drew Sidney back to the islands for meetings and talks. They also brought him a new and extremely pleasurable way of life, for in Barbados he met and renewed a number of important friendships. There was Oliver Messel, the original theatre designer who had once been a frequent guest at Long Barn. Messel even worked on plans for a house for Sidney and Sandra near to the Trees, which were ultimately abandoned, but not without a certain acrimony temporarily interrupting their friendship. There was Claudette Colbert, whom he had known in Hollywood in the 1930s, and who now owned a magnificent house near the beach, full of Impressionist paintings. There were Eileen and Arnold Maremont, whom he had got to know well in California. There was in fact something of that West Coast life here, with its brilliant sunshine and easy friendships, and it was to play an increasingly important part in Sidney's life. In time, the Bernsteins did build their house, a series of imposing coral stone buildings surrounding a central, very open, drawing-room, set in just over an acre of landscaped tropical garden with the beach just beyond the garden gate.

At the beginning, in the early 1960s, the idea for television under a Federal Government looked very possible. Manley had recently been re-elected in Jamaica and appeared to favour the scheme. However it was through Manley himself that it ultimately foundered: not long after the elections, he ordered a referendum to be carried out on the whole question of a federation, and when that was voted down, all talk of Federal and Government Television was abandoned.

To the outside world of labels and pigeon holes, Sidney belongs to that prestigious and never clearly understood fraternity that makes up British Jewry. Born to Orthodox Jewish parents, second generation émigrés from Europe, and grown rich and prosperous in a world in which other Jews have prospered, the fact of his Jewishness seems to have stuck to him particularly closely. It has meant fighting with conviction and passion on behalf of Jews trapped in Nazi Europe in the 1930s; it has meant feeling a sense of belonging and of history, and obeying, when it has seemed right to him, Jewish laws. But equally, he belongs to England. As with most matters about which he cares greatly, however, he says little.

As a member of a prominent Jewish family, it was natural that when Israeli leaders came to London he should be invited to meet them. It was over dinners in London during the 1930s and the post-war years that he met and became friends with people like Golda Meir and Chaim Weizmann, though with few did he get off to such an unpromising start as with David Ben-Gurion who, disgusted by his confession that he was no scholar of the Bible, turned his back on him at their first encounter.

Sidney had never been to Israel, however, until 1962 when he, Sandra and Charlotte flew to Tel Aviv and spent two weeks travelling around the country. What happened to him on that trip altered his feelings considerably. Before that he had thought of Israel with concern, but as a remote corner of his life. Now he came to see it as a spiritual force, increasingly able to provide him with some kind of spiritual base. Since then, there has not been a year when he has not been back at least once.

That April, on arriving in Israel, he had been told that a Romanian ship, bearing immigrants from Romania, was about to dock in Haifa. Sidney went down to the port and stood and watched the people as they filed down the gangplank to the shore, people of all ages and many races, clutching bags, cardboard boxes. What struck him as he stood there looking was not the faith that was drawing them to Israel, but the incredible phenomenon of so many nationalities and backgrounds converging on a single state, a blending of so many languages and histories. He went away much moved by what he had seen and returned to England to set up, with Cecil and his son Alex, the Bernstein Israeli Research Scheme – the only one of the many charitable Bernstein ventures to carry the family name, and then only because it was not stopped in time – an enormously ambitious sociology project masterminded by Max Gluckman at Manchester University and intended to study precisely this pattern of Israeli immigration. In the eighteen years of its existence the Research Scheme has been responsible for ten books, a number of studies and many scholarships. Emmanuel Marx of Tel Aviv's Faculty of Social Sciences, writing to Alex Bernstein, Sidney's nephew and now Chairman of Granada Group, when the tenth and final volume appeared in 1980, said that it was due to the Bernstein Research Fund that social anthropology was established as an academic discipline in Israel.

Not long after Sidney's first visit to Israel, during which he clearly demonstrated great enthusiasm for all he saw, he was asked to advise the Government on matters concerning their public relations with the outside world, and in particular Egypt, which were very bad. Sidney had one message above all to put across, and it was one that he had learnt at the Ministry of Information during the early years of the war: that it is essential to have a Minister of Information who knows precisely what is going on. He does not have to be a Cabinet Minister, but he must have access to the Cabinet. (Sidney had given much the same advice to Ed Murrow, when he was debating whether or not to go and direct public relations for Kennedy.)

The Israeli politicians and industrialists listened carefully to Sidney and replied that Israel did not have such a figure. Then Sidney said: 'Let me tell you what Bruce Lockhart, who was our man in Moscow at the time of the Russian Revolution, told me. Lockhart, who had become a friend of Lenin's, had observed how the civil servants were going over to the Whites, and asked him how he was going to manage without them. Lenin replied: "In Russia, we put a man on a horse and he rides."' There was a silence. Sidney thought that he had made his point. Then one of the group spoke up: 'We once put a man on a horse and he fell off.' There was much laughter.

If Sidney's efforts at public relations were not particularly successful – his advice was not followed – the same was not true of his television work. While in Israel he had spent much time discussing possibilities for a non-profit-making Israeli station. On his return to London he received a letter from Harry Zinder, Director of the Government Information Office, telling him that a Ministerial Committee had been set up by the Cabinet to look at various options for channels. In the event, Sidney lent his help to a project already started and financed by the Rothschild family to provide educational television to schools in the Tel Aviv area. During 1962 and 1963 Reg Hammans and a number of Granada technicians flew out to Israel to work on the service. As the project was coming to an end Lord Rothschild wrote to offer to pay Sidney for the technical work. Sidney thanked him but refused. Just how much money in the course of the years he has actually given to causes of this sort in Israel is not known. He has been active on the Jewish Israel Association, the main charitable body in England raising money for Israel, and he gave a great deal of support to a kibbutz, Yasur in Ashrat on the Syrian border, to which a lot of young people from Manchester went. An insistence on anonymity in all charitable donations runs through his life, and members of the Jewish community in England learned early on that any fund-raising dinner at which donors were expected to declare publicly their contributions was not going to draw a word out of Sidney.

More personally important to Sidney perhaps than any other Jewish cause has been the Jerusalem Committee, on to which he was drawn early in the 1960s through a meeting and instant friendship with Teddy Kollek, Mayor of Jerusalem. The Committee, set up to improve the architectural and cultural life of the city, gathers its distinguished, but not all Jewish, members to Israel for a week every few years when future projects are discussed, debated and settled. Every country is represented except the Arab countries. To these Sidney has given generously of time and money. He loves Jerusalem. 'I find', he says, 'that it gives me some kind of spiritual force every time I go there.' On his eightieth birthday, the city presented him with a scroll: ' . . . With the revival of Israel in our day', it read, 'he gave of his wisdom and his substance with silent generosity to help restore the glory and the beauty of the City of Zion . . . therefore was it solemnly resolved to lay the blessings of Jerusalem upon his gentle head.' Over Israeli politics, he has been careful to have no say.

Sidney's newfound interest in Israel, and the immense business projects that seemed to multiply week by week in the early 1960s and kept him poring over legal documents and moving from meeting to meeting, did not change the fact that television was the dominating interest in his life. He was, and remained, fascinated by television, by what it did, and by what it could be stretched and expanded to do.

In 1960 a new inquiry into broadcasting had been set up under the titular chairmanship of an industrialist called Sir Harry Pilkington, who rode to work every morning on a bicycle, and the more forceful direction of the historian Professor Richard Hoggart. The Pilkington Committee was to take a fresh look at what had happened in the first five years of the independent companies, a somewhat crucial scrutiny given the fact that the BBC was not only insisting on retaining its position as the national instrument of broadcasting, but angling for permission to build a second channel – precisely at the moment when it had lost 70 per cent of its audience to the independent stations.

The members of the committee had been solemnly told by Lord de la Warr that they were discussing a 'force' of almost 'equal importance to the future of mankind ... as nuclear power'. From America they were being made conscious of the warnings of Marshall McLuhan about messages and the medium, while everyday, newspapers in Britain reminded them of the outrageous profits being made by the independent contractors. How could they fail to feel the weight of their task?

None of the independent contractors, however, appeared to take their deliberations very seriously. A jocular, often rather complacent note crept into the reports they consented to deliver to the committee, and rather than explain away their inadequacies, they preferred to attack the ITA for its excessive censorship and demand greater freedom. Even Granada, grown cocky with the praise of years, took a lofty tone. Speaking of the 'Flat iron of censorship', section twelve of their submission reads:

> Among the analogies that come to mind are the effects that 'unfiltered' criticism had upon the now accepted Impressionistic painters. Or the example of Epstein. Take the public reaction to his work through his career and then imagine that a television company had produced a programme analogous to Epstein's *Adam*: we may wonder whether the Authority would have had, or been allowed to have, the courage or the right to keep the company on the air.

In September 1962 the independent companies were delivered a very nasty shock. 'They got', wrote Hugh Carleton Greene, Director General of the BBC, somewhat smugly in a book, *The Third Floor Front*, 'what was coming to them.' The independent companies, Pilkington declared, had failed so miserably to fulfil the conditions of the 1954 Act that the best thing would be to start all over again. Henceforth it proposed that the Authority should plan all the programmes, sell the advertising time, and buy its programmes from contractors. The BBC, by contrast, emerged glowing: the inquiry declared itself full of admiration for its professionalism and awarded it the second channel.

Among the independent contractors there was fury. Peter Cadbury, of Westward TV, celebrated the occasion by holding a garden party at which a giant effigy of the report was burned on a bonfire. Granada's response was more muted. It issued a dignified statement announcing that it totally failed to see itself in the many attacks itemised in the Pilkington Report. In the event, virtually every criticism uttered was completely ignored, and the Tory Government confined itself to strengthening the Authority's powers over the planning of schedules. What else could it have done? Independent television might have its enemies but, as ratings consistently showed, it was vastly popular, and who would have the courage to oppose them?

During the early 1960s, as independent television approached its tenth anniversary, Sidney (with Cecil firmly at his side, since he was the one who went to the meetings) was in fact beginning to emerge as a considerable voice in the statesmanship of the independent contractors, bringing to the deliberations over networking and advertising much of the authority he had once given to the politics of the cinema world. When he spoke out loudly against the new levy, imposed in 1963 by Parliament, and an absolute departure from previous television taxation in that it took its cut not from profits but from advertising revenue (Granada's bill, in a single year, rose from £498,425 to £4,609,196), people were prepared to listen to what he said. When he wrote to *The Times* opposing the introduction of colour television ('Can we really afford another misdirection of resources, which colour would undoubtedly be ... ?) an enormous correspondence developed in the wake of his letter. (Sidney had spoken out loudly, it must be remembered, against independent television, the instrument of his later immense fortune; it was at least partly the introduction of colour that pushed the Group's profits, in 1972, up more than 50 per cent, to £11,537,000.)

He was always planning, always looking for some new corner to make his own. He started a series of annual lectures in the Guildhall, modelled loosely on the Reith Lectures, in conjunction with the British Association for the Advancement of Science, and invited people like Sir Eric Ashby, Professor Eysenck, Professor A. J. Ayer, Alistair Cooke and Sir Kenneth Clark. These were later televised and also published. He started a campaign against the *TV Times*, which he always said he disliked for its trivia, and wanted to start a Northern edition with ABC until they backed out. To compensate, he launched and jointly financed with the BBC a quarterly journal of television under the aegis of the British Film Institute and the editorship of Peter Black. It was called *Contrast* and was intended, Sidney explained in a letter to Lord Hill, by then chairman of the ITA, to be 'critical of programmes' and 'deal with television as a creative force and as a major and continuing technical accomplishment'. After four issues, the magazine failed.

Meanwhile, within the company, he continued to champion his

investigators and when they were attacked to protect them. One of the more famous Granada cases concerned Reginald Maudling, who sued for slander after a 'World in Action' programme alleged that the politician had visited Malta and written to various Maltese politicians in an effort to secure a number of contracts for John Poulson, who was trying to build a hospital on Gozo. *Private Eye* had picked up the story first, but Granada had furthered it. It promised to be very expensive. Sidney engaged solicitors and counsel and prepared for the fight. Then Maudling died; the suit was automatically dropped.

Sidney's own actions, against others, were by now well-known in the legal profession. When the *Express* wrote a story saying that six senior Granada men were walking out because of the terrible working conditions in the company, he sued and managed to get Beaverbrook to pay £1,000 towards the Playing Fields Association, a charity supported by Prince Philip, who was a man Beaverbrook particularly detested. When the *Sunday Express* described Sidney as a 'Socialist millionaire ... who is trying to smash the Equity strike by starving out its members', he sued again, and again when Giles drew a cartoon on the subject of quiz games that had been fixed (though here he settled for an apology). Nearly always, it was the *Express* group, whose interminable vendetta against the independent television companies seemed to lose nothing of its edge with passing time. In the case of Sidney, it was sometimes as if he and Beaverbrook were locked in a private game of cat and mouse, with Beaverbrook making the most preposterous remarks about Granada through his papers, but trying to keep within the law, and Sidney watching and pouncing the moment a paw crossed the line. Their bizarre friendship was, however, to have a gentle ending.

Near the end of his life Beaverbrook learnt that a memoir of Augustus John was being written which included an episode during the First World War in which Beaverbrook had arranged for important painters to go to France and do portraits of all the senior commanding officers who were on duty there at the time. But in his book the biographer had included a detail that Beaverbrook insisted was totally untrue and that offended him greatly. (Sidney did some research on his own and found Beaverbrook to be right.) This was that the British newspaper proprietor had at the same time provided a number of girls for the benefit of the painters. Beaverbrook appealed to Sidney for help. Through his friendships and good relations in the trade, he managed to get the passage removed before publication.

Later, after Beaverbrook's eightieth birthday, Sidney wrote to his son, Max Aitken: 'When there is a pause, and perhaps a moment of silence – or near silence – please convey birthday greetings and respects to your father.' On 1 June 1964, eight days before he died, Beaverbrook himself wrote back: 'I am most grateful to you, as you know, for the help you gave me quite recently. You took a most generous attitude. And I hope our newspapers will always remember it.' The feeling was there; what he had forgotten was that the Beaverbrook newspapers would not go on for ever.

Of all Pilkington's negative remarks, the one most certain to wound Sidney's sense of achievement in television was the attack on the regional performances of the independent companies. The original contract had laid great store by a genuine commitment to the regions. Sidney believed that he had honoured it. Now he had the galling experience of reading the sweeping statement:

> The committee's assessment of the role of regional television in British Broadcasting was a particular disappointment to us. We found little awareness in the report of the degree to which a television service can become identified with the region it serves and of the benefits which can result from that closeness of association.

Hard words indeed for the architect of Granadaland.

Neither were they fair. Sidney had come to Manchester and the North in the mid-1950s full of dreams. He had no Manchester past and no serious Manchester connections but his intention of forming them was absolutely honest. More perhaps than any other original contractor, he was conscious of the responsibility that he had taken on, and there was never anything fake or phoney in his public avowals about his adopted city.

For many years, since he was a very young man, Sidney had been buying pictures for himself, not, he always says, a 'collection' in that his taste in art, like in books, is eclectic. In his houses in London and in the country are a Bonnard, a Gauguin, a Barbara Hepworth sculpture, a Utrillo, several Modiglianis and the first Paul Klee to come to England, but there are also water colours, drawings and oil paintings from every time and every style, including many from early painter friends like Mark Gertler, Frank Dobson and Jacob Epstein. In the 1940s, he bought some Duncan Grant panels intended for the *Queen Mary*. So it was not surprising that almost before the Television Centre in Manchester was finished, Sidney started buying from Northern artists: no offices in England today can have their corridors more densely lined with original paintings. Rather than buy and donate to the local museums, he chose to give money to the curators of the Walker Art

Gallery in Liverpool and the Manchester Gallery, allocating them a fixed sum every year that they were to spend for their collections – the only stipulation being that the works had to come from the North.

Pictures were only the start of his cultural interest in the North. In time, he has endowed a Chair of Drama at Manchester University, one of Landscape Architecture at Sheffield and one in Communications at Keele; he has provided a fellowship in the Arts at Lancaster University as well as scholarships in both the Arts and the Sciences at York and special scholarships at a number of schools. More generally, he and Cecil formed a Granada Foundation, a charitable trust for the North, into which he put £200,000 and Cecil £100,000 with instructions to the trustees – the Bernsteins hold no place on that board – to support any Northern venture that seemed to them worthwhile. (The present value of the Foundation is now over a million pounds.) It is characteristic of Sidney that he grumbles that they don't spend the money fast enough.

In the early years of the Television Centre he also arranged to bring the Amadeus Quartet to York University on a salary, for a two-year contract, during which they were to give only a limited number of concerts. Sidney had learned that they were being overworked.

There was even the day – and no one can say what Sidney really meant by it – when a discursive and rather jocular memorandum circulated among the Granada senior executives. There was no doubt that it came from him. What it proposed was the setting up of a draft constitution for a Northern Office on the lines of the Scottish Office 'with equal or greater autonomy'.

To the old Mancunian families, close knit and prepared to be very wary of this flamboyant and wealthy intruder from the South, Sidney at first appeared to have descended on the city in the guise of a Renaissance benefactor, giving his support to the Civic Trust for the North-West, and holding small and serious dinner parties at which to discuss Northern matters, first at a flat he took in Didsbury, later, when it was ready, in the penthouse flat above the Granada studios. From these occasions were born schemes to plant shrubs and trees in a particularly desolate stretch of the city, and to revive a small patch among the more derelict streets. These people, Northern academics and businessmen, protective and guarded about their city, liked him: they admired the energy he brought to their deliberations and his invariable courtesy.

Of course, there were failures. Some of his dreams were unrealistic, others were not greatly liked by those to whom he described them; in others again, he simply lost interest. From the time when the drama department at Granada had restaged the plays of the Manchester School (the essentially Northern and often working-class plays put on by Mrs Horniman in the Gaiety Theatre between 1907-21) and gone out of its way to recruit Northern playwrights – the first play put out by Granada was set in the North of England – Sidney had imagined the moment when he would set up a theatre in the city, a testing ground for new playwrights and plays. He bought a site not far from the Television Centre and there a small theatre called The Stables opened in 1969. It was not a success. The more obvious popular productions were packed; the unknowns brought in no one. Within three years the venture was considered to be a failure. (It was turned into a club, where people come to drink: this has on the other hand been an immense financial success.)

The failure of The Stables, however, was an exception. Sidney and Cecil became and remained true patrons of the city, and even the traditional Northern contempt for what looked like half-hearted gestures has been muted when it comes to discussing what the family has done for the North. Professor Brook, when introducing Sidney on the day that he was presented with an Honorary Degree by the University of Manchester, spoke for many people when he declared that here was a man who had done much to 'prevent the North of England from becoming a mere colony of London'.

And so it was with a real sense of shock and quite considerable bitterness that Sidney opened the *Guardian*, one day in August 1966, to find a long, closely argued attack by Benedict Nightingale on his Northern credentials. The article spoke of the Granada Group's profits, and compared them unfavourably to the meagre sums of money actually spent in the North; it talked of the trivia and slickness of Granada's ostensibly regional programmes. It referred to promises, unfulfilled. It mentioned Granada staff with their 'dark glasses, and neuroses ... and bright brittle parties'.

Sidney was on holiday at the time. The full extent of his dismay at the tone of the article was deeply revealing, as was the seemingly interminable wrangle with the *Guardian* that broke out in its wake, as point by point, sentence by sentence, Sidney refuted Nightingale's words. Backwards and forwards went letters to and from the *Guardian*'s Editor, Alistair Hetherington, hurt, cross, a little peevish. Sidney issued a writ. In the end, the *Guardian* published an apology. A roneoed booklet, containing a reprint of the original article, the letters that had been published in Sidney's defence, a refutation of the attack and the long exchange of letters, was circulated to all Granada staff.

In June 1967, the ITV contract, which had been extended in 1964 for three years, came up for renewal. The announcement of the result of the Authority's many months of deliberation was in the hands of Lord Hill, former broadcaster as the Radio Doctor, and Postmaster-General at the time of ITV's inception; a short, outspoken figure with a tough *bonhomie*, who had become chairman of the ITA in 1963.

Sidney knew perfectly well what was coming. In the spring he had been called before the Authority to give a testimonial of Granada's faith and to be formally inspected by the committee. He remembers the occasion vividly. The Granada team – Cecil, Victor Peers, Joe Warton, Denis Forman and himself – had been carefully seated on a dais; from below, arranged around a horse-shoe table, the assembled ITA board peered up at them. Towards the end of what was a perfectly amicable meeting, Sir Sidney Caine, a somewhat bellicose figure, then Director of the London School of Economics, pointed out that the file of complaints against Granada was fatter than those of all the other contractors put together. Sidney paused, then said: 'We consider that a compliment.' (When they had left the room, Sidney said:'We have done our best, and we will never discuss this matter again.' Denis Forman interrupted: 'I think you should know that one of those complaints in fact came from Sir Sidney himself, who was furious about the programme Granada had done about LSE.' Sidney asked why he had not told him this before the meeting, and Denis, with a smile, said he thought it might have put him off his stroke.)

However Sidney and Cecil never had any real doubts about Granada's reputation. The exchanges between the ITA and the company had at times been acrimonious, but they had also been challenging. Sidney, Lord Hill was to say, was a figure to behold when defending a programme under criticism: smiling, darting from illogical point to illogical point. The two argued, but they remained friends. So it came as no surprise when, on the Sunday morning before the public announcement about the new contracts, Sidney was summoned to London from Coppings and informed that Granada's contract had been renewed. Nor was he at all surprised to learn that his patch was to be changed: he was to lose Yorkshire, but in return to be granted the full seven-day-week contract for Lancashire. It was something that he had been expecting for years. Lord Hill took barely two minutes to tell Sidney and Denis Forman that their licence had been renewed. Now, from his pocket, Sidney took a prepared statement of grateful acceptance. He had another version, just in case, which read: 'We regret that the Authority has not seen fit to renew our contract. The eleven years in television have been a lot of fun.'

Of Granada's renewal, Lord Hill was to say later that it had been a foregone conclusion. For all the nagging irritations, no one seriously intended taking Granadaland away from the Bernsteins. To the committee members, as they sat debating the appointments day after day, there had never seemed any doubt that Granada was the best of the four original companies, one, as Lord Hill put it, with 'the feel, the life the vigour and the essence of television'. They had provided the North with excellent television; they had conscientiously pursued a programme of educational broadcasting, largely shaped by Sidney's friend Sir Gerald Barry, whom he brought into Granada in the very early years; and they had proved that they were good businessmen: look how cheaply they had been able to lay on programmes like 'University Challenge' and even 'Coronation Street'. More than that, they had been pioneers, and they had taken risks. Alone among the independent companies, Granada believed in the act of broadcasting as a moral and cultural imperative and not one to be subordinate to such considerations as the number of viewers, the desire for quick profits or the need for a quiet life. Changes in the Television Act, when they came, giving television much the same prerogative as newspapers to question and examine, were achieved as a result of repeated representations that the original Act was unworkable – and that was because of repeated infringements of it by Granada. It was not simply that under Sidney and Cecil and their colleagues Granada had grown up: independent television itself had grown up.

No one else, in the contract renewals, proved as fortunate. For when Lord Hill rose to deliver the verdict of the ITA's deliberations, he had a disconcerting message to put across. No one really believed that it was going to be possible to threaten the established sanctity of the pioneers even though independent television was by now the most coveted business operation in England and one widely challenged by other consortia. Lord Hill now proved that it was perfectly possible. He began by telling Rediffusion and ABC that they were going to have to merge, and what was more that 51 per cent of the voting power was going to be in the hands of ABC. He went on to break the news to Lord Derby, chairman of Television West and Wales (TWW) that his group was to be dispossessed altogether of a contract; their crime, he said, had been that they had been too 'London based'. In the papers, even among those who had protested most loudly at the fortunes made by the independent contractors, there was consternation.

Sidney could afford to be well pleased with Granada, which was now safe for a further ten years. And this last victory marked a definite moment in his life. He was sixty-eight, and had a wife and three children with whom he had not spent much time. He had worked very hard indeed for and with his television company for nearly thirteen years. Though he was not actually to relinquish his chairmanship of the television board for several more years, the renewal of the company's licence, that summer day in 1967, was a move in the gradual loosening of his obsessive control over the minutiae of Granada Television affairs.

He became their critic, not their instigator. And he turned, in some small fashion, away, to a fuller family life and to the outside world.

Sidney has received many honours in his lifetime and many of them have pleased him greatly, but none has brought him the satisfaction of his seat in the House of Lords. In May 1969, a few months after his seventieth birthday, Sir Harold Wilson wrote to ask him whether he would accept a Life Peerage, if offered by the Queen, adding that he thought that Sidney had something important to say and should have the opportunity of this particular forum in which to say it.

The letters of congratulation that poured in as his peerage was announced say much for the esteem in which Sidney was held. It was not just the number of them that came to Granada and the Bernstein house in Wilton Crescent: over 550 telegrams and letters. Neither was it the enormous range of people who sent them, from politicians to businessmen, actors to writers, academics to scientists. But a note of unmistakable personal affection seemed to have crept into nearly every one of them. 'I am DELIGHTED you are a peer,' cabled Sir John Betjeman. 'What on earth would Jack Beddington say about us all? Will any head be turned? Yes. Will Yours? No.' (For his crest, Sidney consulted Francis Meynell and Alan Pinnock: between them they came up with a design which included Sidney's motto, 'If I rest, I rust'.)

In his original letter, Wilson had added that there was nothing political in his recommendation, a somewhat surprising statement, given Sidney's unwavering commitment to the Labour Party for well over fifty years. That such a remark was possible however says much about Sidney's position in the world of British politics and especially about how he is actually viewed from within the Labour Party itself. To see and understand this is to take some of the sting out of the much quoted criticism, levelled at many in Sidney's position and very often at him, of the paradox of being a socialist and a very rich man. Both statements in his case are true, much as he hates all reference to his wealth, which is of course enormous; but he has struggled hard against the contradiction.

It is no accident that Sidney has spent his life on the fringes of politics, at Labour Party gatherings (but most often in Kent and Lancashire, and not in Whitehall), at the annual Labour Party Conference (but silent, taking no part at all in debates). Political friends respect his acumen and his intuitions, but they listen to him for his commonsense, not for his political perceptions. He is not, in short, a man of politics at all, lacking almost every one of the attributes that go into political life. He hates prolonged debate, and by contrast enjoys the lonely moment of absolute decision; he is impatient in gatherings where the talk can end in no certainties, and longs always to revert to more general discussion of books and theatre; he loves anecdotes, and possesses a remarkable memory for occasion, but he loathes gossip and is made deeply uncomfortable by all mention of motivation and intrigue. He is a personally very shy man, and has no taste for addressing gatherings, and, for all his physical distinction, has an absolute reluctance to project himself in any way at all. He mistrusts posturing and affectation.

For years, people have puzzled at his position on the side-lines, failing to see that while he relishes the intellectual content of a debate – particularly a political debate – it loses all its charm for him once reduced to caveats and the need to accommodate. The wheedling power of politics is not the kind he enjoys.

What is more, say those who have watched him at Labour Party Conferences, he has a surprisingly unsophisticated view of what politics is, and a respect for those involved that can seem to friends sometimes excessive. He started out in the 1920s as a champion of the underdog, believing that socialism could improve the lot of man, and he continues to believe just that, professing an often uncritical approval of the people who seem to him to be the standard-bearers of his ideals. He is, says one political friend, 'untainted by scepticism or cynicism', an evangelist in politics, a figure of transparent decency and unfaltering standards, and as such greatly respected within the Labour Party. He brings dignity to a discussion, but he does not bring political knowhow. Not even over the question of Israel, where his voice might have been expected to have been heard. Other people, sympathetic to Israel, have formed the Labour Party attitudes without him.

And so, taking pleasure in the atmosphere, enjoying the company of leading Labour figures like Harold Wilson and James Callaghan and Michael Foot, whose political statements and careers he follows closely, he has continued to attend the Conference year after year, arriving in his little Dove when he owned a private plane, taking a suite at the best hotel and holding small parties, and sitting on the platform with other distinguished visitors; but all along he has been listening and not talking and later, unobtrusively, he slips away.

If he has been generous, as he undoubtedly has, to Party funds, he has not been above a certain amount of teasing mockery, especially when it is made too obvious that money is expected of him. In the late 1950s Reg Wallis of the Manchester Labour Party wrote to him indicating that he was expecting something handsome in the way of a contribution to some current local campaign. Sidney by letter asked him exactly what Wallis had in mind. Wallis replied that the highest donation so far was £25 and the lowest five shillings. Sidney sent a cheque for £10. 'Herewith', he wrote, 'my cheque which is somewhere between your rich friends and your honest to God members.'

Sidney received his peerage in the summer of 1969, the same month that Charlotte was married, on a hot summer's day, with the marquee at Coppings full of midsummer flowers and great bowls of wild strawberries. He delayed making his maiden speech for two years, and then chose to give it on the Industrial Relations Bill. Since then, he has attended the House of Lords regularly, but spoken little – on the Common Market, on questions of television, on a few social issues – and never with ease. 'I am', he says of himself, 'a heckler, not an orator.'

When he reached seventy, he says, he started 'backing away'. One by one, he relinquished the absolute control he had always insisted on having of every enterprise around him. The question had long been asked: who would succeed him? Though Granada has remained an intensely family concern, few Bernsteins have worked there.

Cecil had a son, Alex, who joined the company after leaving Cambridge with a First in Economics and made his mark in the television rentals side of the business, unflashily but very competently. In July 1979, when Sidney announced that he was retiring as director and chairman of the company, and became President of the Group for life, Alex took his place. The nature of the seat he inherited was an extraordinary testimonial to a single man's achievements. For though Granada's successes cannot be reckoned without reference to the many others who contributed to them, it is really to Sidney that one has to look. In 1922 the Bernstein company consisted mainly of four suburban theatres. Fifty-seven years later, it was a business empire embracing an extraordinary diversity of concerns, and a profit the previous year of over £34 million. But that was not really the point: far larger fortunes have been made in far less time. What was particular about the growth and spread of the Bernstein interests, from music halls to silent movies, talkies to colour films, theatre to cinema production, television into video, was that they were a mirror of the changing tastes of three generations of the British public. Sidney observed the change: but he was always a little ahead of the game, possessed of a kind of prescience about the way things were going. And there is no doubt at all that sometimes he took a hand in the directing of that very process of change.

Alex's assumption of the chairmanship was not an easy step. In some ways the two men are alike. Alex is widely reported to have brought to the company a greater sense of democracy, while retaining and building on Granada's prosperity, diversifying with shrewdness and great financial success. But there are those who remember Sidney's flamboyance and regret the excitement of the days when, at any moment, unannounced, his tall, brisk figure might be seen striding down a corridor ready to pounce on some unfortunate miscreant, or produce a new, totally impracticable scheme. In any case, they say, Sidney's bravura lives on. Even if the people entering Granada today know nothing of Sidney and his particular style, Granada's stand against revealing its sources in the British Steel case in 1980 is just one proof of the way in which he has imbued his lieutenants with lasting courage. What surprises old Granada hands however is the fact that Sidney, once he had announced his departure, left. There is no brooding presence at Alex's shoulder.

Within the company, as it became clear that Sidney was not going to tamper with anyone's responsibilities, but was liable to keep coming to the office, he soon came to be regarded as the repository of Granada's history, the person who could remember the deals and knew about the company's growth and past, just as once, in Hollywood, thirty years before, he was treated as the authority on the pioneering days of the movie industry. (The two rooms of his files, personal and company, at Granada are indicative of his vision of his own past.) The legends about his famous and unreasonable rages, his impetuosity and his peculiar obsessions live on, as do the stories of his generosity and his charm.

With retirement has come not more leisure – leisure is not a concept that interests him – but more time for other things, the friendships, the travels and the conversation. During the first frantic years of television the weekends at Coppings largely stopped, but with more free time they resumed, with the same excellent food, wine – like Hitchcock, Sidney has built up a cellar he takes pride in – films after dinner and interminable talk.

Some of the great friends are of course dead: Sir Gerald Barry, the gentle, modest man who was the architect of the Festival of Britain, Oliver Messel, Ingrid Bergman, Ed Murrow, Cyril Connolly, Sean O'Casey and Koteliansky. But many of the guests are still those who, like Janet Murrow, Lauren Bacall or Adolph Green, have been visiting Coppings for over thirty years. Others are newer friends, like Bernard Levin or Russell Page, the landscape architect. All speak of his extraordinary capacity for enjoyment and of his energy.

Sidney, who values friendship possibly above all things, treats it with circumspection. He is a man devoid of malice: when he doesn't like someone, he simply withdraws from them, possibly conferring on them at some later stage the most severe title in his repertoire: 'He's a horror.' Those of different political views, yet friends, he tends to call, with affection, 'anarchists'. The private language is peculiar to him; but never whimsy.

A close observer of human fallibility, he forgives it only in his friends.

But once accepted it is hard to fall. 'You can always tell when Sidney really likes someone,' says one friend, 'because he gives a sort of small chuckle every time he mentions their name.' Sidney, somewhat of a puritan in language as in behaviour, flinches from vulgarity and swearing. Lauren Bacall is known to be outspoken. In her, Sidney simply ignores it.

The years have diminished neither his particularly keen sense of curiosity (looking around him in restaurants at what people at neighbouring tables are eating, he will ask the waiter: 'What are those green things on that man's plate?'), nor his delight at turning events into occasions for celebration. One Christmas at Coppings, when there were a great number of people gathered, Sidney, who appointed himself general supervisor, gave to each of the others a job. Russell Page was made Keeper of the Bread; Peter Brook, the director of Entertainment; his wife Natasha the Maker of Salads; while the children were cast in the role of assistant kitchen maids. Bernard Levin was made sommelier. Today, many years later, he continues to hold the same position whenever in Sidney's company.

Sidney loves things being the same, but seizes too on anything new or bizarre or funny, an outing to an unlikely new theatre, a sudden visit to see a house or an exhibition, when he will emerge from the car, much as he always had done, peering around him like a genial and short-sighted bird, smiling a little at the adventure of it all, his eyes darting about in search of the curious or the ridiculous. Old friends feel for him a unique kind of affection, a mixture of respect and fondness. 'I have never known anyone', says one friend, 'who could do something for someone in such an unembarrassing way.'

As when seeing friends in the 1930s, Sidney prefers to be host. Coppings has altered greatly since he bought it in 1936, but now, as then, it is a place to which friends come to talk, to watch films, to relax. The garden, which Sidney loves dearly but knows little about, has been transformed under his own architectural eye and the inspiration of Russell Page. Page has had a hand too in landscaping the grounds surrounding Leigh House, the coral stone house the Bernsteins eventually built in Barbados, close enough to the sea for the break of the waves on the white sand beach to be heard.

Under Sandra, helped by Paul Bevan who has been a constant presence in all the Bernstein decorating ventures, the house has lightened in colour and style, with the highly polished brick floor replaced by carpeting and a scented flowered walk, like an indoor conservatory, with a painted wooden cabinet at the end, leading out from the square front hall. This same partnership has inspired the house in Barbados, to which Sandra had to bring every item of furniture and equipment from London, and the villa overlooking the sea that they owned for some years at Ansedonia in Tuscany. By contrast, the London houses that Sidney has inhabited have always seemed more temporary places, and one in particular was the scene of an especially brutal killing when their butler Julian was murdered in the basement of their house off Belgrave Square by a burglar in search of money.

There is a particular feeling in all the places where Sidney and Sandra live, as if a certain mould has now been perfected and is cast and recast in the same image. It comes from a certain sameness of colour, material, texture and furniture. It comes from the books, hardback, and on every subject, that fill every bedroom and the presence in every living room of a table on which are stacked the most recently published biographies and novels. It comes from the temperature at which the houses are kept, always a little warm. It comes from the kind of food, and the sort of sideplates and the style of glass. The atmosphere is unmistakable: spotless, elegant. There is order. But there is also a rare feeling of ease and informality. People visiting Coppings for the first time are struck by its unpretentiousness, its simplicity and lack of grandeur, a feeling nurtured by both Sidney and Sandra who decided when the children were still very young that they wished to bring them up without ostentation and without spoiling.

Retirement, or at least the kind of retirement that Sidney has gone in for, has brought the time as well for what has turned out to be an unexpected and immense late pleasure: family life. With Sandra, he has travelled extensively, returning often to places like Venice that both enjoy. In the summers, they have been to Sweden to stay on an island and go sailing with Ingrid Bergman, and to Switzerland, to be near the Chaplins. With the children, they have been to Japan and to Russia, to Senegal and to Finland, to Jamaica and to Belgium; they have looked at Niagara Falls and climbed the Chrysler building; and when Sidney realised how unusual and cosmopolitan these travels were becoming, they took a Cross Channel Ferry to France, and visited the Thames locks as well.

Sandra, who never acquired a taste for the committees or formalities of London life, has greatly enjoyed close friendships, both her own, and those of Sidney's early years, and in particular his Hollywood friendships. These people speak of her solidity, her dry sense of deflating humour, her skill in taking on so full and demanding a world, and her eye for good design and good pictures. She has remained reserved, with a horror of attention. She has, they say, fulfilled something essential to Sidney's nature, his absolute lack of all pomposity.

Sandra's great pleasure in family life acted as an immovable base during the demands of the Granada Television years. David and Jane were taken first to an open-air school in Sevenoaks, not far from Coppings, run by two elderly spinsters in fingerless mittens, who bred silk worms. In 1963, when Sandra's mother, who had been living in the oasthouse at Coppings, died, the family moved to spend the weekdays in London. Charlotte went to Queen's College in Harley Street, Jane was sent to St Paul's and David to Westminster, the younger two progressing from junior to senior school. Charlotte studied speech therapy. Afterwards, Jane went off to read Drama at Manchester University – Sidney was especially pleased when he discovered that she had not known that it was he who had endowed the Chair of Drama – and David won a scholarship in Classics to Oxford University.

Family life, say the children, has often been marked by Sidney's desire for perfection in all people and all things, as basic to his nature as his confirmed reluctance to make decisions. He can also, they say, be disconcertingly unobservant: when, after thirty-five years, Cecil shaved off his moustache, Sidney sat opposite him at dinner and never noticed. Hating all games, he delights in gadgets, cameras, video recorders and calculators, but very rarely indeed is able to master the technicalities. For children, and friends of children, he is an extraordinarily approachable figure.

In the 1970s, Sidney's litigiousness reached a peak. A lifetime of cases brought against airline companies and newspapers, against photographers who seemed to be invading his privacy and car manufacturers who lifted what he regarded as his personal company name – some won, some lost, some fair, some absurd – culminated in one enormous and unhappy case against the *Observer*. The fact that he fought it so hard, and minded about it so profoundly, demonstrates the vulnerability of this complicated man.

Sidney and the *Observer* had long been at odds. Early in the 1960s the paper was frequently critical of Granada's programmes, and Sidney, in his customary way, kept up a slightly fractious correspondence with David Astor, finally eliciting the testy reply: 'Some Granada programmes that pretended to be aimed at increasing public awareness and understanding were, in my opinion, in fact aimed at creating a sensational effect through loud and excited controversy, rather than measured meaningful discussion.'

On Sunday 7 October 1973, Sidney was telephoned about an article in the *Observer* entitled 'The £25 million Barranquilla scandal'. The piece, which ran to some six hundred words, was a plain and rather brutal attack on him. It said that over the years, parcels of shares in Barranquilla Investments, a company in which Granada had first become involved in 1962, had 'moved across the City landscape with the smoothness of well guided chips across a poker table'; that 'the ordinary investor . . . has as much chance of getting a slice of the action as he has of hitting the jackpot of Ernie . . . because the big boys have got all but 3.4 per cent of Barranquilla's share capital tied up. Lord Bernstein now owns 64.2 per cent through his master company, Granada Group, as well as having the lion's share of the 7.4 per cent personally owned by the Barranquilla's board . . . '

On the Monday Sidney issued a writ for libel. What was at stake here was not just a question of truth: Sidney himself did not own a single share in Barranquilla. It was a matter of personal honour, and this he cared about very much indeed. John Davis, author of the article, was in effect suggesting that he was a gambler who had succeeded in getting into his hands nearly all the share capital of the company.

A month after the writ had been issued, Sidney wrote to David Astor, asking him whether they might not set an example for cases of this sort, and speed matters up through the courts. There was no question, he made it plain, of accepting an apology. Astor replied that the *Observer* would not shuffle their feet. In the event, the case did not come to court until April 1975, two years later.

Sidney had made the very typical gesture of having the offending article blown up and reproduced, not on flimsy Xerox paper, but on good artwork sheets, and these were handed out to the jury. The case was heard in the High Court, before Mr Justice Bristow and an impressive assortment of barristers. It lasted eight days. During that time the *Observer*'s Counsel, Sir Michael Havers, continued to protest that the article had been nothing other than part of a general attack against City companies with tightly held shares in the hands of a small number of people, who were allowed to have Stock Market quotations without being marketable. John Davis repeatedly declared to Sidney's Counsel, Andrew Bateson, that the article had been written without malice.

At the end of the trial, the jury took two hours to reach their verdict: when they did so, it was in Sidney's favour. What was more, the damages awarded to him were some of the largest ever given in such a suit: £35,000 and costs. The *Observer* appealed.

The appeal was heard before a court presided over by Lord Denning, Master of the Rolls. Shortly before the date set for the hearing, Sidney's legal advisers came to him and suggested that it might be prudent to accept a settlement out of court, and let the appeal drop, since his name had been fully vindicated, and the money was hardly the point at issue. Even Lord Goodman, in his role as friend (being on the board of the *Observer* he could hardly do more), indicated tentatively that it might be wise. Sidney went home to think about it; he talked to Sandra. And then he went back to his solicitors and his Counsel. There was no turning back, he said. He wanted everything to be clear so that there could never again be such a misunderstanding. He wanted it reaffirmed in court. He told his legal advisers that he wished the Appeal Court to be told at the outset of the hearing that if they decided the Judge's summing up was unfair, and his case failed, he would sue again under another judge. He also told them to tell the Court that he would accept whatever damages they awarded.

The clarity was granted him. Lord Denning, in a long and laudatory judgment, upheld the verdict. The damages were confirmed.

What mattered most about the case perhaps was just how much Sidney suffered from it. As day after day he was forced to sit in the court listening to a case that seemed at times to dwell only on his character and integrity, he felt as if his whole life was on trial. The very foundations on which his career had been built, the sense of honour and unshakable probity, were here being challenged: to suggest that he was capable of trickery was to deny everything that he had ever achieved.

After it was all over, after he had taken in the full measure of his success, he regained a sense of composure about his life, although friends say the taste for lawsuits never left him. And since, whenever anyone has asked him what single event has pleased him most in his life, he has replied that it was the day on which Lord Denning spoke up in the High Court and called him 'a most distinguished citizen'.

Sidney Bernstein

Bibliography

Apart from the many hours of conversation that I had with Lord Bernstein over eighteen months, much of the material for this book has come from his papers and archives which were made available to me. They include diaries, letters, speeches, memoranda, records and reports. Unless otherwise specified, the references in the text come from there.

For the earlier chapters I relied on contemporary newspaper accounts, books and the recollections of the few people still alive today who were part of the early English world of the music hall and the cinema. For the later years, a great deal of my information has come from conversations with those who helped create independent television in this country, as well as with many of those who joined Granada as it began.

1 Ilford and the London Suburbs

GLASSTONE, VICTOR. *Victorian and Edwardian Theatres*, Thames and Hudson, London, 1975.
MACQUEEN-POPE, W. *The melodies linger on: the story of the Music Hall*, W. H. Allen, London, 1950.

2 The Music Halls, Bloomsbury and the Film Society

The Journals of Arnold Bennett, 1921-1928, ed. Newman Flower, Cassell and Co., London, 1933.
The Letters of Arnold Bennett, ed. James Hepburn, vol. III 1916-1931,

Bibliography

Oxford University Press, London, 1970.

DRABBLE, MARGARET. *A Biography of Arnold Bennett*, Weidenfeld & Nicolson, London, 1974.

KOMISARJEVSKY, THEODORE. *Myself and the Theatre*, William Heinemann, London, 1929.

MONTAGU, IVOR. *The Youngest Son, Autobiographical Sketches*, Lawrence and Wishart, London, 1970.

TREWIN, J. C. *The Theatre since 1900*, Andrew Dakers, London, 1951.

3 Komisarjevsky and the Super-cinemas

ATWELL, DAVID. *Cathedrals of the Movies, A History of British Cinemas and their audiences*, The Architectural Press, London, 1980.

BETTS, E. *The Film Business*, George Allen & Unwin, London, 1973.

The British Film Industry, Political and Economic Planning, London, 1952.

BROWNLOW, KEVIN. *Hollywood: The Pioneers*, Collins, London, 1979.

FRENCH, PHILIP. *The Movie Moghuls*, Weidenfeld & Nicolson, London, 1969.

HALL, BEN M. *The Best Remaining Seats*, Clarkson N. Potter, New York, 1961.

HALLIWELL, LESLIE. *The Filmgoer's Companion*, Paladin, 1972.

KOMISARJEVSKI, THEODORE. *The Theatre and a Changing Civilisation*, William Heinemann, London, 1936.

LOW, RACHEL. *The History of the British Film 1906-1914, 1914-1918, 1918-1929*, George Allen & Unwin, London, 1948.

MONTAGU, IVOR. *With Eisenstein in Hollywood*, Seven Seas Publishers, Berlin, 1968.

RHODE, ERIC. *A History of Cinema from its origins to 1970*, Allen Lane, 1976.

WALKER, ALEXANDER. *Stardom: the Hollywood Phenomenon*, Stein and Day, New York, 1971.

ZIEROLD, NORMAN. *The Moghuls*, Coward McCann Inc., New York, 1969.

4 The Theatre Years

BELFRAGE, CEDRIC. *Away from it all. An Escapologist's Notebook*, Simon and Schuster, New York, 1937.

COWARD, NOËL. *Present Indicative*, William Heinemann, London, 1937.

GIELGUD, JOHN. *An actor and his time*, Sidgwick & Jackson, London, 1979.

HEPPNER, SAM. *'Cockie'*, Leslie Frewin, London, 1969.

309

MANDER, RAYMOND and JOE MITCHENSON. *The theatres of London*, New English Library, London, 1975.
O'CASEY, EILEEN. *Sean*, Macmillan, London, 1971.
TAYLOR, A. J. P. *Beaverbrook*, Hamish Hamilton, London, 1972.

5 Politics in the 1930s

Archives of Jewish Board of Deputies.
The Burning of the Reichstag: Official Findings of the legal commission of Inquiry, The Relief Committee for the Victims of German Fascism, London, September 1933.
COCKBURN, CLAUD. *The Devil's Decade*, Sidgwick & Jackson, London, 1973.
GERTLER, MARK. *Selected Letters*, ed. Noel Carrington, Rupert Hart-Davis, London, 1965.
HAMILTON, IAIN. *Koestler: A Biography*, Secker & Warburg, London, 1982.
MOSLEY, LEONARD. *Lindbergh: A Biography*, Hodder & Stoughton, London, 1976.
MOWAT, CHARLES LOCH. *Britain between the wars 1918-40*, Methuen & Co., London, 1955.
SKIDELSKY, ROBERT. *Oswald Mosley*, Macmillan, London, 1975.
TOBIAS, FRITZ. *The Reichstag Fire*, Secker & Warburg, London, 1963.
WASSERSTEIN, BERNARD. *Britain and the Jews of Europe 1939-1945*, Institute of Jewish Affairs, London, 1979.

6 Hollywood at War

CALDER, ANGUS. *The People's War, Britain 1939-45*, Jonathan Cape, London, 1969.
HARDY, FORSYTH. *John Grierson: A Documentary Biography*, Faber & Faber, London, 1979.
KORDA, MICHAEL. *Charmed Lives: A family Romance*, Allen Lane, London, 1980.
MORGAN, GUY. *Red Roses every night*, Quality Press, London, 1948.
SHORT, KEN. 'The White Cliffs of Dover', the *Historical Journal of Film, Radio and Television*, vol. II, no. 1, March 1982.
THORPE, FRANCES and NICHOLAS PRONAY. *British Official Films in the Second World War*, Clio Press, Oxford, 1980.
SHINDLER, COLIN. *Hollywood goes to war: Films & American Society 1939-53*, Routledge & Kegan Paul, London, 1979.
VERNON, BETTY D. *Ellen Wilkinson 1891-1947*, Croom Helm, London, 1982.

Bibliography

7 The Propaganda War

BALFOUR, MICHAEL. *Propaganda in war 1939-45*, Routledge & Kegan Paul, London, 1979.

CARROLL, WALLACE. *Persuade or Perish*, Houghton Mifflin, Cony, Boston, 1948.

Documentary News Letters, 49th issue, 'The first six years', Film Centre, London, 1945.

File on War Atrocities Film, ref. Infl/636, Public Record Office, Kew.

JARVIS, I. C. 'Burma Objective. Fanning the Flames: anti-American Reaction to Operation Burma', *Historical Journal of Film, Radio and Television*, vol. I, no. 2, 1981.

WINKLER, ALLAN M. *The Politics of Propaganda: The Office of War Information 1942-45*, Yale University Press, New Haven and London, 1978.

8 With Hitchcock in Hollywood

BERGMAN, INGRID and ALAN BURGESS. *Ingrid Bergman: My Story*, Michael Joseph, London, 1980.

HIGHAM, CHARLES. *Hollywood at Sunset*, Saturday Review Press, New York, 1972.

HOYT, EDWIN P. *Sir Charlie*, Robert Hale, London, 1977.

HOUSEMAN, JOHN. *Run-through 1902-1941* and *Front and Centre 1942-1955*, Simon & Schuster, New York, 1981 and 1979 respectively.

PILAR, OLIVER. *Pegler: Angry man of the Press*, Beacon Press, Boston, 1963.

RUSSELL TAYLOR, JOHN. *Hitch: The life and Work of Alfred Hitchcock*, Faber & Faber, London, 1978.

SMITH, BRADLEY F. *Reaching judgement at Nuremberg*, André Deutsch, London, 1977.

TRUFFAUT, FRANÇOIS. *Hitchcock*, Simon & Schuster, New York, 1967.

9 The Television Franchise
10 Coming on the Air
11 The Creation of Granada
12 'A Most Distinguished Citizen'

A great number of books have been written about the history of television from its opening days at Alexandra Palace to the formation, one by one, of the independent companies. The following were the most relevant to this book:

BLACK, PETER. *The mirror in the corner*, Hutchinson, London, 1972.

Granada: the first 25 years, BFI Dossier no. 9, London, 1981.

FRIENDLY, FRED W. *Due to Circumstances beyond our control*, Random House, New York, 1967.

GOLDIE, G. W. *Facing the Nation: Television and Politics 1936-1976*, The Bodley Head, London, 1977.

GREENE, SIR HUGH. *The Third Floor Front*, The Bodley Head, London, 1969.

HALBERSTEM, DAVID. *The Powers That Be*, Chatto & Windus, London, 1979.

MACKIE, PHILIP. *The Organization*, Quartet Books, London, 1974.

SENDALL, BERNARD. *Independent Television in Britain*, vol. 1: *Origins and Foundations 1946-62*; vol. 2: *Expansion and change 1958-1968*, Macmillan, London, 1982 and 1983 respectively.

SHULMAN, MILTON. *The Ravenous Eye*, Cassell, London, 1971.

TINKER, JACK. *The Television Barons*, Quartet Books, London, 1980.

Year One: The story of the first year of Granada TV Network, Granada, St Albans, 1958.

Index

313

Index

Bernstein Israel Research Scheme, 289
Bernstein Theatres, *see* cinemas, Bernstein
Betjeman, Sir John, 113, 119, 120–1, 299
Betts, Ernest, 51
Beveridge Committee, 197, 210–11
bingo, Granada cinemas used for, 284–5
bioscope, 8
Bishop's Bonfire, The, 228
Bjork, Anita, 193–4
Black, Peter, 247, 249, 292
Blairman, David: letters to, 98; rents houses with Sidney, 68, 73–4; travels with Sidney, 11, 107, 109; also mentioned, 17, 29, 32, 75, 106, 137
Bloomsbury world, Sidney's involvement in, 20–2, 32
Blue Express, The, 66
Blumen in Zimmer, 77
Blumenfeld, R. D., 67
Bogart, Humphrey, 190
Bon Voyage, 162
books, Sidney's interest in, 70, 279
Boulting, Roy, 153, 157
Bournemouth, Sidney meets Zoë at, 75
Bovis Ltd, financial difficulties of, 61–2
Bower, Dallas, 119
Bracken, Brendan, 127–8, 138, 143, 150
Brecht, Bertolt, 180, 190
Brighton, Sidney's convalescence at, 137
British Army Film Unit, 150, 153
British Board of Film Censors, 23, 108
British Information Services Film Division, 145, 147
British Talking Picture System, 45
broadcasting, inquiries into, 197, 210–11, 290–2, 294
Brook, Peter, 274, 280
Brooks, Louise, 100
Brownrigg, Capt. Tom, 231, 249, 250
Brunel, Adrian, 21–2, 23, 25
Buckley, Christopher, 154
Buñuel, Luis, 24
Burma, film of campaign in, 157–8
Bygrave, Ernest George, 16, 18–19

Cabinet of Dr Caligari, The, 24
Café Royal, meetings at, 32
Caine, Sir Sidney, 297
Cairo, Sidney visits, 106–7
Calder-Marshall, Arthur, 156, 162

Callaghan, James, 300
Campbell, Beatrice Stella (Mrs Patrick), 35
Canada: British wartime propaganda in, 144–5; *I Confess* set in, 192–3; television in, Sidney's involvement in, 286
Cape, Jonathan, Granada's share in, 280
Capote, Truman, 209
Capra, Frank, 142, 157
Carroll, Sidney, 66, 73, 80
Caribbean, telecommunications in, 287–8
Carr, Bob, 286
Casalis, Jeanne de, 33, 36, 68
Case to Answer, A, 251
Casson, Sir Lewis, 79
Castle, Molly (later Belfrage), 75, 76, 107, 179, 190
Cecil, Lord, 91
censorship: film, 23–4, 69, 87, 108; TV, by Sidney, 259
Century cinemas, 200
Chalmers-Mitchell, Sir Peter, 108
Chamberlain, Sir Austen, 91–2, 110, 111, 117
Chandos, Lord, 82
Chaplin, Charlie:
  films: incurables entertained by, 15;
    Lloyd George entertained by, 13–4;
    Royal family entertained by, 14
  refusal to be seen on small screen, 135
  Sidney's friendship with, 57, 134–5, 180, 184, 195, 274–5; letters to, 229, 234
charitable functions, Phoenix used for, 66–7
charities, Sidney's support for, 66–7, 289, 290, 295
Chataway, Christopher, 230
Chekhov, Anton, 34
'Chelsea at Nine', 266–7
Cheston, Dorothy, 34, 35, 36
Chief train, Sidney's journey on, 55
Chien Andalou, Un, 24
children: cinema questionnaire for, 185–6; film shows for, 51, 185
Christiansen, Arthur, 93, 107, 220
church, Canadian: *I Confess* script approved by, 193
Churchill, Sir Winston, 117, 124, 127, 148–9

316

Index